CHILDREN OF INCARCERATED PARENTS

Also of interest from the Urban Institute Press:

Child Welfare: The Challenges of Collaboration, by Timothy Ross

Intergenerational Caregiving, edited by Alan Booth, Ann C. Crouter, Suzanne M. Bianchi, and Judith A. Seltzer

Prisoners Once Removed: The Impact of Incarceration and Reentry on Children, Families, and Communities, edited by Jeremy Travis and Michelle Waul

THE URBAN INSTITUTE PRESS
WASHINGTON, DC

CHILDREN
OF INCARCERATED PARENTS
A HANDBOOK FOR RESEARCHERS AND PRACTITIONERS

Edited by J. Mark Eddy and Julie Poehlmann

THE URBAN INSTITUTE PRESS
2100 M Street, N.W.
Washington, D.C. 20037

Library of Congress Cataloging-in-Publication Data

Children of incarcerated parents : a handbook for researchers and practitioners/
edited by J. Mark Eddy and Julie Poehlmann.
    p. cm.
Includes index.
ISBN 978-0-87766-768-1
1. Children of prisoners—United States. 2. Prisoners—Family relationship—
United States. 3. Child welfare—United States. I. Eddy, J. Mark. II. Poehlmann, Julie.
HV8886.U5C45 2010
362.82'950973--dc22

2010034971

Printed in the United States of America

14 13 12 11 10   1 2 3 4 5

THE URBAN INSTITUTE is a nonprofit, nonpartisan policy research and educational organization established in Washington, D.C., in 1968. Its staff investigates the social, economic, and governance problems confronting the nation and evaluates the public and private means to alleviate them. The Institute disseminates its research findings through publications, its web site, the media, seminars, and forums.

Through work that ranges from broad conceptual studies to administrative and technical assistance, Institute researchers contribute to the stock of knowledge available to guide decisionmaking in the public interest.

Conclusions or opinions expressed in Institute publications are those of the authors and do not necessarily reflect the views of officers or trustees of the Institute, advisory groups, or any organizations that provide financial support to the Institute.

Contents

PART II: **Developmental Research**

PART III: **Intervention Research**

Acknowledgments

This book is the result of the efforts and contributions of many people. Most important, we gratefully acknowledge the willingness of incarcerated parents and their families to share their lives with the members of the research community, and to allow us the collective privilege of sharing their stories with others. We are appreciative of Dr. Karen Bogenschneider for sharing her extensive policy expertise—and for her encouragement to assemble an edited volume of scholarly work focused on the children of incarcerated parents—and to Drs. John B. Reid and Patti Chamberlain for sharing their extensive clinical and research experiences with families involved in the juvenile justice and criminal justice systems. We are thankful to each of the contributors to this volume. They represent varied academic disciplines and practical experiences, and we appreciate each perspective. This book could not have been completed without the guidance of Ms. Kathleen Courrier, Mr. Scott Forrey, and Ms. Fiona Blackshaw at the Urban Institute Press. The invaluable assistance of our editorial assistants Ms. Diana Strand and Ms. Sarah Maleck on checking references, organizing materials, contacting contributing authors, compiling information, copyediting, and numerous other tasks was crucial to the completion of this volume.

We are also thankful for the opportunity to work together on this project. We appreciate the unique perspectives that we each bring on the children of incarcerated parents and their families, as well as the contributions that each made in conceptualization, writing, and editing. We contributed equally to the volume, although our contributions were complementary. Finally, we recognize that this book could not have been completed without the patience and warm and generous support provided by our spouses and children.

J. Mark Eddy
Julie Poehlmann

Foreword

Each year in the United States, millions of parents are removed from the community, separated from their children, and sent to prison or jail. Some parents return to their homes after a short time; they are not convicted or they serve sentences of a few weeks or months in a local jail. Others, depending on the crime committed, are sent away for many years; their children grow up while they are in prison. Most prisoners serve sentences of fewer than five years, and many serve sentences of less than two years. No matter the time away, each parent-child separation represents moments of childhood that cannot be put on hold and missed life experiences that may be crucial for a child's well-being and development.

Children and families are often deeply affected by the incarceration of a parent. Incarceration creates new child care responsibilities for family members, presents financial problems related to general living and legal obligations, poses difficulties in maintaining family ties, and presents social and emotional challenges for families and prisoners alike. Children are often confused about the reasons for their parents' absence; they may have limited or no contact with their incarcerated parents, and they often do not know when, or if, their parents will be returning home. Children's lives are often disrupted by moves to other households or schools, new and different expectations from their caregivers, and negative and stigmatizing experiences that are linked to being the child of a person in prison.

Parents who are in prison are removed not only from community living but also from the daily activities associated with child rearing. They are unable to protect their children or provide for them financially, and they have few opportunities to be involved in assuring their children's positive growth and development. Although most incarcerated parents are concerned about their children, few maintain strong connections with their children during incarceration as the result of policies of departments of corrections and their own personal problems. When parents return home, they are often not in a position to assume a responsible parenting role, and their return itself may further disrupt their children's lives.

Although parental incarceration and the challenges it presents for children are long-standing social problems, historically the needs of the children of incarcerated parents have not been a priority for social services agencies, correctional systems, or public policymakers. Conventional wisdom was that parents convicted of crimes, and even those arrested, were unfit parents and undeserving of support. Moreover, their children were not seen as needing any particular assistance. During the past decade, however, a large and steadily increasing prison population, rapidly growing numbers of women in prison, and new concerns about intergenerational crime have been pushing the issue of prisoners' children to the forefront of the national agenda. State legislatures are commissioning reports on parents in prison and their children,[1] national organizations are implementing mentoring programs for prisoners' children (see chapter 11, this volume), and federal and local funds are being provided to develop children's visiting centers in prison, parent education for parents, and support groups for children and their caregivers.[2]

Research and critical analysis of issues and proposals for change have lagged behind the growing interest in program development for children whose parents are incarcerated. The empirical knowledge needed to guide effective policy reform, program development, and practice has been inadequate. The conceptual frameworks that undergird programs, even those widely adopted and promoted as models to emulate, are seldom defined or described, and program evaluation, if done at all, focuses on process rather than outcomes. Anecdotal information and speculation about facts are often used to justify the need for new programs and even the funding of major initiatives. Although the research literature on different aspects of the topics is growing, it is difficult to determine what we really know based on that literature. With few exceptions,[3] the contributions of scholars from different disciplines are not compiled and critiques of various research projects are not published. In some instances, personal observations of individual situations are mistakenly referred to as research findings.

Children of Incarcerated Parents summarizes the current research on children whose parents are incarcerated and discusses the implications of those findings for policy and intervention. The editors, J. Mark Eddy and Julie Poehlmann, and the chapter authors use a developmental perspective to focus this work. Unlike previous volumes that have tackled this topic, they integrate theory with rigorous research and delineate how both resilience processes and contextual factors shape experiences and outcomes for children whose lives are affected by the incarceration of a parent.

The theoretical framework that undergirds this volume is especially important as it provides a reference point for posing meaningful research questions and for understanding and interpreting research findings. Previous works recognize that children's ages and developmental stages are important factors in assessing how children respond to and are affected by parental incarceration. It is generally understood that the experiences of children in middle school can be expected to differ from those of preschoolers and teenagers. Further, the need for data on children's ages and related issues is identified as an area for future research.[4] Compilations and examinations of the literature on children and parental incarceration seldom use child development theoretical frameworks, however, to shape the presentation of critical research findings or the discussion of program models and service priorities.

Similarly, this volume's focus on resilience processes and protective factors provides a useful perspective for understanding families' responses to adversities that can inform policy and program development. The current literature on parents in prison and their children identifies many problems that children experience and barriers and challenges that children's parents and caregivers face in caring for their children and maintaining family ties. Studies show that some children whose parents are incarcerated do poorly in school and have serious social and emotional problems. Other children fare as well or better than their peers whose parents are not, or have not been, involved in the criminal justice system. While scholars reason that parent-child visits, the child's home environment, and other environmental forces matter, the literature falls short in identifying what makes the difference for children and in explaining differential outcomes for children.

Children of Incarcerated Parents provides new insights into old ideas while offering new perspectives about what should be studied and why. The book advances our knowledge in an area where the need is considerable and the interest in doing something for children is becoming more pronounced. Proper use of the scholarly analysis provided here can have significant benefits, with payoffs that extend well into the future.

Creasie Finney Hairston, Ph.D.
Jane Addams College of Social Work
University of Illinois at Chicago

NOTES

1. California, Oregon, and Washington are among the states commissioning reports on incarcerated parents.

2. See J. Mark Eddy, Charles R. Martinez Jr., Tracy Schiffmann, Rex Newton, Laura Olin, Leslie Leve, Dana M. Foney, and Joann Wu Shortt, "Development of a Multisystemic Parent Management Training Intervention for Incarcerated Parents, Their Children, and Families," *Clinical Psychologist* 12, no. 3 (2008): 86–98; and Creasie Finney Hairston, *Focus on Children Whose Parents Are Incarcerated* (Baltimore, MD: Annie E. Casey Foundation, 2007).

3. Exceptions include Katherine Gabel and Denise Johnston, eds., *Children of Incarcerated Parents* (Lanham, MD: Lexington Books, 1995); Creasie Finney Hairston, *Focus on Children Whose Parents Are Incarcerated;* and Cynthia B. Seymour and Creasie Finney Hairston, *Children with Parents in Prison: Child Welfare Policy, Program, and Practice Issues* (New Brunswick, NJ: Transaction Publishers, 2001).

4. See, for example, Creasie Finney Hairston, *Focus on Children Whose Parents Are Incarcerated.*

1

Multidisciplinary Perspectives on Research and Intervention with Children of Incarcerated Parents

J. Mark Eddy and Julie Poehlmann

O ver 1.7 million children in the United States have a parent in prison (Glaze and Maruschak 2008), and possibly millions of children have a parent in jail (Kemper and Rivara 1993). Millions more have parents who were incarcerated or soon will be.[1] For a host of interrelated reasons, over the long run, children of incarcerated parents are at increased risk for behavior problems, attachment insecurity, cognitive delays, and other negative outcomes (e.g., Murray and Farrington 2005; Murray et al. 2009; Poehlmann 2005a, 2005b). Although pioneering advocates, practitioners, and researchers have called attention time and again to the families of inmates, often referring to children and caregivers as "invisible victims" and "collateral damage,"[2] it has taken decades to accumulate a body of scientific knowledge about children of incarcerated parents.

This information has been slow to enter the public consciousness. Even today, the most frequent statistic that appears in the media about these children is that as adults they are six times more likely to be incarcerated than their peers. While this statement makes a compelling introduction to a news story or a speech, the original source is unknown, and no known data verify this claim. For many years, much of what we "know" about the children of incarcerated parents has come from anecdotes and stories such as this, a few small convenience samples, and one large survey of inmates. Fortunately, over the past decade this situation has begun to change, and this book is a testament to the different lines of rigorous inquiry in which

1

a wide variety of scientists are now actively engaged. The majority of this work, however, has been conducted within the United States, which has the highest adult incarceration rate in the world (Pew Center on the States 2009). Thus, the specific historical, cultural, and political contexts within the United States are important to keep in mind while considering the findings and recommendations throughout this book.

Research That Crosses Disciplinary Boundaries

The lives of children affected by parental incarceration intersect with numerous social service systems, from corrections and child welfare to education and health care. Researchers and practitioners from academic disciplines that are traditionally attached to these systems have studied the children of incarcerated parents from time to time, but they have usually worked in isolation from each other. This situation must change. To adequately understand the needs and developmental trajectories of the children of incarcerated parents, knowledge and practices from each relevant academic field are needed. Thus, one goal of this volume is to stimulate future collaborative, multidisciplinary research and intervention efforts focusing on the children of incarcerated parents, their families, and their communities.

In service of this end, this volume reflects a comprehensive, cross-disciplinary approach to understanding the children of incarcerated parents. Representatives from criminology, sociology, law, social work, family studies, education, nursing, psychiatry, prevention science, and developmental and clinical psychology contributed chapters, as did a former corrections and child welfare administrator and scientists from the National Institutes of Health and the Bureau of Justice Statistics. By viewing the children of incarcerated parents through diverse lenses, it is our hope that this volume will not only consolidate a multidisciplinary perspective regarding children's outcomes within the context of parental incarceration, but also stimulate new cross-disciplinary collaborations that generate advances in research, practice, and social policy.

Book Themes

Each chapter in this volume is grounded in five central themes: the importance of a developmental perspective, risk and resilience processes, recognition of the multiple contexts that affect children's development, directions for future developmental and intervention research, and implications for policy and practice. Each theme reflects key issues that are relevant to children of incarcerated parents and have often been ignored in the past literature.

A Developmental Perspective

Some children of incarcerated parents are born while their parent(s) are in prison or jail; most affected minor children are less than 10 years old (Glaze and Maruschak 2008; Mumola 2000). However, many adolescents and adult children have experienced a parent's arrest or incarceration at some point. Because children of incarcerated parents' needs differ dramatically throughout their lives, a developmental perspective is essential. Each chapter in this volume emphasizes developmental theory and research as it applies to children whose parents are incarcerated. In addition, chapter 15 emphasizes a demography perspective that considers children's cumulative risk for experiencing the incarceration of a parent during childhood as well as changes that occur in incarceration rates over time.

Risk and Resilience Processes

Because many children of incarcerated parents experience multiple risks, including separation from parents, poverty, parental substance abuse, and shifts in caregivers, much of the literature focusing on this population has focused on risk and negative outcomes. However, many children of incarcerated parents show resilience, defined as successful adaptation in the face of significant adversity (Luthar, Cicchetti, and Becker 2000). Masten (2001) has argued that resilience is an ordinary process as long as a sufficient array of normative human adaptational systems remains intact, such as positive parent-child relationships and extended family networks. The adequate maintenance of protective systems can be extremely challenging for children and families affected by parental criminality and incarceration, and thus fostering resilience is a primary goal of many intervention efforts. In this volume, each chapter highlights protective factors that can help promote resilience in children of incarcerated parents and offers new ideas for intervention and policies that may better assist children and their families.

Contextual Factors

Like all children, the day-to-day lives of children with incarcerated parents are imbedded in family, school, and community contexts. Unlike other children, however, the lives of children of incarcerated parents are heavily influenced by a powerful fourth context, the criminal justice system, which encompasses various subcontexts with distinct subcultures, including the police, the courts, jails, prisons, and probation and parole.

Of particular importance to consider when interpreting findings about the children of incarcerated parents is the type of setting within which a parent is incarcerated. In this volume, we consider children whose parents are in jail, state prison, or federal prison. The Bureau of Justice Statistics defines jails as locally operated correctional facilities that confine people before or after adjudication. Sentences to jail are usually one year or less (usually for misdemeanors), whereas sentences to state prison are generally more than one year (usually for felonies), although this varies by state. Six states (Connecticut, Rhode Island, Vermont, Delaware, Alaska, and Hawaii) have integrated correctional systems that combine jails and prisons. Compared to prisons, jails are often located closer to the incarcerated individual's family members, possibly affecting visitation frequency. There are fewer federal prisons than state prisons, and federal prisons are often located far from the incarcerated individual's family. In addition, federal prisoners are under the legal authority of the U.S. federal government.[3] Policies and procedures regarding visitation and other forms of contact between family members may vary dramatically depending on the type of facility in which the parent is housed.

Each chapter highlights specific contexts such as these that may directly or indirectly affect children's adaptation and development over time, including what is known about how these factors influence the effectiveness of interventions and policies.

Directions for Future Developmental and Intervention Research

Although developmental and intervention research has progressed significantly over the past decade, there is still much to learn about children affected by parental incarceration and their families. By taking an inventory of current research findings, integrating these findings into a coherent framework, and highlighting knowledge gaps in the literature, this volume offers new directions for research focusing both on child and family development and on interventions designed to ameliorate the negative effects of parental incarceration. Each chapter provides suggestions for areas where further research is needed, and these suggestions are tied together in the final chapter.

Policy and Practice Implications

Accessing the emerging literature on the children of incarcerated parents is difficult for policymakers and practitioners. The integrated and rigorous scholarship presented in this volume provides a springboard not only for increased communication among professionals who are interested in the children of incarcerated parents, but also for the generation of new directions in research that can better inform social policies. To this end, each chapter highlights recent research findings and then discusses the potential implications of these findings for public policy and for practice. In part IV of the volume, these implications are discussed from various perspectives, and comments from throughout the book are tied together.

Historical Background and Current Trends

Over the past several decades, criminal justice policies in the United States have fundamentally changed, leading to exponential growth in the number of incarcerated adults in state and federal prisons and jails (Harrison and Karberg 2004; Mumola 2000). Because most incarcerated adults are parents, this phenomenon has led to an 80 percent increase in the number of children affected by parental imprisonment since 1991 (Glaze and Maruschak 2008). In addition to the children and adolescents affected by a parent in prison, many more have parents who were recently released from prison,[4] and others have parents in jail or who were recently released from jail (Kemper and Rivara 1993). As a result, professionals today are more likely than professionals in any prior generation to encounter children who have or have had parents or other family members in jail or prison or under correctional supervision.

In part I of this volume, Susan D. Phillips discusses the history of criminal justice reforms in relation to current knowledge about how children are affected by parental incarceration and suggests needs for further clarification and reflection. Laura M. Maruschak, Lauren E. Glaze, and

Christopher J. Mumola summarize the most recent U.S. Bureau of Justice Statistics national survey of imprisoned individuals in chapter 3. Findings are presented on the characteristics of imprisoned parents and their children, including rates of parental imprisonment over time, rates of visitation and other forms of contact, and the backgrounds and living arrangements of parents before imprisonment. These two chapters provide important context for the chapters that follow.

Developmental Research

Chapters in part II review the known effects and correlates of parental incarceration for children of different ages, focusing on results from recent cross-sectional and longitudinal studies. Because most mothers and many fathers lived with their children before their incarceration (Glaze and Maruschak 2008) and plan to reunify with their families and children following their release, parental incarceration often results in transitory living arrangements for children. Whereas many children and families strive to maintain contact with the incarcerated parent despite the challenges posed by disrupted living situations, additional stressors—such as financial strain, geographic distance from home to prison, and the ambivalence of family members toward the inmate and visitation—compound the difficulties that families face in remaining connected. Children's caregivers play a vital role in helping maintain ties between the incarcerated parent and child, and the quality of environments that caregivers provide is critical for children's cognitive, academic, and social development during parental incarceration. Chapters 4, 5, 6, and 7 explore these issues in the context of children's attachment relationships and home environments, interactions with schools and communities, and friendships and peer relations. Because African American, Latino, and many other minority children are disproportionately affected by parental incarceration, race, ethnicity, and culture are key contexts for understanding risk and resilience in this population (see chapter 8).

Intervention Research

Numerous interventions have been implemented with incarcerated individuals and their children. This body of intervention research is explored in part III of this volume, including a review of research emanating from prison nursery programs available for women who are pregnant when they enter jail or prison (chapter 9), interventions focusing on improving the communication and parenting skills of incarcerated parents (chapter 10), and mentoring programs for children living in the community (chapter 11). There is growing interest in a multimodal orientation to intervention relevant to the children of incarcerated parents (e.g., Eddy et al. 2008), and thus chapter 12 presents an organizing framework for future interventions of this type.

Implications

In recent years, research has begun to shape policy and practice, particularly within state corrections systems. Various governments have adopted mandates to use evidence-based practices, but there remain many details to work out, including how such practices are defined, implemented, and monitored. Part IV of this volume discusses how research findings might influence future policies, practices, and research relevant to children of incarcerated parents. Chapter 13 in this section focuses on the interface between the corrections and child welfare systems, and chapter 14 focuses on possible applications of empirically based preventive interventions to children of incarcerated parents. Chapter 15 discusses policy implications of the research using a demography perspective. The suggestions for research and intervention that have been developed in the preceding chapters are tied together in chapter 16, providing students, researchers, practitioners, and policymakers a clear starting place to engage in more successful and comprehensive multidisciplinary work and decisionmaking on behalf of children affected by parental incarceration.

Summary

Children of incarcerated parents are a significant and growing population. Researchers from multiple disciplines have learned much about this group of children, especially over the past decade. Here, we bring representatives of these multiple disciplines together, summarize the state of scientific knowledge about the children of incarcerated parents, discuss policies and practices grounded in that knowledge, and offer a blueprint for future research. With over 1 in 31 adults, 1 in 18 men, and 1 in 11 African

Americans under some type of correctional control in the United States (Pew Center for the States 2009), it is no longer tenable for policymakers, practitioners, and researchers to ignore the children of these individuals and their families. This book is our collective attempt to bridge the communication gaps between and among research, practice, and policy-making relevant to children of incarcerated parents, and to encourage further high-quality research to generate the information needed for evidence-based practice and policymaking.

NOTES

1. U.S. Department of Justice, Bureau of Justice Statistics, "Probation and Parole in the United States, 2006," http://www.ojp.usdoj.gov/bjs/pandp.htm (accessed November 25, 2008).

2. See, for example, Travis and Waul (2003).

3. U.S. Department of Justice, Bureau of Justice Statistics, "Terms and Definitions," http://bjs.ojp.usdoj.gov/index.cfm?ty=tda (accessed January 2, 2010).

4. U.S. Department of Justice, Bureau of Justice Statistics, "Probation and Parole in the United States, 2006."

REFERENCES

Eddy, J. Mark, Charles R. Martinez Jr., Tracy Schiffmann, Rex Newton, Laura Olin, Leslie Leve, Dana M. Foney, and JoAnn Wu Shortt. 2008. "Development of a Multisystemic Parent Management Training Intervention for Incarcerated Parents, Their Children, and Families." *Clinical Psychologist* 12(3): 86–98.

Glaze, Lauren E., and Laura M. Maruschak. 2008. *Parents in Prison and Their Minor Children.* NCJ 222984. Washington, DC: U.S. Department of Justice, Bureau of Justice Statistics.

Harrison, Paige M., and Jennifer C. Karberg. 2004. "Prison and Jail Inmates at Midyear 2003." NCJ 203947. Washington, DC: U.S. Department of Justice, Bureau of Justice Statistics.

Kemper, Kathi J., and Frederick P. Rivara. 1993. "Parents in Jail." *Pediatrics* 92:261–64.

Luthar, Suniya S., Dante Cicchetti, and Bronwyn Becker. 2000. "The Construct of Resilience: A Critical Evaluation and Guidelines for Future Work." *Child Development* 71:543–62.

Masten, Ann S. 2001. "Ordinary Magic: Resilience Processes in Development." *American Psychologist* 56:227–38.

Mumola, Christopher J. 2000. *Incarcerated Parents and Their Children.* NCJ 182335. Washington, DC: U.S. Department of Justice, Bureau of Justice Statistics.

Murray, Joseph, and David P. Farrington. 2005. "Parental Imprisonment: Effects on Boys' Antisocial Behaviour and Delinquency through the Life Course." *Journal of Child Psychology and Psychiatry* 46:1269–78.

Murray, Joseph, David P. Farrington, Ivana Sekol, and Rikke F. Olsen. 2009. "Effects of Parental Imprisonment on Child Antisocial Behaviour and Mental Health: A Systematic Review." *Campbell Systematic Reviews* 4:1–105. Oslo, Norway: Campbell Collaboration.

Pew Center on the States. 2009. *One in 31: The Long Reach of American Corrections.* Washington, DC: The Pew Charitable Trusts.

Poehlmann, Julie. 2005a. "Children's Family Environments and Intellectual Outcomes during Maternal Incarceration." *Journal of Marriage and Family* 67:1275–85.

———. 2005b. "Representations of Attachment Relationships in Children of Incarcerated Mothers." *Child Development* 76:679–96.

Travis, Jeremy, and Michelle Waul. 2003. *Prisoners Once Removed: The Impact of Incarceration and Reentry on Children, Families, and Communities.* Washington, DC: Urban Institute Press.

PART I
Historical Background and Current Trends

2

The Past as Prologue

Parental Incarceration, Service Planning, and Intervention Development in Context

Susan D. Phillips

O ver the past several decades, criminal justice policies in this coun try changed fundamentally. As a result, more police were hired, more people were sent to prison, and the amount of time people were held in prison increased. Prisons swelled to capacity and beyond. Today, more people are in prison than ever before, and approximately half of them are parents. For professionals working with children, this means that they are much more likely than in any previous generation to encounter children who have parents or other family members who have been involved with the criminal justice system. This chapter describes the evolution of research on parental incarceration and ongoing service planning and intervention development efforts in the context of these policy reforms.

The Era of Mass Incarceration

In the course of a generation, the criminal justice system in America underwent transformative changes. First, prison populations grew at a historically unparalleled rate. In 1985, only 0.5 million people were in prison; now, there are nearly 2.3 million (Gilliard and Beck 1996; West and Sabol 2008). Second, the composition of prison populations changed. Imprisonment was once reserved for people who committed particularly violent acts (e.g., murder, rape, assault) or especially serious property crimes (e.g., burglary, fraud). Today, because of criminal justice reforms, more people are being sent to prison for crimes stemming from abusing or selling drugs (Caplow and Simon 1999; Mauer 1999; Tonry and Petersilia 1999). Also, changes in mental health policies led to an increased number of people entering prison with mental illnesses (Steadman, Holohean, and Dvoskin 1991). More recently, the number of people detained for violating immigration laws has been increasing because of stepped-up efforts to stem illegal immigration (Phillips and Dettlaff 2009).

Collectively, the criminal justice reforms of the 1980s and 1990s are referred to as mass incarceration policies (e.g., Lynch and Sabol 2004; Meares 2004; Piehl 2004). This term alludes not only to the tremendous growth in the number of prisoners in America, but also to how pervasive the experience of incarceration is among members of some communities. This is particularly true of members of poor, urban communities with high levels of multiple social problems (La Vigne, Visher, and Castro 2004; Skogan 1990; Taylor 1997). Because of the institutional and structural racism African Americans have faced in education, employment, and housing, African Americans are often overrepresented in these communities. Accordingly, mass incarceration policies have had particularly acute consequences for African Americans. For example, in the early 1990s, nearly half the black males age 18 to 35 in neighborhoods in Washington, D.C., and Baltimore were under some form of criminal justice authority (Miller cited in Tonry 1995).

Sending large numbers of people from poor communities to prison may not have had the effect policymakers intended. In fact, high incarceration levels may have paradoxically contributed to depressed economic conditions and weakened social ties in communities and, in turn, unintentionally perpetuated crime (Clear 1996; Rose and Clear 1998). Because of the stigma that follows from having a felony record and various regulations that preclude employers from hiring people with felony convictions, the prospects for employment are poor for individuals who have been to prison (Grogger 1995; Needels 1996). In some neighborhoods, large numbers of people are returning from prisons, leading to a concentration of individuals who are shut off from economic opportunities and public assistance programs (Allard 2002; Hagan and Coleman 2001; Rose and Clear 1998; Travis 2002). Similarly, at the family level, parental incarceration makes it more likely that children's families will experience economic distress and that children will experience repeated disruptions in care (Phillips, Erkanli, Keeler, et al. 2006).

Mass incarceration also gave rise to what some refer to as the prison industrial complex (Donzinger 1996). While one segment of society experienced economic challenges because of the criminal justice reforms of the 1980s and 1990s, others benefited. Expenditures for corrections increased at the extraordinary rate of 423 percent between 1982 and 2003 (Hughes 2006). More jails and prisons had to be built to house the historically unprecedented number of inmates, which created work for architects, construction companies, and others. New jobs emerged throughout the criminal justice system to address the need for additional police officers, correctional officers, court clerks, judges, lawyers, probation officers, parole officers, and so forth. Money flowed to companies supplying everything from uniforms and cars to police departments to food and equipment for prisons.

It is within the context of the socioeconomic fallout of criminal justice reforms that incarcerated parents began attracting the attention of advocates for inmates and of scholars. The advent of mass incarceration policies coincided with a period during which feminist scholars questioned whether theories of crime based on male patterns of offending adequately explained the criminal behaviors of women (Greenfeld and Minor-Harper 1991; Johnston and Gadsen 2003). They also questioned whether correctional programs designed to address the needs of a predominantly male population were appropriate for women (Coll et al. 1997; Harm 1992). Among other things, feminists pointed to differences in the traditional parenting roles of men and women and suggested that separating mothers from their children through incarceration was qualitatively different from separating fathers from their children (Houck and Looper 2002; Lord 1995; Zalba 1964).

Because of this confluence of mass incarceration policies and the feminist criminology movement, much of the research on parents in prison during the 1980s and 1990s focused on incarcerated mothers. A great deal was made of the fact that the female prison population (and, by extension, mothers in prison) increased at a faster *rate* than the male population. Between 1986 and 1991, the number of women in prison increased 75 percent in contrast to a 53 percent increase in men (Snell and Morton 1994). But the difference in the rate of growth (i.e., percent increase) between female and male inmates is largely an artifact of the differences in the size of these two populations.

On any given day, about 1.2 million men are in prison compared with only about 93,000 women. This equates to approximately 130 male inmates for every 10 females. To illustrate how the difference in the absolute size of these two populations affects the rate of growth, consider a prison population of 140 people (130 men and 10 women). If 10 additional men were added to the male population, the male population would increase by approximately 8 percent ($10/130 \times 100$). If 10 women were added to the female population, the increase in the female population would be 100 percent ($10/10 \times 100$). Accordingly, the *rate* of growth in mothers in prison may have exceeded the rate for fathers, but the number of fathers in prisons still vastly exceeds the number of mothers.

Advocacy efforts on behalf of incarcerated mothers also stress the fact that, compared with fathers in prison, a higher percentage of mothers lived with their children before their current prison sentence and have children in foster care or being cared for by relatives. These differences are often presented as prima facie evidence that incarcerating mothers is more damaging to children than incarcerating fathers.

One would expect the incarceration of mothers to have *different* consequences for children than the incarceration of fathers because of differences in the traditional male and female parenting roles. That does not mean, however, that incarcerating record numbers of fathers is benign. As the example above helps illustrate, because there are so many more fathers in prison than there are mothers, more children on any given day have been separated from fathers who were sent to prison than from mothers. Similarly, the number of children in foster care or living with grandparents who have fathers in prison on any given day is also greater than the number with mothers in prison.

Because of the emphasis on differences between mothers and fathers in prison, children of incarcerated mothers and fathers are often discussed as if they are two discrete groups. In fact, this is not always the case. About two-thirds of children whose mothers have been arrested also have fathers who have been arrested (Phillips, Erkanli, Costello, et al. 2006; Wilson 1987), and compared with children of never-arrested fathers, teens whose fathers have been arrested are 11 times more likely to also have mothers who have been arrested (Farrington et al. 2001).

Further, by focusing narrowly on parental incarceration, researchers have overlooked the fact that mass incarceration policies have affected members of children's families other than their parents. In addition to having incarcerated mothers and fathers, children have aunts, uncles, grandparents, and siblings who go to prison (Dallaire 2006, 2007; Glaze and Maruschak 2008). In much the same way that incarceration is more pervasive in some communities than in others, incarceration is more pervasive within some families. Research on how different intrafamily incarceration levels affect children is extremely limited. Nonetheless, available data suggest that the likelihood of children becoming involved in delinquency increases markedly as the number of people within their family networks who have been involved with criminal authorities increases (Farrington, Barnes, and Lambert 1996; Farrington et al. 2001).

Parent-Centered Research and Interventions

Advocacy on behalf of mothers in prison spawned a line of scholarship on the parenting roles of individuals in prison. This parent-centered focus is reflected in titles of publications such as *Imprisoned Mothers and Their Children* (Henriques 1982), *The Impact of the Prison Environment on Mothers* (Clark 1995), and *You Can't Be in Prison and Be a Mother, Can You?* (Baunach 1982). It is also reflected in studies of prison-based parent interventions that often evaluate changes in incarcerated parents' behaviors rather than the impact interventions have on children's outcomes (Boudin 1998; Carlson 2001; Loper and Tuerk 2006; Snyder, Carol, and Mullins 2001).[1] This focus is due, in part, to difficulties in studying inmates' children (Eddy et al. 2001).

Among the programs implemented in correctional facilities that address inmates' parenting roles are various forms of parent education (Hughes and Harrison-Thompson 2002; Loper and Tuerk 2006; Palm 2003), visitation programs that allow parents to engage in parent-child activities (e.g., scouting, reading activities) when their children visit them in prison (Block 1999; Kazura and Toth 2004; Snyder et al. 2001), and prison nurseries that allow mothers who give birth while incarcerated to keep their children with them for a limited time (Carlson 2001).[2] These programs have become more common in the last decade but are still available only on a limited basis. For example, only about 12 percent of parents in state prisons and 26 percent in federal prisons report participating in any type of parenting program while in prison (Glaze and Maruschak 2008).

Limitations of the Parent-Centered Perspective

The parent-centered perspective on parental incarceration has many inherent limitations when it comes to understanding how parental imprisonment affects children. One is that it tends to focus only on parents' current prison sentences when, in actuality, most parents in prison (between 63 and 78 percent) are not new to the criminal justice system but have served previous sentences to probation or incarceration (Mumola 2000). The parent-centered perspective, as it is typically applied, also tends to overlook the fact that inmates' children differ in their prior experiences of parental arrest and incarceration. This may be an important omission given evidence that children experience a greater sense of stigma and shame the first time their parents are sent to prison (Lowenstein 1986), and that the more times parents are incarcerated, the less likely they are to have lived with their children (Harm and Phillips 2001). Any given episode of parental incarceration, therefore, may hold different meaning and have different consequences for children depending on their parents' prior criminal histories.

The parent-centered perspective also tends to overlook differences in the reasons parents are in prison. Discussions of parental incarceration often focus on parents who are in prison for drug-related crimes, because of the role that the criminal justice reforms of the 1980s and 1990s played in increasing the number of nonviolent offenders in prison on drug charges. Parents in prison, however, are serving time for a variety of crimes, some of which involved victimizing members of their families. How the needs of children and families may differ based on the nature of the crimes incarcerated parents commit has not received much attention, but one can certainly anticipate that children whose parents victimized family members (including possibly their children) may have different needs than children whose parents are in prison for other crimes (e.g., drug possession, forgery, or arson).

Finally, the parent-centered perspective also often overlooks the fact that parents are serving sentences of different lengths. Some will be released from prison after serving relatively short sentences, others may not be released until their children are adults, and some (about 1 in 50) will never leave prison alive (Glaze and Maruschak 2008). There is very little information about how variations in parents' prison sentences affect how children and their caregivers cope with parental incarceration. Evaluators, however, noted the importance of understanding such differences when they assessed demonstration projects for children of incarcerated parents that were funded by the federal government several years ago (Bush-Baskette and Patino 2004). Differences in the length of parents' prison sentences were also noted as an important consideration in the design of parenting programs for inmate parents (Loper and Tuerk 2006).

Child-Centered Research and Intervention Development

Whereas many scholars and advocates have applied a parent-focused perspective in understanding and addressing parental incarceration, some others have taken a child-centered approach (Bernstein 2005; Gabel 1992; Johnston 1992; Murray 2007; Myers et al. 1999). A question that arises when parental incarceration is looked at from a child-focal perspective is how sending parents to prison affects children relative to other risk factors that might adversely influence child development.

Developmental Epidemiologic Perspective

Many different risk factors can operate in the lives of children whose parents are in prison. For example, parents in prison have a greater-than-average likelihood of having substance abuse and mental health problems, having histories of family violence, and being inadequately educated (Glaze and Maruschak 2008; Jordan et al. 2002; Phillips, Erkanli, Costello, et al. 2006). These parent problems are well-established correlates of various family risk factors including child abuse and neglect, single-parent households, repeated parent-child separations, residential instability, and extreme poverty. Moreover, a substantial body of research links these parent and family risks to the etiology of childhood functional impairments (e.g., school failure, poor peer relationships), serious childhood emotional and behavioral disturbances, delinquency, and substance abuse (Ammerman et al. 1999; Costello et al. 2002; Cuffe et al. 2005; Oyserman et al. 2000).

The most consistent finding in research on children of incarcerated parents is that they are exposed to a greater total number of risk factors than other children. In other words, *as a group*, children of incarcerated parents are not just more likely to be exposed to parental substance abuse *or* domestic violence *or* inadequately educated parents *or* family disruption or any other single risk factor associated with parent criminality and incarceration. Rather, families in which parents become involved with criminal authorities are more likely to be grappling with multiple problems.

Exposure to a greater total number of risk factors has been documented in studies of children in the general population whose parents have been incarcerated (Murray and Farrington 2005; Phillips, Erkanli, Costello, et al. 2006), as well as in studies of high-risk populations such as teens receiving mental health services (Phillips et al. 2002) and children who come in contact with the child welfare system (Phillips et al. 2004). This is important because the chances of children becoming involved in delinquency rise exponentially as the number of risk factors they experience increases (Biederman et al. 1995; Bry, McKeon, and Pandina 1982). It also suggests that service providers must be prepared to broker and coordinate different services to address multiple needs when working with families in which parents have been incarcerated.

Is Parental Incarceration Causally Linked to Adverse Child Outcomes?   The critical public policy question raised by mass incarceration policies is whether incarcerating parents increases the chances of children developing serious problems, or whether parental incarceration is simply a proxy for numerous other risk factors that just happen to coincide with parental arrest and incarceration (e.g., parental substance abuse, family violence, poverty). Researchers have not yet been able to conclusively answer this question.

Using data from the Cambridge Study in Delinquent Development, researchers in England found that boys who were separated during childhood from their parents because of incarceration were more likely to become involved with criminal authorities than were boys who were separated from their parents during childhood for other reasons such as divorce or illness (Murray and Farrington 2005). This suggests that parental incarceration (or at least something associated with parental incarceration) may have a criminogenic effect on children that other forms of parent-child separation do not. Researchers in other countries, however, have not been able to replicate this finding (Murray, Janson, and Farrington 2007). This may be because of between-country differences in social service systems and the supports generally available to children and families. Accordingly, we cannot automatically assume that the findings of the Cambridge Study generalize to American children.

A study of children in 11 counties in western North Carolina, the Great Smoky Mountains Study, reports that parental incarceration is directly linked to certain adverse family conditions, but not others (Phillips, Erkanli, Keeler, et al. 2006). More specifically, this study finds that when the influences of parental substance abuse, mental illness, and inadequate education are taken into account, parental incarceration is an additional, independent risk factor for children living in families facing economic hardship and for children experiencing repeated disruptions in care. Parental incarceration, however, is not significantly associated with the quality of care children receive or the structure of their families. Parents' problems play a greater role in explaining these latter family circumstances than does parental incarceration. The Great Smoky Mountain Study, however, is based on youth in a rural region of North Carolina where the population is predominantly white or Native American. These findings need to be replicated in other locales to ascertain their applicability to other groups of children.

The Cambridge Study and the Great Smoky Mountains Study are based on children in the general population. The effect of parental incarceration relative to other risk factors has also been studied in several high-risk populations. A study of adolescents who received routine mental health services from providers in Arkansas and Texas examines the relationship between parents' histories of incarceration and adolescents' treatment outcomes six months after children begin an episode of care (Phillips et al. 2002). At intake, the clinical differences between teens whose parents have been to jail or prison and other youth are negligible, but six months after intake teens whose parents have been incarcerated are significantly more likely to have been expelled from school or arrested. This study, however, does not account for differences in the communities in which children live. It is possible that these findings could result from differences in school systems' "no tolerance" policies or patterns of policing rather than parental incarceration.

Finally, a study of a nationally representative sample of children who are subjects of reports of maltreatment finds that having a parent who has recently been arrested is marginally related to children being placed in out-of-home placement (i.e., relative placements, nonrelative foster care, group homes, and so forth) (Phillips et al. 2004). Recent parental arrest, however, is not specifically related to children entering foster care. Instead, placement in nonrelative foster care is linked to the severity of emotional and behavioral problems children are having and the number of different problems parents and families are experiencing.

Service Planning from the Developmental Epidemiologic Perspective. From the child-centered, developmental epidemiologic perspective, the goals of intervention development and service planning for children whose parents experience incarceration are to reduce children's risk exposure and increase protective factors in their lives in order to prevent functional impairments and serious emotional and behavioral problems. Once problems have manifested, a thorough assessment is in order to identify appropriate interventions.

Viewed from the developmental epidemiologic perspective, a crucial shortcoming of many corrections-based programs that address inmate parenting issues is that they typically are not linked with interventions to address parents' underlying problems that place children at risk for developing serious problems (e.g., substance abuse, mental illness). For example, two of three parents in prison (67 percent) have substance abuse problems, a well-recognized risk factor for myriad child problems, but less than half (42 percent) of parents receive substance abuse services in prison (Glaze and Maruschak 2008). The proportion of parents with mental health problems who receive treatment while in prison is even smaller (30 percent). The failure of corrections-based programs to address these problems leaves children vulnerable to re-exposure to these risk factors should their parents reunite with them once released from prison. Further, because many parent risk factors are associated with criminal recidivism, when parents' problems are not addressed while they are in prison, it places children at risk for experiencing additional incarceration-related separations.

When it comes to developing child-centered interventions, it is important to note that (as is the case with parents in prison) children of incarcerated parents are not a homogeneous population. Over a decade ago, Denise Johnston, an advocate and early pleader of efforts to help children of incarcerated parents, pointed out that no single risk factor is universal among children of incarcerated parents (Johnston 1995). This, however, has not prevented groups from employing a one-size-fits-all approach to service planning (e.g., federally sponsored mentoring programs).

Distinctive subgroups of children whose parents have been involved with criminal authorities have different risk factors operating in their lives. For example, researchers studying teens whose mothers had arrest histories identified four distinctive subgroups of children. One group, about 50 percent of the teens, had minimal risk exposure. They were living in households in which there was only occasionally an isolated parent or family risk factor (Phillips, Erkanli, Costello, et al. 2006). The other 50 percent were split almost equally into three additional subgroups. One was made up of children who had histories of physical and sexual abuse. The second group was children who had one or more parents who abused drugs or had mental illnesses. The final group was teens living with extremely poor single mothers who were not providing adequate supervision. Different interventions are indicated for each of these groups. Similar research needs to be conducted with children at various other developmental stages to better understand the differences among children of incarcerated parents.

The limitations of the above study notwithstanding, it points to several important considerations for those involved in planning services or developing interventions for children of incarcerated parents. First, it highlights the fact that not all families with an incarcerated parent are problem ridden. At first glance, this may seem contrary to research showing that cumulative risk is higher among families affected by parental incarceration than among other families, but that is not the case. When we say that families affected by parental incarceration experience a greater number of risk factors, it refers to a collective characteristic of this group—a statistical average. Imagine, for instance, that the average age of a person who reads this book is 35 years. That does not mean that all readers or even most are age 35; some will be younger and some older. Similarly, saying that families affected by incarceration have a greater total number of problems *on average* than other families does not mean that all families that experience parental incarceration have a multitude of problems; some families will have many, and some families will have few or none.

Second, the aforementioned study sends a clear message that a unilateral approach to addressing the needs of children of incarcerated parents is inadequate; different children and families need different interventions. Consistent with this, a few states are bringing together multiple state agencies to identify the needs of the children of incarcerated parents among their constituencies and jointly develop plans for addressing these children's needs (Phillips 2008). In addition to validating the importance of multifaceted planning efforts, this study suggests the need to prepare professionals and volunteers who work with children of incarcerated parents to screen for a range of different problems and the need to establish referral pathways so families can access the particular mix of services that will best address their specific needs.

The Procedural Justice Perspective

Parental incarceration may also be viewed from a procedural justice perspective, which moves the discussion of parental incarceration away from childhood pathology. Procedural justice is concerned with the fairness of processes for settling conflicts (Lind and Tyler 1988). In the case of children of incarcerated parents, we might talk about the *lack* of procedural justice in the process of settling conflicts between the state and individuals who violate the law, a lack that stems from the unintended consequences parental arrest and incarceration have for children. This perspective is seen in the title of a seminal report on children of incarcerated parents, *Why Punish the Children?*

To illustrate the difference between the epidemiologic and procedural justice perspectives, consider that sending parents to prison sometimes causes children to be separated from their parents (Glaze and Maruschak 2008). From the epidemiological point of view, parent-child separation might be of interest as a possible antecedent of grief, disrupted attachment, or economic hardship (Murray and Farrington 2005; Poehlmann 2005). Each possible consequence of incarceration-induced parent-child separation could increase the chances of children developing serious problems. In contrast, from the procedural justice perspective, the fact that sending parents to prison separates children from their parents is of interest simply because the children who are affected have not done anything to warrant being deprived of their parents. Moreover, principles of equity would dictate that children affected by parental incarceration have the same right to an ongoing relationship with their parent as every other child and that they have the same right to compassion and concern in the wake of losing their parent as children who are separated from their parents for other reasons such as divorce, illness, or military service. Accordingly, from a procedural justice perspective, reducing the burden of parental incarceration for children is a matter of justice and does not hinge on demonstrating a relationship between parental incarceration and adverse child outcomes.

The procedural justice framework is incorporated in *The Bill of Rights for Children of Incarcerated Parents,* which was written by the San Francisco Children of Incarcerated Parents Partnership (SFCIPP 2008). The rights defined in *The Bill of Rights* are not rights in the legal sense: they have no basis in law. Instead, they are a list of principles that SFCIPP believes should guide how individuals and systems respond to children whose parents become involved in the criminal justice system. *The Bill of Rights* identifies the rights for children: (1) to be kept safe and informed at the time of their parent's arrest; (2) to be heard when decisions are made about them; (3) to be considered when decisions are made about their parent; (4) to be well cared for in their parent's absence; (5) to speak with, see, and touch their parent; (6) to be supported as they struggle with their parent's incarceration; (7) not to be judged, labeled, or blamed because of their parent's incarceration; and (8) to have a lifelong relationship with their parent.

Groups across the United States have been using *The Bill of Rights* to guide advocacy and service planning efforts. Although *The Bill of Rights* reflects a procedural justice orientation, groups often revert to a parent-centered perspective or an epidemiologic framework in their efforts to make *The Bill of Rights* a reality (Phillips 2008). For example, some groups are pursuing changes because they believe those changes will reduce parents' criminal recidivism (a parent-centered goal) or prevent attachment disorders (an epidemiologic goal). Nonetheless, *The Bill of Rights* reframes discussions about children of incarcerated parents in a way that does not require pathologizing children.

Summary

Since the advent of mass incarceration, children of incarcerated parents have increasingly captured the attention of advocates, researchers, policymakers, and service providers. One thing we know with confidence about these children is that, as a group, they experience numerous risk factors that might adversely affect child development. At the same time, not all these children are equally at risk nor are they at risk for the same reasons. Research suggests that the subgroup of children who are most likely to develop problems are those who live in families with multiple co-occurring problems and with multiple family members who have been involved with the criminal justice system. Ironically, the very families that may most need interventions may also pose the greatest challenges to service providers because they are likely to need an array of integrated services from multiple service systems.

While prisons are increasingly implementing programs that address inmates' parental roles, they are missing important opportunities to address serious parent problems such as substance abuse, mental illness, and inadequate education, problems that place children at risk for developing serious problems. At the same time, service planning and intervention development efforts often target isolated family members (i.e., parents in prison or their children or relatives who care for children while their parents are in prison) or isolated problems (e.g., mentoring, child mental health), resulting in a fragmented response to the needs of children of incarcerated parents.

It is important to address the risk factors that operate in the lives of children of incarcerated parents and to minimize the unintended adverse consequences parental incarceration sometimes has for children. At the same time, it is important to recognize that parents in prison and their children are not a monolithic group. Additional research is needed to better understand how these parents and their children differ from one another and to identify the services and interventions that will be most efficacious for different subgroups.

Finally, not all children whose parents go to prison live in problem-ridden families or develop serious problems. By failing to acknowledge families' resilience, we are actually helping perpetuate negative stereotypes about families that become involved with criminal authorities and contributing to the stigma associated with having a parent in prison.

Ultimately, it is not enough simply to develop new services and interventions to make parental incarceration less noxious for children. Children of incarcerated parents have become a population of interest because, as a society, we elected to use incarceration as the principal means for addressing criminal activity. Criminal activity is most prevalent in neighborhoods in which there are high concentrations of recalcitrant social problems. If we ignore these underlying social problems and simply create new programs that make parental incarceration more palatable for children, we are paving the way for advocates, researchers, and service providers who work with or on behalf of this population to become simply the not-for-profit sector of the prison industrial complex.

NOTES

1. See also Bob Meadows and Vicki Sheff-Cahan, "Moms (and Kids) Behind Bars: A Pioneering Prison in California Lets Inmates Raise Children While Doing Time," *People,* vol. 60, no. 18, November 3, 2003; and Jennifer B. Spring, *The Effect of Parent Education on Knowledge of Parenting Skills and Attitude Change of Incarcerated Mothers,* dissertation/thesis, Indiana State University, Terre Haute, 1998.

2. See also Meadows and Sheff-Cahan, "Moms (and Kids) Behind Bars."

REFERENCES

Allard, Patricia. 2002. *Life Sentences: Denying Welfare Benefits to Women Convicted of Drug Offenses.* Washington, DC: The Sentencing Project.

Ammerman, Robert T., David J. Kolko, Levent Kirisci, Timothy C. Blackson, and Michael A. Dawes. 1999. "Child Abuse Potential in Parents with Histories of Substance Use Disorder." *Child Abuse & Neglect* 23:1225–38.

Baunach, Phyllis J. 1982. "You Can't Be a Mother and Be in Prison. . . . Can You? Impacts of the Mother-Child Separation." In *The Criminal Justice System and Women,* edited by Barbara Raffel Price and Natalie J. Sokoloff (155–69). New York: Clark Boardman.

Bernstein, Nell. 2005. *All Alone in the World: Children of the Incarcerated.* New York: The New Press.

Biederman, Joseph, Sharon Milberger, Stephen V. Faraone, Kathleen Kiely, Jessica Gutie, Eric Mick, et al. 1995. "Family-Environment Risk Factors for Attention-Deficit Hyperactivity Disorder: A Test of Rutter's Indicators of Adversity." *Archive of General Psychiatry* 2:464–70.

Block, Kathleen J. 1999. "Bringing Scouting to Prison: Programs and Challenges." *Prison Journal* 79:269 (215).

Boudin, Kathy. 1998. "Lessons from a Mother's Program in Prison: A Psychosocial Approach Supports Women and Their Children." *Women and Therapy* 21:103–26.

Bry, Breanna H., Patricia McKeon, and Robert J. Pandina. 1982. "Extent of Drug Use as a Function of Number of Risk Factors." *Journal of Abnormal Psychology* 91:273–79.

Bush-Baskette, Stephanie, and Vanessa Patino. 2004. *The National Council on Crime and Delinquency's Evaluation of the Project Development of National Institute of Correction's/Child Welfare League of America's Planning and Intervention Sites Funded to Address Needs of Children of Incarcerated Parents.* Oakland, CA: National Council on Crime and Delinquency.

Caplow, Theodore, and Jonathan Simon. 1999. "Understanding Prison Policy and Population Trends." In *Prisons,* edited by Michael Tonry and Joan Petersilia (63–120). Chicago: University of Chicago Press.

Carlson, Joseph R. 2001. "Prison Nursery 2000: A Five-Year Review of the Prison Nursery at the Nebraska Correctional Center for Women." *Journal of Offender Rehabilitation* 33:75–98.

Clark, Judith. 1995. "The Impact of the Prison Environment on Mothers." *Prison Journal* 75:306–40.

Clear, Todd R., ed. 1996. *Backfire: When Incarceration Increases Crime.* New York: Vera Institute of Justice.

Coll, Cynthia G., Jean B. Miller, Jacqueline P. Fields, and Betsy Mathews. 1997. "The Experiences of Women in Prison: Implications for Services and Prevention." *Women and Therapy* 20:11–29.

Costello, E. Jane, Alaattin Erkanli, John A. Fairbank, and Adrian Angold. 2002. "The Prevalence of Potentially Traumatic Events and in Childhood and Adolescence." *Journal of Traumatic Stress* 15:99–112.

Cuffe, Steven P., Robert E. McKeown, Cheryl L. Addy, and Carol Z. Garrison. 2005. "Family and Psychosocial Risk Factors in a Longitudinal Epidemiological Study of Adolescents." *Journal of the American Academy of Child and Adolescent Psychiatry* 44:121–29.

Dallaire, Danielle H. 2006. "Children with Incarcerated Mothers: Developmental Outcomes, Special Challenges, and Recommendations." *Journal of Applied Developmental Psychology* 28:15–24.

———. 2007. "Incarcerated Mothers and Fathers: A Comparison of Risks for Children and Families." *Family Relations* 56(5): 440–53.

Donzinger, Steven R., ed. 1996. *The Real War on Crime: The Report of the National Criminal Justice Commission.* New York: Harper Collins.

Eddy, Mark A., Melissa Powell, Margaret H. Szubka, Maura L. McCool, and Susan Kuntz. 2001. "Challenges in Research with Incarcerated Parents and Importance in Violence Prevention." *American Journal of Preventive Medicine* 20(1): 56–62.

Farrington, David P., Geoffrey Barnes, and Sandra Lambert. 1996. "The Concentration of Offending in Families." *Legal and Criminological Psychology* 1:47–643.

Farrington, David P., Derrick Jolliffe, Rolf Loeber, Magda Stouthamer-Loeber, and Larry M. Kalb. 2001. "The Concentration of Offenders in Families, and Family Criminality in the Prediction of Boys' Delinquency." *Journal of Adolescence* 24:579–96.

Gabel, Stewart. 1992. "Behavioral Problems in Sons of Incarcerated or Otherwise Absent Fathers: The Issue of Separation." *Family Process* 31:303–14.

Gilliard, Darrell K., and Alan J. Beck. 1996. "Prison and Jail Inmates, 1995." NCJ 161132. Washington, DC: U.S. Department of Justice, Bureau of Justice Statistics.

Glaze, Lauren E., and Laura M. Maruschak. 2008. *Parents in Prison and Their Minor Children.* NCJ 222984. Washington, DC: U.S. Department of Justice, Bureau of Justice Statistics.

Greenfeld, Lawrence A., and Stephanie Minor-Harper. 1991. *Women in Prison.* NCJ 127991. Washington, DC: U.S. Department of Justice, Bureau of Justice Statistics.

Grogger, Jeff. 1995. "The Effects of Arrest on the Employment and Earnings of Young Men." *Quarterly Journal of Economics* 110:51–72.

Hagan, John, and Juleigh P. Coleman. 2001. "Returning Captives of the American War on Drugs: Issues of Community and Family Reentry." *Crime and Delinquency* 47:352–67.

Harm, Nancy J. 1992. "Social Policy on Women Prisoners: A Historical Analysis." *Affilia* 7(1): 90–108.

Harm, Nancy J., and Susan D. Phillips. 2001. "You Can't Go Home Again—or Can You?" *Journal of Offender Rehabilitation* 32(3): 3–21.

Henriques, Zelma W. 1982. *Imprisoned Mothers and Their Children.* Washington, DC: University Press of America.

Houck, Katherine D. F., and Ann B. Looper. 2002. "The Relationship of Parenting Stress to Adjustment among Mothers in Prison." *American Journal of Orthopsychiatry* 72:548–58.

Hughes, Kristen A. 2006. "Justice Expenditures and Employment in the United States, 2003." NCJ 212260. Washington, DC: U.S. Department of Justice, Bureau of Justice Statistics.

Hughes, Margaret J., and Jenee Harrison-Thompson. 2002. "Prison Parenting Programs: A National Survey." *Social Policy Journal* 1:57–74.

Johnston, Denise. 1992. *Children of Offenders.* Pasadena, CA: Pacific Oaks Center for Children of Incarcerated Parents.

———. 1995. "Effects of Parental Incarceration." In *Children of Incarcerated Parents,* edited by Katherine Gabel and Denise Johnston (59–88). New York: Lexington Books.

Johnston, Denise, and Vivian L. Gadsen. 2003. "What Works: Children of Incarcerated Offenders." In *Heading Home: Offender Reintegration into the Family,* edited by Vivian L. Gadsen (123–54). Lanham, MD: American Correctional Association.

Jordan, B. Kathleen, E. Belle Federmal, Barbara J. Burns, William E. Schlenger, John A. Fairbank, and Juesta M. Caddell. 2002. "Lifetime Use of Mental Health and Substance Abuse Treatment Services by Incarcerated Women Felons." *Psychiatric Services* 53:317–25.

Kazura, Kerry, and Kristina Toth. 2004. "Playrooms in Prison: Helping Offenders Connect with Their Children." *Corrections Today* 66:128–32.

La Vigne, Nancy G., Christy A. Visher, and Jennifer Castro. 2004. *Chicago Prisoners' Experiences Returning Home.* Washington, DC: The Urban Institute.

Lind, E. Allan, and Tom R. Tyler. 1988. *The Social Psychology of Procedural Justice.* New York: Plenum Press.

Loper, Ann B., and Elena H. Tuerk. 2006. "Parenting Programs for Incarcerated Parents: Current Research and Future Directions." *Criminal Justice Policy Review* 17(4): 407–27.

Lord, Elaine. 1995. "A Prison Superintendent's Perspective on Women in Prison." *The Prison Journal* 75(2): 257–69.

Lowenstein, Ariela. 1986. "Temporary Single Parenthood: The Case of Prisoners' Families." *Family Relations* 36:79–85.

Lynch, James P., and William J. Sabol. 2004. "Assessing the Effect of Mass Incarceration on Informal Social Control in Communities." *Criminology and Public Policy* 3:267–93.

Mauer, Marc. 1999. *Race to Incarcerate.* New York: The New Press.

Meares, Tracey L. 2004. "Mass Incarceration: Who Pays the Price for Criminal Offending?" *Criminology and Public Policy* 3(2): 295–302.

Mumola, Christopher J. 2000. *Incarcerated Parents and Their Children.* NCJ 182335. Washington, DC: U.S. Department of Justice, Bureau of Justice Statistics.

Murray, Joseph. 2007. "The Cycle of Punishment: Social Exclusion of Prisoners and Their Children." *Journal of Criminology and Criminal Justice* 7(1): 55–81.

Murray, Joseph, and David P. Farrington. 2005. "Parental Imprisonment: Effects on Boys' Antisocial Behaviour and Delinquency through the Life Course." *Journal of Child Psychology and Psychiatry* 46:1269–78.

Murray, Joseph, Carl-Gunnar Janson, and David P. Farrington. 2007. "Crime in Adult Offspring of Prisoners: A Cross-National Comparison of Two Longitudinal Samples." *Criminal Justice and Behavior* 34:133–49.

Myers, Barbara J., Tina M. Smarsh, Kristine Amlund-Hagen, and Suzanne Kennon. 1999. "Children of Incarcerated Mothers." *Journal of Child and Family Studies* 8(1): 11–25.

Needels, Karen E. 1996. "Go Directly to Jail and Do Not Collect? A Long-Term Study of Recidivism, Employment, and Earnings Patterns among Prison Releasees." *Journal of Research in Crime and Delinquency* 33:471–96.

Oyserman, Daphna, Carol T. Mowbray, Paula Allen-Meares, and Kirsten Firminger. 2000. "Parenting among Mothers with Serious Mental Illness." *American Journal of Orthopsychiatry* 70:296–315.

Palm, Glen F. 2003. "Parent Education for Incarcerated Parents: Understanding 'What Works.'" In *Heading Home: Offender Reintegration in the Family*, edited by Vivian L. Gadsen (89–122). Lanham, MD: American Correctional Association.

Phillips, Susan D. 2008. *The Bill of Rights for Children of Incarcerated Parents Technical Assistance Project: Evaluation Report*. Chicago: Jane Addams College of Social Work.

Phillips, Susan D., and Alan J. Dettlaff. 2009. "More than Parents in Prison: The Broader Overlap between the Criminal Justice and Child Welfare Systems." *Journal of Public Child Welfare* 3:3–22.

Phillips, Susan D., Barbara J. Burns, H. Ryan Wagner, and Richard P. Barth. 2004. "Parental Arrest and Children in Child Welfare Services Agencies." *American Journal of Orthopsychiatry* 2:174–86.

Phillips, Susan D., Barbara J. Burns, H. Ryan Wagner, Teresa L. Kramer, and James R. Robbins. 2002. "Parental Incarceration among Youth Receiving Mental Health Services." *Journal of Child and Family Studies* 11(4): 385–99.

Phillips, Susan D., Alaattin Erkanli, E. Jane Costello, and Adrienne Angold. 2006. "Differences among Children Whose Mothers Have a History of Arrest." *Women and Criminal Justice* 17(2/3): 45–63.

Phillips, Susan D., Alaattin Erkanli, Gordon P. Keeler, E. Jane Costello, and Adrienne Angold. 2006. "Disentangling the Risks: Parent Criminal Justice Involvement and Children's Exposure to Family Risks." *Criminology and Public Policy* 5(4): 677–702.

Piehl, Anne H. 2004. "The Challenge of Mass Incarceration." *Criminology and Public Policy* 3:303–308.

Poehlmann, Julie. 2005. "Representations of Attachment Relationships in Children of Incarcerated Mothers." *Child Development* 76:679–96.

Rose, Dina R., and Todd R. Clear. 1998. "Incarceration, Social Capital, and Crime: Implications for Social Disorganization Theory." *Criminology* 26:441–78.

San Francisco Children of Incarcerated Parents Partnership. 2008. *San Francisco Children of Incarcerated Parents Partnership: Who We Are*. San Francisco: San Francisco Children of Incarcerated Parents Partnership.

Skogan, Wesley G. 1990. *Disorder and Decline: Crime and the Spiral of Decay in American Neighborhoods*. New York: The Free Press.

Snell, Tracey L., and Danielle C. Morton. 1994. *Women in Prison*. NCJ 145321. Washington, DC: U.S. Department of Justice, Bureau of Justice Statistics.

Snyder, Zoann K., Teresa A. Carol, and Megan M. C. Mullins. 2001. "Parenting from Prison: An Examination of a Children's Visitation Program at a Women's Correctional Facility." *Marriage and Family Review* 32:33–62.

Steadman, Henry J., Edward J. Holohean, and Joel Dvoskin. 1991. "Estimating Mental Health Needs and Service Utilization among Prison Inmates." *Bulletin of the American Academy of Psychiatry Law* 19(3): 297–307.

Taylor, Ralph B. 1997. "Social Order and Disorder of Street Blocks and Neighborhoods: Ecology, Microecology, and the Systemic Model of Social Disorganization." *Journal of Research in Crime and Delinquency* 34(1): 113–55.

Tonry, Michael. 1995. *Malign Neglect*. New York: Oxford Press.

Tonry, Michael, and Joan Petersilia. 1999. "American Prisons at the Beginning of the Twenty-First Century." In *Prisons,* edited by Michael Tonry and Joan Petersilia (1–16). Chicago: University of Chicago Press.

Travis, Jeremy. 2002. *But They All Come Back.* Washington, DC: Urban Institute Press.

West, Heather C., and William J. Sabol. 2008. "Prisoners in 2007." NCJ 224280. Washington, DC: U.S. Department of Justice, Bureau of Justice Statistics.

Wilson, Harriett. 1987. "Parental Supervision Re-examined." *British Journal of Criminology* 27:273–301.

Zalba, Serapio R. 1964. *Women Prisoners and Their Families.* Sacramento, CA: Department of Social Welfare and Department of Corrections.

3

Incarcerated Parents and Their Children

Findings from the Bureau of Justice Statistics

Laura M. Maruschak, Lauren E. Glaze,
and Christopher J. Mumola

Between 1980 and 2000, the rate at which U.S. residents were held under the jurisdiction of state and federal prison systems more than tripled (Beck and Gilliard 1995; West and Sabol 2008). In the wake of this dramatic increase in the nation's incarceration rate, many researchers began to measure the impacts of incarceration on communities. But the impacts of incarceration on families and children have not received the same attention. While Murray and Farrington (2008) state that this absence of quality research reflects "a lack of academic and public interest in the plight of prisoners' children," identifying incarcerated parents—and through them, their children—remains a challenging endeavor.

A practical reason for this difficulty is that most departments of corrections in the United States do not routinely track either the parental status of their prisoners or any information about the children of prisoners. While many reentry programs recognize the value of maintaining prisoner connections to loved ones in the community, this concern has not translated into systematic efforts by correctional authorities to maintain data on the number of such parents or their children. This data gap may result from prisoners' parental status not being a factor in core decisions regarding facility security. Additionally, even if correctional authorities attempted to systematically collect data on parental status, underreporting may occur. Two-thirds of all parents in prison are fathers who did not live with any of their minor children in the month before their arrest

(Glaze and Maruschak 2008). Many of these fathers may choose not to report their parental status because of fears of additional sanctions for failures to pay child support in the past or for known failings to meet obligations while incarcerated.

As a result of local data collection difficulties, the national estimates of the size and characteristics of this population by the Bureau of Justice Statistics (BJS), the statistical component of the U.S. Department of Justice, have gained wide use in both research and policy work conducted on children of incarcerated parents. These estimates are derived from personal interviews with individual prisoners nationwide, rather than from administrative data. While BJS has conducted similar interviews with local jail inmates, the information provided in this chapter focuses only on parents incarcerated in state and federal prisons in the United States and their affected children. Given the substantial differences in the typical length of stay, the types of criminal offenders housed, and the adjudication status of the inmates held in prisons and jails, the resulting impacts on families and children should be studied separately.

BJS Surveys of State and Federal Prisoners

The BJS surveys are not focused on learning about prisoners' families but rather are designed to collect a rich array of data on the personal and criminal backgrounds of prisoners. The survey datasets contain information on more than 2,000 items and cover such topics as childhood experiences, prior military service, family structure, substance abuse histories, mental and physical health problems, prior convictions, and current offense and sentence. In the context of these wide-ranging interviews, the number of questions about children is fairly limited. However, the abundance of information available in the datasets allows researchers to construct a detailed portrait of parents in prison.

The information collected about these children is obtained from the incarcerated parent, not from other family members, caregivers, social service agencies, or children. The scope of information that can be collected focusing on these children's lives (e.g., school performance, health and development) during the period of parental incarceration is limited given the minimal contact some of these parents have (or had before admission) with their children (Glaze and Maruschak 2008; Mumola 2000). These interviews, conducted in confidential settings in the prison facility through computer-assisted personal interviewing, gathered data on whether prisoners had any children, whether they were living with any of their children before incarceration, how much care they provided for any of their children, the current caregiver of the children, and whether they had had any contact with their children since their incarceration. In addition, the surveys offer a unique resource for gaining in-depth personal information on the lives and criminal careers of parents in prison.

BJS has been conducting national surveys of prisoners for more than 30 years. The series began with the 1974 Survey of Inmates in State Correctional Facilities. Since that time, surveys have been conducted periodically every five to seven years. The surveys have been fielded concurrently with a separate national sample of federal prisoners beginning in 1991. The most recent editions of the prisoner surveys were conducted in 1997 and 2004. For the 2004 surveys, nationally representative samples of 14,499 state prisoners and 3,686 federal prisoners completed interviews. Both the 1997 and 2004 surveys resulted in detailed special reports by BJS focusing on incarcerated parents and the impacts on their children (Glaze and Maruschak 2008; Mumola 2000). This chapter summarizes key findings from these two reports and reflects on future research and data collection efforts with this population.

Parents in Prison

In 2007, an estimated 809,800 parents of minor children were incarcerated in U.S. prisons.[1] The majority of both state (52 percent) and federal (63 percent) prisoners were parents.[2] Since 1991, the number of parents in prison has increased by almost 80 percent, or by an additional 357,300 parents (figure 3.1). While this growth is substantial, the increase is less than the increase in the U.S. prison population over the same period. The most rapid period of growth in the number of incarcerated parents occurred between 1991 and 1997, which was similar to the growth in the U.S. prison population. While the incarcerated parent and the U.S. prison populations continued to increase between 1997 and 2007, both populations increased more slowly.

In addition, during this time, the growth in the incarcerated parent population was outpaced by the growth in the U.S. prison population. One possible explanation for this trend is the aging of the U.S. prison population. Prisoners age 45 and older were the age group least likely to have minor children, and they accounted for a larger share of the prison population in 2007 (20 percent) than in 1991 (11 percent). In contrast, the prisoners most likely to have children, those age 25 to 34,

Figure 3.1. Estimated Number of Parents in Prison, Their Minor Children, and Prisoners in the United States, 1991–2007

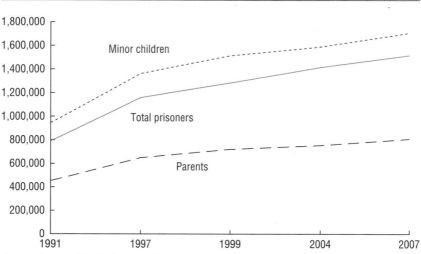

Sources: Bureau of Justice Statistics 1991, 1997, and 2004 Surveys of Inmates in State and Federal Correctional Facilities, and 1991, 1997, 1999, 2004, and 2007 National Prisoner Statistics (NPS) program.

accounted for a smaller share of the prison population in 2007 (34 percent) versus 1991 (45 percent).

In 2007, about 53 percent of men and 61 percent of women in the U.S. prison population were parents. Parents in prison were predominantly male (92 percent). There were 744,200 fathers incarcerated in prison in 2007, and the number of incarcerated fathers had increased by 77 percent since 1991. Although the increase in incarcerated fathers since 1991 is substantial, the number of incarcerated mothers has more than doubled. There were 65,600 mothers in prison in 2007 compared with 29,500 in 1991, reflecting the doubling of the female incarceration rate during that period (Snell and Morton 1992; West and Sabol 2008).[3]

The racial composition of parents in prison was similar to that of the U.S. prison population. In 2007, black men represented the largest portion of men in prison and, consequently, fathers in prison. About 4 in 10 incarcerated fathers were black, another 3 in 10 were white, and about 2 in 10 were Hispanic. About 5 percent of incarcerated fathers were of other races, which included American Indians, Alaska Natives, Asians, Native Hawaiians, other Pacific Islanders, and fathers of two or more races. White women accounted for the largest portion of women in prison and, therefore, mothers in prison. Forty-eight percent of mothers in prison were white, compared with 28 percent who were black, 17 percent who were Hispanic, and another 7 percent who were of other races.

Children of Incarcerated Parents

An estimated 1.7 million children had a parent in state or federal prison in 2007.[4] Because 93 percent of the U.S. prison population was male, about 91 percent of children of incarcerated parents had a father who was incarcerated (West and Sabol 2008). Since 1991, the number of children of incarcerated parents has risen dramatically. Three-quarters of a million more children in the United States had a parent incarcerated in prison in 2007 than in 1991. The substantial increase in the number of children of incarcerated parents reflected the increase in the number of parents incarcerated; the average number of children per parent remained constant at 2.1.

Of the 74 million children in the United States in 2007, about 1 in every 43 had a parent in prison, a rate that has remained fairly stable since 1997. When examined by race, disparities are revealed. Black children were almost eight times more likely than white children and almost three times more likely than Hispanic children to have a parent in prison (table 3.1). In addition, Hispanic children were about three times more

Table 3.1. Minor Children in the U.S. Resident Population with a Parent in Prison, by Race and Hispanic Origin, 2007

	Estimated number of minor children	% of all minor children in U.S. resident population
U.S. total[a]	1,706,600	2.3
White, non-Hispanic	484,100	0.9
Black, non-Hispanic	767,400	6.7
Hispanic	362,800	2.4

Sources: Bureau of Justice Statistics 2004 Survey of Inmates in State and Federal Correctional Facilities and U.S. Census Bureau, Population Division.

Notes: Children were assumed to have the same race/ethnicity as their incarcerated parents. Percentages were calculated based on the U.S. resident population under age 18 as of July 1, 2007.

a. Includes children of other races. Other races include American Indians, Alaska Natives, Asians, Native Hawaiians, other Pacific Islanders, and children of prisoners who specified more than one race.

likely than white children to have had a parent in prison. These racial disparities were consistent with the findings from the 1997 BJS study of incarcerated parents and their children.

About half of all children of parents in U.S. prisons were under the age of 10 years. Additionally, about a quarter of children of parents in state prison and a sixth of children of parents in federal prison were under the age of 4 years. This age composition of children was similar to that found in the 1997 BJS study. It should be emphasized, though, that the ages of the children reported here were determined based on the age of the children at the time of the parents' interviews. Some research indicates that how severely children are affected by parental incarceration is related to certain factors, including the age of the children when they were separated from their parents (Seymour 1998). While age at separation may be important, it is imperative to understand that the separation may not have resulted from the parent's current incarceration. It is possible to use the BJS data to measure children's ages at the time the parents were incarcerated, but the findings could be misleading. As will be discussed later in this chapter, for most children, the separation from a parent occurred before the parents' current incarceration.

Parents in State Prison

In 2007, the large majority (88 percent) of the U.S. prison population was incarcerated in state prison; consequently, the vast majority (85 percent) of incarcerated parents was held in state prison (West and Sabol 2008). These parents in state prison accounted for more than 8 in 10 children in the United States with a parent in prison. Since 1991, the trends in growth of parents in state prison, and their children, have reflected the national trends in growth of the total incarcerated parent population. Although the number of parents in state prison increased substantially over the 16-year period, the prevalence of parents in state prison declined. In 2004, about 52 percent of state prisoners were parents, compared with 55 percent in 1997 and 57 percent in 1991 (Harlow 1994). Despite the decline in the prevalence of parents in state prison, the composition of the parent population has remained fairly stable since 1997. The stability of the characteristics of parents in prison reflected the general stability of the U.S. prison population.

Background of Parents in State Prison

By identifying the attributes of incarcerated parents, social service organizations and governments could improve their prison and community-based programs for incarcerated parents and their children and families. In 2004, the largest portion of parents in state prison was between the ages of 25 to 34 (41 percent), with a median age of 33 years. About half were never married, while about a fifth were either divorced or married. Two-thirds of parents in state prison did not graduate from high school, and about 12 percent had not been educated past the 8th grade. About 6 percent of mothers reported that they were pregnant when admitted to state prison. The typical criminal offenses for which mothers and fathers were serving sentences differed. Fathers were more likely than mothers to be sentenced for a violent offense; mothers were more likely to be convicted of a property or drug offense (figure 3.2).

About 45 percent of parents were on some type of criminal justice status at the time they were arrested for their current offense. About a quarter were on probation, and another fifth were on parole supervision in the community. More than three-quarters of parents had prior criminal histories; the remaining parents were first-time offenders (table 3.2). While 4 in 10 parents in state prison were violent recidivists, a large disparity

Figure 3.2. Current Offense of Parents in State Prison by Gender, 2004

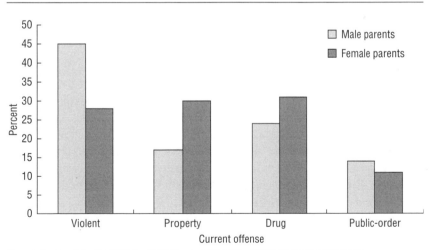

Source: Bureau of Justice Statistics 2004 Survey of Inmates in State Correctional Facilities.

Table 3.2. Criminal Histories of Parents in State Prison, 2004 (percent)

	Total	Male	Female
None	22	21	31
Priors	78	79	69
Violent recidivists[a]	44	46	23
Drug recidivists only	4	4	5
Other recidivists[b]	30	29	41

Source: Bureau of Justice Statistics 2004 Survey of Inmates in State Correctional Facilities.
Note: Includes prior probation, parole, and incarceration sentences.
a. Repeat offenders with at least one current or past violent offense.
b. Includes repeat offenders with unknown offense types.

was found by gender. Fathers (46 percent) were twice as likely as mothers (23 percent) to be violent recidivists. About a quarter of parents in state prison had at least three prior sentences to incarceration: fathers, 24 percent, and mothers, 14 percent.

Impact of Parental Incarceration on Children

Children may be affected by their parents' incarceration in a number of ways, including living arrangements and household composition, ability to stay in contact with incarcerated parents, and parental substance abuse and mental health problems.

Living Arrangement and Household Composition of Parents in State Prison before Incarceration

In 2004, less than half of parents in state prison had been removed from homes where they were living with their children as a result of an arrest or incarceration. Only 48 percent of parents in state prison lived with at least one of their children either in the month before arrest or just before incarceration. While 37 percent lived with at least one of their children in the month before their arrest, the percentage living with them just before incarceration was higher (44 percent). Parents in state prison who lived with their children differed significantly by gender. Mothers were more likely than fathers to report living with at least one of their children both in the month before arrest (55 percent compared with 35 percent) and just before incarceration (61 percent compared with 42 percent).

Because these are measures of parents living with *at least* one of their children, they do not reveal the total number of children affected by the removal of a parent from the household as a result of an arrest or incarceration. What is known from prior research is that over half of incarcerated fathers have children with more than one woman, making it improbable that these fathers were living with all their children before incarceration (Hairston 1995, 1998). Thus, while over half were not living with any of their children before incarceration, an additional unknown percentage of parents lived with at least one child and had other children who did not live with them.

In the month before arrest, mothers were three times more likely to have lived in single-parent households than in two-parent households, whereas fathers were equally likely to have lived in single- or two-parent households.[5] Among all mothers, 42 percent lived in single-parent households and 14 percent lived in two-parent households; the remaining 44 percent did not live with their children. Among all fathers, 17 percent lived in single-parent households and 18 percent lived in two-parent households; the remainder did not live with their children. Some parents in single-parent households were living with boyfriends or girlfriends, and some of these domestic partners may have also been parents of the children living in the household. However, given the way the questions were structured in the surveys, only the prisoner's relationship to household members can be determined; there is no way to determine whether or how these other household members were related to each other. Seventy percent of the fathers living in single-parent households were living with girlfriends. In contrast, less than a quarter of the mothers living in single-parent households were living with boyfriends.

Parental Involvement before Incarceration

Before incarceration, fathers in state prison relied heavily on someone else to care for their children, while mothers in state prison were the primary care providers. Only a quarter of fathers compared with three-quarters of mothers provided primary care. Moreover, about 1 in 10 fathers who lived with at least one of their children before incarceration relied on someone else to provide all the care for their children.

While fathers were less likely than mothers to be responsible for the daily care of their children, they were equally likely to provide primary financial support for their children. Just over half of both mothers and fathers said they were the primary financial supporter of their children. The majority of both mothers (61 percent) and fathers (77 percent) who provided primary financial support reported earning wages or a salary. However, of these parents, mothers relied more heavily than fathers on government transfers, such as welfare, Social Security, or compensation payment (36 percent compared with 10 percent), and on friends (21 percent compared with 9 percent) to provide support for their children.

Care of State Prisoners' Children

Nearly 9 in 10 fathers in state prison had at least one child in the care of the child's mother, compared with about 4 in 10 mothers who had at least one child in the care of the father. Mothers in state prison most commonly identified the child's grandmother (42 percent) as the current caregiver. Mothers (11 percent) were five times more likely than fathers (2 percent) to have had children in the care of a foster home, agency, or institution while in prison. Given that more than half of fathers and around 40 percent of mothers were not living with their children before incarceration, the current caregiver may be the same person who cared for the children before the parents' incarceration. Research specific to incarcerated mothers and their children's risk of placement in foster care revealed that in three-quarters of cases, children were not placed in foster care as a direct result of the incarceration; rather, they had already been placed in foster care before the mother's incarceration (Moses 2006).

Contact between State Prisoner Parents and Their Children

During their incarceration, more than three-quarters of parents in state prison had some contact with at least one of their children, whether minor or adult. Seventy percent of parents in state prison had exchanged letters with their children, 53 percent had spoken with their children over the telephone, and 42 percent had received a personal visit since admission. Mothers were more likely than fathers to have had any contact with their children and to have more frequent contact with their children. For both mothers and fathers, the likelihood of having at least weekly contact with their children decreased as the length of their prison stay increased

Table 3.3. Parents of Minor Children in State Prison Who Reported at Least Weekly Contact with Either Their Adult or Minor Children, by Type of Contact and Time Served, 2004 (percent)

	Time Served Since Admission		
	Less than 1 year	12–59 months	60 or more months
Any type of contact	46	41	34
Mail	33	29	24
Telephone	25	23	20
Personal visits	8	7	5

Source: Bureau of Justice Statistics 2004 Survey of Inmates in State Correctional Facilities.

(table 3.3). This decline in contact was largely due to a decline in the percentage of parents who reported at least weekly mail contact with their children (the most common form of contact).

Because women are typically in prison for less serious offenses than men and serve shorter sentences, on average, it was no surprise that mothers had served less time in prison and expected to be released from prison in a shorter amount of time than fathers. Nearly 4 in 10 mothers compared with 2 in 10 fathers had been in prison less than one year. Further, more than 6 in 10 mothers compared with 4 in 10 fathers expected to be released from prison within a year from the date they were interviewed for the survey.

Family Background of Parents Incarcerated in State Prison

Forty percent of parents in state prison reported growing up in a household that received public assistance; 14 percent reported living in a foster home, agency, or institution at some time during their youth; and 43 percent reported living with both parents most of the time. More than a third of parents in state prison reported that during their youth, their parents or guardians had abused alcohol or drugs. Mothers in state prison were more likely than fathers to have lived in a foster home, agency, or institution and to have had a guardian or parent abuse alcohol or drugs. While the family backgrounds of parents do not differ from nonparents in prison, it is particularly important to address these characteristics because of the possible consequences for their children.

The literature often states that children of prisoners are five to six times more likely to be incarcerated than their peers. However, as Murray and Farrington (2008) and others have commented, both the source and the evidence for this claim are unknown. In their review of several prospective longitudinal studies, Murray and Farrington conclude that "children of prisoners have about three times the risk for antisocial behavior compared to their peers" (2008, 140). The results of a comprehensive meta-analysis of longitudinal studies on how antisocial behavior develops (Lipsey and Derzon 1998) lead to the same conclusion (Eddy and Reid 2003).

In these reviews, antisocial behavior includes, but is not limited to, trouble with police, school, neighbors, and delinquency—behaviors that could lead to incarceration. Given that the outcome measures are broader than just incarceration, it would seem plausible to see a larger disparity between children who had a parent who had been incarcerated and their peers, but that is not the case. Whereas the literature suggests a potentially strong connection between parental incarceration and children's incarceration, among all state prisoners, only about 1 in 5 had a parent who had ever been incarcerated when the prisoner was a minor or an adult (table 3.4). State prisoners are far more likely to have ever had a brother incarcerated than any other immediate family member. More-over, only 4 percent of incarcerated parents of any children (minor or adult) had a child who was ever incarcerated. The meaning of this estimate

Table 3.4. Family Incarceration of State Prisoners by Parental Status, 2004 (percent)

	All prisoners	Parents[a]	Non-parents
Parent	20	23	18
Mother	6	6	5
Father	17	19	15
Brother	32	34	31
Sister	6	7	6
Child	3	4	NA
Spouse	1	2	1

Source: Bureau of Justice Statistics 2004 Survey of Inmates in State Correctional Facilities.

NA not applicable

a. For those who have ever had a child incarcerated, parents include those with minor and adult children.

is unclear, however, because of the large number of parents in the survey with children under the age of 10.

Substance Dependence or Abuse and Mental Health Problems

Substance dependence or abuse (66 percent) and mental health problems (54 percent) are prevalent among the general prison population (James and Glaze 2006).[6] Consequently, parents in state prison have a high prevalence of both. Nearly 7 in 10 parents met the criteria for substance dependence or abuse, and nearly 6 in 10 met the criteria for a mental health problem. While no gender differences were found for substance dependence or abuse problems, mental health problems were more common among mothers than fathers.

About 7 in 10 parents had received treatment at some point in their lives for substance dependence or abuse problems; 43 percent had received treatment since admission to state prison. Among both mothers and fathers, admission to a residential facility or unit for drug or alcohol abuse was the most common treatment they had received since their admission to prison. Less than half (46 percent) of parents in state prison who had mental health problems had ever received treatment in their lives; a third had been treated since their admission to prison.

Imprisoned mothers (71 percent) were more likely than imprisoned fathers (44 percent) to have received mental health treatment at some point in their lives. Mothers were also more likely than fathers to have received treatment since their admission to state prison (53 percent compared with 28 percent). For both mothers and fathers, prescription medication was the most common type of treatment they had received both in their lifetimes and since their admission to state prison. It is important to note that many prisoners had substantial time left to serve on their sentences at the time they were interviewed and therefore may eventually participate in substance abuse and mental health treatment programs before their release from prison. As a result, these figures represent conservative estimates of treatment rates.

Program Participation among Parents in State Prison

Incarceration provides an opportune time not only for treatment for substance abuse or mental health problems, but also for participation in programs designed to improve life skills. Parents in prison may participate in life-skills programs such as work, education, and self-help programs. About two-thirds of mothers and slightly more than half of fathers attended self-help or improvement classes while incarcerated. A third of mothers and fathers, respectively, participated in employment programs, which included vocational, job training, and employment-counseling programs. In addition, a third of each participated in education programs. However, mothers (27 percent) were two and half times more likely than fathers (11 percent) to participate in parenting or childrearing classes.

Comparison between Resident and Nonresident Parents

Analysis of the characteristics of resident and nonresident parents reveals very few differences between the two groups, particularly among fathers.[7] Resident fathers were more likely than nonresident fathers to have had contact with their children since their admission to prison. Some notable differences, however, were found among mothers. Resident mothers were more likely than nonresident mothers to have had at least weekly contact with a child, to have received work assignments within the prison, and to have participated in parenting or childrearing classes. In addition, resident mothers were less likely than nonresident mothers to have been physically or sexually abused in the past, and to have had any substance dependence or abuse problems. These findings may provide insight into the reasons these nonresident mothers were not living with their children in the first place.

Parents in Federal Prison

Nearly two-thirds of federal prisoners in 2007 were parents: 63 percent of men and 56 percent of women. The prevalence of parents in federal prison remained stable between 1991 and 2007. However, the number of parents in federal prison more than tripled over the 16-year period. The dramatic increase in the number of parents in federal prison between 1991 and 2007 was driven by the increase in the federal prison population, which also tripled during that time (Bureau of Justice Statistics 1995; West and Sabol 2008). The growth in the federal prison population was primarily the result of a significant increase in the number of drug offenders, specifically those convicted of a drug trafficking offense, between 1991 and 2007. Drug offenders accounted for half the growth in the federal prison population over these 16 years (Bureau of Justice Statistics 1997; West and Sabol 2008).

Notable Characteristics of Parents in Federal Prison

For the most part, the profile of incarcerated parents is very similar in both state and federal prisons, but there are some notable characteristics of parents in federal prison. Overall, parents in federal prison were older, more likely to be married, and had higher levels of educational attainment than parents in state prison. Further, given the larger share of federal prisoners sentenced for immigration offenses and international drug trafficking activity, it is not surprising to find that parents in federal prison (17 percent) were almost three times as likely as those in state prison (6 percent) to be noncitizens. However, federal prisoners who were noncitizens were equally likely as those who were citizens to be parents. In addition, among federal prisoners who were parents, citizens and noncitizens had the same average number of children (about 2.2).

In 2007, an estimated 21,200 noncitizens in federal prison were parents, and they had an estimated 45,700 children. After these parents complete their sentences, most will be deported from the United States, thereby either leaving children behind in the United States or possibly being reunited with their children living in other countries.[8] The implications are important for social service organizations to be aware of when creating programs for parents in federal prison and their children.

Given that violent offenders compose 9 percent of the federal prison population, compared with 53 percent of the state prison population, it is not surprising to find that parents in federal prison (12 percent) were far less likely to be incarcerated for a violent offense than parents in state prison (West and Sabol 2008). Half the federal prison population is sentenced for a drug trafficking offense; consequently, more than 5 in 10 parents in federal prison had been incarcerated for drug trafficking (West and Sabol 2008). Parents in federal prison were almost half as likely as those in state prison to have had a criminal justice status at the time of their current arrest (26 percent compared with 45 percent) and less likely to report a prior criminal history (68 percent compared with 79 percent). A smaller percentage of parents in federal prison (16 percent) had at least three prior incarcerations than parents in state prison (23 percent).

Over half of parents in federal prison lived with at least one of their children either in the month before arrest or just before incarceration, including about 8 in 10 mothers. Parents in federal prison were more likely to have lived in two-parent households (27 percent) than in single-parent households (21 percent) in the month before arrest. About 9 in 10 had had contact with their children since admission; 85 percent had had telephone contact, 84 percent had exchanged mail, and 55 percent had had personal visits.

Parents in federal prison were less likely than those in state prison to have grown up in a household that received public assistance or to have lived in a foster home, agency, or institution. While growing up, fewer parents in federal prison had a parent or a guardian who had abused alcohol or drugs. In addition, they were less likely than parents in state prison to have had a parent incarcerated. Parents in federal prison were also less likely than those in state prison to have substance dependence or abuse and mental health problems.

Future Research and Data Collection

While these national estimates of the size and characteristics of incarcerated parents may be useful for policymakers, researchers, and the public at large, demands for such state and local data and for further direct information about children are pervasive. The BJS prisoner surveys are conducted on a sample of prisoners designed to be nationally representative; the number of interviews collected in most states is insufficient to provide valid estimates at the state level. Various state and local social service agencies and nonprofit organizations have contacted BJS for state-specific data in recent years, simply to get a sense of how many imprisoned parents and children may need services in a given community, county, or state. To meet this demand, BJS is considering various options. One approach would be to expand the sample to a sufficient size to produce more state-specific estimates. While this would not be feasible in all states, generic estimates could be developed for those states not self-representing in the survey sample. The use of audio computer-assisted self-interviewing (ACASI) technology may assist efforts to increase sample size. ACASI interviews will allow for group administration while adding a measure of privacy by replacing the interviewer with touch-screen laptops and audio instructions delivered via headphones.

Another approach would be to explore estimation techniques that could produce reliable state-specific data for all states. Currently, BJS is exploring the possibility of producing state-specific estimates of the numbers of incarcerated parents using the administrative data submitted by correctional administrators under the National Corrections Reporting Program. About forty state departments of corrections each year submit prisoner-level administrative data on the basic demographic characteristics, criminal offenses, sentence length, and time served of their prison admissions, one-day prison populations, and exiting prisoners. If a model could be developed for predicting the likelihood of a prisoner being a parent of a child using BJS's most recent prisoner surveys, that model could be applied to these state-specific administrative data to produce valid state estimates of parents in prison. This would allow each state's estimate of incarcerated parents to reflect the specific characteristics of their prisoner population.

Other possible approaches involve obtaining direct information about children in states and communities through matching data across several systems (e.g., corrections, child welfare, schools), although there are barriers to these approaches such as those related to confidentiality. Even if such barriers to access are overcome, researchers may encounter serious difficulties in linking parents and children across data systems.

A recent effort by the Urban Institute is sobering in regards to these challenges. The project involved three large cities, two of which had already maintained integrated databases combining information from government agencies statewide, such as jail and prison bookings, child welfare cases, foster care cases, substance abuse and mental health treatment clients, and juvenile delinquency cases. Even in jurisdictions with such integrated data resources, the project report still concluded that "all three sites in this study restricted their analyses to incarcerated mothers because they could not locate datasets that consistently and reliably linked incarcerated fathers to their children" (Brazzell 2008, 1–2). With mothers making up only 8 percent of incarcerated parents, the limitations of this effort powerfully illustrate the challenges facing future efforts at such data linking.

In the face of such obstacles, future research might be best directed toward greater use of other data resources, such as the Bureau of Labor Statistics' National Longitudinal Survey of Youth, and future data sources like the new National Children's Study.[9] These longitudinal surveys hold the prospect of tracking child adjustment through various stages of development. Parents may experience alternating periods of confinement and freedom during their criminal careers, and longitudinal studies would enable researchers to study the impacts of repeated parental incarcerations on children. Such longitudinal studies could also shed light on whether these impacts persist after a parent's release from custody.

Lastly, the field may also benefit from an effort to better understand how parental incarceration may or may not have unique impacts on children. Murray and Farrington (2008), for example, note that the research on the impacts of divorce on children is "extensive," and this literature would seem to offer a fertile point of comparative analysis. Likewise, how do the impacts associated with parental incarceration compare with those associated with parental death and parental separation due to military deployment or other work assignments? Comparative research of this kind could greatly benefit public policy directed at assisting families affected by incarceration by placing such policy within a larger context of assisting children experiencing a parental loss of any kind.

NOTES

1. To provide the most recent estimates of the number of parents in prison, and their minor children, the distributions from the 2004 prisoner surveys were applied to the most recent prison population counts at the time to yield 2007 estimates.

2. "Parents" refers to state and federal prisoners who reported having at least one minor child, unless otherwise stated.

3. Imprisonment rate is the number of prisoners sentenced to serve more than 1 year per 100,000 U.S. residents.

4. "Children" refers to minor children under the age of 18, unless otherwise stated.

5. A single-parent household is a household where the parent lived with at least one of his or her children and either did not have a spouse or the spouse did not live in the household. A two-parent household is a household where the parent and his or her spouse lived with at least one of his or her children.

6. Inmates meet the criteria for a mental health problem if they have had a recent history of a mental health problem in the year before arrest or since admission, or if they have experienced, in the 12 months before the interview, symptoms of mental health disorders. See James and Glaze (2006).

7. In this paragraph, the term "resident" parents refers to parents who lived with at least one of their children in either the month before arrest or before incarceration.

8. While the 2004 BJS study does not allow for reliable estimation of noncitizen parents' countries of origin, the Federal Bureau of Prisons reports such data for its general prisoner population (http://www.bop.gov). As of May 30, 2009, 66 percent of noncitizen federal prisoners were Mexican citizens; no other country accounted for more than 5 percent of noncitizen federal prisoners.

9. According to the official web site (http://www.nationalchildrensstudy.gov), the following federal agencies are conducting the study: the National Institute of Child Health and Human Development, the National Institute of Environmental Health Sciences, the Centers for Disease Control and Prevention, and the U.S. Environmental Protection Agency.

REFERENCES

Beck, Allen J., and Darrell K. Gilliard. 1995. *Prisoners in 1994.* NCJ 151654. Washington, DC: U.S. Department of Justice, Bureau of Justice Statistics.

Brazzell, Diana. 2008. *Using Local Data to Explore the Experiences and Needs of Children of Incarcerated Parents.* Washington, DC: The Urban Institute.

Eddy, J. Mark, and John B. Reid. 2003. "The Adolescent Children of Incarcerated Parents." In *Prisoners Once Removed: The Impact of Incarceration and Reentry on Children, Families, and Communities,* edited by Jeremy Travis and Michelle Waul (233–58). Washington, DC: Urban Institute Press.

Glaze, Lauren E., and Laura M. Maruschak. 2008. *Parents in Prison and Their Minor Children.* NCJ 222984. Washington, DC: U.S. Department of Justice, Bureau of Justice Statistics.

Hairston, Creasie Finney. 1995. "Fathers in Prison." In *Children of Incarcerated Parents,* edited by Katherine Gabel and Denise Johnston (31–40). New York: Lexington Books.

———. 1998. "The Forgotten Parent: Understanding the Forces That Influence Incarcerated Fathers' Relationships with Their Children." *Child Welfare* 77(5): 617–39.

Harlow, Carolyn W. 1994. *Comparing Federal and State Prison Inmates, 1991.* NCJ 145864. Washington, DC: U.S. Department of Justice, Bureau of Justice Statistics.

James, Doris J., and Lauren E. Glaze. 2006. *Mental Health Problems of Prison and Jail Inmates.* NCJ 213600. Washington, DC: U.S. Department of Justice, Bureau of Justice Statistics.

Lipsey, Mark W., and James H. Derzon. 1988. "Predictors of Violent or Serious Delinquency in Adolescence and Early Adulthood." In *Serious and Violent Juvenile Offenders: Risk Factors and Successful Interventions,* edited by Rolf Loeber and David P. Farrington (86–105). Thousand Oaks, CA: SAGE Publications.

Moses, Marilyn C. 2006. "Does Parental Incarceration Increase a Child's Risk for Foster Care Placement?" *National Institute of Justice Journal* 255:12–14.

Mumola, Christopher J. 2000. *Incarcerated Parents and Their Minor Children.* NCJ 182335. Washington, DC: U.S. Department of Justice, Bureau of Justice Statistics.

Murray, Joseph, and David P. Farrington. 2008. "The Effects of Parental Imprisonment on Children." In *Crime and Justice: A Review of Research,* vol. 37, edited by Michael Tonry (133–206). Chicago: University of Chicago Press.

Seymour, Cynthia B. 1998. "Children with Parents in Prison: Child Welfare Policy, Program, and Practice Issues." *Child Welfare* 77(5): 469–93.

Snell, Tracy L., and Danielle C. Morton. 1992. *Prisoners in 1991.* Washington, DC: U.S. Department of Justice, Bureau of Justice Statistics.

U.S. Department of Justice, Bureau of Justice Statistics. 1995. *Correctional Populations in the United States, 1992.* Washington, DC: U.S. Department of Justice, Bureau of Justice Statistics.

———. 1997. *Correctional Populations in the United States, 1995.* NCJ 163916. Washington, DC: U.S. Department of Justice, Bureau of Justice Statistics.

West, Heather C., and William J. Sabol. 2008. *Prisoners in 2007.* NCJ 224280. Washington, DC: U.S. Department of Justice, Bureau of Justice Statistics.

PART II
Developmental Research

4

Longitudinal Research on the Effects of Parental Incarceration on Children

Joseph Murray

This chapter reviews longitudinal research on the effects of parental incarceration on children. Longitudinal studies follow the same people over time, using repeated assessments. By studying people over time, longitudinal studies have many advantages over cross-sectional studies, which collect data at only one point in time. Longitudinal studies can be used to investigate children's natural development as they grow. They can be used to investigate continuity and change in behavior over time. They can be used to study how life events and other influences in childhood predict and cause later life outcomes. When two generations of participants are included in a study, patterns of behavior and influence from parents to children can be investigated.

Dozens of large longitudinal studies have investigated the development of antisocial and criminal behavior over time, using representative community samples of at least several hundred participants with five or more years of data collection and many measures of different variables (Farrington and Welsh 2007; Thornberry and Krohn 2003). Despite the breadth of research in this area, only recently have children of incarcerated parents been studied in longitudinal research. The lack of extensive study of this topic represents one of several forms of social exclusion of children of incarcerated parents (Murray 2007).

The few longitudinal studies on the effects of parental incarceration on children have benefited from in-depth qualitative research. Careful studies of children's experiences during parental incarceration have documented the difficulties that can occur, at least for some children. These include psychological distress, confused explanations given to children, changes in child care arrangements, difficulties in maintaining contact with incarcerated parents, loss of family income, stigma associated with parental incarceration, and home and school moves.[1] This suggests that parental incarceration might cause multiple strains for children and might contribute to the development of mental health problems or antisocial behavior.

For two reasons, it should not be assumed that parental incarceration causes undesirable outcomes for children. First, even if children of incarcerated parents show more problems than their peers, this might be because of parental criminality or other disadvantages before parental incarceration, not because parental incarceration itself has causal effects. Second, separation from an abusive or antisocial parent by incarceration might actually decrease the likelihood of behavior problems for some children because it removes a disruptive and antisocial influence from their lives (see, e.g., Jaffee et al. 2003). Thus, the effects of parental incarceration need to be empirically tested. Longitudinal research is needed to examine the possible effects on children throughout their development.

This review of longitudinal research on the children of incarcerated parents is divided into the following sections. First, key questions for research are presented. Second, methodological issues are discussed. Third, 10 longitudinal studies on child outcomes following parental incarceration are summarized. Fourth, the findings are drawn together and critical research needs are identified for the future.

Key Questions for Research

A first key question for research is whether parental incarceration predicts undesirable outcomes for children. If parental incarceration does not predict child outcomes, then it is unlikely to causally affect them.

However, even if parental incarceration predicts child problem behavior, such a finding does not imply that it causes those problems. Parental incarceration is associated with many other risk factors that might explain children's outcomes, such as parental criminality, antisocial behavior, and mental health problems; poor parenting practices; family poverty and low socioeconomic status; and residing in deprived neighborhoods (Huebner and Gustafson 2007; E. Johnson and Waldfogel 2004; Murray and Farrington 2005; Phillips et al. 2006). Risk factors associated with parental incarceration are called confounds, which need to be taken into account when estimating causal effects. Thus, even if parental incarceration predicts child problem behavior, further tests are required to answer the second key question for research: Does parental incarceration cause an increase in child problem behavior?

As well as testing for overall causal effects, it is important to understand the mechanisms by which parental incarceration affects children. Mechanisms are the causal pathways linking parenting incarceration and child outcomes. Four key theories about how parental incarceration might affect children are discussed extensively elsewhere (Hagan and Dinovitzer 1999; Murray and Farrington 2008a). First, social bonding and attachment theory suggests that parental incarceration might harm children because traumatic parent-child separation disrupts children's attachment relations and quality of care. Parental incarceration involves a number of potential threats to children's attachment security that might increase children's vulnerability for undesirable outcomes (Murray and Murray 2010; Poehlmann chapter 5, this volume). Second, strain theory (Agnew 1992) suggests that the loss of family income and other negative life events after parental incarceration might cause an increase in child antisocial behavior. Third, social learning theory suggests that parental incarceration might affect children through reduced quality of care and supervision, while families and caregivers cope with emotional and financial difficulties. Fourth, labeling theory suggests that social stigma and official bias following parental incarceration might cause an increase in the probability of children developing a delinquent identity and being charged or convicted for criminal behavior. Different interventions to support children will be required depending on which mechanisms explain children's outcomes (Murray and Farrington 2006). Thus, a third key question for research is: Which mechanisms explain the effects of parental incarceration on children?

A fourth major issue for research is understanding variability in children's reactions to parental incarceration. Children might react differently, and show different outcomes after parental incarceration, because of different child characteristics, parent characteristics, aspects of the family environment, and wider social and penal contexts (see Murray and

Farrington 2008a for a review). For example, children might experience parental incarceration differently according to their developmental stage at the time of the incarceration (Johnston 1995), and this might moderate its effects on children. Maternal incarceration might have worse consequences for children than paternal incarceration (Murray and Farrington 2008a; Parke and Clarke-Stewart 2003). The effects might also differ according to whether children were living with their parent before the incarceration (Parke and Clarke-Stewart 2003). A study of young children in the United States suggests that children might be less affected by parental incarceration if they receive stable, quality parenting during the separation (Poehlmann 2005). Factors that explain variability in children's outcomes after parental incarceration are called moderators. Identifying moderators can help understand resilience and why some children do better or worse than other children after parental incarceration. Accordingly, a fourth major question for longitudinal research is: Which factors moderate the effects of paternal incarceration on children?

Methodological Issues

While longitudinal studies have many strengths, there are great challenges to conducting a large study over many years. It is important to bear in mind the desirable qualities in longitudinal research when reviewing existing studies. Methodological quality issues for longitudinal research in general are discussed elsewhere (e.g., Murray, Farrington, and Eisner 2009). Some key issues that are most relevant to research on children of incarcerated parents are highlighted here.

No large longitudinal study has been designed and conducted specifically to examine the effects of parental incarceration on children. Instead, researchers have investigated this topic using relevant data from studies that were conducted for other purposes. Not surprisingly, these data have limitations.

An important issue is the quality of measurement of parental incarceration in these studies. If parental incarceration is not accurately measured, children can be misclassified as experiencing the event or not, and studies can produce misleading results. Often, parental incarceration has been measured by asking children's caregivers about parental incarceration at any time in the past. Caregiver reports about other parents' incarceration might not be reliable (Bendheim-Thoman Center for Research on Child Wellbeing 2002), and this measure does not always specify who was incarcerated or when the incarceration occurred. Sometimes, parental incarceration might even have occurred before children were born, which seems less likely to affect children than parental incarceration during childhood.

A major difficulty in longitudinal research is estimating causal effects of parental incarceration on children. In the absence of randomized experiments, the best way to investigate causal effects is to test (a) whether child outcomes change from before to after parental incarceration, and (b) whether these changes remain even after taking into account confounding variables associated with parental incarceration (Murray et al. 2009). Studies that do not analyze change, or do not take into account important confounds (e.g., through matching or regression analyses), are likely to be biased in their estimates of causal effects.

Detailed, time-ordered data are very desirable to investigate causal effects, mediating mechanisms, and moderators. Often confound variables are only measured after parental incarceration. If confounds are not measured before parental incarceration, they can be confused with mediating mechanisms (which occur after parental incarceration). For example, if low family income is measured only after parental incarceration, it will be unclear whether this represents a preexisting family situation (i.e., a confound) or a consequence of the incarceration (i.e., a mediating mechanism). Controlling for such variables (e.g., in regression analyses or other modeling techniques) can result in underestimating the causal effects of parental incarceration on children. Therefore, studies should ideally start data collection before parental incarceration, conduct intensive assessments during the incarceration, and assess families and children afterward.

Longitudinal Research Published to Date

An extensive previous review (Murray and Farrington 2008a) examined cross-sectional studies as well as longitudinal studies of children of incarcerated parents. This chapter reviews key longitudinal studies published to date, including several that were not in the Murray and Farrington review. The following five criteria were used to select studies for this chapter. The study must be published; have a longitudinal design; include both children of incarcerated parents and comparison children without incarcerated parents; have at least 100 participants (for reviews of smaller and qualitative studies, see Murray 2005 and Murray and Farrington 2008a); and measure child antisocial behavior or mental health as an outcome. Antisocial behavior (including criminal behavior) and mental health (referring mainly to anxiety and depression) are chosen as outcomes for this review because they are the main psychological outcomes that have been studied in this population (for a review of other possible outcomes, see Murray and Farrington 2008a).

For each study, where possible, results are summarized separately for boys and girls, and separately for antisocial behavior and mental health. To assess the strength with which parental incarceration predicts child outcomes, individual results are extracted from each study based on the best measures available. Strength of prediction is determined by comparing outcomes for children of incarcerated parents and outcomes for a comparison group of children from the general population without incarcerated parents.

The measure of strength of prediction used in this review is the odds ratio [OR]. The odds of an outcome is equal to the number of children with the outcome divided by the number of children without the outcome. The OR represents how more or less likely children of incarcerated parents are to experience an outcome than other children. An OR less than 1.0 indicates that children of incarcerated parents are less likely to have an outcome than other children. An OR larger than 1.0 shows an increased probability of an outcome after parental incarceration; an OR of 2.0 or larger indicates strong prediction (Cohen 1996). Where studies present other statistical results, for example correlation coefficients, they are converted into ORs for this review to compare findings between studies more easily. (Such conversions are marked with an asterisk.)

Where available, results are also extracted from each study to estimate the causal effects of parental incarceration on child outcomes. Causal effects are measured as "adjusted" ORs. Adjusted ORs indicate the number of times greater (or smaller) the odds of an outcome for children of incarcerated parents compared with other children, after taking into account effects of confounding variables, such as parental criminality.

Huebner and Gustafson: United States

Huebner and Gustafson (2007) investigated the effects of maternal incarceration on children's criminal outcomes in the National Longitudinal Survey of Youth. This is a nationally representative longitudinal study of males and females in the United States, who ranged between 14 and 22 years old in 1979, and the women's children. In 2000, the children ranged between 18 and 24 years old. Huebner and Gustafson compared 31 children whose mothers were incarcerated between 1979 and 2000, and 1,666 children whose mothers were not incarcerated. This is a rare longitudinal study that focuses on the effects of maternal incarceration on children. Fathers' incarceration was not measured. Adult convictions of the children were measured using self-reports between 1994 and 2000. No adult conviction occurred before maternal incarceration.

Twenty-six percent of children with incarcerated mothers were convicted as adults, compared with 10 percent of comparison children. This translates into an OR of 3.1 (95 percent confidence interval [CI] = 1.4–7.1), showing that maternal incarceration strongly predicted children's convictions. Huebner and Gustafson also estimated the causal effects of maternal incarceration on children's convictions, by taking into account a number of possible confounds in statistical analyses. The confounds that were controlled for were child delinquency and education; maternal absence; maternal delinquency; maternal education; maternal smoking during pregnancy; adolescent mother; parental supervision; home environment; peer pressure; and the age, sex, and race of the child. There were strong and significant effects of maternal incarceration on adult conviction (OR = 3.0; CI = 1.4–6.4) even after controlling for the confounds listed above.

These results are consistent with the hypothesis that maternal incarceration causally contributes to children's own criminal outcomes. However, change in child outcome from before to after maternal incarceration was not analyzed, which means that this study might have overestimated causal effects. It is also possible that there is bias in the other direction. Many confounds (including child delinquency) were measured after maternal incarceration might have occurred. Controlling for variables measured after maternal incarceration (especially child delinquency) might underestimate the effects of maternal incarceration on children.

Johnson: United States

Johnson (2009) investigated the effects of parental incarceration on children in the Panel Study of Income Dynamics. This is a longitudinal study of a nationally representative sample of families recruited in the United States in 1968, and it includes over 3,500 children studied from 1997. Johnson compared children who had a parent incarcerated during three different stages of childhood (0–5, 6–10, and 11–16 years) with children who did not have a parent incarcerated. This is an important study of how the effects of parental incarceration on children might differ according to children's age at the time of the incarceration.

Maternal and paternal incarceration were measured by identifying whether parents were incarcerated at each interview wave until 2005, and by asking them, in 1995, whether and when they had previously served time in jail or prison. Five hundred and eighty-four children had a father incarcerated, but it was not reported how many children had a mother who was incarcerated, or the number of children who had a parent incarcerated at different times during childhood. Children's caregivers reported on children's internalizing problems (anxiety and depression) and antisocial behavior in 1997 and again in 2002–03. Data were available for 3,540 children ranging in age from 3 to 17 years. Only occasions of parental incarceration occurring before the child outcome were used in analyses.[2] To estimate causal effects of parental incarceration, Johnson statistically controlled for a number of confounds, including parental incarceration at other times in childhood and before the child's birth; neighborhood quality; neighbor policing for drugs; family member with alcohol problems; religiosity; parental education; whether the mother was married; and the child's sex, age, and race.

Converting Johnson's results into ORs, large effects of parental incarceration on child outcomes were observed. Adjusted ORs[*] for internalizing problems were 2.6 (CI = 1.1–6.1) for parental incarceration at age 0–5; 1.8 (CI = 0.8–4.0) at age 6–10; and 4.7 (CI = 1.1–19.1) at age 11–16. Adjusted ORs for antisocial behaviors were 2.1 (CI = 1.1–4.1) for parental incarceration at age 0–5; 1.6 (CI = 0.8–3.1) at age 6–10; and 5.2 (CI = 1.6–17.2) at age 11–16. Some confounds were measured after parental incarceration, which may have resulted in underestimating the causal effects on children. Change in child outcome was not analyzed, which might have resulted in overestimating the effects.

Kandel and Colleagues: Denmark

Kandel and colleagues (1988) compared 92 sons of fathers who had at least one prison sentence with 513 sons of fathers who had never been registered with the police, in a birth cohort of 1,944 males born between 1936 and 1938 in Copenhagen. Fourteen hundred men were targeted for follow-up in this study. The study report suggests that 795 participants were excluded from analyses because their father had been arrested and not incarcerated. Details were not provided, but it appears that paternal incarceration might have occurred any time until 1972, when sons' records were searched. Therefore, paternal incarceration might have occurred before birth, during childhood, or even after the son's criminal outcome. Maternal incarceration was not measured.

Of sons with incarcerated fathers, 39 percent received at least one prison sentence themselves by age 34–36. Of sons in the comparison group, 7 percent received at least one prison sentence. This translates into an OR of 8.5 (CI = 5.0–14.6). This might overestimate the strength of prediction of child outcomes after paternal incarceration because sons whose fathers had other kinds of criminal record (e.g., an arrest record) were excluded from the comparison group. Causal effects were not estimated, for example by statistically controlling for confounds.

Kinner, Alati, Najman, and Williams: Australia

Kinner and colleagues (2007) compared 137 children of incarcerated fathers with 2,262 controls in the Mater University Study of Pregnancy. This is a longitudinal survey of 8,458 women who were pregnant in Australia in 1981 and the children arising from the pregnancy. When the children were age 14, mothers were asked whether their current partner had ever been detained in prison. Therefore, paternal incarceration does not necessarily refer to the child's biological father, and it might have occurred before children were born. Maternal incarceration was not measured. Child internalizing and antisocial problems were measured at the same time in mother and child questionnaires. The following confounds were measured between birth and age 5: maternal age and education, family income, maternal anxiety and depression, maternal substance use, dyadic adjustment, domestic violence, and parenting style. Analyses were conducted on 2,399 adolescents for whom complete data were available. This is an important, large, population-based study of child adjustment following parental incarceration.

Paternal incarceration predicted internalizing problems with ORs* of 1.2 (CI = 0.5–3.0) for boys and 2.0 (CI = 1.0–3.9) for girls. ORs for antisocial problems were 1.7 (CI = 0.9–3.3) for boys and 1.5 (CI = 0.7–3.4) for girls. After controlling for the confounds listed above, adjusted ORs for internalizing problems were 1.1 (CI = 0.4–3.0) for boys and 1.9 (CI = 1.0–3.8) for girls. Adjusted ORs for antisocial problems were 1.3 (CI = 0.6–2.5) for boys and 1.2 (CI = 0.5–2.9) for girls. Because confounds were measured after paternal incarceration might have occurred, these results might underestimate the causal effects of paternal incarceration on children. Change in child outcome was not analyzed, which might result in over-estimating causal effects.

Murray and Farrington: England

Murray and Farrington (2005, 2008b) investigated the effects of parental incarceration on boys' antisocial behavior and mental health problems in the Cambridge Study in Delinquent Development. This is a longitu-dinal study of 411 boys born in 1953 and living in South London in 1963. Data were collected through interviews with the study males, their par-ents, their teachers, and through searches of criminal records until age 50. The criminal records of the boys' mothers and fathers were repeatedly searched until 1994. Murray and Farrington compared 23 boys whose parents were incarcerated in the boys' first 10 years of life and 382 boys who did not experience parental incarceration any time before age 18. None of the 23 boys who had a parent incarcerated had been permanently separated from their parent before the incarceration. This study used reli-able measures of parental incarceration and was able to investigate very long term outcomes of parental incarceration for boys.

To examine the strength of prediction for this review, boys whose par-ents were incarcerated in their first 10 years of life were compared with all boys whose parents were not incarcerated from the boys' birth until age 18. The outcomes examined were internalizing problems at age 48 and the boy's own criminal conviction between ages 18 and 50. Parental incarceration up to age 10 was a strong predictor of these outcomes: OR = 3.2 (CI = 1.3–8.0) for internalizing problems; OR = 4.7 (CI = 2.0–11.5) for conviction.

To estimate the causal effects of parental incarceration, boys whose par-ents were incarcerated during childhood (birth to age 10; $n = 23$) were compared with boys whose parents were incarcerated only before the boy's birth ($n = 17$). The logic of this comparison is that children whose parents are incarcerated only before their birth do not experience the incarcera-tion but might have similar family backgrounds to children whose parents are incarcerated during childhood. Other confounds that were statistically controlled for were the number of convictions of the boy's parents, the boy's IQ, whether the boy was "daring," and family size (which were the most important confounding variables in this study; see Murray and Farrington 2005, 2008b).

Comparing boys whose parents were incarcerated during childhood with boys whose parents were incarcerated only before their birth, while taking into account the confounds listed above, adjusted ORs were 2.9 (CI = 0.4–19.0) for internalizing problems and 1.5 (CI = 0.3–7.2) for conviction. However, this study did not analyze change in child outcomes from before to after parental incarceration, and the confounds were measured after parental incarceration, which might have biased the results.

Murray, Janson, and Farrington: Sweden

Murray and colleagues (2007) compared children whose parents were incarcerated between birth and age 18 with children whose parents were not incarcerated in Project Metropolitan. This is a longitudinal study of all 15,117 children born in 1953 who lived in Stockholm in 1963. Parental incarceration was measured by searching the criminal records of the father (or the mother, if information was not available about the father) until 1972, when children were age 19. It is not known exactly how many mothers' records were searched, and parental incarceration refers primarily to fathers' incarceration in this study. Children's own criminal convictions were identified in records between 19 and 30 years old. For this review, children whose parents were incarcerated between birth and 6 years of age (early childhood; $n = 75$) and between 7 to 18 years (late childhood-adolescence; $n = 146$) were compared with children whose parents were not incarcerated from the child's birth up to age 18 ($n = 14,834$). Children whose parents were incarcerated in both early childhood and late childhood-adolescence were excluded from the analyses.

Parental incarceration in early childhood predicted conviction in adulthood (age 18–30) with ORs of 1.7 (CI = 0.8–3.5) for boys and 5.2 (CI = 2.1–12.4) for girls. Parental incarceration in late childhood-adolescence predicted conviction in adulthood with ORs of 3.5 (CI = 2.2–5.5) for boys and 1.6 (CI = 0.6–4.3) for girls. To produce estimates of causal effects for this review, children whose parents were incarcerated any time between birth and age 18 ($n = 283$) were compared with children whose parents were incarcerated only before the child's birth ($n = 245$). When making this comparison, the number of criminal convictions of the parents (until the child was age 18) and the social class of the family at age 10 were also taken into account. The adjusted ORs for adult conviction were 1.6 (CI = 0.9–2.9) for boys and 1.4 (CI = 0.5–3.6) for girls. However, this study did not analyze change in child outcome, and confounds were measured after parental incarceration, which might have biased the results.

Pakiz, Reinherz, and Giaconia: United States

Pakiz and colleagues (1997) investigated predictors of children's antisocial behavior, including parental incarceration, in the Simmons Longitudinal Study. This is a longitudinal study of 777 children who were 5 years old in 1977. At age 18, parental incarceration history was measured in interviews about family environment. It was not reported how many children had a parent incarcerated. At age 21, children's antisocial behavior was measured in interviews. The following confounds were measured for males at age 5–18: family disadvantage, childhood behavior problems, school grades, physical abuse in the family, and participant marijuana use or dependency. For females, the following were measured: childhood hostility, self-esteem, school suspension, attention problems, parental divorce, antisocial behavior, sexual abuse in family, and need for social support. Analyses were based on 188 males and 187 females with complete data up to age 21.

For males, having an incarcerated parent by age 18 significantly predicted age 21 antisocial behavior (OR* = 5.4; CI = 1.6–20.7), but for females it did not. It was not possible to estimate an OR for females, because only a "nonsignificant" finding was reported. This study might have underestimated the effects of parental incarceration on children because confounds (including children's antisocial behavior) were measured after parental incarceration. Change in child outcome was not analyzed.

Roettger: United States

Roettger (2008) compared rates of serious and violent delinquency between 784 males whose fathers had ever been incarcerated and 5,344 males whose fathers had never been incarcerated in the National Longitudinal Study of Adolescent Health (AddHealth).[3] This is a study of about 20,000 adolescents who were in grades 7 through 12 in 1994–95. A subsample of about 7,500 male participants was eligible for a longitudinal survey including follow-up interviews at age 18–24. In these interviews, participants were asked, "Has your biological father ever served time in jail or prison?" Maternal incarceration was not measured. Self-reported serious and violent delinquency was measured using 15 questionnaire items. Paternal incarceration predicted serious and violent delinquency with an OR of 1.8 (CI = 1.3–2.7).

The following confounds were also measured in the study: the participant's race, alcohol or substance abuse, family structure, parental strictness, father involvement, physical abuse, care by social services, school attachment, high school dropout, employment, marriage, cohabitation, poverty, and the racial and educational characteristics of the neighborhood. Taking these confounds into account, the adjusted OR for serious and violent delinquency following paternal incarceration was 1.6 (CI = 1.2–2.2). However, confounds in this study were measured after paternal incarceration might have occurred, and change in child outcome was not analyzed, which might have biased the results.

Stanton: United States

In a pioneering study of the effects of maternal incarceration on children, Stanton (1980) compared children of 54 mothers in jail and 21 children with mothers on probation. The logic of this comparison is that, if children of probation mothers have similar backgrounds as children of jailed mothers, then differences in their outcomes should indicate causal effects of mothers being jailed rather than being put on probation. The mothers had a total of 166 children, ranging in age from 4 to 18 years. Children had been living with their mother before her arrest. Stanton first collected data from the children's mothers, children's outside caregivers, and children's teachers during the mothers' incarceration. Stanton also re-interviewed the mothers one month after their release from jail. At that time, the mothers reported whether their children had been in trouble with the police, the school, or neighbors. Of 24 children of jailed mothers, 42 percent had been in trouble, compared with 24 percent of 17 children with mothers on probation. This translates into an OR of 2.3 (CI = 0.6–9.3).

Comparison of the incarcerated mothers and the mothers on probation showed that the groups differed in their prior criminal history, marital history, socioeconomic status, unemployment rates, and educational levels. Because these differences were not taken into account in the analyses of child outcomes, the results are likely to be biased. Moreover, four of the probation mothers had previously been incarcerated, confounding the comparison between their children and children of jailed mothers. Change in child outcome from before to after maternal incarceration was not analyzed.

Wilbur and Colleagues: United States

Wilbur and colleagues (2007) compared internalizing and antisocial behaviors of 31 children with incarcerated fathers and 71 children without incarcerated fathers, in a cohort of 252 children born in Boston between 1990 and 1993. Infants were originally selected for the study to investigate the effects of in utero cocaine exposure on children, and approximately half of the original sample ($n = 123$) had been exposed to cocaine. When children were 6, 8, 9, and 11 years old, children's caregivers were asked whether the child's father had been incarcerated in the previous two years or since the last interview. Wilbur and colleagues compared children whose fathers had been incarcerated when the children were 6 to 11 years old ($n = 31$) with children whose fathers had not been incarcerated during this period ($n = 71$). Children who had an incarcerated mother ($n = 5$) were excluded from the analyses. The latest measure of child behavior after the father's incarceration was used as the outcome.

Wilbur and colleagues estimated the causal effects of paternal incarceration on children by comparing children of incarcerated fathers with children whose fathers were not incarcerated, while statistically controlling for confounds. The confounds that were taken into account in the final analyses were child age, gender, and cocaine exposure in utero (the most important confounds in the study). The adjusted ORs* associated with a father's incarceration were 1.1 (CI = 0.5–2.5) for internalizing problems, indicating almost no effect, and 2.3 (CI = 1.0–5.4) for antisocial problems, indicating a strong relationship. Change in child outcome was not analyzed, which means that these results might overestimate causal effects of parental incarceration on children.

Discussion

This chapter reviewed 10 longitudinal studies of the effects of parental incarceration on children. The first question of interest was whether parental incarceration predicts child behavior problems. Although some individual results were not statistically significant, taken together the 10 studies show that parental incarceration predicts an increased risk of antisocial behavior or mental health problems for children. Strength of prediction was strong in most studies.

The second question was whether parental incarceration causes an increase in child problem behavior. All studies that investigated possible causal effects of parental incarceration suggested undesirable effects on children. If parental incarceration does have undesirable effects on children, a range of support programs could be used to mitigate these effects (Eddy and Reid 2003; Murray and Farrington 2006; Parke and Clarke-Stewart 2003; see also chapters 9–14, this volume). However, the studies reviewed here had important limitations. None examined change in child outcome from before to after parental incarceration, and confounding variables were often measured after parental incarceration. Many studies did not control for the criminality of children's parents. Therefore, estimates of causal effects seem likely to be systematically biased in these studies. New studies, with improved designs, are needed to draw more confident conclusions.

There is little longitudinal evidence concerning the third question: what are the mechanisms explaining effects of parental incarceration on children? Findings from the Cambridge Study in Delinquent Development suggested some conclusions about mediating mechanisms. In this study, separation because of parental incarceration predicted more antisocial and mental health problems for children than separation from parents for other reasons (Murray and Farrington 2005, 2008b). Thus, separation per se did not seem to be the main explanation for children's outcomes. Rather, the particularly traumatic nature of events surrounding parental incarceration was implicated.

Another possible mechanism considered in the Cambridge Study was official (police and court) bias toward children of incarcerated parents, which might make them more likely to be arrested or convicted for their crimes than other children. To examine this hypothesis, two outcomes (self-reported crime and officially recorded crime) were compared after parental incarceration. If official bias were important, one would expect stronger effects of parental incarceration on officially recorded crime than on self-reported crime. The effects of parental incarceration on these two outcomes were similar, which suggested that official bias did not explain children's criminal outcomes in this study (Murray and Farrington 2005). Other possible mediators that could inform intervention efforts, such as the quality of care provided for children during parental incarceration, and opportunities for contact between children and their incarcerated parent, should be focused on in future studies.

Scant longitudinal research has been conducted on the last question: what are the moderators of the effects of parental incarceration on children? Two studies that examined whether children's outcomes differed according to child age at the time of parental incarceration did not show any clear moderating effect of age (R. Johnson 2009; Murray et al. 2007). Two studies that examined the effects of maternal incarceration on children did not show markedly stronger effects than studies focusing on paternal incarceration (Huebner and Gustafson 2007; Stanton 1980). However, the possible different effects of maternal and paternal incarceration should be examined more rigorously. Particularly needed are new studies that include both mothers and fathers. Many other possible child and parent moderators, such as whether children were living with their parent, and the quality of parent-child relationships before the incarceration, should also be investigated in future longitudinal research.

Ecological theory (Bronfenbrenner 1979) suggests that the effects of parental incarceration on children might also be moderated by the wider social and penal context in which it takes place. Using carefully matched samples from England and Sweden, Murray, Janson, and Farrington (2007) found that the effects of parental incarceration on children were much stronger in England than in Sweden. This might be explained by shorter prison sentences in Sweden, more family-friendly prison policies, a welfare-oriented juvenile justice system, an extended social welfare system, or more sympathetic public attitudes toward prisoners. Most studies reviewed in this chapter were conducted in the United States, where effects of parental incarceration on children also appear stronger than in Sweden. Further, carefully matched, cross-national comparisons should be used to identify promising social and penal policies to mitigate harmful effects of parental incarceration on children. Because prison populations have changed dramatically over the past few decades in many countries, new studies are needed using recent samples.

In conclusion, longitudinal studies have clearly shown that parental incarceration predicts undesirable outcomes for children. Research to date also suggests possible causal effects on children, but these effects need to be tested more rigorously in studies designed specifically for this purpose. Future research also needs to investigate mediating mechanisms to understand these effects, and moderating factors that explain why some children develop problem behaviors after parental incarceration while others do not.

NOTES

1. See Boswell (2002); Braman and Wood (2003); Henriques (1982); Kampfner (1995); Pellegrini (1996); Poehlmann (2005); Richards et al. (1994); Sack (1977); Sack, Seidler, and Thomas (1976); and Skinner and Swartz (1989).

2. Rucker Johnson, personal communication with the author, 2008.

3. Results on parental incarceration in AddHealth were published in Guo, Roettger, and Cai (2008) but, for this review, findings are taken from Roettger (2008) because these are more detailed and more easily converted into odds ratios.

REFERENCES

Agnew, Robert. 1992. "Foundation for a General Strain Theory of Crime and Delinquency." *Criminology* 30(1): 47–88.

Bendheim-Thoman Center for Research on Child Wellbeing. 2002. "Incarceration and the Bonds among Parents." Fragile Families Research Brief 12. Princeton, NJ: Princeton University.

Boswell, Gwyneth. 2002. "Imprisoned Fathers: The Children's View." *Howard Journal* 41(1): 14–26.

Braman, Donald, and Jenifer Wood. 2003. "From One Generation to the Next: How Criminal Sanctions Are Reshaping Family Life in Urban America." In *Prisoners Once Removed: The Impact of Incarceration and Reentry on Children, Families, and Communities*, edited by Jeremy Travis and Michelle Waul (157–88). Washington, DC: Urban Institute Press.

Bronfenbrenner, Urie. 1979. *The Ecology of Human Development*. Cambridge, MA: Harvard University Press.

Cohen, Patricia. 1996. "Childhood Risks for Young Adult Symptoms of Personality Disorder: Method and Substance." *Multivariate Behavioral Research* 31(1): 121–48.

Eddy, J. Mark, and John B. Reid. 2003. "The Adolescent Children of Incarcerated Parents." In *Prisoners Once Removed: The Impact of Incarceration and Reentry on Children, Families, and Communities*, edited by Jeremy Travis and Michelle Waul (233–58). Washington, DC: Urban Institute Press.

Farrington, David P., and Brandon C. Welsh. 2007. *Saving Children from a Life of Crime: Early Risk Factors and Effective Interventions*. Oxford: Oxford University Press.

Guo, Guang, Michael E. Roettger, and Tianji Cai. 2008. "The Integration of Genetic Propensities into Social-Control Models of Delinquency and Violence among Male Youths." *American Sociological Review* 73:543–68.

Hagan, John, and Ronit Dinovitzer. 1999. "Collateral Consequences of Imprisonment for Children, Communities, and Prisoners." In *Crime and Justice: A Review of Research, Vol. 26: Prisons*, edited by Michael Tonry and Joan Petersilia (121–62). Chicago: University of Chicago Press.

Henriques, Zelma W. 1982. *Imprisoned Mothers and Their Children: A Descriptive and Analytical Study*. Washington, DC: University Press of America.

Huebner, Beth M., and Regan Gustafson. 2007. "The Effect of Maternal Incarceration on Adult Offspring Involvement in the Criminal Justice System." *Journal of Criminal Justice* 35(3): 283–96.

Jaffee, Sara R., Terrie E. Moffitt, Avshalom Caspi, and Alan Taylor. 2003. "Life with (or without) Father: The Benefits of Living with Two Biological Parents Depend on the Father's Antisocial Behavior." *Child Development* 74:109–26.

Johnson, Elizabeth I., and Jane Waldfogel. 2004. "Children of Incarcerated Parents: Multiple Risks and Children's Living Arrangements." In *Imprisoning America: The Social Effects of Mass Incarceration*, edited by Mary Pattillo, David Weiman, and Bruce Western (97–131). New York: Russell Sage Foundation.

Johnson, Rucker. 2009. "Ever-Increasing Levels of Parental Incarceration and the Consequences for Children." In *Do Prisons Make Us Safer? The Benefits and Costs of the Prison Boom*, edited by Stephen Raphael and Michael Stoll (177–206). New York: Russell Sage Foundation.

Johnston, Denise. 1995. "Effects of Parental Incarceration." In *Children of Incarcerated Parents*, edited by Katherine Gabel and Denise Johnston (59–88). New York: Lexington Books.

Kampfner, Christina J. 1995. "Post-Traumatic Stress Reactions in Children of Imprisoned Mothers." In *Children of Incarcerated Parents*, edited by Katherine Gabel and Denise Johnston (89–102). New York: Lexington Books.

Kandel, Elizabeth, Sarnoff A. Mednick, Lis Kirkegaard-Sorensen, Barry Hutchings, Joachim Knop, Raben Rosenberg, and Fini Schulsinger. 1988. "IQ as a Protective Factor for Subjects at High Risk for Antisocial Behavior." *Journal of Consulting and Clinical Psychology* 56(2): 224–26.

Kinner, Stuart A., Rosa Alati, Jake M. Najman, and Gail M. Williams. 2007. "Do Paternal Arrest and Imprisonment Lead to Child Behaviour Problems and Substance Use? A Longitudinal Analysis." *Journal of Child Psychology and Psychiatry* 48(11): 1148–56.

Murray, Joseph. 2005. "The Effects of Imprisonment on Families and Children of Prisoners." In *The Effects of Imprisonment*, edited by Alison Liebling and Shadd Maruna (442–92). Cullompton, England: Willan.

———. 2007. "The Cycle of Punishment: Social Exclusion of Prisoners and Their Children." *Criminology and Criminal Justice* 7(1): 55–81.

Murray, Joseph, and David P. Farrington. 2005. "Parental Imprisonment: Effects on Boys' Antisocial Behaviour and Delinquency through the Life Course." *Journal of Child Psychology and Psychiatry* 46(12): 1269–78.

———. 2006. "Evidence-Based Programs for Children of Prisoners." *Criminology and Public Policy* 5(4): 721–36.

———. 2008a. "The Effects of Parental Imprisonment on Children." In *Crime and Justice: A Review of Research*, vol. 37, edited by Michael Tonry (133–206). Chicago: University of Chicago Press.

———. 2008b. "Parental Imprisonment: Long-Lasting Effects on Boys' Internalizing Problems through the Life Course." *Development & Psychopathology* 20(1): 273–90.

Murray, Joseph, and Lynne Murray. 2010. "Parental Incarceration, Attachment, and Child Psychopathology." *Attachment & Human Development* 12(4):289–309.

Murray, Joseph, David P. Farrington, and Manuel P. Eisner. 2009. "Drawing Conclusions about Causes from Systematic Reviews of Risk Factors: The Cambridge Quality Checklists." *Journal of Experimental Criminology* 5(1): 1–23.

Murray, Joseph, Carl-Gunnar Janson, and David P. Farrington. 2007. "Crime in Adult Offspring of Prisoners: A Cross-National Comparison of Two Longitudinal Samples." *Criminal Justice and Behavior* 34(1): 133–49.

Pakiz, Bilge, Helen Z. Reinherz, and Rose M. Giaconia. 1997. "Early Risk Factors for Serious Antisocial Behavior at Age 21: A Longitudinal Community Study." *American Journal of Orthopsychiatry* 67(1): 92–101.

Parke, Ross, and Kimberly A. Clarke-Stewart. 2003. "The Effects of Parental Incarceration on Children: Perspectives, Promises, and Policies." In *Prisoners Once Removed: The Impact of Incarceration and Reentry on Children, Families, and Communities,* edited by Jeremy Travis and Michelle Waul (189–232). Washington, DC: Urban Institute Press.

Pellegrini, Anna Maria. 1996. "Children Coping with a Father in Prison: Psychological Tasks." Paper presented at the NEPACS conference, "The Child and the Prison," Grey College, Durham, England, September 28.

Phillips, Susan D., Alaattin Erkanli, Gordon P. Keeler, E. Jane Costello, and Adrian Angold. 2006. "Disentangling the Risks: Parent Criminal Justice Involvement and Children's Exposure to Family Risks." *Criminology & Public Policy* 5(4): 677–703.

Poehlmann, Julie. 2005. "Representations of Attachment Relationships in Children of Incarcerated Mothers." *Child Development* 76(3): 679–96.

Richards, Martin, Brenda McWilliams, Lucy Allcock, Jill Enterkin, Patricia Owens, and Jane Woodrow. 1994. *The Family Ties of English Prisoners: The Results of the Cambridge Project on Imprisonment and Family Ties.* Cambridge: Centre for Family Research, University of Cambridge.

Roettger, Michael E. 2008. "Three Essays on Social Inequality and the U.S. Criminal Justice System." Ph.D. diss., University of North Carolina at Chapel Hill.

Sack, William H. 1977. "Children of Imprisoned Fathers." *Psychiatry* 40:163–74.

Sack, William H., Jack Seidler, and Susan Thomas. 1976. "The Children of Imprisoned Parents: A Psychosocial Exploration." *American Journal of Orthopsychiatry* 46(4): 618–28.

Skinner, Donald, and Leslie Swartz. 1989. "The Consequences for Preschool Children of a Parent's Detention: A Preliminary South African Clinical Study of Caregivers' Reports." *Journal of Child Psychology and Psychiatry* 30(2): 243–59.

Stanton, Ann M. 1980. *When Mothers Go to Jail.* Lexington, MA: Lexington Books.

Thornberry, Terence P., and Marvin D. Krohn. 2003. *Taking Stock of Delinquency: An Overview of Findings from Contemporary Longitudinal Studies.* New York: Kluwer/ Plenum.

Wilbur, MaryAnn B., Jodi E. Marani, Danielle Appugliese, Ryan Woods, Jane A. Siegel, Howard J. Cabral, and Deborah A. Frank. 2007. "Socioemotional Effects of Fathers' Incarceration on Low-Income, Urban, School-Aged Children." *Pediatrics* 120(3): E678–85.

5

Attachment in Infants and Children of Incarcerated Parents

Julie Poehlmann

Scholars and practitioners have raised concerns about disrupted attachment relationships in children following parental incarceration because it limits parent-child contact (e.g., Johnson and Waldfogel 2002; Myers et al. 1999). According to attachment theory and research, disrupted attachments significantly affect children's developmental outcomes and mental health (Bowlby 1973; Dozier et al. 2001). Children of incarcerated parents experience elevated risk for internalizing and externalizing behavior problems, school failure, substance abuse, and other negative outcomes (see Murray and Farrington 2008 and Murray et al. 2009 for reviews). Attachment problems, in addition to other risk factors, possibly contribute to such child outcomes (Murray and Murray 2010; Poehlmann, Park, et al. 2008). Although pioneering attachment scholars recorded their observations of infants with incarcerated mothers decades ago (e.g., Spitz 1956), empirical studies of attachment relationships in children of incarcerated parents have only recently emerged. Several recent studies have increased researchers' understanding of the complex relationship processes in children affected by parental imprisonment, although researchers still have much to learn.

This chapter presents attachment theory as a conceptual framework that can guide research focusing on infants and children of incarcerated parents and their families, giving special attention to theoretical considerations regarding disrupted attachments. Studies that have assessed attachment in affected infants and children are reviewed and areas for future developmental and intervention research with children of incarcerated parents are highlighted, linking attachment processes to risk and resilience while emphasizing the importance of context. Finally, policy and practice implications of the research are discussed.

Attachment as a Key Developmental Process

Forming an attachment is a key developmental task in infancy and early childhood, although attachments continue throughout the lifespan (Bowlby 1982). Attachment theory describes the origins of a child's developing relationship with primary caregivers and the implications of these early relationships for later development. A child who develops a secure attachment derives comfort from contact with the attachment figure if distressing or threatening situations arise (safe haven) and uses the attachment figure as a base from which to explore the environment with increasing confidence over time (secure base) (Ainsworth et al. 1978; Sroufe and Waters 1977). How a child organizes his or her behaviors around an attachment figure emerges from a history of repeated interactions with that caregiver and correlates with the caregiver's sensitive responsiveness and emotional and physical accessibility to the child (Ainsworth et al. 1978; Vondra, Shaw, and Kevenides 1995). Although dyadic interactions are a cornerstone of developing attachments (Bowlby 1982), these interactions occur in the context of broader familial and social relations (e.g., Cowan 1997; Davies et al. 2002).

For children of incarcerated parents, a key context for the development of attachment relationships is the caregiving environment(s) in which the children live during the parents' imprisonment (Poehlmann 2005b; Poehlmann, Park, et al. 2008), which may differ from the environment in which they lived before the incarceration. Many children of incarcerated mothers live with their grandparents during the imprisonment, whereas 80 to 90 percent of children whose fathers are incarcerated continue to live with their mothers (Glaze and Maruschak 2008). Aspects of the caregiving environment that may influence attachment quality include the caregiver's access to such resources as social support, the nature of the caregiver's relationship with the incarcerated parent (Enos 2001; Poehlmann 2005a), the caregiver's responsivity to children (Poehlmann, Park, et al. 2008), and the sociodemographic and psychosocial risks present. Social stigma associated with parental imprisonment is also a key contextual risk (Murray 2007) that may relate to children's attachment relationships and social interactions (e.g., Shlafer and Poehlmann 2010).

In the language of attachment theory, children's cognitive and emotional expectations about relationships are referred to as internal working models or representations of attachment. Bowlby (1973, 1982, 1988) hypothesizes that children develop internal working models of self and others during the toddler years, based on their early interactions and experiences with caregivers. As children's symbolic development and capacity for language increase, these representations become more elaborated, refined, and enduring (Bretherton 1990, 1993). Children's cognitive and emotional expectations about relationships are thought to function as a lens for interpreting future interpersonal experiences (Bretherton and Munholland 1999), thus forming developmental pathways leading toward social and emotional competence or psychopathology (Bowlby 1988). Although young children likely hold both global and specific representational models of relationships and some integration of models occurs over time, we do not clearly understand how this process unfolds (Bretherton and Munholland 1999; Lynch and Cicchetti 1991; Poehlmann 2005b). In research focusing on families affected by parental incarceration, children's representations of attachment relationships with caregivers and imprisoned parents do not significantly differ (Poehlmann 2005b; Shlafer and Poehlmann 2010), possibly reflecting generalized expectations about family relationships or the potential effects of one attachment on other relationships.

Attachment Relationships and Disruptions

Attachment theory and research suggest that children's cognitive and emotional expectations for close relationships are less optimal when attachment figures are unavailable and unresponsive (Bowlby 1973; Toth et al. 2002). Disruptions that dramatically diminish or eliminate the availability and responsiveness of an attachment figure occur during a separation or when discontinuity in care occurs (Bowlby 1973). Disruptions in attachments may be temporary (e.g., a time-limited separation) or permanent (e.g., parental death or abandonment). When parents who have cared for a child go to jail or prison, the child-parent relationship is typically disrupted because of the physical separation that is initiated (Poehlmann 2005b) and the limited contact that follows (Glaze and Maruschak 2008). Because incarcerated mothers are more likely to live with their children before arrest than incarcerated fathers (Glaze and Maruschak 2008), scholars have speculated that children of imprisoned mothers may be at higher risk for disrupted attachments than children of imprisoned fathers (Dallaire 2007; Murray and Murray 2010). In addition, compared to children of incarcerated fathers, children of incarcerated mothers are more likely to be exposed to their parents' criminal activity, arrest, and sentencing (Dallaire and Wilson 2010). These events may be traumatizing for children and contribute to their feelings of distress or insecurity. However, no studies have directly compared children's attachments to incarcerated mothers versus incarcerated fathers.

Following a relationship disruption or separation, young children often experience acute anxiety and distress (Bowlby 1973). Many children of incarcerated parents exhibit sadness, fear, anger, and confusion following a parent's imprisonment (Shlafer and Poehlmann 2010). Other commonly reported reactions include worry, acting out, loneliness, developmental regression, sleep problems, and indifference or detachment (Poehlmann 2005b). Children's reactions to separation resulting from parental incarceration are similar to the reactions recorded for children whose parents are hospitalized (e.g., Bowlby 1979; Robertson 1953). However, when a parent is incarcerated, the separation from the child is typically longer than for hospitalization, especially if the parent is in prison rather than jail,[1] and the social context is likely to differ.

How the child handles a relationship disruption following the initial separation may depend on multiple factors. Although the empirical research is limited, theory suggests that these factors may include the child's age and gender, the quality of the previous attachments, the quality of caregiving following the disruption (including the coparenting alliance with the incarcerated parent), the frequency and quality of contact with the incarcerated parent, and the availability of other support systems. Infants and young children do not possess the language and communication skills to understand why their mother or father is leaving them, and they do not comprehend the concept of incarceration. In addition, many young children of incarcerated mothers show cognitive delays, further limiting their capacity for understanding the situation (Poehlmann 2005a). In contrast, a newborn or very young infant may not even be aware that a parent has left. For children of any age, the role of the child's caregiver is thought to be crucial regarding how the child handles the separation and

children's subsequent adaptation in families affected by parental incarceration (Cecil et al. 2008; Poehlmann 2003). In a study of infants in foster care, Dozier and colleagues find that infants organize their attachment
behaviors around the new caregivers' availability (Dozier et al. 2001). It
is also possible that if the parent was abusive or significantly impaired
because of substance abuse, a separation may eventually result in positive
changes for a child.

Although any significant relationship disruption can be difficult for
young children, parent-child separation resulting from parental incarceration may be particularly challenging for several reasons. Incarcerated parents are not free to leave the correctional facilities to visit their children.
Many prisons have policies stating that inmates may only place collect
calls. Because of restrictions such as these as well as other factors, children's
contact with incarcerated parents is often sporadic, and few children have
regular visits (Glaze and Maruschak 2008). Visits and contact are often
regulated by children's caregivers, especially when children are young
(Enos 2001; Roy and Dyson 2005; Shlafer and Poehlmann 2010). Further, there is much social stigma associated with parental incarceration
(Murray 2007), which may cause secrecy and distorted communication in the family (Hagen and Myers 2003; Poehlmann 2005b) or may
prompt acting-out behaviors in children who are teased (Shlafer and
Poehlmann 2010). Finally, children may experience trauma such as witnessing the parent's arrest (Dallaire 2007; Dallaire and Wilson 2010) or
they may feel frightened visiting a jail or prison, depending on the context and the hospitality of the visitation environment (e.g., Murray
2007; Poehlmann et al. 2010). These factors may influence a child's
ability to cope with a disrupted relationship resulting from parental
incarceration.

Although many children affected by parental incarceration may be
at risk for experiencing disrupted attachments, there is potential for
resilience, or the process of successful adaptation in the face of significant
adversity (e.g., Luthar, Cicchetti, and Becker 2000; Masten 2001). Masten
(2001, 2007) has argued that resilience following adversity is the most
common response when normative human adaptational systems, such as
positive family relationships, effective parenting, and age-appropriate
cognitive development, remain intact and protective. Indeed, young children who live with their grandparents when their mothers are incarcerated have more positive attachment representations when their caregivers
report less depression; in addition, these children exhibit fewer behavior

problems when their caregiving environments are more responsive and their attachment representations are more positive (Poehlmann, Park, et al. 2008).

Individual Differences in Patterns of Attachment

When an infant develops an attachment relationship with a parent or caregiver, one of several different patterns can be formed, including secure, insecure-avoidant, insecure-ambivalent/resistant, and disorganized attachment. An infant classified as secure gains comfort from contact with his attachment figure and is confident exploring his environment in the attachment figure's presence. An infant classified as insecure-avoidant does not seek contact with his attachment figure when distressed but rather maintains some distance between them. An infant classified as insecure-ambivalent seeks contact with his attachment figure when distressed but does not gain comfort; instead, he acts angry and may alternate between pushing away his attachment figure and trying to achieve contact (Ainsworth et al. 1978). In contrast to these organized patterns, an infant classified as disorganized does not have a clear pattern of approaching his attachment figure when distressed but may appear dazed, confused, or fearful (Main and Hesse 1990).

A fairly recent meta-analysis finds that about 15 percent of children in low-risk families show the disorganized pattern, whereas the rates of disorganized patterns are up to 80 percent in high-risk samples (van IJzendoorn, Schuengel, and Bakermans-Kranenburg 1999). The meta-analysis also finds that in low-risk samples, about 60 percent of infants show secure attachments. In higher-risk samples, the rate of security is lower (e.g., children of depressed parents, 41 percent; children in families with low socioeconomic status, 48 percent; children of substance-abusing mothers, 26 percent; children who have been maltreated, 9 percent).

The validity and usefulness of classifying children into these different attachment patterns hinge on empirical associations between attachment patterns and observed interactions in the home during the child's first year (Ainsworth et al. 1978) as well as children's subsequent social-emotional adjustment (Thompson 2008). For example, previous research has found that children who have secure attachments during infancy are more ego resilient and curious, have more optimal interactions with parents and peers, display better emotion regulation, and exhibit more compliance and cooperation with adults than children with insecure attachments (see Thompson 2008 for a review).

Because of their status as "organized" patterns of attachment, insecure-avoidant and resistant attachment classifications are seen as more adaptive than disorganized attachment. Insecure attachment can be viewed as a nonspecific risk factor for psychopathology, as it may eventually result in several different child outcomes depending on a host of factors, including children's environments and individual competencies (see Cicchetti and Toth 2009 for a discussion, and Dozier, Stovall-McClough, and Albus 2008 for a review). However, because of their relatively high base rates in typically developing children, insecure patterns have proved less useful in predicting psychopathology than the disorganized pattern (Green and Goldwyn 2002). In recent years, disorganized attachment in children has been shown as a strong predictor of clinical psychopathology (see Lyons-Ruth and Jacobvitz 2008 for a review). Such findings have implications for understanding children's development in the context of risk and for interpreting research that measures children's developmental outcomes in attachment security and attachment disorganization.

Assessment of Attachment Relationships

Studies focusing on children of incarcerated parents have used a range of methods for assessing attachment security and organization, in part depending on the child's age, the feasibility of conducting direct observations, and whether access to incarcerated parents and caregivers is possible. Attachment assessments have been designed for children of different ages, and several of these have been used in studies of children whose parents are incarcerated.

The Strange Situation Procedure (SSP; Ainsworth et al. 1978), a laboratory procedure that involves coding children's responses to reunion with the attachment figure following brief separations, is considered the gold standard for assessing infants' and toddlers' attachment to a particular caregiver (Solomon and George 2008). To date, two studies have successfully used the SSP with infants of incarcerated mothers, one within the context of a prison nursery intervention (Byrne, Goshin, and Joestl 2010) and one within the context of a jail diversion program (Cassidy et al. 2010). However, in part because of difficulties conducting direct observations of parent-infant interactions in corrections settings and accessing infants who live in the community apart from their incarcerated parents, no studies have used the SSP with infants of incarcerated fathers or infants of incarcerated mothers who have not spent time in prison nursery or jail diversion settings.

For older children, who have developed the capacity for symbolic representation and verbal expression, several approaches are available for measuring attachment security. These methods involve analyzing children's responses to pictures depicting separations (e.g., Walsh, Symons, and McGrath 2004); examining children's reunion behaviors following separation, similar to a modified SSP;[2] or coding children's enactments of their solutions to attachment-relevant story stems (e.g., Bretherton, Prentiss, and Ridgeway 1990). This last technique is particularly promising for working with children of incarcerated parents.

Story stem assessments such as the Attachment Story Completion Task (ASCT; Bretherton, Ridgeway, and Cassidy 1990) use props and dolls to facilitate children's enactments and verbal narratives to attachment-related themes. Children's representations of attachment are then inferred from their verbal and nonverbal responses, with prototypically secure responses reflecting portrayals of adults as nurturing and responsive authority figures, a lack of intense violence, some degree of organization, lack of avoidance, and coherence (e.g., Gloger-Tippelt et al. 2002; Poehlmann 2005b). The discriminate and concurrent validity of story stem techniques has been established with young children from middle and low socioeconomic backgrounds, including children who have experienced family disruptions (e.g., Bretherton, Ridgeway, et al. 1990; Grych, Wachsmuth-Schlaefer, and Klockow 2002; Oppenheim et al. 1997; Toth et al. 2002). The ASCT has been used to assess attachment representations in preschool and elementary school children whose mothers are imprisoned (Poehlmann 2005b; Poehlmann, Park, et al. 2008). No studies with children of incarcerated parents have examined the relation between SSP classifications and the ASCT, although such links have been demonstrated with typically developing children (e.g., Bretherton, Ridgeway, et al. 1990).

Several methods are available for assessing attachment in older children, including self-report questionnaires, narrative discourse methods, and family drawings; however, unlike in infancy, there is no gold standard for assessing attachment in middle childhood. Examples of such assessments include the Attachment Interview for Children and Adolescents (AICA; Ammaniti et al. 2000), the Inventory of Parent and Peer Attachment (IPPA;

Armsden 1986; Armsden and Greenberg 1987; or the revised version, Gullone and Robinson 2005), and the Security Scale (Kerns, Klepac, and Cole 1996). The IPPA is a self-report measure that focuses on children's feelings of trust, anger, and communication regarding mothers and fathers. In contrast, many narrative discourse methods like the AICA indirectly access a child's state of mind surrounding attachment in addition to the quality of children's specific relationships.

Although few attachment measures have been used with children affected by parental imprisonment, Shlafer and Poehlmann (2010) have used the IPPA with 9- to 15-year-old children whose parents are incarcerated, and Dallaire, Wilson, and Ciccone have used family drawings with 4- to 14-year-old children whose parents are in jail.[3] In using the IPPA, Shlafer and Poehlmann find that some children would not complete the measure because they felt they had no relationship with the incarcerated parent. Like the SSP and many other attachment assessments (Zeanah et al. 2005), the IPPA focuses on assessing the quality of a relationship rather than assessing whether an attachment is present or absent. In contrast, the Important People Interview is an assessment that focuses on identifying children's attachment figures and is appropriate for children age 6 to 12 years.[4] In addition, Kerns and her coauthors' (1996) Security Scale measures the degree to which children believe an attachment figure is available and responsive, including their reliance on the attachment figure in times of stress. However, neither of these assessments has been used with children affected by parental incarceration.

Attachment in adults is an important consideration when assessing the attachment of children. The Adult Attachment Interview (AAI)[5] is considered the gold standard for assessing an adult's state of mind regarding attachment, and it is appropriate for adolescents as well (e.g., Allen et al. 2007). The AAI involves interviewing the individual regarding his or her experiences with each parent. When used with adolescents, slight modifications are made to the 18 questions to make them more easily understandable (e.g., Allen et al. 2007). The AAI can be coded using the AAI Classification System or the AAI Q-set.[6] Both coding systems reference process characteristics (e.g., coherence, secure versus anxious strategies) and the content of responses. Although no published studies have used the AAI with adolescents affected by parental incarceration, Borelli and colleagues (2010) have used the AAI to assess attachment states of mind in imprisoned mothers.

Studies of Attachment in the Children of Incarcerated Parents

Only a few studies have been conducted focusing on children's attachments to their caregivers and incarcerated parents. Table 5.1 summarizes the most rigorous of such studies. In this section, these studies are reviewed according to the age of the children studied.

Studies with Infants in Prison and Jail Nurseries

Two recent studies have focused on children in prison nursery programs available for women who are pregnant when they enter prison, and one study has focused on children whose mothers are in a jail diversion program (see Byrne, this volume). In these programs, infants live with their mothers in the prison or jail diversion setting until the mother is released or until infants reach a certain age (which ranges widely by location and setting). Then, the infants must transition to living in the community, either with the released mother or with a nonmaternal caregiver. Each study has provided some information about attachment processes in infants whose mothers are incarcerated.

Byrne and her coauthors (2010) assess attachment security in a subset of 30 infants drawn from a larger longitudinal intervention study focusing on maternal and child prison nursery coresidence. They find that infants who reside with their mothers in the prison nursery intervention program for at least one year are more likely to have secure attachments to their mothers than infants discharged from the nursery program before one year. In addition, the SSP distributions for both groups are compared with previously published meta-analytic findings of clinical and community samples. Sixty percent of infants are classified secure (75 percent who coresided a year or longer and 43 percent who coresided less than a year), which is within the range of normative community samples.

In another intervention study, Cassidy and her coauthors (2010) implement the Circle of Security perinatal program (Hoffman et al. 2006) with mothers who are pregnant when they enter a jail diversion program. Mothers give birth while living in the diversion program and then live with their infants for six months in the secure residential setting, after which the infants transition to the community. Mothers receive not only

Table 5.1. Summary of Studies on Attachment in Children of Incarcerated Parents

Author(s)	Age of children	Sample size	Comparison group?	Method of assessing attachment	Parental incarceration
Byrne et al. (2010)	12–28 months	42	No	Strange Situation Procedure; Adult Attachment Interview	Mother in NY prison nursery program
Cassidy et al. (2010)	12 months	20	No	Strange Situation Procedure; Experiences in Close Relationships Scale	Mother in MD jail diversion nursery program
Baradon et al. (2008)	1 week–9 months	27	No	Parent Development Interview	Mother in UK prison nursery program
Poehlmann (2005b)	2.5–7.5 years	60	No	Attachment Story Completion Task; emotions checklist	Mother in WI state prison
Poehlmann, Park, et al. (2008)	3–7.5 years	37	Yes	Attachment Story Completion Task	Mother in WI state prison
Dallaire, Wilson, and Ciccone (2009)	4–14 years	32	Yes	Family drawings	Father and/or mother in VA jail
Shlafer and Poehlmann (2010)	4–15 years	57	No	Inventory of Parent and Peer Attachment (with 27 children 9 and older); Revised Inventory of Parent Attachment	Father and/or mother in WI prison or jail

Note: "Sample size" refers to the number of children with an incarcerated parent who participated in the study; "comparison group" refers to whether the study collected data on a group of children not affected by parental incarceration.

intervention during their stay in the program, but also support services for six months following discharge (i.e., wraparound services). All mothers have a history of substance abuse, and women who engage in violent crime are not included in the program. For mothers who receive the full 15-month intervention (from their third trimester of pregnancy until the infants turn 12 months), the proportion of infants classified as securely attached to their mothers as assessed via the SSP (70 percent) approximates that of low-risk community samples (compared with previously published meta-analytic findings), similar to Byrne and her coauthors' results.

An additional study conducted in the United Kingdom focuses on an attachment-based intervention in a prison nursery but only reports indirect data reflecting infant attachment. Baradon and colleagues (2008) examine New Beginnings, a short-term intervention program implemented in the mother-baby units of two women's prisons. The program was piloted with 27 dyads in 2004 and 2005. Baradon and her coauthors report preliminary evaluation data from 15 mothers assessed during the pilot phase using the Parent Development Interview (PDI)[7] before and following program participation. The PDI focuses on mothers' thoughts and feelings about their infants, including mothers' reflective capacity regarding the child. Although qualitative analyses of the PDI indicate a significant increase in maternal reflective functioning over the course of treatment, post-treatment scores are considered below the normative level. The lack of longitudinal data from the nonintervention group and small sample size preclude causal inference regarding potential treatment effects; however, Baradon and colleagues suggest that New Beginnings appears to benefit some infant-mother relationships in the prison nursery setting, although no direct assessment of infant attachment was conducted.

Although these studies are intriguing and provide important descriptive information about attachment in infants raised in jail diversion or prison nursery programs, the meaning of the findings is not entirely clear because the studies did not have randomized designs (see Byrne, this volume, for a discussion and rationale). Instead, Byrne and coauthors' and Cassidy and coauthors' studies compare their SSP findings to SSP distributions drawn from 25 studies summarized in a meta-analytic review (van IJzendoorn et al. 1999); samples included a range of risk factors, including low socioeconomic status, maternal substance abuse, maternal depression, and maternal clinical diagnoses.

Studies with Young Children

Two published studies have measured attachment relationships in young children of incarcerated mothers. In the first of these studies, Poehlmann (2005b) examined representations of attachment relationships and behavioral and emotional reactions to separation in 54 children age 2.5 to 7.5 years whose mothers were incarcerated in a state prison. Children participated in videotaped interviews in their homes using the ASCT, and nonmaternal caregivers and incarcerated mothers were interviewed about children's reactions to maternal incarceration and visitation. Poehlmann finds that most children (63 percent) hold representations of insecure relationships with mothers and caregivers (26 percent in the highly ambivalent-disorganized group and 37 percent in the avoidant-detached group). Children who have lived continuously with one caregiver since their mother's incarceration are significantly more likely to have a secure relationship with the caregiver than children who have changed placements one or more times.

From an attachment perspective, developing relationships with consistently available alternative adults can ease the negative effects of parental loss and facilitate resilience processes, whereas experiencing multiple shifts in caregivers undermines this process. Yet research has not examined whether secure attachment to a caregiver or parent is sufficient to promote positive outcomes for children of incarcerated parents, especially when the children are exposed to multiple risk factors.

Other research has highlighted contextual factors that relate to continuity of care for children of incarcerated parents. An analysis of a larger dataset finds that children are more likely to live in continuous caregiving arrangements when incarcerated mothers choose the caregiver, when children are able to live with their fathers, and when the mother-caregiver relationship is more positive (Poehlmann, Shlafer, et al. 2008). Similarly, in their analysis of data from incarcerated parents drawn from a nationally representative probability sample of state and federal prisoners, Johnson and Waldfogel (2002) find that children experiencing more contextual risks—such as maternal single marital status, having more children in the family, maternal history of drug use, and receipt of public assistance—are more likely to be placed in nonparental care (although attachment is not measured). These studies highlight the importance of contextual factors that may indirectly relate to attachment via their influence on the caregiving environment.

Poehlmann (2005b) also finds that children are slightly more likely to hold positive representations of caregivers when they are told about the mother's incarceration in simple, honest, and developmentally appropriate ways, underscoring the importance of emotionally open and sensitive communication within the family (Bretherton 1990, 1995). There also is a trend for children who have visited their mothers in prison to have slightly less positive representations of mothers than children who have not visited. One possible explanation for these findings is that a recent visit may activate the child's attachment system without affording opportunities to work through intense feelings about the relationship. Young children may need additional emotional support and reassurance to cope effectively with such visits so they maintain and strengthen parent-child relationships, rather than cause stress. The results of the Poehlmann (2005b) study highlight the need for support in families affected by maternal imprisonment to promote stable, continuous placements for children. However, weaknesses of the study include its lack of longitudinal data, inability to assess children's attachment quality before maternal incarceration, lack of direct observations of mother-child interactions, and lack of a comparison group.

Only two studies focusing on attachment relationships in children of incarcerated parents have used comparison groups that experienced risks other than parental incarceration. The first of these was conducted by Poehlmann, Park, and their coauthors (2008), who compared attachment representations in 37 children raised by custodial grandparents due to maternal incarceration with those in 42 children raised by custodial grandparents due to other reasons. Children ranged from 3 to 7.5 years old. Children's representations of family relationships were examined in relation to grandparents' responsivity and depression, family sociodemographic risks, and children's behavior problems. Findings suggest that global representations of family relationships in children of incarcerated mothers and children living with grandparents for other reasons do not significantly differ. In addition, children include more relationship violence in their representations when grandparents report elevated depressive symptoms. Finally, children exhibit fewer externalizing behavior problems when grandparents are more responsive to them and when children hold representations of positive attachment relationships (measured using the ASCT). These findings suggest that the caregiving context is important for the development of children's relationships and behavioral functioning in these high-risk families. The second study to use a comparison group was conducted with older children and is described next.

Studies with Older Children

Dallaire, Wilson, and Ciccone compared 32 children, age 4 to 14 years, whose parents were incarcerated in a regional jail with 30 children separated from their parents for other reasons (besides parental death or military service).[8] Half the 32 children had incarcerated mothers and half had incarcerated fathers. Children were asked to create family drawings, and these representations of attachment relationships were assessed using the coding system presented in Fury, Carlson, and Sroufe (1997). Similar to Poehlmann, Park, and their coauthors (2008), the authors find no differences in mean attachment codes between groups (Dallaire, Ciccone, and Wilson 2008). They find that more frequent visitation with incarcerated parents is associated with higher scores on codes that reflect attachment insecurity (e.g., role reversal, tension/anger, etc.), controlling for children's age and gender. However, frequency of visitation is not associated with family drawing variables for children separated from their parents for reasons other than incarceration. The authors interpret these results as suggesting that traditional visitations at jails (e.g., behind Plexiglas) can be stressful for children and may undermine their sense of attachment security.

In a study of 57 children who participated in a mentoring program for children of incarcerated parents, Shlafer and Poehlmann (2010) use a mixed method longitudinal design to investigate children's relationships and behavioral adjustment. Children in the study ranged in age between 4 and 15 years, although only 27 children age 9 and older completed the self-report measure of attachment (IPPA). Most children had incarcerated fathers (86 percent), although 4 children had incarcerated mothers (7 percent), and in 4 cases, both parents were incarcerated (7 percent). Because mostly fathers were incarcerated, the majority of children lived with their biological mothers (79 percent). Although 100 percent of the participants in the program agreed to participate in the research, 28 percent left the mentoring program at the six-month mark. Monthly interviews were conducted with children, caregivers, and mentors during the first six months of program participation, and questionnaires were administered at intake and six months to assess caregiver-child and incarcerated parent–child relationships, contact with incarcerated parents, and children's behavior problems. In addition, 40 caregivers completed the Revised Inventory of Parent Attachment (Johnson, Ketring, and Abshire 2003), a self-report measure focusing on caregivers' perspectives of the caregiver-child relationship. However, direct access to incarcerated parents was not possible.

Findings indicate that many children report ambivalent feelings about their relationships with incarcerated parents, including feelings of sadness, anger, and resentment. Although some children view their incarcerated parent as a positive attachment figure, other children report negative feelings toward or no relationship with incarcerated parents. In addition, children age 9 and older who have contact with incarcerated parents report fewer feelings of alienation toward them than children with no contact, although most contact occurs through telephone calls or letters rather than visits. Visits are sporadic, and no child who discusses a visit reports having a positive experience. Another key finding is that children's behavior problems are a primary concern for many caregivers and teachers; most behavior problems have a negative relational component, including reactions to social stigma associated with parental imprisonment. Finally, caregivers who feel less positively about their children have children rated by caregivers and teachers as exhibiting more externalizing behavior problems, controlling for earlier behavior problems.

Shlafer and Poehlmann's findings highlight the importance of the caregiving context for children whose parents are incarcerated. Weaknesses of the study include its high rates of missing data from caregivers and teachers, lack of access to incarcerated parents, and lack of assessments of children's attachments before parental incarceration. Strengths included its longitudinal design and inclusion of children affected by paternal as well as maternal incarceration.

Summary and Discussion

In some cases, children perceive their incarcerated parents as meeting some of their attachment needs (Byrne et al. 2010; Shlafer and Poehlmann 2010). In a prison nursery setting, when infants and mothers live together for at least 12 months, most children develop secure attachments to their mothers in the context of an intervention (Byrne et al. 2010). However, few children of incarcerated parents are raised in prison nursery settings. For the typical child who lives in the community after his caregiving parent goes to prison, attachment processes may be more vulnerable to various risk factors (e.g., poverty, changes in living arrangements, social stigma, challenges associated with visits).

Although the studies reviewed in this chapter have enhanced our understanding of attachment in families affected by parental incarceration, we still have much to learn, especially regarding the influence of children's prior attachments on the quality of their relationships during and following parental incarceration and the processes that occur following reunion. It is possible that some children never formed an attachment with the parent or the relationship was insecure before the parent's incarceration, perhaps affecting the child's developmental trajectory. It is also possible that a secure attachment could deteriorate following separation from the parent, especially if the child experiences limited or no contact with the parent or if the alternate caregiving environment is not stable or supportive. Reunification processes are complex and likely to be emotionally challenging as well.

When children live in the community during their parents' incarceration, the caregiving environment is a crucial setting for the development of attachment relationships (Poehlmann, Park, et al. 2008), similar to children in foster care (Dozier et al. 2001). Several factors may be particularly important, including whether the child remains with one consistent caregiver or is shifted from one home to another (Poehlmann 2005b) and whether the caregiver is functioning well or is suffering from problems such as significant depression (Poehlmann, Park, et al. 2008). Other issues of importance include the quality of communication in the home, the nature of the relationship between the caregiver and the incarcerated parent, the feelings of the caregiver toward the child, the presence of contextual risks such as social stigma, and the challenges a family faces related to visitation and other forms of contact. Additional research is needed to better clarify the roles and importance of these issues, and the interactions among them.

Implications for Developmental and Intervention Research

Three studies that have assessed children's attachment relationships have suggested that visitation and other forms of contact with incarcerated parents are key issues affecting children's relationships with caregivers and imprisoned parents (see Poehlmann et al. 2010). Many caregivers think that visitation and other forms of contact with incarcerated parents are associated with children's behavior problems, whereas others argue for the importance of visitation and other forms of contact. Prison and jail visiting environments can be frightening or stressful for children in some cases, and in other cases the environments can be welcoming and supportive (Arditti 2003; Arditti and Few 2006, 2008; Loper et al. 2009). We know little about how programs that facilitate visitation between children and incarcerated parents affect children or whether potential effects vary on the basis of the child's age or other variables (Bruns 2006; Poehlmann et al. 2010). Clearly, further work is needed to understand basic issues such as these.

It is important for intervention programs to acknowledge that children's attachment systems may become activated during visitation (Poehlmann 2005b). Interventions must not only communicate this information to caregivers but also help caregivers develop the skills to assist children in labeling and organizing their thoughts and feelings before and following a visit. Additional research focusing on attachment in children of incarcerated parents is needed, especially research that incorporates a developmental perspective, includes appropriate comparison groups, and assesses risks and resilience processes in children within their key developmental contexts.

In particular, perusal of table 5.1 suggests several research needs, such as studies focusing on attachment in infants or young children of incarcerated fathers, studies with larger samples, studies with comparison groups, and studies focusing on attachment in adolescents whose parents are incarcerated. The use of comparison groups of children who have experienced other familial risks or separations may help researchers tease apart the effects of parental incarceration on children's attachments relative to the effects of other risks (e.g., parental substance abuse). The effects of short-term and long-term incarceration (i.e., jail versus prison) should also be examined. The field also needs longitudinal studies that can examine the direction of effects and follow children as they adjust to the multiple transitions involved when a parent goes to jail or prison and eventually returns to the community. In addition, most commonly used attachment measures assess quality of relationships rather than the presence or absence of attachments (Zeanah et al. 2005). Additional research on identifying conditions under which an attachment with an incarcerated parent (or the child's caregiver) is present or not and determining the quality of the relationship may be important for understanding the effects of visitation and the reunification process for children and families. Attachment theory and research indicate that it is critical that children develop an attachment relationship with some consistent figure, be it the parent or another caregiver (Bowlby 1982;

Thompson 2008). Of course, conditions that promote secure attachments should be encouraged.

Tentative evidence regarding the potential efficacy of attachment-based interventions implemented in prison nursery settings is emerging but scant. Because randomized controlled trials have not been conducted, it is possible that the findings may have resulted from keeping infants and mothers together for a certain period, rather than reflecting effects of the attachment interventions per se. In addition, we know virtually nothing about how children raised in prison nurseries fare in the years following their release into the community.

The field also needs investigations on the effects of other intervention programs that may facilitate development of secure attachments in children of incarcerated parents, especially with children who live in the community. To date, no published studies have focused on attachment interventions for children of incarcerated parents living with caregivers in the community, despite the importance of these contexts for children's development. Research with maltreated children suggests that the potential efficacy of dyadic psychotherapy techniques with young children and their caregivers (e.g., Toth et al. 2002) could be investigated in families affected by parental imprisonment. Older children may benefit from school-based interventions grounded in attachment theory as children's contexts widen to include peers (Lopez and Bhat 2007). In addition, studies examining the effects of parenting interventions for incarcerated individuals (e.g., Loper and Tuerk 2006) or multimodal interventions with parents in corrections settings should consider assessment of children's attachment relationships to document additional program effects.

Overall, theory and research suggest that many children of incarcerated parents are at risk for developing insecure or disorganized attachments to their parents and other caregivers. In the studies that use comparison groups, the level of risk for insecure attachment in children of incarcerated parents appears similar to that of children who experience separation from parents for other reasons. However, more research is needed to understand the processes leading from risks to attachment insecurity or resilience in children of incarcerated parents. Some children have no attachment to incarcerated parents, especially when parents and children no longer have contact with each other. Yet this is less concerning if the child has developed a secure attachment to an alternate caregiver. However, nothing is known about the efficacy of attachment interventions with older children of incarcerated mothers or children of incarcerated fathers, suggesting needs for future research and interventions with this population.

Implications for Policy and Practice

To date, research findings suggest that if families and society fail to attend to the needs of high-risk children, including their attachment relationships, we may decrease their chances of developing into competent and caring adults. For children with incarcerated parents, this failure could cause taxpayers and society to bear additional costs beyond that of the parent's incarceration. One fundamental need of all children is to have a physical and emotional connection with a consistent primary caregiver. For parents who are convicted of crimes, serious consideration of sentences that provide opportunities for connection, such as in well-supervised jail diversion programs and prison nurseries or in corrections facilities that encourage regular visitation in child-friendly settings, seems warranted. When such sentences are not possible or the inmate's children are in foster care or kinship arrangements, it is important to find ways to support new caregivers in developing positive attachment relationships with children and to maintain positive placements for the duration of the parent's prison or jail stay. Work in both areas will be facilitated through improved cooperation and joint planning by child welfare and corrections systems, as well as mental health and substance abuse services, early intervention programs, and schools.

Findings from attachment research also point to the urgent need for jails and prisons to review and improve visitation policies, practices, and settings for children of incarcerated parents. A recent review (Poehlmann et al. 2010) suggests that visitation with incarcerated parents relates to positive child outcomes, such as secure attachment, only in the context of interventions, whereas mail correspondence relates to positive child outcomes even when interventions are not in place. However, visitation with children appears to have fairly consistent benefits for incarcerated parents.

Because of the complex issues related to visitation that arise in families affected by parental incarceration, institutions and families should take steps to improve the likelihood that a child's visit with an incarcerated parent is a positive experience. This may include better preparing family members for visits, improving the settings in which visits occur, and working with incarcerated parents and caregivers on communication issues that arise during and following visits. Institutions can also encourage and support alternatives (or supplements to) in-person visits with children, such as letter writing, audiotape production, scrapbook development, and artwork exchange. As systems strive to improve visitation, it is critical that evaluations of policies and programs be conducted not only from the incarcerated individual's perspective, but also from the perspectives of children of various ages and developmental capacities.

Attachment research with children of incarcerated parents has both negative and positive implications. The bad news is that many children affected by parental imprisonment are at risk for developing insecure attachments, thus placing them at risk for future problems. The good news, however, is that attachment research has identified multiple routes that could be pursued to facilitate resilience processes in this vulnerable population.

NOTES

1. Bureau of Justice Statistics, "All Terms and Definitions," http://bjs.ojp.usdoj.gov/index.cfm?ty=tda (accessed January 2, 2010).

2. Jude Cassidy and Robert S. Marvin, "Attachment Organization in Three- and Four-Year-Olds: Procedures and Coding Manual," unpublished coding manual, University of Virginia, 1992.

3. Danielle H. Dallaire, Laura Wilson, and Anne E. Ciccone, "A Comparative Analysis of Family Drawings Made by Children with Incarcerated Parents and Children Separated from Their Parents for Other Reasons," manuscript under review, 2009.

4. Roger Kobak and Natalie Rosenthal, "The Important People Interview," unpublished manuscript, department of psychology, University of Delaware, Newark, 2003.

5. Carol George, Nancy Kaplan, and Mary Main, "Adult Attachment Interview, 3rd ed.," unpublished manuscript, department of psychology, University of California, Berkeley, 1996.

6. For the AAI Classification System, see Mary Main and Ruth Goldwyn, "Adult Attachment Scoring and Classification System," unpublished manuscript, University of California, Berkeley, 1998. For the AAI Q-set, see George, Kaplan, and Main, "Adult Attachment Interview," 1996.

7. Arietta Slade, J. Lawrence Aber, Ivan Bresgi, Brenda Berger, and Merryle Kaplan, "The Parent Development Interview—Revised," unpublished master's protocol, The City University of New York, 2004.

8. Dallaire, Wilson, and Ciccone, "A Comparative Analysis of Family Drawings."

REFERENCES

Ainsworth, Mary S., Mary C. Blehar, Everett Waters, and Sally Wall. 1978. *Patterns of Attachment: A Psychological Study of the Strange Situation*. Oxford: Lawrence Erlbaum.

Allen, Joseph P., Maryfrances Porter, Christy McFarland, Kathleen McElhaney, and Penny Marsh. 2007. "The Relation of Attachment Security to Adolescents' Paternal and Peer Relationships, Depression, and Externalizing Behavior." *Child Development* 78:1222–39.

Ammaniti, Massimo, Marinus H. van IJzendoorn, Anna M. Speranza, and Renata Tambelli. 2000. "Internal Working Models of Attachment during Late Childhood and Early Adolescence: An Exploration of Stability and Change." *Attachment and Human Development* 2:328–46.

Arditti, Joyce A. 2003. "Locked Doors and Glass Walls: Family Visiting at a Local Jail." *Journal of Loss and Trauma* 8:115–38.

Arditti, Joyce, and April Few. 2006. "Mothers' Reentry into Family Life Following Incarceration." *Criminal Justice Policy Review* 17:103–23.

———. 2008. "Maternal Distress and Women's Reentry into Family and Community Life." *Family Process* 47:303–21.

Armsden, Gay C. 1986. "Attachment to Parents and Peers in Late Adolescence: Relationships to Affective Status, Self-Esteem, and Coping with Loss, Threat, and Challenge." *Dissertation Abstracts International* 47:1751–52.

Armsden, Gay C., and Mark T. Greenberg. 1987. "The Inventory of Parent and Peer Attachment: Relationships to Well-Being in Adolescence." *Journal of Youth and Adolescence* 16:427–54.

Baradon, Tessa, Peter Fonagy, Kirsten Bland, Kata Lenard, and Michelle Sleed. 2008. "New Beginnings: An Experienced-Based Programme Addressing the Attachment Relationship between Mothers and Their Babies in Prisons." *Journal of Child Psychotherapy* 34:240–58.

Borelli, Jessica L., Lorie Goshin, Sarah Joestl, Juliette Clark, and Mary W. Byrne. 2010. "Attachment Organization in a Sample of Incarcerated Mothers: Distribution of Classifications and Associations with Substance Abuse, Depressive Symptoms, Perceptions of Parenting Competency, and Social Support." *Attachment & Human Development* 12:355–74.

Bowlby, John. 1973. *Attachment and Loss, Volume II: Separation: Anxiety and Anger.* New York: Basic Books.

———. 1979. *The Making and Breaking of Affectional Bonds.* London: Tavistock.

———. 1982. *Attachment and Loss, Volume I: Attachment.* 2nd ed. New York: Basic Books.

———. 1988. "Developmental Psychiatry Comes of Age." *American Journal of Psychiatry* 145:1–10.

Bretherton, Inge. 1990. "Open Communication and Internal Working Models: Their Role in the Development of Attachment Relationships." In *Nebraska Symposium on Motivation*, vol. 36, edited by Ross A. Thompson (59–113). Lincoln: University of Nebraska Press.

———. 1993. "The Origins of Attachment Theory: John Bowlby and Mary Ainsworth." *Developmental Psychology* 28:759–75.

———. 1995. "A Communication Perspective on Attachment Relationships and Internal Working Models." In *Caregiving, Cultural, and Cognitive Perspectives on Secure-Base Behavior and Working Models*, edited by Everett Waters, Brian E. Vaughn, German

Posada, and Kiyomi Kondo-Ikemura (310–29). *Monographs of the Society for Research in Child Development*, vol. 60. Hoboken, NJ: Wiley-Blackwell.

Bretherton, Inge, and Kristine Munholland. 1999. "Internal Working Models in Attachment Relationships: A Construct Revisited." In *Handbook of Attachment: Theory, Research, and Clinical Applications*, edited by Jude Cassidy and Phillip R. Shaver (89–114). New York: Guilford Press.

Bretherton, Inge, Charlynn Prentiss, and Doreen Ridgeway. 1990. "Family Relationships as Represented in a Story-Completion Task at Thirty-Seven and Fifty-Four Months of Age." *New Directions for Child Development* 48:85–105.

Bretherton, Inge, Doreen Ridgeway, and Jude Cassidy. 1990. "Assessing Internal Working Models of the Attachment Relationship: An Attachment Story Completion Task for 3-Year-Olds." In *Attachment in the Preschool Years: Theory, Research, and Intervention*, edited by Mark T. Greenberg, Dante Cicchetti, and E. Mark Cummings (273–308). Chicago: University of Chicago Press.

Bruns, Deborah A. 2006. "Promoting Mother-Child Relationships for Incarcerated Women and Their Children." *Infants and Young Children* 19:308–22.

Byrne, Mary W., Lorie S. Goshin, and Sarah S. Joestl. 2010. "Intergenerational Transmission of Attachment for Infants Raised in a Prison Nursery." *Attachment & Human Development* 12:375–93.

Cassidy, Jude, Yair Ziv, Brandi Stupica, Laura J. Sherman, Heidi Butler, Andrea Karfgin, Glen Cooper, Kent Hoffman, and Bert Powell. 2010. "Enhancing Attachment Security in the Infants of Women in a Jail-Diversion Program." *Attachment & Human Development* 12:333–53.

Cecil, Dawn K., James McHale, Anne Strozier, and Joel Pietsch. 2008. "Female Inmates, Family Caregivers, and Young Children's Adjustment: A Research Agenda and Implications for Corrections Programming." *Journal of Criminal Justice* 36(6): 513–21.

Cicchetti, Dante, and Sheree L. Toth. 2009. "The Past Achievements and Future Promises of Developmental Psychopathology: The Coming of Age of a Discipline." *Journal of Child Psychology and Psychiatry* 50:16–25.

Cowan, Phillip A. 1997. "Beyond Meta-Analysis: A Plea for a Family Systems Perspective on Attachment." *Child Development* 68:600–603.

Dallaire, Danielle H. 2007. "Children with Incarcerated Mothers: Developmental Outcomes, Special Challenges, and Recommendations." *Journal of Applied Developmental Psychology* 28:15–24.

Dallaire, Danielle H., and Laura Wilson. 2010. "The Impact of Exposure to Parental Criminal Activity, Arrest, and Sentencing on Children's Academic Competence and Externalizing Behavior." *Journal of Child and Family Studies* 19:404–18.

Dallaire, Danielle H., Anne E. Ciccone, and Laura C. Wilson. 2008. "A Comparative Analysis of Family Drawings Made by Children with Incarcerated Parents and Children Separated from Their Parents for Other Reasons." Poster presented at the fall annual convention of the Virginia Psychological Association, Virginia Beach, October.

Davies, Patrick T., Gordon T. Harold, Marcie C. Goeke-Morey, and E. Mark Cummings. 2002. "Child Emotional Security and Interparental Conflict." *Monographs of the Society for Research in Child Development* 67(3): Serial No. 270.

Dozier, Mary, K. Chase Stovall-McClough, and Kathleen E. Albus. 2008. "Attachment and Psychopathology in Adulthood." In *Handbook of Attachment: Theory, Research, and Clinical Applications,* 2nd ed., edited by Jude Cassidy and Phillip R. Shaver (718–44). New York: Guilford Press.

Dozier, Mary, K. Chase Stovall, Kathleen E. Albus, and Brady Bates. 2001. "Attachment for Infants in Foster Care: The Role of Caregiver State of Mind." *Child Development* 72:1467–77.

Enos, Sandra. 2001. *Mothering from the Inside: Parenting in a Woman's Prison.* Albany: State University of New York Press.

Fury, Gail, Elizabeth A. Carlson, and L. Alan Sroufe. 1997. "Children's Representations of Attachment Relationships in Family Drawings." *Child Development* 68:1154–64.

Glaze, Lauren E., and Laura M. Maruschak. 2008. *Parents in Prison and Their Minor Children.* NCJ 222984. Washington, DC: U.S. Department of Justice, Bureau of Justice Statistics.

Gloger-Tippelt, Gabriele, Beate Gomille, Lilith Koenig, and Juergen Vetter. 2002. "Attachment Representations in 6-Year-Olds: Related Longitudinally to the Quality of Attachment in the Infancy and Mother's Attachment Representations." *Attachment & Human Development* 4:318–39.

Green, Jonathan, and Ruth Goldwyn. 2002. "Annotation: Attachment Disorganization and Psychopathology: New Findings in Attachment Research and Their Potential Implications for Developmental Psychopathology in Childhood." *Journal of Child Psychology and Psychiatry* 43:835–46.

Grych, John H., Tonya Wachsmuth-Schlaefer, and Laura L. Klockow. 2002. "Interparental Aggression and Young Children's Representations of Family Relationships." *Journal of Family Psychology* 16:259–72.

Gullone, Eleonora, and Kym Robinson. 2005. "The Inventory of Parent and Peer Attachment-Revised (IPPA-R) for Children: A Psychometric Investigation." *Clinical Psychology and Psychotherapy* 12:67–79.

Hagen, Kristine Amlund, and Barbara J. Myers. 2003. "The Effect of Secrecy and Social Support on Behavioral Problems in Children of Incarcerated Women." *Journal of Child and Family Studies* 12:229–42.

Hoffman, Kent T., Robert S. Marvin, Glen Cooper, and Bert Powell. 2006. "Changing Toddlers' and Preschoolers' Attachment Classifications: The Circle of Security Intervention." *Journal of Consulting and Clinical Psychology* 74:1017–26.

Johnson, Elizabeth I., and Jane Waldfogel. 2002. "Parental Incarceration: Recent Trends and Implications for Child Welfare." *Social Service Review* 76:460–79.

Johnson, Lee N., Scott A. Ketring, and Carla Abshire. 2003. "The Revised Inventory of Parent Attachment: Measuring Attachment in Families." *Contemporary Family Therapy: An International Journal* 25:333–49.

Kerns, Kathryn A., Lisa Klepac, and Amy Cole. 1996. "Peer Relationships and Preadolescents' Perceptions of Security in the Child-Mother Relationship." *Developmental Psychology* 32:457–66.

Loper, Ann B., and Elena H. Tuerk. 2006. "Parenting Programs for Incarcerated Parents: Current Research and Future Directions." *Criminal Justice Policy Review* 17:407–27.

Loper, Ann Booker, L. Wrenn Carlson, Lacey Levitt, and Kathryn Scheffel. 2009. "Parenting Stress, Alliance, Child Contact, and Adjustment of Imprisoned Mothers and Fathers." *Journal of Offender Rehabilitation* 48:483–503.

Lopez, Caroline, and Christine Suniti Bhat. 2007. "Supporting Students with Incarcerated Parents in Schools: A Group Intervention." *Journal for Specialists in Group Work* 32:139–53.

Luthar, Suniya S., Dante Cicchetti, and Bronwyn Becker. 2000. "The Construct of Resilience: A Critical Evaluation and Guidelines for Future Work." *Child Development* 71:543–62.

Lynch, Michael, and Dante Cicchetti. 1991. "Patterns of Relatedness in Maltreated and Nonmaltreated Children: Connections among Multiple Representational Models." *Development & Psychopathology* 3:207–26.

Lyons-Ruth, Karlen, and Deborah Jacobvitz. 2008. "Attachment Disorganization: Unresolved Loss, Relational Violence, and Lapses in Behavioral and Attentional Strategies." In *Handbook of Attachment: Theory, Research, and Clinical Applications*, 2nd ed., edited by Jude Cassidy and Phillip R. Shaver (666–97). New York: Guilford Press.

Main, Mary, and Erik Hesse. 1990. "Parents' Unresolved Traumatic Experiences Are Related to Infant Disorganized Attachment Status: Is Frightened and/or Frightening Parental Behavior the Linking Mechanism?" In *Attachment in the Preschool Years*, edited by Mark T. Greenberg, Dante Cicchetti, and E. Mark Cummings (161–82). Chicago: University of Chicago Press.

Masten, Ann S. 2001. "Ordinary Magic: Resilience Processes in Development." *American Psychologist* 56:227–38.

———. 2007. "Resilience in Developing Systems: Progress and Promise as the Fourth Wave Rises." *Development & Psychopathology* 19:921–30.

Murray, Joseph. 2007. "The Cycle of Punishment: Social Exclusion of Prisoners and Their Children." *Criminology and Criminal Justice* 7:55–58.

Murray, Joseph, and David P. Farrington. 2008. "The Effects of Parental Imprisonment on Children." In *Crime and Justice: A Review of Research*, vol. 37, edited by Michael Tonry (133–206). Chicago: University of Chicago Press.

Murray, Joseph, and Lynne Murray. 2010. "Parental Incarceration, Attachment, and Child Psychopathology." *Attachment & Human Development* 12(4): 289–309.

Murray, Joseph, David P. Farrington, Ivana Sekol, and Rikke F. Olsen. 2009. "Effects of Parental Imprisonment on Child Antisocial Behaviour and Mental Health: A Systematic Review." *Campbell Systematic Reviews* 4:1–105. Oslo, Norway: Campbell Collaboration.

Myers, Barbara J., Tina M. Smarsh, Kristine Amlund-Hagen, and Suzanne Kennon. 1999. "Children of Incarcerated Mothers." *Journal of Child and Family Studies* 8(1): 11–25.

Oppenheim, David, Ayelet Nir, Susan Warren, and Robert N. Emde. 1997. "Emotion Regulation in Mother-Child Narrative Co-construction: Association with Children's Narratives and Adaptation." *Developmental Psychology* 33:284–94.

Poehlmann, Julie. 2003. "An Attachment Perspective on Grandparents Raising Their Very Young Grandchildren: Implications for Intervention and Research." *Infant Mental Health Journal* 24:149–73.

———. 2005a. "Incarcerated Mothers' Contact with Children, Perceived Family Relationships, and Depressive Symptoms." *Journal of Family Psychology* 19:350–57.

———. 2005b. "Representations of Attachment Relationships in Children of Incarcerated Mothers." *Child Development* 76:679–96.

Poehlmann, Julie, Danielle Dallaire, Ann B. Loper, and Leslie Shear. 2010. "Children's Contact with Their Incarcerated Parents: Research Findings and Recommendations." *American Psychologist* 65:575–98.

Poehlmann, Julie, Rebecca J. Shlafer, Elizabeth Maes, and Ashley Hanneman. 2008. "Factors Associated with Young Children's Opportunities for Maintaining Family Relationships during Maternal Incarceration." *Family Relations* 57:267–80.

Poehlmann, Julie, Jennifer Park, Lydia Bouffiou, Joshua Abrahams, Rebecca Shlafer, and Emily Hahn. 2008. "Attachment Representations in Children Raised by Their Grandparents." *Attachment & Human Development* 10:165–88.

Robertson, Joyce. 1953. "Some Responses of Young Children to the Loss of Maternal Care." *Nursing Times* 49:382–86.

Roy, Kevin M., and Omari L. Dyson. 2005. "Gatekeeping in Context: Babymama Drama and the Involvement of Incarcerated Fathers." *Fathering: A Journal of Theory, Research, & Practice about Men as Fathers* 3:289–310.

Shlafer, Rebecca J., and Julie Poehlmann. 2010. "Attachment and Caregiving Relationships in Families Affected by Parental Incarceration." *Attachment & Human Development* 12:395–415.

Solomon, Judith, and Carol George. 2008. "The Measurement of Attachment Security and Related Constructs in Infancy and Early Childhood." In *Handbook of Attachment: Theory, Research, and Clinical Applications*, 2nd ed., edited by Jude Cassidy and Phillip R. Shaver (383–418). New York: Guilford Press.

Spitz, Rene. 1956. "The Influence of the Mother-Child Relationship, and Its Disturbances." In *Mental Health and Infant Development, Vol. I: Papers and Discussions*, edited by Kenneth Soddy (103–08). Oxford: Basic Books.

Sroufe, L. Alan, and Everett Waters. 1977. "Attachment Is an Organizational Construct." *Child Development* 48:1184–99.

Thompson, Ross A. 2008. "Early Attachment and Later Development: Familiar Questions, New Answers." In *Handbook of Attachment: Theory, Research, and Clinical Applications*, 2nd ed., edited by Jude Cassidy and Phillip R. Shaver (348–65). New York: Guilford Press.

Toth, Sheree L., Angeline Maughan, Jody T. Manly, Mary Spagnola, and Dante Cicchetti. 2002. "The Relative Efficacy of Two Interventions in Altering Maltreated Preschool Children's Representational Models: Implications for Attachment Theory." *Development & Psychopathology* 14:877–908.

van IJzendoorn, Marinus H., Carlo Schuengel, and Marian J. Bakermans-Kranenburg. 1999. "Disorganized Attachment in Early Childhood: Meta-Analysis of Precursors, Concomitants, and Sequelae." *Development & Psychopathology* 11:225–49.

Vondra, Joan I., Daniel S. Shaw, and M. Cristina Kevenides. 1995. "Predicting Infant Attachment Classification from Multiple, Contemporaneous Measures of Maternal Care." *Infant Behavior & Development* 18:415–25.

Walsh, Trudi M., Douglas K. Symons, and Patrick J. McGrath. 2004. "Relations between Young Children's Responses to the Depiction of Separation and Pain Experiences." *Attachment & Human Development* 6:53–71.

Zeanah, Charles H., Anna T. Smyke, Sebastian F. Koga, and Elizabeth Carlson. 2005. "Attachment in Institutionalized and Community Children in Romania." *Child Development* 76:1015–28.

6

Middle Childhood

Family, School, and Peer Contexts for Children Affected by Parental Incarceration

Danielle H. Dallaire and Lauren Aaron

According to recent national figures, 30 to 34 percent of parents in state and federal prisons have children between the ages of 5 and 9, and an additional 32 to 35 percent have children between the ages of 10 and 14 (Glaze and Maruschak 2008). Thus, the majority of parents in state and federal prisons have a child in the developmental period of middle childhood. There is a growing literature on children in this age group affected by parental incarceration, particularly concerning key developmental issues during middle childhood such as children's attainment of socioemotional and academic competencies.

This chapter considers how parental incarceration affects the development of children's age-appropriate competencies during middle childhood (roughly, the ages of 6 to 12). After briefly reviewing applicable developmental and ecological theories, research is reviewed that examines the impact of parental incarceration on children's socioemotional and academic development. The chapter focuses specifically on the need to explore moderating influences and children's experiences of risks in their proximal environments (family, school, and peer contexts). Lastly, the more limited literature highlighting mechanisms of resilience in this population is reviewed and implications for policy are discussed.

Applicable Theoretical Perspectives

Erikson's theory (1950) provides a useful framework for understanding children's age-appropriate developmental tasks during middle childhood. Erikson suggests that industry is the major task during this stage. To be industrious, Erikson posits that one must develop competencies and skills in the tools of society; in our society, industry during middle childhood can be best conceptualized as academic and peer competency. Of particular interest here is how badly parental incarceration disrupts the development of these key competencies as parental incarceration exposes children to greater risks that may undermine their potential to attain academic and social competence.

These risks to children's environments will be examined herein from an ecological perspective (Bronfenbrenner 1979). These environments include children's immediate developmental contexts, or their microsystems (e.g., home and school settings), as well as settings that affect them indirectly, including their exosystems (e.g., a parent's workplace) and the larger culture in which they are a part, or the macrosystem (cultural norms and expectations). Interactions between microsystems (such as parents' involvement with their children's school and with their children's teachers), or mesosystems, will also be considered.

Taking such an approach in this chapter is essential, as exploring how key micro-, meso-, and exosystems interact to influence children's academic and social functioning allows better understanding of the complex and multifaceted stressor of parental incarceration and its impact during middle childhood. Because of the many and unique stresses their parents or caregivers may experience, children in this age range with incarcerated parents may be exposed to more proximal risk factors in key microsystem contexts, including more harsh, unresponsive parenting practices in the familial context (e.g., Phillips et al. 2004), teacher stigmatization in the academic context (e.g., Nesmith and Ruhland 2008), and risk for association with delinquent peers in the peer context (e.g., Hanlon et al. 2005). Children of incarcerated parents also face risks outside their immediate developmental contexts. For example, research has demonstrated that parental incarceration depletes families' economic resources (Arditti, Lambert-Shute, and Joest 2003; Western and Wildeman 2009) and that after release, convicted felons have difficulty finding employment (Arditti and Few 2006; Travis and Waul 2004).

Though micro-, meso-, and, to a lesser extent, exosystem factors are the primary focus of this chapter, macrosystem forces are also important to consider when trying to understand a child's response to parental incarceration. For instance, during incarceration, children and families may feel that they cannot grieve publicly or that they cannot discuss the loss of their family member because of cultural stigma (see Arditti 2005). Unlike the array of resources available to children who have lost a parent to death or divorce, western society has no formal rituals or ceremonies and few formal support systems to help children cope with the loss of an incarcerated parent. Such macrosystem forces may influence children's adjustment to parental incarceration; however, an in-depth consideration of factors at the macro level is beyond the scope of this chapter.

The Effect of Parental Incarceration on Children's Socioemotional and Academic Competence

Generally, research examining children's well-being during middle childhood indicates that parental incarceration interferes with the development of age-appropriate social and academic competencies. However, recent research findings have highlighted the diversity of children's responses to parental incarceration. Such findings suggest the need to explore important moderating influences that may protect children from adverse experiences, as well as specific risk experiences, such as witnessing a parent's arrest, that may be associated with worse outcomes at this stage of development.

Research Findings Showing No Impact of Parental Incarceration

Several recent studies have used large, archival datasets and sophisticated data analytic techniques and found little evidence of the negative effects of maternal incarceration on children's academic and socioemotional outcomes. For example, Cho (2009a, 2009b) examines differences in the effect of maternal imprisonment versus short-term jail stays on children's grade retention and performance on standardized tests. This dataset includes mothers of 4,135 elementary school children who experienced long-term (e.g., one-year) maternal imprisonment. The comparison sample includes mothers of 9,346 elementary school children who experienced their mother's short-term (e.g., a few days) jail stay. Cho finds no negative effects of maternal imprisonment relative to maternal jail stays on children's likelihood of grade retention (2009a) or performance on math and reading standardized tests (2009b). Cho, however, was unable to use a comparison group of children not exposed to maternal imprisonment or jail stays; thus, children's adjustment relative to peers was not examined.

Given that certain risk experiences, such as witnessing maternal arrest or criminal activity, are likely common among children affected by both maternal jail and imprisonment, it would be important to include a comparison group of children who have not experienced maternal arrest. Phillips and Erkanli (2008) make such a comparison when they examine a large-scale, nationally representative sample for differences between children whose mothers had been arrested ($n = 735$) and children whose mothers had never been arrested ($n = 1,609$). Phillips and Erkanli find no significant differences between mothers' reports of socioemotional problems in children whose mothers had been arrested and children of never-arrested mothers among children age 11 and older. However, the sample employed by Phillips and Erkanli consists of families who have been investigated by Child Protective Services for reports of child maltreatment. Thus, the results may not be generalizable because of the high level of risk in this population.

Research Findings Showing a Negative Impact of Parental Incarceration

Findings from other studies suggest that parental incarceration is related to both academic problems and socioemotional difficulties. In their report on how parental incarceration affects children's antisocial behavior throughout the life span, Murray and Farrington (2005) describe several academic-related outcomes for children at age 10. Their dataset was compiled in the early 1960s in inner-city London, and it included 23 male children separated from (mainly) fathers before age 10 because of incarceration, 227 male children not separated from their fathers, 138 male children separated from their fathers before age 10 for other reasons, and 17 male children whose fathers were incarcerated before their birth. Murray and Farrington find that compared to children whose fathers have never been incarcerated, boys whose fathers have been incarcerated during their first decade of life show lowered IQ scores and lowered achievement on standardized tests. However, there are no significant differences on academic-related outcomes between children whose fathers have been incarcerated before the child's birth and children whose fathers have been incarcerated in the first decade of their life.

Wilbur and colleagues (2007) examine the effects of parental incarceration on children's socioemotional well-being in a sample of children age 6 to 11, originally recruited from hospitals to study in utero exposure to cocaine. In the sample of 102 children, 31 of whom experienced paternal incarceration, Wilbur and colleagues find that paternal incarceration is associated with higher depressive symptoms and greater externalizing behaviors, according to both child and teacher report. These findings are robust after accounting for children's experience of other risk factors.

These mixed results underscore the need to further examine risk factors specific to the experience of parental incarceration to understand how parental incarceration can negatively influence children's development.

Risk Experiences Specific to Experiencing Parental Incarceration

In the following sections, school-age children's experience of parental incarceration and associated risk experiences will be examined in the framework of important contexts of development, including the family, school, and peer contexts.

Within Children's Familial Context

The impact of parental incarceration on children's proximal familial relations varies. In some cases, parental incarceration may be associated with positive changes in the child's caregiving environment. In others, there may be little change in the child's daily life. In still other instances, parental incarceration may be associated with detrimental changes in the child's caregiving environment. Recent studies have looked at types of risks that school-age children with incarcerated parents face in their home environments and whether they experience increased risks in relation to peers whose parents are not incarcerated. Evidence from this line of research suggests that children's social and academic reactions to parental incarceration are affected by (a) the experience of sociodemographic risk factors, within the family, including the increased likelihood of experiencing poverty and low parental education, (b) risks associated with their caregiver's mental health, including caregiver stress and psychopathology, (c) children's risk experiences in their interactions with their caregivers, including the experience of harsh parenting behaviors and maltreatment, and (d) children's experience of specific events related to parents' criminal activity, arrest, and sentencing.

In studies using different archival datasets, Susan Phillips and her colleagues have identified risk experiences faced by children with incarcerated parents (Phillips et al. 2004, 2006). In a sample of 5,504 child participants age 15 and younger whose families had contact with child welfare services, 12.5 percent of children experienced parental (mostly maternal) incarceration. Phillips and colleagues (2004) report that the children with histories of parental incarceration faced more sociodemographic and familial risk experiences. Specifically, compared with children whose parents were not incarcerated, these children experienced higher rates of poverty, parental substance use, and parental mental illness. They were also more likely to be the recipients of impaired parenting behaviors (e.g., inappropriate discipline) and were exposed to more domestic violence.

Phillips and colleagues found similar results in 2006 when they examined risk experiences of 306 children between the ages of 9 and 13 whose mothers had histories of arrest and compared them with classmates of never-arrested mothers. Consistent with the earlier findings, children whose mothers had been arrested were more likely than their peers to experience sociodemographic risk factors like living in a large family, experiencing poverty, and parental unemployment. Phillips and colleagues also found that these children experienced greater caregiver risks (such as having a familial history of substance abuse and mental illness), more harsh and punitive parenting, and less parental supervision. Children of mothers with arrest histories were also more likely than other children to have suffered both physical and sexual abuse.

Many more recent findings using large-scale datasets replicate and extend the findings of previous studies that used smaller datasets and examined children with incarcerated fathers. For example, Gabel and Shindledecker (1992, 1993) find that compared with children (mean age 7.4 years) at the same residential facility whose fathers have never been incarcerated, children whose fathers have been incarcerated are more likely to have experienced maltreatment and parental substance abuse. In their examination of the functioning of families with an incarcerated parent, Arditti, Lambert-Shute, and Joest (2003) find that two-thirds of the 56 caregivers report that the family has suffered economic problems, and half report experiencing physical health problems since the parent's incarceration. In a study with children attending a faith-based summer camp for children of incarcerated mothers, Mackintosh, Myers, and Kennon (2006) find that the caregivers of these 69 children (mean age 9 years) report high stress levels. Also, compared with published norms on the measure of parental warmth they employed, these caregivers report expressing less warmth. Such stress and lack of warmth may relate to children's social and emotional difficulties. In fact, child reports of caregiver rejection in this sample relate to caregivers' reports of children's externalizing behaviors. These smaller, more focused studies support the findings of Phillips and colleagues and others that show parental incarceration affects the number of risk factors experienced by children and families.

Collectively, these studies indicate that children with incarcerated parents not only face greater sociodemographic risk experiences, but they also may experience more negative family dynamics, including receiving more harsh and sometimes abusive parenting behaviors than children who have not experienced parental incarceration. Yet, the impact of familial and sociodemographic risks on the socioemotional and academic competence of children of incarcerated parents has not been examined in conjunction with the impact of parental incarceration. Thus, several important questions remain: How does parental incarceration affect children beyond the experience of other risk factors in these children's lives? Many studies have also not addressed whether the impact of parental incarceration is direct, or how much it is mediated by familial dynamics, such as conflict within the family. Further, it is unclear how the incarceration of a parent affects a child's interactions with the incarcerated parent as well as the child's interactions with his or her caregiver.

In an attempt to address the above issues, Aaron and Dallaire (forthcoming) analyzed the Children-at-Risk dataset (see Harrell, Cavanagh, and Sridharan 1999) to assess the impact of family dynamics on children with incarcerated parents. Family dynamics constitute parent-child interactions (e.g., parent-child conflict), as well as interactions between and behaviors of other members of the household (e.g., sibling delinquency), and significant experiences of household members (e.g., parental drug use, family victimization). This dataset includes a sample of 874 children age 10 to 14 (mean age 12.36 years) recruited from high-risk neighborhoods in four U.S. cities, 18 percent of whom had an incarcerated parent at some point during their lives, and 4 percent of whom had an incarcerated parent during the two-year study. In hierarchical regression analyses, after controlling for children's experience of sociodemographic risk factors (e.g., parental unemployment, drug use), history of parental incarceration predicts problematic family processes (including family victimization) and higher levels of sibling delinquency. History of parental incarceration is also associated with higher levels of parent-reported child delinquency. However, after accounting for these problematic family processes, history of parental incarceration no longer predicts child delinquency. These results suggest that although parental incarceration is associated with negative family processes and children's delinquent behavior, when familial factors are accounted for, parental incarceration may no longer predict child delinquency.

Aaron and Dallaire (forthcoming) also find that recent parental incarceration (i.e., within the course of the two-year study) predicts higher parent-child conflict. This finding is robust after controlling for sociodemographic risk experiences and previous exposure to parental incarceration. These results suggest that a recent parental incarceration may worsen family processes and interactions following the parent's release from prison, and that the negative impact of parental incarceration on children's well-being may be at least partially mediated by problematic parent-child interactions.

The diversity of children's responses to parental incarceration may also relate to their experience of their parent's arrest as this is a very proximal, personal risk experience. Though estimates of the number of children who witness parental arrest vary, Dallaire and Wilson (2010) find that 26 percent of incarcerated parents report that their children witnessed their arrest. Witnessing a parent's arrest is likely traumatic for a child: seeing police arrive (likely without warning), watching their parent handcuffed and driven away in the back of a police car, and other aspects of an arrest create a chaotic scene. This event may be particularly traumatic during middle childhood as these children may better understand the ramifications of parental arrest than younger children, and if the arrest occurred in view of neighbors and classmates, the children may be embarrassed and ashamed. Dallaire and Wilson (2010) find evidence that children's witnessing of parental criminal activity, arrest, and sentencing negatively affects their socioemotional and academic competence. In a sample of 32 children (mean age 10.74 years) with incarcerated parents, parents' reports of children's experience of these events predict caregivers' reports of children's anxiety and depression, children's self-reports of emotion dysregulation, and poor child performance on a receptive language vocabulary test, even after controlling for other negative life events.

Overall, research examining children's likelihood of experiencing risks in their familial environment when parents are incarcerated has indicated that children are exposed to greater sociodemographic risks and poorer quality of parenting behaviors, including abusive and neglectful parenting. Several studies have documented that children with incarcerated parents in this age group have experienced maltreatment at higher rates than children not affected by parental incarceration (Gabel and Shindledecker 1993; Phillips et al. 2006). Studies focusing on the effects of child maltreatment have demonstrated that maltreated children experience strained social relations (Bolger and Patterson 2001), emotional problems (Smith and Walden 1999), and academic difficulties (Eckenrode, Laird, and Doris 1993). Children with incarcerated parents may be particularly vulnerable to maltreatment because of the confluence of serious problems in some families with incarcerated parents that, in turn, place their children at much higher risk for abusive and neglectful parenting, including concurrent poverty and social isolation (see Arditti 2005; Belsky 1993; and Mackintosh et al. 2006). The great variability seen in children's responses to parental incarceration may stem from the variability in their experiences of parental incarceration within the family context and, specifically, their experiences of negative parenting behaviors, maltreatment, and personal events related to their parent's arrest and incarceration.

Within Children's School Context

In addition to their home environments, children may face risks to their socioemotional and academic competence in their school environments. Although teachers can provide valuable support to children with incarcerated parents, very little data exist examining the impact of parental incarceration on children's interactions with their teachers and in school contexts. However, the available information suggests that children with incarcerated parents may face stigmatization within the school setting (Dallaire, Ciccone, and Wilson 2010; Nesmith and Ruhland 2008).

All 34 children (age 8 to 17 years) recruited from communities with high rates of adult incarceration who participated in Nesmith and Ruhland's qualitative examination of children with incarcerated parents "seemed keenly aware of negative assumptions that might be made about them because they had a parent in prison" (2008, 1123). A major issue that emerged from this work is the social challenges these children experienced concerning fears of stigmatization by teachers and peers. Some specific fears included not being able to talk with friends or others about their situation. Nesmith and Ruhland identified an intense internal tension between children wanting to talk about their parent's incarceration and fear of the negative consequences of discussing it. They noted that "the children who suffered from social stigma and isolation were at times able to locate some supportive resources; but on the whole, they were without role models, unable to connect to others like themselves, or to find trustworthy people who would help them feel less marginalized in general" (2008, 1123). Such feelings of isolation from peers and other adults, including teachers, can hamper children's development of supportive, intimate peer relations, thus undermining emerging social and academic competence.

Dallaire and colleagues (2010) interviewed 30 teachers about their experiences with children and families affected by incarceration. These teachers saw several ways that parental incarceration negatively affected their students' academic achievement. The teachers identified various risk factors, including the instability of children's home situations. Home instability was associated with behaviors that made success at school difficult, such as misplacing book bags or leaving textbooks and other important educational materials at various locations. Teachers also identified several emotional reactions, such as "falling apart," which manifested themselves in the classroom and made concentrating difficult. Developmentally, these teachers felt that parental incarceration was more detrimental to elementary and middle school–age children than to adolescents. Though most teachers noted that it would be helpful for them to know about a child dealing with parental incarceration, they also noted that they have witnessed their colleagues be "unsupportive," be "unprofessional," and have lowered expectations for children with incarcerated parents.

In a follow-up experiment with elementary school teachers, Dallaire and colleagues (2010) find further evidence for teacher stigmatization. In this study, 73 elementary school teachers rated their expectations for the competency of a fictitious child new to their classroom because of maternal incarceration. Teachers randomly assigned to a scenario describing a new student who recently moved in with his or her grandmother because the mother was "away at prison" rated the child as less competent than teachers randomly assigned to scenarios in which the child's mother was described as either "away," "away at rehab," or "away at school."

Facing stigmatization and feeling isolated because of parental incarceration in the school context could negatively affect children's interactions with teachers and peers, as well as academic performance and feelings of acceptance and belonging in an academic environment. Adolescent children with incarcerated mothers are more likely to drop out of school (Trice and Brewster 2004; Shlafer and Poehlmann, this volume). Perhaps the cumulative effect of stigmatization and negative interactions at school, combined with the family risks discussed above, contributes to a disinclination to persist in academic endeavors.

Within Children's Peer Context

Though several research studies cited here have examined children's socioemotional and academic functioning in relation to their peers, very few studies have examined how parental incarceration may affect children's peer contexts. In one of just a handful of studies examining this issue, Hanlon and colleagues (2005) assess peer relations in a sample of 88 children (mean age 11.5 years) of incarcerated substance-abusing mothers. Despite noting several positive indicators of development in their sample, Hanlon and colleagues also note important areas of concern. These included a tendency for children affected by parental incarceration to affiliate with deviant peers, and an increased likelihood of experiencing some sort of social problem, like fighting or getting in trouble with a teacher. Similarly, in a study using a nationally representative sample, Huebner and Gustafson (2007) report outcomes for children affected by maternal incarceration at age 10 ($n = 31$) compared with children not affected by maternal incarceration ($n = 1,666$). Huebner and Gustafson find a trend (approaching statistical significance) for the children affected by parental incarceration to be more likely to associate with deviant peers.

Whether children witnessed their parent's arrest and/or sentencing may also have implications for children's social development. In an ongoing study of elementary school–age children ($n = 210$, mean age $= 9.08$) in an inner-city, low–socioeconomic status, high-risk environment, among the children who experienced parental incarceration ($n = 66$), Dallaire finds preliminary evidence to suggest that witnessing parental arrest worsens children's peer relations. In this sample, children who witnessed their parent's arrest or sentencing (according to their parent's report) report receiving fewer prosocial behaviors from their peers (e.g., being cheered up when they are sad) than their classmates who did not witness parental arrest or sentencing.[1] However, these data are still being collected as this book goes to press, and these findings are considered tentative.

Though a paucity of research examines the impact of parental incarceration within children's peer context of development, the available research suggests that children with incarcerated parents may be at greater risk for association with delinquent peers. This is a fruitful area for future research because the risks experienced in children's familial context likely influence their experiences in the peer context. For example, children's social competence may be affected by the quality of attachment they have with their parents. Children who do not experience sensitive, responsive parenting and who are not securely attached have difficulties in peer relationships, whereas securely attached children have better social skills and are relatively popular (Kerns, Klepac, and Cole 1996). The challenges in peer relations associated with attachment are of particular concern for children with incarcerated parents, who may experience insecure attachment because of separation from their parents and other risks. This is illustrated by Poehlmann's (2005) finding that 63 percent of a sample of 60 young children with incarcerated mothers have insecure attachment classifications.

Fostering Resilience in Children Affected by Parental Incarceration within Their Familial, School, and Peer Contexts

Important protective factors may mitigate children's experiences of risks within their family, school, and peer contexts of development. In stark contrast to the number of studies examining children's risk experiences, relatively few studies have examined factors associated with promoting resilience in this population during middle childhood. In work with school-age children attending a summer camp for children with incarcerated mothers, Hagen, Myers, and colleagues identify important intra- and interpersonal processes that can serve as protective factors. Specifically, Hagen, Myers, and Mackintosh (2005) identify hope as a protective factor against internalizing and externalizing behavior in a sample of 65 children (mean age 9.02 years). Hagen and Myers (2003) find that social support interacted with children's ability to keep a secret to predict both internalizing and externalizing behaviors. They find that when children feel they have adequate social support, their level of secrecy does not predict problem behaviors. However, children who report low social support and low secret-keeping behavior display high levels of problem behaviors. These results suggest that it is important for children to identify supportive individuals in their environment in whom they can confide; if children can do this, they have some protection against exhibiting problem behaviors.

Articles published concerning intervention work with children in the school context indicate a growing awareness of this issue among school personnel, and activities and school-based interventions for children dealing with parental incarceration may foster resilience. For example, Lopez and Bhat (2007) initiated a support group for elementary school–age children with incarcerated parents at their school. They were compelled to start this group because, in their experience as school counselors, half the children referred for services were children with incarcerated parents. Lopez and Bhat outline the objectives and activities of eight group sessions and how the group and group activities can be structured to support resilience. The children who participated describe feeling more confident in peer groups and feeling pride in accomplishing goals set in group meetings. Springer, Pomeroy, and Johnson (1999) write about two school-based interventions they led with elementary school–age children. They document the obstacles they faced in the first group assembled and how they learned from their mistakes to make the second group productive. By the end of the second group, the children commented that they could better express their emotions and that their behavior in class and with peers had improved. Such groups, when structured and executed effectively, may help promote resilience in this population of children.

In terms of children's resilience and academic success, Nesmith and Ruhland (2008) find that most children in their study (53 percent) report that they are doing well in school. Even if children are not participating in a school-based support group or intervention, other organized school activities, like sports organization or clubs, may contribute to resilience. Nesmith and Ruhland report that participating in such activities benefits children in their sample in several ways. For instance, participation gives children an outside activity to engage in that may promote the development of self-competence in a new skill area and opportunities for friendship, and the activity could provide the child with an outlet for frustrations or anger.

Though no study has documented this, an important step toward fostering resilience in these children would be to increase connections among important influences in children's lives. Such connections would enrich children's mesosystems. For example, Poehlmann and colleagues (2008) have demonstrated that when incarcerated mothers and children's caregivers have a stronger alliance, the child experiences greater stability. Other possible mesosystem connections that may promote children's resilience could entail encouraging conversations between caregivers and supportive teachers. Additionally, as Mackintosh and colleague's (2006) work indicates, caregivers are highly stressed; perhaps support groups could help caregivers connect with others. Some school- and faith-based organizations offer support groups for grandparents caring for grandchildren. School-based support groups may help caregivers feel less isolated from other individuals and help connect them with important resources related to the child's educational experiences.

Future Research Directions

The research reviewed in this chapter falls into one of two categories. In category one, analyses were conducted on an archival dataset that allowed questions about parental incarceration to be tested, as well as more complex relations and interactions, though the measures in the dataset were not intended to examine such questions. In category two, the data were collected as part of a relatively small research study (e.g., with sample sizes rarely larger than 50) designed to examine very specific questions pertaining to parental incarceration. Studies in the latter group often contained rich qualitative data and interesting results, but with insufficient power to detect more complex relations and interactions.

Both types of studies have advantages and disadvantages. Analysis of archival data allows testing of complex modeling and relations among variables and covariates. Also, with large sample sizes, greater power exists to detect small effects and to examine moderating and mediating factors. A significant disadvantage is that the complexity of children's experiences of parental incarceration often cannot be examined thoroughly. None of the large-scale studies reviewed here could account for children's experience of witnessing their parent's arrest, or whether children had to move because of the parent's arrest or incarceration. In contrast, the smaller-scale studies can better account for children's diverse experiences of parental incarceration. These smaller studies, however, lack the sufficient statistical power to examine the multiple influences that may co-occur for children with incarcerated parents.

These methodological problems could be remedied with a purposefully planned, well-funded, large-scale research project focusing on how parental incarceration affects children and families throughout childhood. Such a study could better address important questions related to factors that may moderate children's reactions to parental incarceration, including the influence of family dynamics and gender, for example. None of the studies cited in this chapter addressed either parent or child gender, for example, or the possible interaction between parent and child gender. A large-scale study, even if cross-sectional, would be a critical next step in this line of research.

A further step would entail examining longitudinal relations for a cohort of children who are followed across important periods of development. Questions might include "How does separation from mothers during infancy due to incarceration affect children's peer relations at school age?" or "How does witnessing parental arrest during middle childhood affect children's association with deviant peers during adolescence?" A longitudinal study would also allow researchers to address important questions related to how parental incarceration affects a family's dynamics and how strongly family dynamics influence child development during and after a parent's incarceration.

Additional areas for future research concern children's experiences of parental incarceration in peer and school contexts as well as further examination of risk and resilience. In comparison to research focusing on the familial context of risk, significantly less research focuses on children's experiences of parental incarceration in school and peer contexts. Evidence is accumulating that parental incarceration influences these contexts of development, and there is much to be learned about how parental incarceration may color children's experiences with their teachers and peers. This area is especially relevant to research during middle childhood, when important experiences in children's lives increasingly occur outside the family context. Also, compared with the amount of research examining children's risk experiences in relation to parental incarceration, relatively less research focuses on environmental and personal characteristics that foster children's resilience, especially during middle childhood. Finally, future research should be directed at better understanding how specific experiences related to parental incarceration (e.g., witnessing arrest) may undermine children's achievement of socioemotional and academic competencies.

Policy Implications

Policy implications relevant to the development period of middle childhood concern how children at this stage may handle the arrest of their parent and how parental incarceration may affect children's school experiences. In contrast to younger age ranges, children in middle childhood are cognizant of what is happening when their parent is arrested. In these instances, it would be helpful to have officers trained in child development to help children understand the context of parental arrest. However, if a parent is arrested and taken away when a child is at school, then the child would likely return home to an empty home with no knowledge of what has happened. This is particularly troubling if the arrested parent is a single parent, which is often the case when mothers are arrested and imprisoned (Glaze and Marushak 2008).

The criminal justice system rarely considers whether individuals being arrested have minor children (see Smith and Elstein 1994). Parents are not routinely given the opportunity to contact a secondary caregiver for their children when they are arrested, and police officers are not routinely trained to deal with families and children of criminal suspects. Nor are officers under instruction to act differently when arresting an individual with young children in the home, though there are notable exceptions and model programs in San Francisco, California; New Haven, Connecticut; and Clearwater, Florida. Specialized training might focus on helping children better understand what is going on in a developmentally appropriate way. Requiring officer training in handling such situations may help lessen some potential problems that arise when children witness a parent's arrest.

The other policy-relevant area for middle childhood concerns children's interactions in the school context. Following the arrest or imprisonment of a student's parent, teachers and administrators are usually only informed of the situation by word of mouth, and many teachers may never know that their students are affected by parental incarceration. As studies have shown that adolescent's academic competency is detrimentally affected by parental incarceration (e.g., Trice and Brewster 2004), it is important that teachers understand how a parent's incarceration may influence academic and behavior in the school setting during middle childhood. Privacy concerns, however, may make informing teachers of such events difficult or unlikely, and these concerns are well founded, as children who know that their teachers are informed about their home situation may be even more sensitive to perceived stigmatization from peers (e.g., Nesmith and Ruhland 2008). Despite these limitations, however, policies that allow administrators and teachers to be aware of how parental incarceration affects their students are important to help raise awareness and to help circumvent school-related problems associated with parental incarceration.

NOTE

1. Danielle H. Dallaire, "The Impact of Parental Incarceration on Children's Peer Relations," unpublished raw data, 2010.

REFERENCES

Aaron, Lauren, and Danielle H. Dallaire. Forthcoming. "Parental Incarceration and Multiple Risk Experiences: Effects on Family Processes and Children's Delinquency." *Journal of Youth and Adolescence.*

Arditti, Joyce A. 2005. "Families and Incarceration: An Ecological Approach." *Families in Society: The Journal of Contemporary Social Services* 86:251–60.

Arditti, Joyce A., and April L. Few. 2006. "Mothers' Reentry into Family Life Following Incarceration." *Criminal Justice Policy Review* 17:103–23.

Arditti, Joyce A., Jennifer Lambert-Shute, and Karen Joest. 2003. "Saturday Morning at the Jail: Implications of Incarceration for Families and Children." *Family Relations* 52:195–204.

Belsky, John. 1993. "Etiology of Child Maltreatment: A Developmental-Ecological Analysis." *Psychological Bulletin* 114:413–33.

Bolger, Kerry E., and Charlotte J. Patterson. 2001. "Developmental Pathways from Child Maltreatment to Peer Rejection." *Child Development* 72:549–68.

Bronfenbrenner, Urie. 1979. *The Ecology of Human Development: Experiments by Nature and Design.* Cambridge, MA: Harvard University Press.

Cho, Rosa M. 2009a. "The Impact of Maternal Imprisonment on Children's Probability of Grade Retention: Results from Chicago Public Schools." *Journal of Urban Economics* 65:11–23.

———. 2009b. "The Impact of Maternal Incarceration on Children's Educational Achievement: Results from Chicago Public Schools." *Journal of Human Resources* 44(3): 772–97.

Dallaire, Danielle H., and Laura C. Wilson. 2010. "The Relation of Exposure to Parental Criminal Activity, Arrest, and Sentencing to Children's Maladjustment." *Journal of Child and Family Studies* 19:404–18.

Dallaire, Danielle H., Anne Ciccone, and Laura Wilson. 2010. "Teachers' Experiences with and Expectations of Children with Incarcerated Parents." *Journal of Applied Developmental Psychology* 31:281–90.

Eckenrode, John, Molly Laird, and John Dorris. 1993. "School Performance and Disciplinary Problems among Abused and Neglected Children." *Developmental Psychology* 29:53–62.

Erikson, Erik H. 1950. *Childhood and Society.* New York: Norton.

Gabel, Stewart, and Richard Shindledecker. 1992. "Incarceration in Parents of Day Hospital Youth: Relationship to Parental Substance Abuse and Suspected Child Abuse/Maltreatment." *International Journal of Partial Hospitalization* 8:77–87.

———. 1993. "Characteristics of Children Whose Parents Have Been Incarcerated." *Hospital and Community Psychiatry* 44:656–60.

Glaze, Lauren E., and Laura M. Marushak. 2008. *Parents in Prison and Their Minor Children.* NCJ 222984. Washington, DC: U.S. Department of Justice, Bureau of Justice Statistics.

Hagen, Kristine A., and Barbara J. Myers. 2003. "The Effect of Secrecy and Social Support on Behavioral Problems in Children of Incarcerated Women." *Journal of Child and Family Studies* 12:229–42.

Hagen, Kristine A., Barbara J. Myers, and Virginia H. Mackintosh. 2005. "Hope, Social Support, and Behavioral Problems in At-Risk Children." *American Journal of Orthopsychiatry* 75:211–19.

Hanlon, Thomas E., Robert J. Blatchley, Terry Bennett-Sears, Kevin E. O'Grady, Marc Rose, and Jason M. Callaman. 2005. "Vulnerability of Children of Incarcerated Addict Mothers: Implications for Preventive Intervention." *Children and Youth Services Review* 27(1): 67–84.

Harrell, Adele, Shannon Cavanagh, and Sanjeev Sridharan. 1999. "Evaluation of the Children at Risk Program: Results 1 Year after the End of the Program." NCJ 178914. Washington, DC: U.S. Department of Justice, Office of Justice Programs, National Institute of Justice.

Huebner, Beth M., and Regan Gustafson. 2007. "The Effect of Maternal Incarceration on Adult Offspring Involvement in the Criminal Justice System." *Journal of Criminal Justice* 35:283–96.

Kerns, Kathryn A., Lisa Klepac, and AmyKay Cole. 1996. "Peer Relationships and Preadolescents' Perceptions of Security in the Mother-Child Relationship." *Developmental Psychology* 32:457–66.

Lopez, Caroline, and Christine S. Bhat. 2007. "Supporting Students with Incarcerated Parents in Schools: A Group Intervention." *Journal for Specialists in Group Work* 32:139–53.

Mackintosh, Virginia H., Barbara J. Myers, and Suzanne S. Kennon. 2006. "Children of Incarcerated Mothers and Their Caregivers: Factors Affecting the Quality of Their Relationship." *Journal of Child and Family Studies* 15:581–96.

Murray, Joseph, and David P. Farrington. 2005. "Parental Imprisonment: Effects on Boys' Antisocial Behavior and Delinquency through the Life Course." *Journal of Child Psychology and Psychiatry* 46:1269–78.

Nesmith, Ande, and Ebony Ruhland. 2008. "Children of Incarcerated Parents: Challenges and Resiliency, in Their Own Words." *Children and Youth Services Review* 30:1119–30.

Phillips, Susan D., and Alaattin Erkanli. 2008. "Differences in Patterns of Maternal Arrest and the Parent, Family, and Child Problems Encountered in Working with Families." *Children and Youth Services Review* 30:157–72.

Phillips, Susan D., Barbara J. Burns, H. Ryan Wagner, and Richard P. Barth. 2004. "Parental Arrest and Children Involved with Child Welfare Services Agencies." *American Journal of Orthopsychiatry* 74:174–86.

Phillips, Susan D., Alaattin Erkanli, E. Jane Costello, and Adrian Angold. 2006. "Differences among Children Whose Mothers Have Been in Contact with the Criminal Justice System." *Women and Criminal Justice* 17:43–61.

Poehlmann, Julie. 2005. "Representations of Attachment Relationships in Children of Incarcerated Mothers." *Child Development* 76:679–96.

Poehlmann, Julie, Rebecca J. Shlafer, Elizabeth Maes, and Ashley Hanneman. 2008. "Factors Associated with Young Children's Opportunities for Maintaining Family Relationships during Maternal Incarceration." *Family Relations* 57:267–80.

Smith, Barbara E., and Sharon G. Elstein. 1994. "Children on Hold: Improving the Response to Children Whose Parents Are Arrested and Incarcerated." Chicago: American Bar Association Center on Children and the Law.

Smith, Maureen, and Tedra Walden. 1999. "Understanding Feelings and Coping with Emotional Situations. A Comparison of Maltreated and Nonmaltreated Preschoolers." *Social Development* 8:93–116.

Springer, David W., Elizabeth C. Pomeroy, and Toni Johnson. 1999. "A Group Intervention for Children of Incarcerated Parents: Initial Blunders and Subsequent Solutions." *Groupwork* 11:54–70.

Travis, Jeremy, and Michelle Waul, eds. 2004. *Prisoners Once Removed: The Impact of Incarceration and Reentry on Children, Families, and Communities.* Washington, DC: Urban Institute Press.

Trice, Ashton D., and JoAnne Brewster. 2004. "The Effects of Maternal Incarceration on Adolescent Children." *Journal of Police and Criminal Psychology* 19:27–35.

Western, Bruce, and Christopher Wildeman. 2009. "The Black Family and Mass Incarceration." *Annals of the American Academy of Political and Social Science* 621:221–42.

Wilbur, MaryAnn B., Jodi E. Marani, Danielle Appugliese, Ryan Woods, Jane A. Siegal, Howard J. Cabral, and Deborah A. Frank. 2007. "Socioemotional Effects of Fathers' Incarceration on Low-Income, Urban, School-Aged Children." *Pediatrics* 120:678–85.

7

Adolescence in the Context of Parental Incarceration
Family, School, and Community Factors

Rebecca J. Shlafer and Julie Poehlmann

In 2004, nearly 250,000 youth between 15 and 17 years old had a parent incarcerated in a state or federal prison (Glaze and Maruschak 2008). These figures underestimate the total number of adolescents affected by a parent's incarceration, as they do not account for more than 700,000 adults who were held in local jails during that same year (Sabol and Minton 2008). Between 1997 and 2004, the number of adolescents between 15 and 17 years old affected by parental incarceration increased 15 percent (Glaze and Maruschak 2008; Mumola 2000). In addition, it is estimated that more than one-third of children with incarcerated parents will turn 18 years old before their parent is released (Glaze and Maruschak 2008). Adequately serving the growing population of adolescents with incarcerated parents requires understanding the challenges and needs of this age group, including their cognitive, social, and emotional development within multiple contexts.

Developmental Considerations in Adolescence

Adolescence is characterized by significant changes in cognitive, social, and emotional capacities. Throughout this developmental period, improvements in decisionmaking capabilities, abstract thinking, and moral reasoning skills become apparent. Although peers become increasingly important in adolescence, parents and other family members continue to play significant roles. Thus, the incarceration of a parent alters each developmental task that adolescents face. Recent studies have focused on the family, school, and community contexts of adolescents affected by parental incarceration, including youths' social experiences, peer acceptance, and behavioral outcomes. This chapter examines the developmental outcomes of adolescents with incarcerated parents, including adolescents' interactions with their parents, peers, teachers, and communities. Implications for prevention, intervention, policy, and future research are discussed.

Cognitive and Language Development in the Context of Parental Incarceration

Adolescence is characterized by dramatic changes in cognitive skills, including an increased capacity for formal operational thinking and the development of more complex decisionmaking and moral reasoning skills (Keating 1990). Although the individual, familial, and community processes surrounding parental incarceration are complex and can be confusing for a child at any age, adolescents with incarcerated parents may be better equipped to understand the complexities of a parent's incarceration than younger children. Much of this understanding may relate to improvements in language and communication skills that occur throughout adolescence, including the ability to comprehend and use abstract and complex language. For example, Murray (2007) describes younger children experiencing parental incarceration in a state of "linguistic isolation." Compared with adolescents, younger children cannot understand the basic facts about their parent's imprisonment, they have fewer capacities to process the loss, and they lack the language and cognitive capacities to express their preferences about placement or contact.

Many adolescents, however, can understand the complex issues related to their parent's incarceration. Adolescents typically develop the cognitive capacities to understand right from wrong, abstractions related to rules and laws, and the potential consequences of their actions and the actions of others. Thus, many adolescents are capable of understanding why a parent was incarcerated, whereas younger children are not as likely to understand the concept of laws, the basics of the legal system, or the consequences of breaking a law. For example, some children between the ages of 6 and 12 with incarcerated mothers express disgust about their mothers' drug use or stealing, whereas others counsel their mothers to "be good" or "straighten up" (Myers 2009). Unlike younger children, adolescents are also capable of verbally expressing their thoughts about these issues. They may ask questions, express their feelings about the parent's behaviors, or communicate their preferences about placement and contact during a parent's incarceration. For example, one 13-year-old boy in Shlafer and Poehlmann's (2010) sample states, "I'm not sad or anything, but I wouldn't be mad if he called me." However, empirical research examining adolescents' preferences for placement or contact, and how those preferences are considered in custody and visitation arrangements during a parent's incarceration, is sorely lacking.

Most adolescents can compare alternative solutions to a problem, express their opinions on a topic, and weigh hypothetical outcomes before making a decision. In the context of a parent's incarceration, adolescents may be better able than younger children to express their opinions regarding contact with their parent. Caregivers typically regulate children's contact with incarcerated parents, particularly when children are young (Enos 2001; Poehlmann et al. 2008). However, little is known about other important issues such as adolescents' preferences for contact or how, on their own volition, adolescents maintain contact with the imprisoned parent. Caregivers of younger children are often "gatekeepers," controlling children's contact with the incarcerated parent (Shlafer and Poehlmann 2010). However, adolescents often have contact with an incarcerated parent facilitated by someone other than the primary caregiver, bypassing the caregiver's gatekeeping role. Some adolescents communicate with a relative of the incarcerated parent who is responsible for arranging contact between the adolescent and the incarcerated parent. Other adolescents indicate that they communicate with the incarcerated parent by using personal cell phones, writing letters, or arranging visits to the prison without their caregiver's knowledge or permission.

Increased cognitive capacities may benefit adolescents in numerous ways. However, the circumstances surrounding a parent's incarceration are typically complex and confusing, even for the adults involved. Having some understanding of these complexities, but lacking the cognitive capacities to completely understand, may be overwhelming for adolescents and may be a source of additional stress. Research is needed exploring adolescents' understanding of their parent's incarceration, their preferences for placement or contact, and how these issues affect adolescents' cognitive, social, and emotional developmental outcomes.

Adolescent Social and Emotional Development in the Context of Parental Incarceration

Family Relationships. Although adolescence is characterized by important cognitive and emotional transformations that alter the attachment system (Allen 2008), attachment to parents and other significant adults is no less important than it was during infancy and childhood (Marvin and Britner 2008). Maintaining contact during a parent's incarceration can be difficult for many reasons, including location of the prison, cost of travel or telephone calls, and conflicted family relationships (Myers et al. 1999; Poehlmann 2005b). The frequency, consistency, and quality of contact between an adolescent and an incarcerated parent may influence the adolescent's expectations of the parent's emotional availability. When contact with the incarcerated parent is infrequent, inconsistent, or poor, adolescents may have unclear expectations about their parents' availability.

Although findings from probability samples of prisoners in the United States suggest that few incarcerated parents receive regular visits from their children, statistics regarding the frequency and type of contact with the incarcerated parent have not been examined according to the child's age (Glaze and Maruschak 2008; Mumola 2000). Most incarcerated parents, however, communicate with their children through mail correspondence (Glaze and Maruschak 2008). Few studies have examined the impact of contact during a parent's incarceration on adolescents' outcomes. The research that has examined these associations has focused primarily on the perceptions and attitudes of incarcerated parents (e.g., Snyder, Carlo, and Mullins 2001; Tuerk and Loper 2006) or outcomes among younger children (Poehlmann 2005c).

Two recent studies, however, provide some information about adolescents. In a sample of children who range in age from 9 to 15, Shlafer and Poehlmann (2010) find that children who have contact with their incarcerated parent report fewer feelings of alienation and anger toward the parent than children who have no contact. However, the authors find no differences between contact groups regarding children's feelings of trust, communication, or overall feelings about the incarcerated parent (as measured using the Inventory of Parent and Peer Attachment; see Armsden and Greenberg 1987). Further, in a sample of families affected by maternal incarceration, Trice and Brewster (2004) find that adolescents who communicate more with their incarcerated mothers are less likely to drop out of school or to be suspended from school than those who experience less communication, although there are no significant group differences in either noncompliance rates at home (i.e., not completing household chores, arriving home after curfew) or police arrests between the contact groups.

Other theoretical perspectives that emphasize the importance of supervision, modeling, and guidance are valuable when examining adolescent social and emotional development within the family context (Dishion et al. 1994; Patterson, DeBaryshe, and Ramsey 1990). As is the case for all adolescents, caregivers provide a crucial context for development. The quality of the adolescent-caregiver relationship and the caregiver's ability to provide adequate supervision and support likely depend on the history of personal interactions, as well as broader family resources. In particular, the role of the caregiver before a parent's incarceration, the consistency and dependability of the caregiver during the parent's incarceration, and the caregiver's psychological and tangible resources are likely to influence adolescents' developmental outcomes. In the context of parental incarceration, caregivers commonly experience multiple socioeconomic and psychological risk factors. Caregivers are often single parents with limited financial resources, low educational attainment, and poor mental health (Poehlmann 2005a). Combined, these risk factors can alter adolescents' living environments and the quality of adolescent-caregiver relationships.

Despite its obvious importance, few researchers have examined the caregiver's role in adolescent development during a parent's incarceration. In one exception, Shlafer and Poehlmann (2010) examine attachment and caregiving in a sample of youth whose parents are incarcerated. They find high rates of children exhibiting internalizing (19 percent) and externalizing (33 percent) symptoms that are borderline or clinically significant. In analyses examining outcomes among the oldest children (age 7 to 15), Shlafer and Poehlmann find that when caregivers report less positive feelings about the children, teachers and caregivers both report children exhibiting more externalizing behavior problems six months later, even after controlling for externalizing problems at intake. These results suggest that the caregiver-child relationship may be important for children's behavioral outcomes in families affected by parental incarceration, although the findings await replication.

Peer Relationships. The caregiver-child relationship also shapes adolescents' other relationships, including relationships with peers. Securely attached adolescents relate more positively to their peers than insecurely attached adolescents, and they are described as competent, empathic, and self-confident (Thompson 2000). Some adolescents of incarcerated parents, however, have been described as rejecting their peers, lacking self-confidence, and doubting their friendships (Shlafer and Poehlmann 2010). The influence of peers and friends becomes increasingly important during adolescence. Perceived relational support by peers generally increases, whereas perceived parental support decreases (Meeus 2003). This developmental period is characterized by increasing concerns about peers' impressions and the need for approval from friends. This trend is relevant to parental incarceration in a number of ways. Parental incarceration can be socially stigmatizing and isolating, particularly as peer relationships and intimacy in friendships become increasingly important. Despite the theoretical and anecdotal writings on this topic (e.g., Adalist-Estrin 2005), few empirical studies have examined the effects of social stigma, secrecy, and isolation regarding parental incarceration on adolescents.

In one exception, Nesmith and Ruhland (2008) interview children and teens between 8 and 17 years old who are affected by a parent's incarceration. Through qualitative analyses of interviews, these researchers identify a theme that they label "social challenges," which captures children's and adolescents' feelings of social stigma, isolation, and secrecy in the context of parental incarceration. Nesmith and Ruhland find that adolescents frequently report challenges in their social lives, including circumstances that inhibit or interfere with their abilities to connect to individuals outside their families, difficulties developing a sense of belonging to their neighborhoods and communities, and trouble making friends and relating to peers. The researchers' consideration of the adolescents' perspectives is particularly valuable and should be incorporated in future research with this population. Additionally, empirical work should consider how social stigma and isolation relate to adolescent's subsequent outcomes.

Behavior Problems and Psychopathology. As peer relationships grow increasingly important, teens face challenges related to peer pressure. Unlike with young children, experimentation and some risk-taking behavior are considered normative for teenagers. Because of the obvious developmental importance and consequences for long-term adjustment, adolescent behavior problems, antisocial outcomes, and psychopathology have been studied extensively in the context of parental incarceration. For example, research by Kinner and colleagues (2007) finds that girls whose mothers' partners have ever been imprisoned are more likely to use alcohol and tobacco at age 14 than girls whose mothers' partners have never been incarcerated. Kinner and colleagues also find that the partners' histories of arrest (but not imprisonment) are associated with boys' use of alcohol and tobacco at age 14.

Other researchers have examined the effects of parental incarceration on adolescents' behavior problems. In their analysis of prospective data from the Cambridge Study on Delinquent Development, Murray and Farrington (2005, 2008b) find that boys separated from a parent before age 10 because of parental incarceration are more likely to exhibit antisocial behaviors and internalizing symptoms in adolescence and adulthood than boys who experience other types of childhood separations from parents. For example, 61 percent of boys who experience parental incarceration before age 10 show antisocial personality characteristics at age 14, whereas only 16 to 33 percent of boys in the comparison groups show such characteristics at age 14 (Murray and Farrington 2008b). Further, boys separated within the first 10 years of life because of a parent's imprisonment have the highest rates of co-occurring internalizing and antisocial problems in adolescence. These findings remained significant even after controlling for parental criminality and other family risks. While these findings are intriguing, similar analyses using data from a Swedish longitudinal study do not replicate these findings (Murray, Janson, and Farrington 2007; also see Murray, this volume, for a review of longitudinal research focusing on the effects of parental incarceration).

Other researchers have examined associations between parental incarceration and adolescents' internalizing and externalizing symptoms. Kinner and colleagues (2007) find that a history of incarceration among mothers' current partners is associated with more internalizing and externalizing symptoms in adolescents (as rated by their mothers) compared with adolescents whose mothers' partners do not have a history of incarceration. Further, a history of incarceration for mothers' current partners is associated with self-reported internalizing symptoms among girls, although it is unrelated to self-reported externalizing symptoms among girls. In addition, the incarceration of mothers' partners does not significantly relate to self-reported behavior problems among boys. However, after controlling for other risk factors (i.e., maternal age and education, family income, maternal anxiety and depression, maternal alcohol and tobacco consumption, dyadic adjustment, domestic violence, and parenting style), the associations between arrest and incarceration and children's outcomes become nonsignificant, suggesting that a history of incarceration in the mother's partner may not be a unique risk factor for less optimal outcomes when examined in the context of other socio-demographic and family risk factors.

These studies also suggest strong associations between parents' and adolescents' antisocial behaviors. Such behaviors include, but are not limited to, violating the rights of others, breaking the law, and disregard for social standards or the legal system. Although one cannot equate incarceration with the full range of antisocial behaviors, incarcerated individuals have most likely engaged in some antisocial behavior (e.g., stealing, assault, drug use). Scholars have offered numerous and wide-ranging explanations for intergenerational associations in antisocial behavior, including parental modeling of negative behaviors, family socialization regarding the acceptance of deviant behaviors, and lack of supervision (e.g., Patterson et al. 1990); the heritability of potential genetic markers relevant to antisocial behaviors (e.g., Carey and Goldman 1997); and the accumulation of risks relevant to children's antisocial behaviors (e.g., Rutter 1997).

Dannerbeck (2005) compares juvenile offenders with and without histories of parental incarceration. In her sample, approximately one-third (32 percent) of juvenile offenders report a history of parental incarceration. Further, compared with adolescents without histories of parental incarceration, adolescents with incarcerated parents are more likely to report that they have a parent with a mental health disorder and a history of substance abuse. Adolescents with a history of parental incarceration are more likely to report a history of abuse and out-of-home placement, more likely to have experienced a parenting style described as "severely ineffective," and are referred to the juvenile authorities at a younger age than those who have not experienced the incarceration of a parent.

It is often assumed that most adolescents with parents involved in the criminal justice system will grow up to be criminals themselves. Although research has documented an increased risk for offending among youth whose parents are involved in the criminal justice system (e.g., Farrington, Barnes, and Lambert 1996; Murray et al. 2007; Robins 1979), discontinuity between generations is also considerable (Bijleveld and Wijkman 2009). Having an incarcerated parent by no means determines whether an adolescent will follow the same developmental path (see Murray, this volume). Research on this topic must consider how antisocial and criminal behaviors are and *are not* transmitted across generations.

The specific processes that explain the intergenerational transmission of antisocial behavior remain unclear. There is a need for additional research that examines parents' functioning before incarceration (e.g., criminal behavior witnessed by the adolescent, harsh or neglectful parenting, mental health and substance use) and adolescents' subsequent outcomes. It should also be noted that race is often used as a risk indicator in studies examining intergenerational patterns of antisocial behavior. Ethnic minorities are overrepresented in both the adult (Glaze and Maruschak 2008) and juvenile correction systems (Snyder and Sickmund 2006). Therefore, it is important that researchers continue to examine race in future research on parental incarceration and developmental outcomes in adolescence.

In addition to the research documenting adolescents' risk for behavior problems, other research has explored psychopathology among adolescents with incarcerated parents (e.g., Phillips et al. 2002). Phillips and colleagues find that among youth (between 11 and 18 years old) receiving mental health services, those with a history of parental incarceration have more lifetime risk factors (abuse or neglect, poverty, parental drug or alcohol abuse) and have experienced more recent negative life events in the past six months (witnessed violence and family crises). At intake, adolescents with a history of parental incarceration are more likely to have diagnoses for conduct disorder or attention-deficit/hyperactivity disorder, but they are less likely to be diagnosed with major depression. However, these findings may not be widely generalizable because they focus on adolescents receiving mental health services.

School and Community Contexts for Adolescents Affected by Parental Incarceration

School is a particularly important context for children affected by parental incarceration. As previously discussed, parental incarceration may significantly affect adolescents' relationships with peers and teachers, as well as their behaviors and achievement in the school setting. Previous research has documented a range of problems that adolescents with incarcerated parents experience within school settings; however, little is known about the processes that influence adolescents' school success or failure. Although cognitive delays and the experience of risk (e.g., prenatal substance exposures) that predispose children to developmental problems and the need for special education have been documented in younger children of

incarcerated mothers (Poehlmann 2005a), these risks have not been documented with adolescent samples. It is unknown whether (and to what
extent) adolescents with incarcerated mothers or fathers experience cognitive delays or prenatal risks that affect their long-term school outcomes.
However, initial findings have documented a range of school-related
problems associated with parental incarceration. These problems include
truancy, suspension, expulsion, failing classes, dropping out of school,
and violence.

For example, Hanlon and colleagues (2005) examine self-reports of
children age 9 to 14 who have substance-abusing incarcerated mothers.
Forty-five percent of the children express little or no interest in school,
33 percent report failing a grade, 27 percent have spent time in special
education classes, and 35 percent report being in multiple fights. Further,
49 percent of the adolescents report a history of school suspension (18 percent of the sample five or more times) and 10 percent report expulsion.
In particular, older youth, boys, and adolescents who experience more
risk factors (e.g., more peer deviance, poor parental monitoring) report
more delinquent activity and school problems. Trice and Brewster (2004)
find that compared to their best friends, adolescents with incarcerated
mothers are significantly more likely to have dropped out of school or to
have been suspended during the last school year. Additionally, adolescents with incarcerated mothers have more disciplinary school conferences, are more likely to have failed a class, and are more likely to report
being absent from school 20 or more days than adolescents who did not
experience maternal imprisonment. Similarly, in the Cambridge Study on
Delinquent Development, Murray and Farrington (2008a) find that at
age 14, 74 percent of the boys who experienced parental incarceration
before age 10 have been truant, compared with 22 to 35 percent in the
control groups. Sixty-eight percent of the 14-year-old boys who experience parental incarceration fail out of school compared with 19 to 33 percent in the control groups.

Taken together, these results indicate that parental incarceration may
be a risk marker for negative school performance and behaviors. The findings also suggest the importance of identifying affected children early and
intervening to prevent problems in the school context. Certainly, support
and education offered in the school setting have been presented as ame-
liorating some of these problems (Lopez and Bhat 2007). Clopton and East
(2008), for example, provide suggestions for teachers and school administrators working with children of incarcerated parents, although Clopton

and East focus on younger children. However, there are no studies of school-based interventions for children of incarcerated parents. Research is needed addressing how schools can effectively assist children of all ages who face difficulties as a result of a parental incarceration.

Community and after-school activities are also important contexts for adolescent development. Although adolescents' involvement in the community (e.g., church, volunteerism) and participation in after-school activities may be protective factors for some children (e.g., Masten and Coatsworth 1998), the positive youth development literature has not included children affected by parental incarceration. More research is needed examining adolescents' involvement in community activities, as well as how these experiences relate to their adjustment in the context of parental imprisonment and how these settings can be used for interventions among youth with incarcerated parents.

Resilience and Ecological Approaches for Studying Adolescents with Incarcerated Parents

The research that has emerged within the past decade has provided important information about the development of adolescents with incarcerated parents. However, this research has been overwhelmingly problem focused (Eddy and Reid 2003). Scholars should examine the outcomes of adolescents with incarcerated parents using a resilience framework (e.g., Masten 2001). It is vital that researchers and practitioners begin to understand how and why some adolescents adapt successfully, despite the risks associated with parental incarceration. Further, it is important for researchers to begin to understand the factors that promote resilience so they can guide practitioners to capitalize on protective factors.

Research with adolescents of incarcerated parents should consider protective factors that are suggested by theory and previous developmental research, including positive family relationships, supportive relationships with nonfamily members (e.g., a teacher, mentor, or coach), youths' self-efficacy, supervision in the home, and positive peer relationships (Grossman et al. 1992; Rutter 1987; Werner and Smith 1992). In one recent example, Nesmith and Ruhland (2008) discuss risk and protective factors among older children and teens with incarcerated parents using a resilience framework. Through qualitative analyses of interviews with youth, Nesmith and Ruhland find that religion and faith are particularly important among older children and adolescents who are effectively coping with their parent's incarceration. In addition, youth receive extended support and reduced social isolation through their involvement in their faith communities. Finally, Nesmith and Ruhland note that youth who are well adjusted are also likely to have supportive, positive peer relationships. These findings should be replicated both qualitatively and quantitatively with larger samples.

More resilience-focused research with this population is greatly needed. However, to fully understand the factors that promote resilience, researchers must consider the multiple contexts of adolescent development. In particular, it is important to consider adolescents' development at home and at school, as well as their interactions with the criminal justice system as a result of their parents' incarceration. Additionally, attention should be paid to adolescents' involvement in extracurricular activities (e.g., athletic practices, religious participation) and other contexts unique to this developmental period, including any after-school or weekend working environments.

An ecological model (Bronfenbrenner 1986) may be particularly valuable when addressing the needs of adolescents with incarcerated parents. Consistent with this model, future research should consider adolescents' adaptation within and between contexts before, during, and after their parent's incarceration. For example, using an ecological perspective, Arditti (2005) discusses risk and protective factors across systems and the impact of incarceration on the family. Within the microsystem (i.e., settings in which the adolescent is directly involved), Arditti notes the importance of parent-child relationships and social support for family members during the incarceration period. Within the mesosystem (i.e., links between settings in which the adolescent is involved), issues related to visitation and family-friendly visiting environments are addressed.

The fit of similar models to the data should be considered when examining the effects of parental incarceration on adolescents. For example, social stigma and isolation in the context of parental incarceration may influence adolescents' academic functioning, including school failure, dropping out, and behavior problems as well as peer relations. An ecological approach is equally valuable when examining successful adaptation and competence. For example, supportive and stable relationships between adolescents and their caregivers may combat stigma and influence adolescents' interactions with peers and ultimately their social and emotional adjustment across these systems. Researchers examining adolescents' outcomes in the context of parental incarceration should consider using both ecological and resilience frameworks.

Although Trice and Brewster (2004) do not explicitly apply an ecological or resilience framework, their research provides one example of how researchers can examine positive outcomes across multiple domains in the context of parental incarceration. Trice and Brewster examine the adjustment of adolescents with incarcerated mothers. Adolescents are 13 to 20 years old, and caregivers report on the adolescents' adjustment at home, at school, and within their communities. Trice and Brewster find that adolescents placed with family members are the least likely to drop out of school compared with adolescents placed in foster care or with friends. When adolescents' academic outcomes are examined, Trice and Brewster find that when caregivers report adolescents as having positive experiences at school (e.g., participation in athletics and receiving good grades), fewer academic problems are reported compared with students whose caregivers do not report positive experiences. Although Trice and Brewster note the high risk status of their sample, they also draw attention to factors across multiple systems that may promote positive outcomes in the context of parental incarceration (e.g., inmate education, stability in the caregiving environment, and counseling and services for children).

Directions for Future Research, Intervention, and Policy

Research Recommendations

Our current understanding of the needs and outcomes of adolescents with incarcerated parents is quite limited. Although there is a tremendous need for more research focusing on this population, research grounded in a developmental perspective will be most valuable to the field. Researchers and practitioners should consider adolescents' adjustment before, during, and after a parent's incarceration, as well as within and across multiple systems of development. Further, resilience-focused research—empirical work that recognizes and examines factors associated with adolescents' successful adaptation despite the considerable adversities they experience in the context of parental incarceration—is increasingly needed. Finally, researchers should consider adolescents' perspectives, in addition to incarcerated parents' and caregivers' perspectives.

Additional research is needed examining adolescents' relationships with caregivers and incarcerated parents from multiple perspectives. More research is needed examining the effects of these relationships on adolescent outcomes. For example, incarcerated parents and caregivers may model negative (e.g., their own risk-taking behavior) and positive behaviors (e.g., religious participation) for adolescents. The processes through which these behaviors are modeled for adolescents need to be better understood. Future research should also examine how supervision and support provided by caregivers relates to adolescent outcomes, including school achievement and risk-taking behaviors.

Replication and extension of recent findings is particularly needed. For example, Murray and Farrington's research (2005, 2008b) examining the effects of parental incarceration on boys' outcomes should be replicated with comparable samples of girls. In addition, because maternal and paternal incarceration may have different effects on children and adolescents (Murray and Murray 2010), parental gender should be considered in future analyses. Because boys and older children may be at higher risk for developing antisocial outcomes and school problems than girls or younger children (e.g., Murray and Farrington 2008a; Hanlon et al. 2005), studies should examine different pathways for girls and boys as well as following children through adolescence. Further, additional prospective, longitudinal samples with children in the United States are needed, especially since the United States incarcerates more individuals than any other country in the world (Pew Center on the States 2008).

Eddy and Reid (2003) note that a fundamental challenge with research on this topic is that none of the relevant academic disciplines (i.e., child development, psychology, sociology, social work, criminology, nursing, public health) has identified children of incarcerated parents as a population of particular interest. Although this is a current shortcoming of our knowledge base and disciplinary isolation, it is also an incredible opportunity for interdisciplinary collaboration. The most comprehensive and accurate knowledge will come when researchers bridge their areas of expertise; only then will researchers have the knowledge necessary to design and implement successful intervention and preventions programs targeting this growing population of children and adolescents affected by parental incarceration.

Prevention and Intervention

Despite the growing number of adolescents with incarcerated parents, few programs or initiatives are targeted at engaging adolescents. Mentoring has recently come to the attention of policymakers and practitioners as one intervention strategy. Many researchers have called for supportive, adult role models to help address the needs of this population of youth. For example, Nesmith and Ruhland (2008) recommend more African American adult role models for youth with incarcerated parents. Further, in their examination of 9- to 14-year-olds with incarcerated addict mothers, Hanlon and colleagues (2005, 82) conclude that as high-risk children enter adolescence, the need for concerned adults who possess the time, motivation, and energy to support these children is critical:

> Although requiring considerable investment of outside resources, the implementation of a culturally sensitive, prevention-oriented mentoring approach appears to be an ideal one for this set of circumstances . . . Because of their multiple needs, many of these families require the provision of comprehensive caseworker support services as well, particularly in cases in which birth mothers and surrogate parents disagree on the advisability of the mothers' future assumption of the parenting role.

However, the impact of mentoring on high-risk populations is not well understood, and the cost-benefit analyses conducted with lower-risk populations are not entirely promising (Aos et al. 2004; Rhodes, Haight, and Briggs 1999). Further, mentoring programs that have targeted children with incarcerated parents have primarily included younger participants. For instance, less than 20 percent of the children in Public/Private Venture's Amachi initiative was between the ages of 13 and 18, and only 1 percent was over the age of 16 (Farley 2004; Jucovy 2003). Thus, it may be inappropriate to generalize Amachi's initial findings to adolescents with incarcerated parents. Further, although the evaluation of Amachi has methodological strengths (e.g., continued monitoring of matches; interviews with program developers, staff, pastors, volunteer coordinators, and mentors), reports to date are primarily descriptive, and much more information is needed about the long-term outcomes of children participating in the program.

Intervention efforts should also be directed toward caregivers of adolescents with incarcerated parents (e.g., Hanlon, Carswell, and Rose 2007). Caregivers provide supervision and support for adolescents during parental incarceration. They may be instrumental in preventing negative school outcomes (e.g., truancy, school failure), substance abuse, and other delinquent behaviors. Caregivers may be key in fostering positive outcomes as well, such as involvement in extracurricular activities. More research is needed documenting caregivers' roles in intervention, as well as how their involvement can shape adolescents' outcomes.

Policy Implications

Research focusing on adolescents affected by parental incarceration also has implications for local, state, and national policies. A 2006 report to the Washington State legislature focusing on children of incarcerated parents made several recommendations that are relevant for adolescents (Russell et al. 2006). Recommendations were made based on information collected during interviews with offenders, service providers, caregivers, and adult children of offenders. The authors also considered research on children of incarcerated parents and existing policies and programs targeting this population. Russell and colleagues' recommendations included (a) gathering child data during the court hearing process to help plan services for children and adolescents; (b) developing arrest protocols for adults with children; (c) educating human service, judicial, and education professionals about the needs of children and adolescents with incarcerated parents; (d) developing family resource centers to serve families affected by parental incarceration; (e) implementing systemic programs that increase communication among systems and with families to increase the chances of family reunification; and (f) promoting the economic stability of affected families.

In addition to these recommendations, providing support to adolescents around arrest, sentencing, visitation, and reunification issues would be useful. These efforts could become part of corrections policies and programs or through coordination with other systems. Researchers should implement school-based interventions, especially those that begin early, and investigate their outcomes. Increased communication among systems, including criminal justice, schools, and child welfare, will help identify children affected by parental incarceration early and allow for interventions that attempt to decrease social isolation and stigma, increase opportunities for positive youth development (especially interactions with nondeviant peers and supportive adults), and promote adolescents' school attendance and completion of academic work. It will also help affected adolescents if society attempts to decrease social stigma by better reintegrating formerly incarcerated parents back into society and into roles that promote positive civic engagement, including helping with issues related to employment, education, and voting. Alternatives to incarceration for individuals with children should also be considered to decrease family disruption and minimize the impact on the next generation. Further, alternatives should be considered for adolescents who engage in negative behaviors; providing offending adolescents a chance at rehabilitation and corrective experiences may help prevent intergenerational cycles of antisocial behavior and incarceration.

REFERENCES

Adalist-Estrin, Ann. 2005. "Mentoring Children of Prisoners." *Family and Corrections Network Report* 39:1–3.

Allen, Joseph P. 2008. "The Attachment System in Adolescence." In *Handbook of Attachment,* 2nd ed., edited by Jude Cassidy and Phillip R. Shaver (419–35). New York: Guilford Press.

Aos, Steve, Roxanne Lieb, Jim Mayfield, Marna Miller, and Annie Pennucci. 2004. *Benefits and Costs of Prevention and Early Intervention Programs for Youth.* Olympia: Washington State Institute for Public Policy.

Arditti, Joyce A. 2005. "Families and Incarceration: An Ecological Approach." *Families in Society: The Journal of Contemporary Social Services* 86:251–60.

Armsden, Gay C., and Mark T. Greenberg. 1987. "The Inventory of Parent and Peer Attachment: Relationships to Well-Being in Adolescence." *Journal of Youth and Adolescence* 16:427–54.

Bijleveld, Catrien J. H., and Miriam Wijkman. 2009. "Intergenerational Continuity in Convictions: A Five-Generation Study." *Criminal Behavior and Mental Health* 19:142–55.

Bronfenbrenner, Urie. 1986. "Ecology of the Family as a Context for Human Development: Research Perspectives." *Developmental Psychology* 22(6): 723–42.

Carey, Gregory, and David Goldman. 1997. "The Genetics of Antisocial Behavior." In *Handbook of Antisocial Behavior,* edited by David M. Stoff, James Breiling, and Jack D. Maser (243–54). Hoboken, NJ: John Wiley & Sons.

Clopton, Kerri L., and Katheryn K. East. 2008. " 'Are There Other Kids Like Me?' Children with a Parent in Prison." *Early Childhood Education Journal* 36:195–98.

Dannerbeck, Anne M. 2005. "Differences in Parenting Attributes, Experiences, and Behaviors of Delinquent Youth with and without a Parental History of Incarceration." *Youth Violence and Juvenile Justice* 3(3): 199–213.

Dishion, Thomas J., Terry Duncan, J. Mark Eddy, Beverly I. Fagot, and Rebecca Fetrow. 1994. "The Words of Parents and Peers: Coercive Exchanges and Children's Social Adaptation." *Social Development* 3:255–68.

Eddy, J. Mark, and John B. Reid. 2003. "Adolescent Children of Incarcerated Parents: A Developmental Perspective." In *Prisoners Once Removed: The Impact of Incarceration and Reentry on Children, Families, and Communities,* edited by Jeremy Travis and Michelle Waul (233–58). Washington, DC: Urban Institute Press.

Enos, Sandra. 2001. *Mothering from the Inside: Parenting in a Women's Prison.* Albany, NY: State University of New York Press.

Farley, Chelsea. 2004. "Amachi in Brief." Philadelphia, PA: Public/Private Ventures.

Farrington, David P., Geoffrey Barnes, and Sandra Lambert. 1996. "The Concentration of Offending in Families." *Legal and Criminological Psychology* 1:47–63.

Glaze, Lauren E., and Laura M. Maruschak. 2008. *Parents in Prison and Their Minor Children.* NCJ 222984. Washington, DC: U.S. Department of Justice, Bureau of Justice Statistics.

Grossman, Frances K., Jack Beinashowitz, Luleen Anderson, Mariko Sakurai, Laura Finnin, and Margery Flahery. 1992. "Risk and Resilience in Young Adolescents." *Journal of Youth and Adolescence* 21(5): 529–50.

Hanlon, Thomas E., Steven B. Carswell, and Marc Rose. 2007. "Research on the Caretaking of Children of Incarcerated Parents: Findings and Their Service Delivery Implications." *Children and Youth Services Review* 29:348–62.

Hanlon, Thomas E., Robert J. Blatchley, Terry Bennett-Sears, Kevin E. O'Grady, Marc Rose, and Jason M. Callaman. 2005. "Vulnerability of Children of Incarcerated Addict Mothers: Implications for Preventive Interventions." *Children and Youth Services Review* 27(1): 67–84.

Jucovy, Linda. 2003. *Amachi: Mentoring Children of Prisoners in Philadelphia.* Philadelphia, PA: Public/Private Ventures.

Keating, Daniel. 1990. "Adolescent Thinking." In *At the Threshold: The Developing Adolescent,* edited by Shirley S. Feldman and Glen Elliot (54–90). Cambridge, MA: Harvard University Press.

Kinner, Stuart A., Rosa Alati, Jake M. Najman, and Gail M. Williams. 2007. "Do Paternal Arrest and Imprisonment Lead to Child Behaviour Problems and Substance Use? A Longitudinal Analysis." *Journal of Child Psychology and Psychiatry* 48(11): 1148–56.

Lopez, Caroline, and Christine S. Bhat. 2007. "Supporting Students with Incarcerated Parents in Schools: A Group Intervention." *Journal for Specialists in Group Work* 32:139–53.

Marvin, Robert S., and Preston A. Britner. 2008. "Normative Development: The Ontogeny of Attachment." In *Handbook of Attachment,* 2nd ed., edited by Jude Cassidy and Phillip R. Shaver (269–94). New York: Guilford Press.

Masten, Ann S. 2001. "Ordinary Magic: Resilience Processes in Development." *American Psychologist* 56(3): 227–38.

Masten, Ann S., and J. Douglas Coatsworth. 1998. "The Development of Competence in Favorable and Unfavorable Environments: Lessons from Research on Successful Children." *American Psychologist* 53(2): 205–20.

Meeus, Wim. 2003. "Parental and Peer Support, Identity Development, and Psychological Well-Being in Adolescence." *Psychology: The Journal of the Hellenic Psychological Society* 10(2/3): 192–201.

Mumola, Christopher J. 2000. *Incarcerated Parents and Their Children.* NCJ 182335. Washington, DC: U.S. Department of Justice, Bureau of Justice Statistics.

Murray, Joseph. 2007. "The Cycle of Punishment: Social Exclusion of Prisoners and Their Children." *Criminology and Criminal Justice* 7(1): 55–81.

Murray, Joseph, and David P. Farrington. 2005. "Parental Imprisonment: Effects on Boys' Antisocial Behaviour and Delinquency through the Life Course." *Journal of Child Psychology and Psychiatry* 46(12): 1269–78.

———. 2008a. "The Effects of Parental Imprisonment on Children." In *Crime and Justice: A Review of Research*, vol. 37, edited by Michael Tonry (133–206). Chicago: University of Chicago Press.

———. 2008b. "Parental Imprisonment: Long-Lasting Effects on Boys' Internalizing Problems through the Life Course." *Development & Psychopathology* 20(1): 273–90.

Murray, Joseph, and Lynne Murray. 2010. "Parental Incarceration, Attachment, and Child Psychopathology." *Attachment & Human Development* 12(4): 289–309.

Murray, Joseph, Carl-Gunnar Janson, and David P. Farrington. 2007. "Crime in Adult Offspring of Prisoners: A Cross-National Comparison of Two Longitudinal Samples." *Criminal Justice and Behaviors* 34:133–49.

Myers, Barbara J. 2009. "What Do Children of Incarcerated Mothers Say about Their Lives?" Paper presented at the biennial meeting of the Society for Research in Child Development, Denver, CO, April.

Myers, Barbara J., Tina M. Smarsh, Kristine Amlund-Hagen, and Suzanne Kennon. 1999. "Children of Incarcerated Mothers." *Journal of Child and Family Studies* 8(1): 11–25.

Nesmith, Ande, and Ebony Ruhland. 2008. "Children of Incarcerated Parents: Challenges and Resiliency, in Their Own Words." *Children and Youth Services Review* 30:1119–30.

Patterson, Gerald R., Barbara DeBaryshe, and Elizabeth Ramsey. 1990. "A Developmental Perspective on Antisocial Behavior." *American Psychologist* 44:329–35.

Pew Center on the States. 2008. *One in 100: Behind Bars in America 2008.* Washington, DC: Pew Charitable Trusts.

Phillips, Susan D., Barbara J. Burns, H. Ryan Wagner, Teresa L. Kramer, and James R. Robbins. 2002. "Parental Incarceration among Youth Receiving Mental Health Services." *Journal of Child and Family Studies* 11(4): 385–99.

Poehlmann, Julie. 2005a. "Children's Family Environments and Intellectual Outcomes during Maternal Incarceration." *Journal of Marriage and Family* 67:1275–85.

———. 2005b. "Incarcerated Mothers' Contact with Children, Perceived Family Relationships, and Depressive Symptoms." *Journal of Family Psychology* 19:350–57.

———. 2005c. "Representations of Attachment Relationships in Children of Incarcerated Mothers." *Child Development* 76:679–96.

Poehlmann, Julie, Rebecca J. Shlafer, Elizabeth Maes, and Ashley Hanneman. 2008. "Factors Associated with Young Children's Opportunities for Maintaining Family Relationships during Maternal Incarceration." *Family Relations* 57:267–80.

Rhodes, Jean E., Wendy L. Haight, and Ernestine C. Briggs. 1999. "The Influence of Mentoring on the Peer Relationships of Foster Youth in Relative and Nonrelative Care." *Journal of Research on Adolescence* 9(2): 185–201.

Robins, Lee N. 1979. "Sturdy Childhood Predictors of Adult Outcomes: Replications from Longitudinal Studies." In *Stress and Mental Disorder*, edited by James E. Barrett, Robert M. Rose, and Gerald L. Klerman (219–35). New York: Raven Press.

Russell, Kathleen Z., Belinda D. Stewart, Betsy Rodgers, and Dee Crocker. 2006. "Children of Incarcerated Parents: Final Report of the Oversight Committee to the Governor and the Legislature of Washington." Olympia: Washington State Oversight Committee.

Rutter, Michael. 1987. "Psychosocial Resilience and Protective Mechanisms." *American Journal of Orthopsychiatry* 57(3): 316–31.

———. 1997. "Antisocial Behavior: Developmental Psychopathology Perspectives." In *Handbook of Antisocial Behavior,* edited by David M. Stoff, James Breiling, and Jack D. Maser (115–24). Hoboken, NJ: John Wiley & Sons.

Sabol, William J., and Todd D. Minton. 2008. "Jail Inmates at Midyear 2007." NCJ 221945. Washington, DC: U.S. Department of Justice, Bureau of Justice Statistics.

Shlafer, Rebecca J., and Julie Poehlmann. 2010. "Attachment and Caregiving Relationships in Families Affected by Parental Incarceration." *Attachment & Human Development* 12:395–415.

Snyder, Howard N., and Melissa Sickmund. 2006. *Juvenile Offenders and Victims: 2006 National Report.* NCJ 212906. Washington, DC: U.S. Department of Justice, Office of Justice Programs, Office of Juvenile Justice and Delinquency Prevention.

Snyder, Zoann K., Teresa A. Carlo, and Megan M. Mullins. 2001. "Parenting from Prison: An Examination of Children's Visitation Program at a Women's Correctional Facility." *Marriage and Family Review* 32:33–61.

Thompson, Ross A. 2000. "The Legacy of Early Attachments." *Child Development* 71:145–52.

Trice, Ashton D., and JoAnne Brewster. 2004. "The Effects of Maternal Incarceration on Adolescent Children." *Journal of Policy and Criminal Psychology* 19(1): 27–35.

Tuerk, Elena H., and Ann B. Loper. 2006. "Contact between Incarcerated Mothers and Their Children: Assessing Parenting Stress." *Journal of Offender Rehabilitation* 43:23–43.

Werner, Emmy E., and Ruth S. Smith. 1992. *Overcoming the Odds: High-Risk Children from Birth to Adulthood.* New York: Cornell University.

8

Contexts of Race, Ethnicity, and Culture for Children of Incarcerated Parents

Keva M. Miller, Eleanor Gil-Kashiwabara,
Harold E. Briggs, and Schnavia Smith Hatcher

As the U.S. prison population has increased over the past few decades, so has the attention given to the impact of parental incarceration on children. In various studies, the children of incarcerated parents have been found vulnerable to prolonged parent-child separation, family instability, economic hardship, social demarcation and exclusion, and involvement with child welfare agencies (e.g., Johnson and Waldfogel 2008; Johnston 1995; Myers et al. 1999; Phillips et al. 2006; Swann and Sylvester 2006). These vulnerabilities are linked to attachment-related issues, delinquency, diminished academic performance, and internalizing and externalizing behaviors (e.g., Bocknek, Sanderson, and Britner 2009; Foster and Hagan 2007; Murray and Farrington 2005, 2008; Phillips et al. 2004; Poehlmann 2005a, 2005b).

It is well documented that racial and ethnic minority men and women are overrepresented in America's state and federal prisons (Beck 2000; Harrison and Beck 2006; Mumola 2000; Sabol, West, and Cooper 2009; Western and Wildeman 2009). Consequently, parental incarceration and associated vulnerabilities are much more likely to affect children of color. The disproportional racial and ethnic representation and disparate rates between racial and ethnic minority and white children are alarming. While African American/black children account for only 15 percent of the general U.S. population, they represent 45 percent of children of incarcerated parents (Federal Interagency Forum on Child and Family Statistics

2008; Glaze and Maruschak 2008). Hispanic/Latino children make up about 21 percent of both the general population and the children-of-incarcerated-parents population. In contrast, white children represent 57 percent of the general population but only 28 percent of children with an imprisoned parent. Put another way, Hispanic children are 2.5 times more likely and African American/black children are 7.5 times more likely than white children to have an incarcerated parent (Glaze and Maruschak 2008). American Indian/Alaskan Native and mixed-race children are similarly overrepresented.

Given that children of color are more likely to experience parental incarceration, the need and opportunity exist to examine a greater dynamic beyond simply reporting race/ethnicity statistics. It is imperative that scholars and practitioners examine how the contexts of race, ethnicity, and culture interact with risks and protective processes to better understand how these factors function as contributing indicators of children's functioning (Mays, Cochran, and Ponce 2004). However, the study of race, ethnicity, and culture is often confounded with political, environmental, and social risks, thus making it difficult to identify the true effects that they have on children's development and outcomes (Murry, Smith, and Hill 2001). The variations in cultural experiences within races and ethnicities make it difficult for researchers to discern how strongly culture affects children and for practitioners to provide culturally responsive services.

This chapter presents a conceptual framework on the interplay between race, ethnicity, and culture and how risk and protective processes are present within these contexts for children of incarcerated parents, potentially influencing their development and outcomes. The few studies that consider racial or ethnic variables in this population are presented; however, there is a clear need for research that provides an in-depth examination of how these variables influence children's development and outcomes. The chapter concludes with a discussion of implications for policy and practices for the children of incarcerated parents and their families.

Contexts of Race, Ethnicity, and Culture

Formulating a theoretical and conceptual framework pertaining to issues concerning *race, ethnicity,* and *culture* is essential to understanding how these factors shape the overall functioning of children with incarcerated parents. *Race* is typically operationalized as a distinct human type based on inherited biological or physical characteristic such as skin color, hair, or facial features (Healey and O'Brien 2004; Thomas and Schwarzbaum 2006). However, race may also be characterized as a social construct created by individuals for a social or political purpose (Takaki 1993). *Ethnicity* refers to individuals with a collective identity based on perceptions of common ancestry/heritage or language/dialect (McMahon and Watts 2002; Western States Center 2003). In contrast, *culture* is the created environment constructed by individuals who live within its context. Culture is the subjective shared community experience acquired over a lifetime of socialization (Draguns 1996).

Race and ethnicity are usually presented as categorical terms and used for comparisons. However, in practice, these terms often reflect an underlying construct—culture. Conceptualizing culture as a latent construct helps broaden understanding of human functioning and experiences because culture has a unifying effect within and between racial and ethnic groups (Murry, Smith, et al. 2001). Cultural similarities between racial and ethnic groups within the United States deserve increased attention within the literature on the children of incarcerated parents, and may have significant policy implications. At the same time, significant within-group cultural differences must be explored in future research and have significant implications for policy and practice.

Historical, political, and social issues that precede individuals' lives influence a person's worldview, perceived opportunities, and livelihood (Thomas and Schwarzbaum 2006). For many communities of color, such experiences have left an ineradicable mark on the well-being of families and children. Many African Americans have a history rooted in the transatlantic slave trade, centuries of chattel slavery, the convict leasing program, Jim Crow laws and segregation, and the civil rights movement (Gabbidon 2010; Miller 2007). For centuries, American Indians were driven from their lands, displaced, stripped of their sovereignty, subjected to spiritual and cultural genocide, and had their children taken and placed in boarding schools (Sanchez, Batchelder, and McRoy 1998). Restrictive immigration legislation, citizenship and deportation, inequitable pay for labor, and pressure to assimilate have been constant struggles among the Hispanic community (Gabbidon 2010; Sanchez et al. 1998). Although people of color have diverse experiences, they share common thread, namely an increased vulnerability to pathogenic conditions and formidable challenges that have contributed to adverse outcomes as well as adaptive protective processes to cope with risk exposure. In many respects, risk exposure and adaptive development have created a unifying cultural minority experience that includes underlying factors and processes manifested as racial or ethnic experiences.

Culture of Risk Exposure

As discussed throughout this volume, many children of incarcerated parents are exposed to significant risks that are concerning and merit attention. The argument set forth here is that the experiences of children of color are distinguishable from other children of incarcerated parents in that they encounter a host of multilayered inequalities rooted in broad structural systems (e.g., political, economic, societal). Exposure to such inequalities is arguably magnified and presented as a unique experience that potentially creates an increased vulnerability to maladaptive functioning and poor outcomes. For children of color, parental incarceration may be part of a more complicated dynamic, one with numerous inequalities and injustices within multiple social contexts. Most notably, children of color with parents in prison are disproportionally affected by disparities in drug and sentencing policies and potentially have an increased vulnerability to intergenerational poverty, adverse community conditions and neighborhood dynamics, inadequate health care, and multisystem involvement (i.e., child welfare, juvenile justice) (Foster and Hagan 2007; Western and Wildeman 2009).

Throughout U.S. history, the criminal justice system has served as a means for political, social, and economic subordination of racial and ethnic minorities (Romper and Pence 1999). Many scholars attribute discriminatory policies and biased penal system practices as determinants for disproportionality and disparity in the U.S. criminal justice system (Human Rights Watch 2002). One of the most apparent forms of discrimination in recent years is reflected in the racial biases in state and federal drug laws. The war on drugs imposed harsh mandatory minimums and increased penalties for possession and sale of crack cocaine, a primary drug of choice for African Americans from impoverished communities (American Civil Liberties Union 2006; The Sentencing Project 2009). Although there are recent efforts to reform legislation on some of the stringent mandatory sentencing and drug policies, the unintentional consequences that these policies had on children of color were far-reaching.

To understand how mandatory minimums and drug sentencing policies affected children on multiple fronts, it is essential to address the interrelated dynamics of criminal justice, public assistance, and child welfare practices and policies. For example, a drug felony conviction creates barriers to accessing resources. Welfare assistance programs have policy stipulations that deny individuals with drug convictions access to public assistance benefits and subsidized housing (Covington 2003; Jacobs 2001; Smith and Young 2003). Mandatory minimum sentences contribute to extended parent-child separations and the potential risks for child welfare involvement. The combination of child welfare involvement and long sentences for felony drug convictions can preclude a parent's, in most cases a mother's, ability to reunite with her children upon release. Many children of incarcerated parents become a part of separate agencies with unique goals that are too often at odds with the needs of children and their families (Enos 2008).

Children of color with incarcerated parents encounter broad-based structural and service-related inequalities within multiple fields of practice. Chief among these issues is that no one particular field of practice takes ownership for addressing the unique racial, ethnic, and cultural considerations of working with this population of children. As an example, it is well documented that children of color are disproportionately and disparately represented in child welfare systems across the country (Courtney et al. 1996; Harris and Hackett 2008; Hill 2006; Wells and Daniels 2008). Among all U.S. children, African American and American Indian children have the highest rates of foster care placements despite having similar substantiated rates of child maltreatment as white children (Child Welfare League of America 2003; Hill, Jackson, and Waheed 2008). African American children are overrepresented in child welfare systems in all 50 states, American Indians in 24 states, and Latino children in 10 states (Hill et al. 2008). Across the county, African American and American Indian children are also more likely to remain in the child welfare system for extended periods compared with other children (Child Welfare League of America 2003).

The overrepresentation of children of color in the child welfare system appears to parallel the overrepresentation of children of color with incarcerated parents. Whether there is a connection between African American children's length of stays in foster care and lengthy sentences for drug felony convictions is unclear. However, a few studies have examined associations between child welfare involvement (e.g., assessment for child maltreatment, foster care placements) and parental incarceration. For example, Hayward and Depanfilis (2007) use data from the

Adoption and Foster Care Analysis and Reporting System (AFCARS) to examine reunification for the children of incarcerated parents. African American children are overrepresented among those with an incarcerated parent, and they are the least likely to reunify with their parents. Whether African American children are more likely than other children to have a parent convicted on a drug felony charge is not evident, but it remains an important factor to examine in future studies.

In another study, Phillips and colleagues (2004) use a nationally representative sample of children assessed by child welfare agencies using data from the National Survey of Child and Adolescent Well-Being (NSCAW) to compare differences in demographic characteristics and parental risk factors between children of parents with and without an arrest history. African American children are affected disproportionately by parental arrests. Only 28 percent of the children assessed by child welfare are African American, although they represent 43 percent of the children of parents with an arrest history. While this study again provides important population data on the disproportionate representation of African American children of criminal justice–involved parents within the child welfare population, there remains a lack of inquiry into whether there are correlates of this inequality between these two systems, as well as a tendency to ignore the implications for children and families. For example, a few child welfare agencies across the country (e.g., California, New York, Oregon) work jointly with correctional systems to provide services to children, families, and the incarcerated. However, it is not evident that these programs make a concerted effort to be culturally responsive, considering the interrelated dynamics between multisystem involvement, cultural risks, and children's development and outcomes.

Racial and ethnic disproportionality in the juvenile justice system is another pervasive issue within communities of color. In 2006, 40 percent of the 92,854 juvenile offenders were African American, and an estimated 63 percent of African American juvenile offenders were detained for drug trafficking.[1] Dannerbeck (2005) examines parental factors associated with youth delinquency and life experiences among a sample of 1,112 youth with juvenile justice involvement and finds that 31 percent have a parent with a history of incarceration. African American youth are disparately affected by parental incarceration. Approximately 70 percent of African American compared with 25 percent of white youth in Dannerback's sample report having a parent with a history of incarceration. Compared with youth without an incarcerated parent, youth with parental incarceration histories experience additional risks (e.g., parental substance abuse, poor parenting, out of home placements).

While some studies have found an association between parents' and children's criminal justice involvement, the causal link remains unclear. Parental incarceration is inextricably linked to numerous social, political, and environmental risks (Myers et al. 1999; Phillips et al. 2002). Children of incarcerated parents are often exposed to the same risks as their parents. The concentration of risks found within many families and communities of color, such as poverty, adverse neighborhood conditions, and violence exposure, may be predictive of an intergenerational cycle of criminality.

Cultural Protective Processes

Despite historical, political, and social traumas and the resultant risks, people of color have survived against incredible odds, across multiple generations, and they have seemingly become resistant to absolute destruction (Greene 1995; McCullough-Chavis and Waites 2004). In the face of such adversity, people of color, under necessity, have developed and refined cultural strengths and protective processes that are resources for the family's well-being. Familial collectivism (nuclear, extended, and fictive kinships), flexibility of gender roles, value of children, spirituality and religiosity, and a reverence for elders are examples of potential resources found within racial and ethnic communities (Murry, Brown, et al. 2001). These positive cultural traits can have a significant impact on children of incarcerated parents. In fact, anecdotal and some empirical evidence suggest that not all children with incarcerated parents exhibit developmental problems or poor outcomes; in fact, many are faring quite well (Hanlon et al. 2005). Yet the literature has not adequately examined the extent that between- and within-cultural protective factors foster positive development and outcomes for children of color with incarcerated parents.

Links with family and community are important resources that buffer against political, societal, and environmental risks. These connections help facilitate coping mechanisms against risk and stressful life situations (Cook et al. 2007; Dulmus and Hilarski 2003; Runyan et al. 1998; Werner and Smith 1992). The formation and maintenance of strong family ties is a cultural strength that is commonly entrenched in many racial/ethnic families, where *familial collectivism, familism,* or *colectivismo,* rather than the individual, is emphasized to create solidarity and support for family members. Familial collectivism is a powerful asset for social, emotional, and economic survival, which in turn can foster overall child well-being. A commitment to familial relationships can also help children maintain a sense of belonging and identity in the midst of stress associated with parental incarceration. The protective element of familial collectivism may decrease the potential effects of societal shame and stigma associated with a parent's incarceration (Gabel 1992). Additionally, the pervasiveness of incarceration among many racial and ethnic groups, particularly within African American and Latino families, has made this particular social phenomenon a "normative" life experience in some communities (Swisher and Waller 2008; Western and Wildeman 2009). This does not necessarily mean that engaging in criminogenic behaviors and activities is acceptable, but, rather, that incarceration is part of the minority experience.

Familism and normalizing the incarceration experience may help incarcerated parents maintain an important role within their children's lives, which includes engagement in co-parenting with children's current caregivers. Hairston (2008) suggests the racial and ethnic identity of the parent may partially predict whether a child maintains contact with an incarcerated parent, and that African American parents are more likely than other ethnic minorities to have contact with their children during parental incarceration. In an analysis of 1997 survey data, Hairston and Rollins (2003) find that 24 percent of black, 20 percent of Hispanic, and 21 percent of white mothers report monthly visits during their incarceration. Thirty-three percent of black mothers receive weekly phone calls, whereas 22 percent of Hispanic and 26 percent of white mothers received weekly calls. Swisher and Waller (2008) examine single father engagement with their children using longitudinal data from the Fragile Families Child Well-Being Study. They find that race and ethnicity moderate the relationship between paternal incarceration (present and past) and nonresident fathers' contact with their children. Black incarcerated fathers are more likely to have contact with their children than white incarcerated fathers. Moreover, mothers are more likely to distrust black or Latino incarcerated fathers than mothers of children with white incarcerated fathers.

Families are social extensions of a larger context that provides strength and support within many racial and ethnic minority communities. Families that structure their lives so essential mechanisms are in place to effectively deal with persistent adversities are better able to adapt to challenging conditions and promote the well-being of all family members (Walsh 1998). Some of these adaptations are found in the acceptance of flexible roles within formal and informal family networks. For most children, there is no substitute for a parent. However, within many communities of color, children often maintain close relationships with extended family members and others on whom they rely heavily for child-rearing responsibilities. For example, fictive kin, individuals not related by blood or marriage who have the same rights and responsibilities as blood relatives, are often sought after as substitute caregivers. This adaptive mechanism is particularly prominent in African American families, and it appears to predate the enslavement of African individuals in the United States (Chatters, Taylor, and Jayakody 1994). American Indian families also value the role of extended family networks, blood relatives, and non-blood relatives (Sanchez et al. 1998). These patterns are found among Latino families, as child care responsibilities are shared among extended family, and children without parents are often informally adopted by members within the Latino community (Sanchez et al. 1998).

Extended families can be accessed as important resources for maintaining sibling connections and averting child welfare placements, thereby sustaining sibling relationships and providing continuity of placement with caregivers who are important attachment figures. These resources are likely to promote healthy development and outcomes for children. For example, Enos (2008) conducted a qualitative study of incarcerated mothers and found that race and ethnicity are associated with child placement decisions. African American and Latina mothers are more likely to request that family members care for their children than white mothers. A study conducted by Hanlon and colleagues (2005) illustrates how extended family networks can allay adverse outcomes. Eighty-eight adolescents with incarcerated mothers, most of whom were African American, were assessed for adjustment following their mothers' incarceration. Findings indicated that while some children exhibited problematic behaviors, the majority of youth showed no significant adjustment or functional deficits. Results were partially attributed to extended family caregiving (in most cases, the grandmother) as a protective element that is rooted in African American culture. However, most youth were cared for by their grandmothers before their mothers' incarcerations.

Variations within Racial and Ethnic Groups

Although the members of racial and ethnic minority groups often experience both an increased vulnerability to deleterious political, social, and environmental challenges as well as a tendency to develop protective mechanisms to cope in the presence of risk, important and significant within-group differences must be considered. Careful considerations of the variation and diversity within racial and ethnic groups should be made when using or reporting population-based data. Thus, researchers must move beyond simply accounting for the numbers of participants from each racial and ethnic group. Ideally, studies would expand to include variables that reliably and validly index cultural factors experienced between *and* within racial and ethnic groups.

Of particular note is the great influx of individuals from other countries that has occurred within recent decades. Recent immigration has significant implications for considering the meaning of race, ethnicity, and especially culture. For example, the migration of many peoples from Mexico, Central America, South America, Africa, and the Caribbean has led to diverse populations with significant differences from those who share similar race or ethnicity but have lived in the United States for multiple generations. The historical narratives of these people differ dramatically from those of individuals who have been in the United States for many generations. Their experiences upon arrival will have commonalities as well as uniqueness to those from century-old populations. This makes the delivery of culturally appropriate interventions complicated, especially when people of a given race or ethnicity are seen as more similar to each other than different.

Implications for Research, Practice, and Policy

The lives of children with incarcerated parents are complicated. Although the scientific knowledge on the population has increased, the extent that the contexts of race, ethnicity, and culture interact with risks *and* protective processes is understudied. There is a need for research that provides in-depth analyses on the distinct experiences and differential outcomes for children of color in the context of parental incarceration. Moreover, policymakers and practitioners must implement social policies and programs that can help the population transcend formidable conditions that accompany parental incarceration.

Implications for Future Research

The National Institutes of Health require that racial and ethnic diversity be represented in research study samples. The expectation is that the development of scientific evidence will inform policy and practice and encourage advances in implementing programs that are inclusive of and responsive to the members of all racial and ethnic groups. While people of color have been represented in studies of the children of incarcerated parents, most studies only report the percentage of participants of a given race and ethnicity. This surface analysis is insufficient to provide the field with in-depth knowledge about children of color and their families. It is time to move beyond this type of work and examine the distinct experiences, and the variability among, children of color.

As findings accrue, more sophisticated analyses can be conducted on how risks *and* protective mechanisms influence racial and ethnic minority children of incarcerated parents. Parental incarceration may be a symptom of or proxy for broader complex risks. For children of color, these risks include exposure to social exclusion or demarcation, intergenerational poverty, fewer educational opportunities, and other noxious contextual risks. Further studies are needed on how, why, and whether these risks differentially affect children of color. Important questions to ask in future studies include: Does race/ethnicity predict parental incarceration and intergenerational criminal justice involvement over and above other factors? Are the correlates of race/ethnicity *and* exposure to adverse environments more predictive of maladaptive development and poor outcomes than parental incarceration alone? Moreover, protective processes that promote healthy development and outcomes should be examined within empirical studies. For example, inquiries are needed on such questions as: To what extent does familial collectivism decrease the risks for attachment- and trauma-related disorders? Does access to social and familial capital (i.e., church community, connections with extended and fictive kinships) provide adaptive mechanisms that ameliorate feelings of abandonment, guilt, and shame?

As the prison population increases among minority women, their children become more vulnerable to extended stays in foster care. An important consideration for future research is the extent that multisystem involvement (i.e., child welfare, juvenile justice) affects the lives of the incarcerated and their children. Presumably, involvement with multiple systems increases family stress. Thus, it is necessary to examine whether multiple system involvement increases the probability of adverse outcomes. Another important research question to investigate is the process through which law enforcement places children in the care of child welfare and whether race/ethnicity is a significant predictor of such decisions.

Implications for Practice and Policy

As practitioners work with children of incarcerated parents, it is important to identify and access cultural strengths. Acknowledging the strengths of racial/ethnic minority individuals and families provides a solid foundation for understanding how to access these strengths and better serve the population. As identified, many minority groups value the culture of collective responsibility—particularly when it comes to raising the children within their communities. Joining with families and communities as true partners to address the issues concerning the needs of children with incarcerated parents would be an important first step. In the collaborative process, identifying members of the family system as experts on their family is beneficial in assisting families with children's adaptation and coping. Practitioners may seek to identify familial and communal strengths in an effort to provide culturally relevant services, thus building upon the "culture of family and community" that is prevalent among racial and ethnic minorities.

Most pertinent systems do not effectively articulate appropriate protocols for working with incarcerated parents, their children, or children's caregivers. Rarely do criminal justice or child welfare policies provide clear direction on how to address the needs of children and their families upon arrest, during incarceration (i.e., jail, courts, prison), and upon reentry (i.e., community corrections and supervision) (Enos 2008; From 2008; Hairston 2008). Collaborative cross-system policy initiatives could help allay many of the adverse outcomes associated with parental criminal justice involvement (From 2008; Hairston 1999; Porterfield, Dressel, and Barnhill 2000). Hairston (2008) proposes policies that implement services at the time of parental arrest, during incarceration, and upon reentry. As new policies are developed, considering the unintended consequences of past policies and how they contributed to the current state of affairs for children of color is paramount. Policymakers from criminal justice and child welfare must recognize the racial and ethnic disproportionality that occurs within each system, and respond. It is essential that these systems work together, and that policymakers mandate that culturally responsive and effective services be available for incarcerated parents and their children.

A financial investment into resources that collect and track data across service systems (i.e., criminal justice, child welfare, juvenile justice) about the individual characteristics of parents and their children, including race and ethnicity, will bring attention to the parallels of disproportionality and disparity between systems, and hopefully provide incentive to address these problems. Policymakers and administrators would then be challenged to provide an explanation for the disproportionate numbers, to clarify the extent of systems overlap with families, and to develop solutions to rectify the overrepresentation of people of color within these systems.

Conclusion

The contexts of race, ethnicity, and culture are important factors in the lives of many children of incarcerated parents. It is imperative that researchers, policymakers, and practitioners make a more concerted effort to consider how these contexts affect children. Attention to this issue is needed immediately, as children of color today have an increased vulnerability to parental incarceration and co-occurring risks. Yet these children and their families also have access to protective factors, and these too need to be examined and ways found to build on such strengths. It is the responsibility of scholars and practitioners to identify, understand, and access protective mechanisms to allay the risks and to promote healthy development and improved outcomes for all children of incarcerated parents.

NOTE

1. Office of Juvenile Justice and Delinquency Prevention, "Statistical Briefing Book: Juveniles in Corrections, Custody Data (1997–Present)," http://ojjdp.ncjrs.gov/ojstatbb/corrections/qa08201.asp?qaDate=2006.

REFERENCES

American Civil Liberties Union. 2006. Testimony of Jesselyn McCurdy, legislative counsel, American Civil Liberties Union Washington National Office, to the United States Sentencing Commission on Cocaine and Sentencing Policy, November 14.

Beck, Allen J. 2000. "Prisoners in 1999." NCJ 183476. Washington, DC: U.S. Department of Justice, Bureau of Justice Statistics.

Bocknek, Erika L., Jessica Sanderson, and Preston A. Britner. 2009. "Ambiguous Loss and Post-Traumatic Stress in School-Age Children of Prisoners." *Journal of Children and Family Studies* 18:323–33.

Chatters, Linda M., Robert J. Taylor, and Rukmalie Jayakody. 1994. "Fictive Kinship Relations in Black Extended Families." *Journal of Comparative Family Studies* 25:297–312.

Child Welfare League of America. 2003. *Children of Color in the Child Welfare System: Overview, Vision, and Proposed Action Steps.* Washington, DC: Child Welfare League of America.

Cook, Alexandra, Joseph Spinazzola, Julian Ford, Cheryl Lanktree, Margaret Blaustein, Caryll Sprague, Marylene Cloitre, et al. 2007. "Complex Trauma in Children and Adolescents." *Focal Point* 21(1): 4–8.

Courtney, Mark E., Richard P. Barth, Jill D. Berrick, Devon Brooks, Barbara Needell, and Linda Park. 1996. "Race and Child Welfare Services: Past Research and Future Directions." *Child Welfare* 75(2): 99–137.

Covington, Stephanie S. 2003. "A Woman's Journey Home: Challenges for Female Offenders." In *Prisoners Once Removed: The Impact of Incarceration and Reentry on Children, Families, and Communities,* edited by Jeremy Travis and Michelle Waul (67–103). Washington, DC: Urban Institute Press.

Dannerbeck, Anne M. 2005. "Differences in Parenting Attributes, Experiences, and Behaviors of Delinquent Youth with and without Parental History of Incarceration." *Youth Violence and Juvenile Justice* 3(3): 199–213.

Draguns, Juris G. 1996. "Universal and Culturally Distinctive: Charting the Course of Cultural Counseling." In *Counseling across Cultures,* edited by Paul B. Pedersen, Juris G. Draguns, Walter J. Lonner, and Joseph E. Trimble (1–20). Thousand Oaks, CA: SAGE Publications.

Dulmus, Catherine N., and Carolyn Hilarski. 2003. "When Stress Constitutes Trauma and Trauma Constitutes Crisis: The Stress-Trauma Crisis Continuum." *Brief Treatment and Crisis Intervention* 3:27–35.

Enos, Sandra. 2008. "Incarcerated Parents: Interrupted Childhood." *CW360°: A Comprehensive Look at a Prevalent Child Welfare Issue* (spring): 18.

Federal Interagency Forum on Child and Family Statistics. 2008. *America's Children in Brief: Key National Indicators of Well-Being, 2008.* Washington, DC: U.S. Government Printing Office.

Foster, Holly, and John Hagan. 2007. "Incarceration and Intergenerational Social Exclusion." *Social Problems* 54(4): 399–433.

From, Sarah B. 2008. "When Mom Is Away: Supporting the Families of Incarcerated Mothers." *CW360°: A Comprehensive Look at a Prevalent Child Welfare Issue* (spring): 19.

Gabbidon, Shaun L. 2010. *Race, Ethnicity, Crime, and Justice: An International Dilemma.* Thousand Oaks, CA: SAGE Publications.

Gabel, Stewart. 1992. "Behavioral Problems in Sons of Incarcerated or Otherwise Absent Fathers: The Issue of Separation." *Family Process* 31(3): 303–14.

Glaze, Lauren E., and Laura M. Maruschak. 2008. *Parents in Prison and Their Minor Children.* NCJ 222984. Washington, DC: U.S. Department of Justice, Bureau of Justice Statistics.

Greene, Beverly. 1995. "African American Families: A Legacy of Vulnerability and Resilience." *National Forum* 75(3): 29–32.

Hairston, Creasie Finney. 1999. "Kinship Care When Parents Are Incarcerated." In *Kinship Care: Improving Practice through Research,* edited by James P. Glesson and Creasie Finney Hairston (189–214). Washington, DC: CWLA Press.

———. 2008. "Children with Parents in Prison: Child Welfare Matters." *CW360°: A Comprehensive Look at a Prevalent Child Welfare Issue* (spring): 4.

Hairston, Creasie Finney, and James Rollins. 2003. "Social Capital and Family Connections." *Women, Girls, and Criminal Justice* 4(5): 67–68, 76.

Hanlon, Thomas E., Robert J. Blatchley, Terry Bennett-Sears, Kevin E. Grady, Marc Rose, and Jason M. Callaman. 2005. "Vulnerability of Children of Incarcerated Addicted Mothers: Implications for Preventative Interventions." *Children and Youth Services Review* 27:67–84.

Harris, Marian S., and Wanda Hackett. 2008. "Decision Points in Child Welfare: An Action Research Model to Address Disproportionality." *Children and Youth Services Review* 30:199–215.

Harrison, Paige M., and Allen J. Beck. 2006. "Prison and Jail Inmates at Midyear 2005." NCJ 213133. Washington, DC: U.S. Department of Justice, Bureau of Justice Statistics.

Hayward, Anna R., and Diana Depanfilis. 2007. "Foster Children with an Incarcerated Parent: Predictors of Reunification." *Children and Youth Services Review* 29(10): 1320–34.

Healey, Joseph F., and Eileen T. O'Brien. 2004. *Race, Ethnicity, and Gender.* Thousand Oaks, CA: SAGE Publications.

Hill, Robert B. 2006. *Synthesis of Research on Disproportionality in Child Welfare: An Update.* Washington, DC: Casey Alliance on Racial Equity.

Hill, Robert B., Sondra Jackson, and Kahatib Waheed. 2008. "Reducing Racial and Ethnic Disproportionality and Disparities in Child Welfare: Promoting Racial Equity." Presentation at the joint meeting on adolescent treatment effectiveness, Washington, D.C.

Human Rights Watch. 2002. "Race and Incarceration in the United States." Press backgrounder. Washington, DC: Human Rights Watch.

Jacobs, Ann. 2001. "Give 'em a Fighting Chance: Women Offenders Re-enter Society." *Criminal Justice* 16(1): 44.

Johnson, Elizabeth, and Jane Waldfogel. 2008. "Trends in Parental Incarceration and Implications for Child Welfare." *CW360°: A Comprehensive Look at a Prevalent Child Welfare Issue* (spring): 6–7.

Johnston, Denise. 1995. "Effects of Parental Incarceration." In *Children of Incarcerated Parents,* edited by Katherine Gabel and Denise Johnston (59–88). New York: Lexington Books.

Mays, Vickie M., Susan D. Cochran, and Ninez A. Ponce. 2004. "Thinking about Race and Ethnicity in Population-Based Studies of Health." In *Race and Research: Perspectives on Minority Participation in Health Studies,* edited by Bettina M. Beech and Maurine Goodman (79–100). Washington, DC: American Public Health Association.

McCullough-Chavis, Annie, and Cheryl Waites. 2004. "Genograms with African American Families: Considering Cultural Context." *Journal of Family Social Work* 8(2): 1–19.

McMahon, Susan D., and Roderick J. Watts. 2002. "Ethnic Identity in Urban African American Youth: Exploring Links with Self-Worth, Aggression, and Other Psychosocial Variables." *Journal of Community Psychology* 30(4): 411–31.

Miller, Keva M. 2007. "Risk and Resilience among African American Children of Incarcerated Parents." *Journal of Human Behavior in the Social Environment* 15(2/3): 25–37.

Mumola, Christopher J. 2000. *Incarcerated Parents and Their Children.* NCJ 182335. Washington, DC: U.S. Department of Justice, Bureau of Justice Statistics.

Murray, Joseph, and David P. Farrington. 2005. "Parental Imprisonment: Effects on Boys' Antisocial Behaviour and Delinquency through the Life Course." *Journal of Child Psychology and Psychiatry* 46(12): 1269–78.

———. 2008. "Parental Imprisonment: Long-Term Effects on Boys' Internalizing Problems through the Life Course." *Development & Psychopathology* 20:273–90.

Murry, Velma M., Emilie P. Smith, and Nancy E. Hill. 2001. "Race, Ethnicity, and Culture in Studies of Families in Context." *Journal of Marriage and Family* 63:911–14.

Murry, Velma M., P. Adama Brown, Gene H. Brody, Carolyn E. Cutrona, and Ronald L. Simons. 2001. "Racial Discrimination as a Moderator of the Links among Stress, Maternal Psychological Functioning, and Family Relationships." *Journal of Marriage and Family* 63:915–26.

Myers, Barbara, Tina M. Smarsh, Kristine Amlund-Hagen, and Suzanne Kennon. 1999. "Children of Incarcerated Mothers." *Journal of Child and Family Studies* 8:11–25.

Phillips, Susan D., Barbara J. Burns, H. Ryan Wagner, and Richard P. Barth. 2004. "Parental Arrest and Children Involved with Child Welfare Services Agencies." *American Journal of Orthopsychiatry* 74(2): 174–86.

Phillips, Susan D., Barbara J. Burns, H. Ryan Wagner, Teresa L. Kramer, and James M. Robbins. 2002. "Parental Incarceration among Adolescents Receiving Mental Health Services." *Journal of Child and Family Studies* 11(4): 385–99.

Phillips, Susan D., Alaattin Erkanli, Gordon P. Keeler, E. Jane Costello, and Adrian Angold. 2006. "Disentangling the Risks: Parent Criminal Justice Involvement and Children's Exposure to Family Risks." *Criminology and Public Policy* 5(4): 677–702.

Poehlmann, Julie. 2005a. "Children's Family Environments and Intellectual Outcomes during Maternal Incarceration." *Journal of Marriage and Family* 67:1275–85.

———. 2005b. "Representations of Attachment Relationships in Children of Incarcerated Mothers." *Child Development* 76:679–96.

Porterfield, Jeff, Paula Dressel, and Sandra Barnhill. 2000. "Special Situations of Incarcerated Parents." In *To Grandmother's House We Go and Stay: Perspectives on Custodial Grandparents,* edited by Carole B. Cox (184–202). New York: Springer Publishing Company.

Romper, R. H., and D. J. Pence. 1999. "Critical Race Theory in Social Justice." In *Social Justice/Criminal Justice: The Maturation of Critical Theory in Law, Crime, and Deviance,* edited by Bruce A. Arrigo. Belmont CA: West/Wadsworth.

Runyan, Desmond K., Wanda M. Hunter, Rebecca R. S. Socolar, Lisa Amaya-Jackson, Diana English, John Landsverk, Howard Dubowitz, Dorothy H. Browne, Shrikant I. Bangidiwala, and Ravi M. Mathew. 1998. "Children Who Prosper in Unfavorable Environments: The Relationship to Social Capital." *Pediatrics* 101:12–18.

Sabol, William J., Heather C. West, and Matthew Cooper. 2009. *Prisoners in 2008.* NCJ 228417. Washington, DC: U.S. Department of Justice, Bureau of Justice Statistics.

Sanchez, Gina, Michelle Batchelder, and Ruth McRoy. 1998. *African Americans: Cultural Diversity Curriculum for Social Workers and Health Practitioners.* Austin: Texas Department of Health.

Smith, Carrie J., and Diane S. Young. 2003. "The Multiple of TANF, ASFA, and Mandatory Drug Sentencing for Families Affected by Maternal Incarceration." *Children and Youth Services Review* 25(7): 535–52.

Swann, Christopher A., and Michelle Sheran Sylvester. 2006. "The Foster Care Crisis: What Caused Caseloads to Grow?" *Demography* 43(2): 309–35.

Swisher, Raymond R., and Maureen R. Waller. 2008. "Confining Fatherhood: Incarceration and Paternal Involvement among Unmarried White, African American, and Latino Fathers." *Journal of Family Issues* 29(8): 1067–88.

Takaki, Ronald. 1993. *A Different Mirror: A History of Multicultural America.* New York: Back Bay Books/Little, Brown and Company.

The Sentencing Project. 2009. *Federal Crack Cocaine Sentencing.* Washington, DC: The Sentencing Project.

Thomas, Anita J., and Sara Schwarzbaum. 2006. *Culture & Identity: Life Stories for Counselors and Therapists.* Thousand Oaks, CA: SAGE Publications.

Walsh, Froma. 1998. *Strengthening Family Resilience.* New York: Guilford Press.

Werner, Emily E., and Ruth S. Smith. 1992. *Overcoming the Odds: High-Risk Children from Birth to Adulthood.* New York: Cornell University Press.

Western, Bruce, and Christopher Wildeman. 2009. "The Black Family and Mass Incarceration." *Annals of the American Academy of Political and Social Science* 621: 221–42.

Western States Center 2003. *Dismantling Racism: A Resource Book for Social Change Groups.* Portland, OR: Western States Center.

Wells, Susan J., and Meredith Daniels. 2008. "Racial Disparities in Child Welfare." *CW360°: A Comprehensive Look at a Prevalent Child Welfare Issue* (spring): 13.

PART III
Intervention Research

9

Interventions within Prison Nurseries

Mary W. Byrne

The concept of a prison nursery is contradictory. Hearing about this phenomenon can conjure up the frequently used and inaccurate media notion of "babies behind bars" (Brodie 1982),[1] with the suggestion that infants who live with their mothers in prison are being concurrently punished. This impression is reinforced by the paucity of information available about prison nurseries, with reports scattered across disciplines and comprising largely anecdotal content. The scholarly literature on this topic is nascent.

This chapter presents historical and international perspectives on prison nurseries. It provides a contextual overview, within which the scant literature addressing prison nurseries is synthesized. The chapter also identifies results from the sparse outcome studies that exist and assesses the potential of the nursery as an intervention and policy direction in the United States.

Historical and International Overview: What Is Known about Prison Nurseries

What is a prison nursery? There are variations, but essentially it is a setting within a criminal justice facility where incarcerated pregnant women can reside following delivery and be the primary caregivers for their newborn infants while also fulfilling their prisoner role and penal sentences. Since the 1800s there have been records of U.S. children living with their incarcerated mothers, frequently under conditions of deprivation and suffering as documented by the philanthropic reformer Elizabeth Fry (Ryder 1884; see Craig 2009 for review). Gender and racial inequalities in society and its penal systems continue to taint contemporary programs (Vainik 2008). Today, an unknown number of incarcerated women live with their infants and children in prison nursery settings throughout the world, and a relatively minuscule number do so in the United States.

The National Alliance of Nongovernmental Organizations (NGOs) on Crime Prevention and Criminal Justice conducted the most recent multinational survey of programs for incarcerated women with infants (Weintraub 1987). Of the 70 nations responding, only four had a policy of customarily separating children from their imprisoned mothers: the Bahamas, Liberia, Suriname, and the United States. A 1999 collection of essays highlighted the comparative issues of women imprisoned in the United States, Canada, England, New Zealand, Poland, and Thailand (Cook and Davies 1999). Together the papers identified these diverse populations as universally neglected and invisible to society. A common theme for women prisoners was their interrupted role as mothers and their painful concerns for their children's welfare, whether coresiding or separated.

None of these book-length reports concluded with a strong endorsement of prison coresidence for dependent children. The National Alliance of NGOs cautioned that keeping children with imprisoned mothers was psychologically harmful and sometimes physically inadequate, and it noted that children residing with mothers in prison served primarily as an alternative to child welfare in impoverished countries (Weintraub 1987). In addition to the four countries surveyed that did not routinely allow infants or children in prison, three others that legally permitted children in prison (New Zealand, Ireland, and Luxembourg) actively discouraged the practice. The National Alliance of NGOs recommended institutionalization alternatives for the mother whenever feasible and facilities separated from the incarcerated general population for children who did have to stay inside prison communities. This is in keeping with the counsel of the United Nations Committee on the Rights of the Child (2006), which has emphasized the best interest of the child in decisionmaking regarding placement of children in prison with their mothers and cautioned about unmet needs for adequate facilities, connections to the outside environment, and preparation for eventual separations.

Nevertheless, in individual countries, prison nursery programs have persisted and advocates have attempted to develop supportive resources. Available reports provide limited information from Europe, the United States, Australia, and New Zealand, with even less circulated from Africa, Asia, and Central or South America. Following extensive fact-finding efforts, the Women's Prison Association (WPA) Institute on Women and Criminal Justice described international practices briefly in an appendix to a national report that included small amounts of information on prison nurseries in Canada, Germany, Iceland, Ghana, India, Egypt, Mexico, and Chile (WPA 2009).

Longer reports for selected countries can be pieced together from both published literature and nontraditional sources, including Quaker United Nations Office reports (Quaker Council for European Affairs 2007; Robertson 2008), the Internet, graphic arts exhibits, and personal networking. In Germany, for example, a century-old maximum security prison for women in Preungesheim offers what has been hailed as the most comprehensive program in the world for imprisoned women and their children (Kauffman 2001; Robertson 2008). Mothers are divided by security risk categories into two groups with infants and children up to 3 years old, one confined to the prison grounds and the other with "open house" access to the adjoining Frankfurt community. Children receive prison-based or community day care while mothers participate in prison programs or employment. During the work-release phase, mothers can spend time with their children of all ages in their homes in the city and return to prison at night. Spain also maintains programs for incarcerated women and children through age 3 (Jiménez and Palacios 2003). Convicted women choose whether to take infants and young children into prison with them or leave them in the care of others. Two prison options are provided: "mother centers" in prisons or, for women nearing the end of their sentences, dependent units in open residences integrated in the community. Because their experiences have been documented by international photographer Diana Matar, it is known that families, including children, can opt to live with an incarcerated adult in some prisons in Mexico. Visual evidence for life experiences of mothers and children in states with and without prison nurseries have also been memorialized by an Oregon videographer (Jacobs 2008) and a midwife/photographer from Washington State.[2] In New Zealand, the Roper Committee recommended in 1989 that when the imprisoned mother was the sole caregiver, children up to the age of 2 should be kept with her in a nursery unit

(Morris and Kinghi 1999). For many years, the policy allowed for co-residence until the infant was age 6 to 9 months. It was not until 2008 that the political climate supported a legislative extension to two years, but the Family Help Trust reports the funding to support this change was still not approved by the end of 2009.[3]

In the United States, the New York State Department of Correctional Services prison nursery program is in a maximum-security facility as old as that of the German program. In 1990, the program was expanded to include an adjacent medium-security facility. Its history since 1901 has evolved from placement in a reformatory to incorporation into the highest security facility established later at the same location. It is the longest continually operated prison nursery program in the United States.

In the U.S. penal system, the reformatory movement in the early 1900s included establishment of cottage units where children could live with their mothers up to age 2. Such units existed in several states and in one federal prison for women (Alderson, West Virginia) from 1930 to the 1960s (Craig 2009). Responses from 70 institutions to a mid-century national survey revealed that the 13 states with statutory provisions governing children born to inmates all allowed these children to remain with their mothers for up to two years (Shepard and Zemans 1950). Over the next two decades, prison nursery programs closed until only one, in New York, remained (Boudouris 1983; Morton and Williams 1998). Reasons cited for closing included prison security and management, liability, and concerns about child development and separation (Radosh 1988). Ironically, during this period of general decline in prison nursery programs nationwide, New York State made dramatic, developmentally oriented changes in its prison nursery environment. Under the direction of a dynamic civilian contractee, Elaine Roulet, the New York State prison program developed a children's center in the 1970s with comprehensive distance parenting activities and community ties (Roulet, O'Rourke, and Reichers 1993).

With the approach of the 21st century, several trends converged to promote renewed development of prison nurseries (Goshin and Byrne 2009). A dramatic upswing in female incarceration was outpacing that of men (Belknap 2007; Mumola 2000) and associated with strict drug trafficking laws (Snell and Morton 1994). Societal support swelled for toughness on crime (Acoca and Raeder 1999; Belknap 2007). Yet, increasing advocacy was building identifying children with incarcerated parents as a vulnerable and unrecognized group in need of multiple social services (Bloom 1993, 1995; Gabel and Johnston 1995). At the same time, corrections departments and legislators were newly interested in reentry transition projects aimed at preventing criminal recidivism (National Institute of Justice 2005).

These events coalesced to create a slow upward trend in reintroduction of state prison nurseries. Nebraska added a nursery program in 1994 (Carlson 1998); South Dakota, Massachusetts, Montana, Ohio, and Washington did so by 2001 (Pollock 2002). As of 2009, there are nine prison nurseries in eight states (California, Indiana, Illinois, Nebraska, New York, Ohio, South Dakota, and Washington; see WPA 2009), with legislation passed for a future nursery in West Virginia.[4] In addition, there are an unknown number of jail-based residential mother-baby programs; the Rose M. Singer Center at the Rikers Island jail in New York City may be the best known and is the only one named in the WPA (2009) national report of criminal justice facilities for women with children.

The Federal Bureau of Prisons (BOP) has been acclaimed for the clearest standards among correctional systems for accommodating the special health care needs of female prisoners (Fearn and Parker 2004), but there has not been a federal prison nursery since 1960. In the mid-1980s, BOP created the Mother and Infant Nurturing Together program for pregnant inmates who could be transferred to contracted community residences following birth and remain with their infants for up to three months, at which time the mothers would give up their infants to the custody of someone they had previously designated in the community. The National Association of Women Judges (2007) is advocating for new legislation to support reintroducing prison nurseries into the federal system (Byrne 2008).

Measured Outcomes for Prison Nurseries

Despite the long history of children residing inside prisons, there has been little effort toward measuring outcomes in prison nurseries. Rather, this history has been largely invisible, with few official records kept on children in prison settings. Programs have emerged and been discontinued erratically with little report of aims and content from which outcomes could be evaluated. Additionally, prison nursery programs have not been consistently designated or designed as interventions, although typically assumptions have been made that they will improve infant-mother relationships and reduce criminal recidivism (Byrne, Goshin, and Joestl 2010). These assumptions are only recently being tested.

Spitz's Findings

Unfortunately, one of the oldest scientific outcome studies that included infants raised in prison nurseries has been largely ignored because these children served as controls. The much-heralded work of psychoanalyst René Spitz brought to light the severe depression and developmental delays that resulted for children reared in institutions (Spitz 1945). Spitz documented that even when physical needs were adequately met, impersonal care imposed "hospitalism syndrome" on institutionalized children, while those reared by their mothers in a prison nursery thrived on the attention lavished on them (Spitz 1956). While improvements in hospitals and orphanages came to the fore following this study, the significance of the positive outcomes for the control infants' development was lost.

Inmate Observations from Federal and State Nurseries

Interestingly, the most detailed reports of daily life for women and children in prison have been those of former women prisoners who observed children in prison and wrote books about them. Elizabeth Flynn, a communist labor organizer confined to the Alderson federal prison in West Virginia from 1955 to 1957, wrote that the daily mothering of the babies coresiding in cottages evoked a humanizing effect on both inmates and staff (Flynn 1963). She also described the overwhelming grief experienced by these mothers when their infants were removed at the mandatory age of a few months, and she advocated for longer coresidence. Two decades later, Jean Harris, headmistress of a prestigious academy for girls and focus of media attention for the murder of her lover,[5] was sentenced to the Bedford Hills Correctional Facility in New York State. During her incarceration, she spent years assisting and observing in the prison children's center and infant day care setting, and she later wrote a book and articles describing the women and children she came to know. She highlighted the women's many hardships on the path to prison, recalled Spitz's insights on care patterns, and advocated for more funding for prison nurseries (Harris 1988, 1993).

Survey Reports

Survey methods have also been used to catalog prison- and jail-based parenting programs ranging from adult classes to mother-infant prison nursery arrangements (Boudouris 1983; Shepard and Zemens 1950; Weintraub 1987). Boudouris (1983) surveyed all types of programs for incarcerated mothers and their children in 55 correctional institutions in all 50 states, representing a total population of 14,610 women. He concluded that it was not clear whether having children reside within correctional institutions was either good or bad for the children, inmates, or institution. In 1988, Radosh published a survey of programs established by state legislatures for incarcerated mothers' in-house care of their children and noted that the vast majority of imprisoned women had children outside the prison walls, with a considerable portion in the infancy to preschool ages (Radosh 1988). More recently, Pollock's (2002) national survey of prison-based parenting programs noted the range from adult classes lasting a few hours to a small number of long-term prison nurseries and called for more programs. The WPA's recent catalogue of current national prison nursery and community-based residential parenting programs for criminal justice–involved mothers shows little increase.

Studies Based on Interviews, Official Records, and External Observer Reports

More formal studies addressing prison nursery outcomes have used interviews as the primary study methodology, sometimes combined with observation or administrative records. Baunach (1985) used interviews and observations to understand the effects on mother-infant relationships achieved by community-linked programs (alternatives to prison nurseries) for pregnant inmates in two sites: Daniel Boone Career Development Center in Kentucky and Purdy Treatment Center for Women in Washington State. She also interviewed women participants from three prisons, staff, and community foster mothers. Again, the overriding theme was the inevitable separation layered on maternal feelings of loss, failure, guilt, bitterness, and stigma. Baunach also addressed legal termination of parental rights on the basis of equating incarceration to voluntary abandonment as held in *In re Jameson* versus the views of Palmer (1972 as cited in Baunach 1985), who recommended legislative reform encompassing protection for incarcerated mothers to live with their children through age 2; community release programs, making it possible for mothers to live with their children outside prison; and restructured visiting rooms, where dependent children can interact with mothers in a fashion free from blatant security oversight.

Gabel and Girard (1995) reported results of interviews with a convenience sample of the 26 women who could be accessed in the New York State prison nurseries at Bedford Hills and Taconic Correctional Facilities. In contrast with mothers in the previously cited studies who were separated early from their infants, these women expressed that the coresidence program provided them with a sense of bonding, improved parenting skills, and self-respect, although they complained about crowding, lack of privacy, and negative interactions with some corrections officers and staff. The authors' conclusion that a lack of research on prison nurseries made it impossible to argue either for or against such programs echoed the conclusions of Boudouris (1983) a decade earlier.

Pennix (1999) later reported impressions of incarcerated mothers in the federal prison system. Based on interviews with 100 women imprisoned from the 1970s through the 1990s, Pennix discovered that the women valued the Alderson Federal prison program, Linking Inmate Families Together, which provided parenting education, a visiting room, and social service assistance with child custody problems. Every mother interviewed cited the agony of being separated from her children and the resulting emotional turmoil, including shame, depression, anger, sorrow, and rejection, along with an overwhelming fear that children would never understand the separation.

Enos (2001) developed a carefully constructed grounded theory of mothering from prison through extensively interviewing women incarcerated without their children in Rhode Island. These women continued psychological strategies begun before arrest in which they separated their mother-identity from their criminal, substance-abusing, or other socially unacceptable identities. They highly valued their children and the maternal role but engaged in role reversal in which their children were perceived as critical resources and a last hope. Pregnant inmates looked to the potential redemptive value of their unborn children. Mothers with a history of forced separation from their young children reported that they did not feel any maternal connection with those offspring.

As a graduate student Schehr (2004) conducted extensive field journaling based on participant observations over several months with 23 women in a prison nursery. Eight years later, she found 10 of these women and selected for extensive interviews three whom she deemed best able to reflect on the effects of the prison nursery. Analyses included writing a poem that synthesized each woman's experience as well as extensive qualitative analyses from which emerged the meta-themes of safety, affiliation, change, and resilience. All women had to struggle against major reentry challenges related to housing, child care, and family relationships, and even years later they reported longing to reconnect with their previously supportive peers in the nursery program and with the nursery manager.

Descriptive Reports and Process Analyses

Evaluation studies have been published for three of the more recently established prison nursery programs. In Nebraska, Carlson (1998, 2001, 2009) described that state's prison nursery near its outset and conducted five-year and ten-year reviews when 42 and 65 participants, respectively, had completed the program. Consistent outcomes included reductions in prison misconduct reports and subsequent recidivism. In the five-year review, misconduct reports declined 13 percent, comparing the time participants resided in the general population versus their time in the nursery; misconduct was less for the ten-year review but could only be made by self-report. Criminal recidivism, defined as conviction for a new crime within three years of release, was 9 percent versus 33 percent in the five-year review and 17 percent versus 50 percent in the ten-year review, comparing cohorts of nursery participants with pregnant inmates who were separated from their infants during the four years before establishment of the nursery. Detailed expenditures were reported and compared favorably with the state's foster-care cost estimates. Similar to the earlier New York sample described by Gabel and Girard (1995), the women avowed that the prison nursery brought them closer to their infants with whom they anticipated a lifelong relationship. However, at the five-year review, only 57 percent of the mothers actually retained post-release custody of their children (Carlson 2001), and by the ten-year review, the investigator found it impossible to maintain contact to determine maternal custody (Carlson 2009). The earlier report is comparable to the New York estimates of 62 percent maternal custody for 37 participants for whom records could be located three years following release from the Taconic Correctional Facility prison nursery program (State of New York Department of Correctional Services 2002).

Kauffman (2002) described and analyzed an early stage of the prison nursery opened at the Ohio Reformatory for Women in 2001 and intended for healthy pregnant inmates with short sentences and nonviolent crimes. Relying on reports of nurseries with longer histories, Kauffman maintained that the presence of infants contributed to a sense of well-being for staff and inmates and predicted that the Ohio program would run smoothly and result in lower recidivism rates than those of the general population. These expectations were repeated in a corrections online journal ("Ohio Baby Program" 2003). After 55 women had completed the program, a corrections internal report, based on a comprehensive inspection, partly substantiated the early predictions and highly praised the environmental cleanliness, the child development resources in the Achieving Baby Care Success program, and the community links consistent with the program's parallel universe strategy, which premises that life inside prison should mirror life outside (Correctional Institution Inspection Committee 2005).

Five years after the Residential Parenting Program opened in the Washington Correctional Center for Women in 1999, Fearn and Parker (2004) conducted an extensive process analysis of the approximately 90 dyads that had completed the program. They described the community partnerships established by the prison system to help the program meet prenatal health needs, build positive mother-child relationships, and serve as a bridge to community services that would facilitate reentry resources and success for the women and their children. Despite the length and detail in Fearn and Parker's report, they lacked sufficient information to determine whether the program resulted in reduced criminal recidivism or increased successful postrelease family relationships.

Infant and Child Developmental Outcomes Studies

Children's outcomes following their stays in prison nursery programs were not directly addressed again from the time of Spitz's (1956) control group results until recently. Perhaps the most widely quoted, and often misquoted, study of children's outcomes for a prison nursery sample is the one conducted by Liza Catan in the United Kingdom (Catan 1988, 1992). In two mother-baby units for incarcerated women and their infants, Catan assessed 74 children during stays averaging 13 weeks and compared them with 33 control children whose imprisoned mothers chose to have the child cared for in the community by family members or the foster care system. Scores on the Griffith mental development scale were comparable between groups at baseline but had significantly declined in motor and cognitive domains by 4 months of age for the babies in the prison units. This was attributed to inadequate opportunity for developmental stimulation, and the report apparently led to environmental and protocol changes in the units, although details have not been published in peer-reviewed professional literature (Her Majesty's Prison Service 2007). When the American Medical Association conducted a scientific review of bonding programs for women prisoners and newborns, they incorrectly concluded that Catan's study had demonstrated inadequate infant-mother attachment, although Catan did not assess this variable.

The Spanish ministries for social service and internal affairs commissioned a study carried out by Seville University to discover the developmental level of children brought up in that country's prisons and the quality of stimulation the children received (Jiménez and Palacios 1998, 2003). Scores on the Brunet-Lezine scale (Josse 1997) showed development similar to the community infant population, but the Home Observation for Measurement of the Environment (HOME; see Bradley and Caldwell 1978) indicated concerns about provision of play materials and varied experiences. Further, infants who had low HOME scores experienced a significant drop in developmental quotients after 18 months of age. Similar to the UK study, suggestions for improvement targeted environmental changes that should be made in the prison setting. For the infants in the UK study, Catan had recommended more opportunity for motor activity and less time restrained in baby carriages. For the older infants and toddlers in the Spain study, Jiménez and Palacios recommended training in child development for the predominantly low-education mothers, improved prison nursery school programs, and integrated community experiences.

Studies in New York State Prison Nursery System Conducted by a Visiting Scientist

In 2000, I initiated a program of research assessing both the maternal and child outcomes of the prison nursery program in New York State.[6] Ethnographic and cross-sectional studies were followed by a longitudinal study that extended from nursery admission through length of nursery stay and the infants' first reentry year. Multiple methods and measures were employed, including participant observation, interviews, videotaping, questionnaires, prison records, child development assessments using the Bayley Scales of Infant Development (Bayley 1993), and inter-generational attachment measures using the Adult Attachment Interview (AAI)[7] and the Strange Situation Procedure (SSP; see Ainsworth et al. 1978). Ethnographic methodologies (Spradley 1979, 1980) were used to define a theory tentatively called "claiming the parenting self," a long-term process moving through self-construction stages of identification, nourishment, and integration. This section summarizes the findings from these studies.[8]

In the exploratory, cross-sectional study, 58 mothers with 60 infants were recruited across two years. Participants completed a battery of well-established questionnaires and a private interview, and permitted me to conduct developmental assessments of their infants. Attachment and separation were key areas of concern expressed by the mothers. Mothers focused on these issues so much that the family history originally placed at the beginning of the interview was moved to a later point in the protocol, so trust and empathy could be established before the mothers' sorrow was evoked.

Mothers reported good physical but worrisome mental health as measured by the Medical Outcomes Study Short Form 36 (see Ware, Kosinski, and Gandek 2000) and the Center for Epidemiologic Studies Depression Scale (see Radloff 1977). Unanticipated high levels of self-esteem (Self-Esteem Scale; see Rosenberg 1964) and existential well-being (Spiritual Well-Being Scale; see Paloutzian and Ellison 1982) were also reported, as well as self-perceptions of highly valuing the parent role and parenting competence (Parent Sense of Competency; see Gibaud-Wallston 1977). The latter finding contrasted with observed knowledge gaps in parenting, particularly around child development at age 6 months and older. For all infants, developmental screening indicated performance appropriate for age (Denver Developmental Screening Test, see Frankenberg and Dodds 1992; CAT-CLAMS, see Capute and Accardo 1996; Early Language Milestones, see Coplan 1993). Motor skills were more advanced than verbal skills, however, and there was some suggestion of borderline language competencies for a small number of older infants.

First Longitudinal Study of Mother and Child Prison Nursery Outcomes

Subsequently, a National Institutes of Health–funded longitudinal study of maternal and child outcomes was conducted with 97 consenting nursery participants and their 100 infants living together in the New York

State Department of Correctional Services prison nursery program at Bedford Hills Correctional Facility and Taconic Correctional Facility.[9] An intervention design was used, adding tailored nurse practitioner visits to the parenting education and infant day care resources already present in the nursery. A two-group positive control experiment was used. Participants were assigned to one of two treatment arms emphasizing either child health or mother-infant relationship synchrony, and each was compared against normative standards. All study participants received weekly visits from a nurse practitioner on the research team and biweekly telephone calls and mailings during the first reentry year.

Legal and ethical constraints made it impossible to randomize imprisoned women to an experimental and true control group and will continue to do so through the foreseeable future. Statute 611 under Article 21 of the New York State Criminal Law provides that pregnant incarcerated women can live with their newborns.[10] Applications are screened within the facility for eligibility based on no history of child-related crimes, no violent crimes, and satisfactory discipline record during incarceration, with the latter two conditions sometimes waived on a mother's appeal of her denied application. Acceptance to the program and any subsequent removal are ultimately determined by the prison administrators in accord with the current provisions of statute 611. All determinations for inclusion are made before the mother's return from the birthing site. There are no waiting lists or later admissions of community-born infants. Altering selection of women by randomization would deny their legal rights as well as unethically impose maternal separation on randomly selected control infants and, therefore, was not done.

Based on scores on the AAI completed at time of nursery (and study) entry, two-thirds of the mothers in the prison nursery intervention study had internalized insecure attachment representations with their own parent figures, the inverse of profiles found in low-risk community samples (Borelli et al. 2010). For the infants available for the SSP starting at age 1 (the earliest that the SSP can be conducted), 75 percent who lived a full year in the prison nursery were classified as securely attached to their mothers (Byrne, Goshin, and Joestl 2010). Strikingly, only 25 percent of these mothers had been coded autonomous (secure) on the AAI at time of prison nursery entry. Compared with meta-analyzed samples using the SSP (Van IJzendoorn, Schuengel, and Bakersman-Kranenburg 1999), this proportion of secure infants was similar to 15 U.S. low-risk community samples and significantly higher than many high-risk samples, including

7 samples in low-socioeconomic studies, 9 in studies with maternal depression, 4 with parental substance abuse, and 5 with maternal maltreatment. Thus, the research suggests the intervention facilitated maternal change, making it possible for women who had not previously internalized security to raise infants in the nursery who were securely attached. For these infants, who will encounter multiple maternal and environmental stress factors, infant secure attachment would be expected to provide a measure of resilience over time (Sroufe 2005).

Infants' development was assessed with the Bayley Scales of Infant Development every three months in prison. Twice during the reentry year, children's development was measured either in the research office using the Bayley Scales or with the Ages and Stages Questionnaire (see Squires, Potter, and Bricker 1999) completed by the mother or alternate caregiver. At all ages tested from 3 to 24 months, children met the appropriate developmental milestones for mental and motor domains. However, nine children, all from the health treatment arm, demonstrated measured lags in the behavioral domain during the toddler year when tested at 15 to 24 months. All were successfully referred to their community's early intervention program for further evaluation.

The nursing intervention was continued after release by mail and phone contact, and 76 infants and caregivers were successfully followed throughout the entire first reentry year. Children transferred to alternate caregivers while mothers completed the remainder of their sentences showed signs of child dysregulation, exhibited as changes in sleeping and eating patterns and excessive crying. However, when there was only one primary alternate caregiver during this interim, these issues resolved in three to four weeks. Of greater concern was persistent regression associated with separations abruptly initiated by the corrections system and with those that resulted in multiple shifts in caregivers.

Criminal recidivism for mothers in the prison nursery intervention who were followed for one full reentry year was 10 percent for parole violations and 0 percent for new court convictions. Reentry challenges were many and resources few, with continuing concerns regarding employment, housing, relationships, and child care. Intervention advice was tailored to meet individual needs, the most common of which were child behavioral concerns, locating community services, and social isolation. Similar to findings from previously discussed qualitative studies, many women wished they could have contact during reentry with selected nursery peers—the few women they had met and befriended inside the prison nursery. Mothers and alternate caregivers volunteered multiple unsolicited endorsements of the experimental nursing intervention conducted in prison and continued during reentry. The prison program has now initiated a similar telephone support outreach for mothers returning from the nursery to the community.

Some differential effects between the two treatment arms match theoretical expectations. Infant and toddler behavioral competencies were measurably of concern only in a subset of families who participated in the health arm of the intervention. More mothers who participated in the synchrony arm of the intervention overcame their own insecure attachment representations to raise secure infants. Mothers in both the health and synchrony intervention arms showed increased maternal sensitivity, responsiveness and contingency, child care knowledge, and sense of parent competency from entry to completion of the nursery program. Future analyses comparing cross-sectional and longitudinal outcomes will partially answer which outcomes can be attributed to the prison nursery routines alone or to the program as enhanced by the NP intervention. Anticipated changes in one large New York county's sentencing procedures may make it possible to randomize such maternal-infant dyads to a prison nursery or alternative community facility, but the legal underpinning for such a plan remains tentative (Byrne et al. 2007). Descriptive comparative studies contrasting outcomes between states with and without prison nurseries are a more likely although less rigorous design option for future studies.

Additional Attachment-Based Research with Criminal Justice–Involved Mothers

In addition to this author's research focusing on infant-mother attachment in a prison nursery setting, one other published study reports an attachment-based intervention with mothers coresiding with infants in a prison nursery. A small group program based on reflective assessment has been piloted in a UK mother-baby unit (Baradon et al. 2008). The psychoanalytic approach used trained therapists from the community who visited the units to conduct eight two-hour sessions on topics with evidence-based potential to activate the attachment relationship. The program encouraged these mothers to examine issues that critically affect their parenting. Their ability to reflect significantly improved ($p = 0.003$) as measured by Wilcoxon Signed Ranks one-tailed test of pre- and post-intervention reflective functioning codes (Fonagy et al. 1998), which were derived from transcripts of the Parent Development Interview.[11] While promising, one concern is that incarcerated women may not have the resources between intervention sessions within prison to confront and resolve all that has surfaced. Programs such as these require supportive mental health services as well as a safe therapeutic milieu, which may be challenging to create in the traditionally controlled prison environment.

Prison Nurseries as Interventions: Essential Components, Alternative Approaches, and Recommendations for Research and Policy

Research assessing outcomes in prison nursery settings is in its infancy, and much remains to be discovered. It is not even clear if all programs are truly interventions or if they are simply relatively safe prison coresidence alternatives to confinement with an incarcerated general population. Yet, prison nurseries potentially provide a rich opportunity to create a positive parenting and change environment for an otherwise vulnerable and hard-to-reach mother-baby population that has few alternative resources.

When the reports and studies available are considered together, some consensus can be inferred on the essential components for an effective nursery program (Byrne 2009). As sparse as the evidence is for positive maternal and child outcomes for nursery participants, the most persuasive evidence comes from programs that address the mothers' psychological issues and the infants' developmental needs, as well as reentry preparation and resources for both.

A coherent theoretical model is needed to guide prison nursery activities. Within whatever model used, essential program components include parenting support, provision of health resources, integrated substance abuse treatment, and fostering community ties, all within the context of gender specificity. More than 10 years ago, it was argued that successful rehabilitative programs in women's prisons had to include both strong female role models and development of supportive peer networks (Morash, Bynum, and Koons 1998). These goals are challenging but not impossible in a hierarchical environment established around control and punishment. For example, a former long-term prisoner shared how she and an incarcerated peer successfully co-facilitated psychosocial groups to examine and improve mothering while imprisoned (Boudin 1998). Peer support can be similarly fostered in the nursery setting and facilitated in reentry through changes in policy allowing women who shared nursery time to communicate with each other following release.

Gender specificity encompasses recognizing that the needs of incarcerated women differ in key ways from those of their male counterparts. Gender regard needs to imbue occupational training, health care, mental health treatment (including substance abuse recovery), and reentry preparation. It is important to combine required care of children within prison nurseries with respite so mothers can engage in opportunities for education and occupational training. Incarcerated mothers need to prepare for the working mother role that they will inevitably have to play outside prison. Thirty percent of women in state prisons and 34 percent in federal prisons headed single-parent households before arrest (Mumola 2000) and can be expected to do so following reentry.

Reports of poor standards for perinatal care and general health care in prison have not changed appreciably over time (Amnesty International 1999, 2006; McCall, Casteel, and Shaw 1985; Sered and Norton-Hawk 2008; Siefert and Pimlott 2001; Vainik 2008), although health status is critical for parenting and optimum development of children. The Health Promoting Prison movement, which has influenced prison reform in 25 European countries and New Zealand (Whitehead 2006), has yet to change the United States. Substance abuse, often triggered by violent victimization and abuse, plays a strong role in many women's pathways to prison (DeHart 2008; Radosh 2002). As in the outside community, the recidivistic nature of addictive disease, the reliance on male-oriented prevention programs, and the failure to integrate programs with parenting issues (Shearer 2003) may explain recovery lapses even for women who are offered repeated prison-based substance abuse interventions.

Substance abuse recovery may especially benefit from criminal justice community partnerships. The California Department of Corrections and Rehabilitation (2009) reports that offenders who completed both in-prison and community follow-up substance abuse treatment programs showed substantially reduced return-to-custody rates, with striking drops for women (from 43.7 to 16.5 percent two years after release). But the data were admittedly biased by only including those who completed both programs.

Alternative community residential programs have also quantified success in recidivism and cost savings. Women and Infants at Risk, Summit

House, Hour Children, and Tamar's Children are four positive examples from different areas of the country.

In Michigan, the Women and Infants at Risk (WIAR) program was developed following a needs assessment conducted by social work students under the auspices of a city council. WIAR moved incarcerated pregnant women with substance abuse histories into community residences for pre-natal, postpartum, and infant care supervised by nurse midwives (Siefert and Pimlott 2001) in lieu of creating a prison nursery, which was opposed by corrections administrators. An evaluation conducted after 45 births over four years indicated birth outcomes superior to those that occurred during the needs assessment. Maternal relapse during the year after birth remained a problem, and the evaluators recommended funding a comprehensive after-care program.

In North Carolina, the Summit House prison alternative program offers comprehensive counseling, vocational, educational, and parenting services to substance-abusing women and their children. In 2009 it reported a three-year re-incarceration rate of 6.5 percent, compared with the state rate of 36.2 percent, and annual taxpayer savings approaching $750,000.[12] Hour Children in New York City has reported broad positive outcomes since 1995 for its program of multiple services to support and reunite incarcerated and formerly incarcerated women and their children.[13] Tamar's Children, a jail diversion program in Baltimore, offered wraparound social services and an adapted attachment-based Circle of Security program to selected women and children from 2001 to 2004.[14] Attachment outcomes are strikingly similar to those in the Byrne prison nursery study (Cassidy et al. 2010).

It is difficult to compare the effectiveness of alternative, multiservice programs to one another or to prison-based programs because they tend to report success following program completions but exclude outcomes of those who leave. Critical questions for future research are what predicts completion of effective programs, how those who complete them differ from those who do not, and how this information can be used to tailor interventions for individuals who have not succeeded. How to create integration and synergy across prison-based, reentry, and community-based efforts is also a critical question.

Linking prison programs to community agencies, as collaborators or as alternative options, seems logical and critical if imprisonment is to lead to successful reentry for child-rearing women. Incorporating outside health and social service expertise highlights attention to community standards.

Mental health consultants can provide relief to staff members who hold conflicting roles as advocates for both prisoners and the prison system (Silverman 2005). The development of working arrangements with invested external service professionals and interested scientists can provide not only precise, credible, research-based interventions but top-quality evaluations. To achieve such requires negotiations around such issues as access and collaborative strategies so historical suspicion and obstacles can be transcended (Byrne 2005; Zwerman and Gardner 1986).

There is now long-awaited data-based evidence that, at their best, prison nurseries foster positive mother-child relationships, optimum child development, and interruption of maternal criminal recidivism. These outcomes enhance the protective factors that contribute to resilience and balance risks for child-rearing women and their children. For such effective outcomes to occur, adequate resources are essential, such as those associated with the more successful programs described. Financing needs to be considered concurrently with enabling legislation. Programming within prison nurseries is enhanced by the input of civilian professionals who are keenly aware of community standards and are a valuable resource. Civilian relationships can be established through contracts for services, advisory boards, and volunteer programs.

Future policymaking related to prison nursery programs needs to incorporate a broad approach that encompasses these programs, creates links between prison-based and community-based services, and establishes community alternative programs for criminal justice–involved mothers. Prison nursery programs and their community alternatives should not exist in isolation from the events that precede women's incarceration and follow reentry. In a more ideal society, the need for prison nurseries would be largely negated by education in personal relationships and reproductive health that begins in childhood and by accessible community services that address substance abuse recovery, domestic violence, mental health, and employability for women. Meanwhile, the prison nursery provides a unique opportunity—and perhaps the only remaining one—to provide multiple needed services to a small but significant portion of underserved women and infants, and to do so at a time of unique susceptibility and readiness for change.

Yet the constraints of a punitive and authoritarian environment are difficult to overcome and may readily thwart programs oriented toward self-help and autonomy. Connections between prison-based and community programs can enhance behavioral change and provide a bridge for support during reentry. Alternative sentencing programs for some criminal justice–involved child-rearing women may offer an even more effective approach and a milieu that more closely matches community realities.

Considerable gaps in knowledge remain that must be filled to advance knowledge for prison nursery programs. Little is known about the comparative effectiveness of prison nurseries and community alternative programs or the populations for which each is appropriate. Criteria describing who should be admitted to a prison nursery are not empirically established and are a grave concern for criminal justice systems. Most nursery programs define their lowest risk populations as eligible participants: women with nonviolent crimes, short sentences, and no histories with child protective agencies. On the other hand, the women in this author's longitudinal study fit a higher risk criminal and psychosocial profile, consistent with those of most incarcerated mothers, and notably positive outcomes were measured.

The notion of providing services to all in need rather than those with the lowest risks could take the options a step further. Comprehensive therapeutic nurseries exist in the community for depressed and victimized mothers and for other families at risk for such problems as child abuse and neglect; while those with prison nursery experience have discussed this type of approach, it has not been formally attempted within corrections environments. Good decisions around eligibility and types of nurseries cannot be made until more is known about the outcomes of current programs. To advance this dialogue, common ground needs to be broken around the concept of risk. Correctional security risks, child welfare risks, and maternal psychosocial risks are different conversations that have not yet been shared across professions and systems.

Documenting outcomes of prison nurseries and related community alternative programs must continue. In the absence of randomized controlled trials, much can still be learned from descriptive comparative, longitudinal, and quasi-experimental approaches (Morgan and Winship 2007). Researchers should direct their efforts toward innovative design alternatives that offer strong causal inference, rigor, and feasibility for studying problems to which trials cannot be applied (Vaughan 2008; West et al. 2008).

Enhanced demographic recording and reporting within departments of corrections (DOC) would provide helpful baseline data that should be made available to researchers and policymakers while maintaining appropriate attention to privacy and confidentiality for both incarcerated mothers and their children. Allowing and facilitating research by external scientists who fully comply with legislative protections for human subjects and are experienced in study designs is the best way for DOCs and alternative community services to credibly measure their programs' maternal and child outcomes. Toward this end, positive and ongoing relationships between corrections departments with universities and with individual highly credentialed researchers are key to conducting research (Byrne 2005). While criminal justice systems are understandably interested in recidivism, learning more about broader maternal outcomes related to family roles and child development is equally important to understanding how to achieve reentry success.

Another aspect barely addressed is the influence of the nursery on prison personnel and culture. The comments on humanizing effects created by the presence of infants interacting with their mother were recorded by a prisoner a half-century ago (Flynn 1963) and have been echoed since. Mismatched values and priorities related to nurseries and their participants have been recorded among corrections administrators, officers, staff, and civilians as well as across these diverse groups but have been poorly explored. Understanding these differences and their impact can lead to design and evaluation of policies and continuing education programs for prison personnel aimed at achieving consistent and effective support for prison nursery coresidents.

Ultimately, the knowledge base required to inform research, policy, and practice concerning prison nurseries depends on an ethical foundation to which society should subscribe. While ostensibly removed from society, nursery participants are also part of society and are expected to return to the free community. Pathways to prison, experiences inside the prison, bridges to the outside community, and resumption of a meaningful place in that community are all parts of the journey that have ethical and societal implications. Quinney (1991) has long advocated for a peacemaking approach to the study of crime and its prevention based on consideration of all that has preceded the criminal act as well as the characteristics of the criminal and the crime and not just to retribution and punishment. Peacemaking principles are uniquely applicable to preventing child-rearing women's criminal activities, to addressing them when they occur, and to productively integrating convicted women and their children into society without increasing their cumulative painful life experiences (Radosh 2002). The peacemaking paradigm can inform current prison nursery systems aspiring to optimum effectiveness. It may also offer for the future a social environment capable of addressing women's criminal acts and their consequences for children through early prevention and long-term healing.

NOTES

1. See also Vicki Haddock, "Babies Behind Bars," *San Francisco Chronicle,* May 24, 2006, E1; and Lucius Lomax, "Babies Behind Bars," *Austin Chronicle,* July 26, 2004.

2. See Cheryl Hanna-Truscott, "Protective Custody: Within a Prison Nursery at the Washington Corrections Center for Women. Gallery," http://www.protectivecustody.org/gallery.

3. Libby Robins, director, Family Help Trust, electronic communications with the author, November 8, 2008, and December 17, 2009.

4. Mannix Porterfield, "W. Virginia's Prison Nursery Program Receives World-wide Attention," *Beckley Register-Herald,* March 16, 2007.

5. "Death of the Diet Doctor," *Time,* March 24, 1980.

6. Mary W. Byrne, "Maternal and Child Outcomes of a Prison Nursery Program: Key Findings," http://www.nursing.columbia.edu/byrne/prison_nursery.html.

7. Carol George, Nancy Kaplan, and Mary Main, "Adult Attachment Interview," 3rd ed., unpublished manuscript, department of psychology, University of California, Berkeley, 1996.

8. See also Byrne, "Maternal and Child Outcomes."

9. Byrne, "Maternal and Child Outcomes."

10. New York State Correction Law, article 22, § 611, "Births to inmates of correctional institutions and care of children of inmates of correctional institutions."

11. Arietta Slade and J. Lawrence Aber, "The Parent Development Interview—Revised," unpublished protocol, City University of New York, 2004.

12. See http://www.summithouse.org.

13. See the "History" and "Supportive Services" pages of the organization's web site, http://www.hourchildren.org.

14. Circle of Security, "COS Projects: Early Intervention Program for Parents and Children," http://www.circleofsecurity.net/cos_projects.html.

REFERENCES

Acoca, Leslie, and Myrna Raeder. 1999. "Severing Family Ties: The Plight of Nonviolent Female Offenders and Their Children." *Stanford Law and Policy Review* 11:133–43.

Ainsworth, Mary D. S., Mary C. Blehar, Everett Waters, and Sally Wall. 1978. *Patterns of Attachment: A Psychological Study of the Strange Situation.* Hillsdale, NJ: Lawrence Erlbaum and Associates.

Amnesty International USA. 1999. *Not Part of My Sentence: Violations of the Human Rights of Women in Custody.* New York: Amnesty International USA.

———. 2006. "Abuse of Women in Custody: Sexual Misconduct and Shackling of Pregnant Women." New York: Amnesty International USA.

Baradon, Tessa, Peter Fonagy, Kirsten Bland, Kata Lenard, and Michelle Sleed. 2008. "New Beginnings: An Experience-Based Programme Addressing the Attachment Relationship between Mothers and Their Babies in Prison." *Journal of Child Psychotherapy* 34:240–58.

Baunach, Phyllis J. 1985. *Mothers in Prison.* New Brunswick, NJ: Transaction Books.

Bayley, Nancy. 1993. *Bayley Scales of Infant Development.* 2nd ed. San Antonio, TX: The Psychological Corporation Harcourt Brace and Company.

Belknap, Joanne. 2007. *The Invisible Woman: Gender, Crime, and Justice.* Belmont, CA: Thompson-Wadworth.

Bloom, Barbara. 1993. *Why Punish the Children? A Reappraisal of the Children of Incarcerated Mothers in America.* San Francisco, CA: National Council on Crime and Delinquency.

———. 1995. "Imprisoned Mothers." In *Children of Incarcerated Parents,* edited by Katherine Gabel and Denise Johnston (21–30). New York: Lexington Books.

Borelli, Jessica, Lorie Goshin, Sarah Joestl, Juliette Clark, and Mary W. Byrne. 2010. "Attachment Organization in a Sample of Incarcerated Mothers: Distribution of Classifications and Associations with Substance Abuse History, Depressive Symptoms, Perceptions of Parenting Competency, and Social Support." *Attachment & Human Development* 12:355–74.

Boudin, Kathy. 1998. "Lessons from a Mother's Program in Prison: A Psychosocial Approach Supports Women and Their Children." *Women and Therapy* 21:103–25.

Boudouris, James. 1983. *Parents in Prison: Addressing the Needs of Families.* Lanham, MD: American Correctional Association.

Bradley, Robert H., and Bettye M. Caldwell. 1978. "Screening the Environment." *American Journal of Orthopsychiatry* 48:114–29.

Brodie, Donna L. 1982. "Babies Behind Bars: Should Incarcerated Mothers Be Allowed to Keep Their Newborns with Them in Prison?" *University of Richmond Law Review* 16:677–92.

Byrne, Mary W. 2005. "Conducting Research as a Visiting Scientist in a Women's Prison." *Journal of Professional Nursing* 21(4): 223–30.

———. 2008. "Evidence from a Prison Nursery." Paper presented at the third annual Congressional Caucus for Women's Issues and National Leaders of the Judiciary, Washington, D.C., June 25.

———. 2009. "Before the Next Surge: An Assessment of the Contemporary Prison Nursery Movement." *Women, Girls, and Criminal Justice* 10(5): 65, 74, 77–79.

Byrne, Mary W., Lorie S. Goshin, and Sarah Joestl. 2010. "Intergenerational Attachment for Infants Raised in a Prison Nursery." *Attachment & Human Development* 12:375–93.

Byrne, Mary W., Gina Hajjawi, Mary Hughes, and Teresa Fabi. 2007. "Successful Reentry of Women and Children: Against All Odds." 12th national workshop on adult and juvenile female offenders, Association on Programs for Female Offenders, Baltimore, Md., October 23.

California Department of Corrections and Rehabilitation. 2009. *Annual Report: Division of Addiction and Recovery Services.* Sacramento: State of California.

Capute, Arnold, and Pasqual Accardo. 1996. "The Infant Neurodevelopmental Assessment: A Clinical Interpretive Manual for CAT-CLAMS in the First Two Years of Life, Part 1." *Current Problems in Pediatrics* 26(7): 238–57.

Carlson, Joseph R. 1998. "Evaluating the Effectiveness of a Live-In Nursery within a Women's Prison." *Journal of Offender Rehabilitation* 27(1/2): 73–85.

———. 2001. "Prison Nursery 2000: A Five-Year Review of the Prison Nursery at the Nebraska Correctional Center for Women." *Journal of Offender Rehabilitation* 33(3): 75–97.

———. 2009. "Prison Nurseries: A Pathway to Crime-Free Futures." *Corrections Compendium* 34(1): 17–22.

Cassidy, Jude, Yair Ziv, Brandi Stupica, Laura J. Sherman, Heidi Butler, et al. 2010. "Enhancing Attachment Security in the Infants of Women in a Jail-Diversion Program." *Attachment & Human Development* 12:333–53.

Catan, Liza. 1988. "The Development of Young Children in HMP Mother and Baby Units." Working Papers in Psychology. East Sussex, UK: University of Sussex.

———. 1992. "Infants with Mothers in Prison." In *Prisoners' Children: What Are the Issues?*, edited by R. Shaw (13–28). London: Routledge.

Cook, Sandy, and Susanne Davies. 1999. *Harsh Punishment: International Experiences of Women's Imprisonment.* Boston: Northeastern University Press.

Coplan, James. 1993. *Early Language Milestones.* Austin, TX: Pro-Ed.

Correctional Institution Inspection Committee. 2005. "Evaluation and Inspection Report on the Ohio Reformatory for Women." Columbus, OH: Correctional Institution Inspection Committee.

Craig, Susan C. 2009. "A Historical Review of Mother and Child Programs for Incarcerated Women." *The Prison Journal* 89(1 Suppl): 35S–53S.

DeHart, Dana D. 2008. "Pathways to Prison: Impact of Victimization in the Lives of Incarcerated Women." *Violence Against Women* 14(12): 1362–81.

Enos, Sandra. 2001. *Mothering from the Inside.* Albany: State University of New York Press.

Fearn, Noelle E., and Kelly Parker. 2004. "Washington State's Residential Parenting Program: An Integrated Public Health, Education, and Social Service Resource for Pregnant Inmates and Prison Mothers." *California Journal of Health Promotion* 2(4): 34–48.

Flynn, Elizabeth G. 1963. *The Alderson Story: My Life as a Political Prisoner.* New York: International Publishers.

Fonagy, Peter, Mary Target, Harold Steele, and Miriam Steele. 1998. *Reflective-Functioning Manual.* Version 5. London: University College London.

Frankenberg, William K., and Josiah B. Dodds. 1992. *Denver II Training Manual.* Denver, CO: Denver Developmental Materials, Inc.

Gabel, Katherine, and Kathryn Girard. 1995. "Long-Term Care Nurseries in Prisons: A Descriptive Study." In *Children of Incarcerated Parents*, edited by Katherine Gabel and Denise Johnston (237–54). New York: Lexington Books.

Gabel, Katherine, and Denise Johnston, eds. 1995. *Children of Incarcerated Parents*. New York: Lexington Books.

Gibaud-Wallston, Jonathan A. 1977. "Self-Esteem and Situational Stress: Factors Related to Sense of Competence in New Parents." Ph.D. diss. in psychology, George Peabody College for Teachers.

Goshin, Lorie S., and Mary W. Byrne. 2009. "Converging Streams of Opportunity for Prison Nursery Programs in the United States." *Journal of Offender Rehabilitation* 48:1–21.

Harris, Jean. 1988. *They Always Called Us Ladies*. New York: Macmillan.

———. 1993. "Babies in Prison." *Zero to Three* 13(3): 38–41.

Her Majesty's Prison Service. 2007. *The Management of Mother and Baby Units*. 3rd ed. London: Her Majesty's Prison Service.

Jacobs, Randi. 2008. *Sentence for Two*. Portland, OR: Angel Productions.

Jiménez, Jesús M., and Jesús Palacios. 1998. *Ninos y Madres en Prisión: Desarrollo Psico-Sociobiologico de los Ninos Residents en Centros Penitenciaros*. Madrid: Ministerio del Interior y Ministerio de Trabajo y Asunto Sociales.

———. 2003. "When Home Is in Jail: Child Development in Spanish Penitentiary Units." *Infant and Child Development* 12:461–74.

Josse, Denise. 1997. *Brunet-Lezine Révisé: Échelle de Développement Psychomoteur de la Première Enfance*. Paris: Etablissement d'Applications Psychotechniques.

Kauffman, Kelsey. 2001. "Mothers in Prison." *Corrections Today* 63(1): 62–65.

———. 2002. "Prison Nurseries: New Beginnings and Second Chances." *Women, Girls, and Criminal Justice* 3(1): 1–2, 14–15.

McCall, Carolyn, Jan Casteel, and Nancy S. Shaw. 1985. "Pregnancy in Prison: A Needs Assessment of Perinatal Outcome in Three California Penal Institutions." Sacramento: California Department of Health Services.

Morash, Merry, Timothy S. Bynum, and Barbara A. Koons. 1998. "Women Offenders: Programming Needs and Promising Approaches." NCJ 171667. Washington, DC: U.S. Department of Justice, National Institute of Justice.

Morgan, Stephen M., and Christopher Winship. 2007. *Counterfactuals and Causal Inference: Methods and Principles for Social Science*. New York: Cambridge University Press.

Morris, Allison, and Venezia Kinghi. 1999. "Addressing Women's Needs or Empty Rhetoric? An Examination of New Zealand's Policy for Women in Prison." In *Harsh Punishment: International Experiences of Women's Imprisonment*, edited by Sandy Cook and Susanne Davies (142–59). Boston: Northeastern University Press.

Morton, Joanne B., and Deborah M. Williams. 1998. "Mother/Child Bonding." *Corrections Today* 60(7): 98–104.

Mumola, Christopher J. 2000. *Incarcerated Parents and Their Children*. NCJ 182335. Washington, DC: U.S. Department of Justice, Bureau of Justice Statistics.

National Association of Women Judges. 2007. *Annual Report 2007*. Washington, DC: National Association of Women Judges.

National Institute of Justice. 2005. "Reentry Programs for Women Inmates." *NIJ Journal* 252.

"Ohio Baby Program Yields Early Success." 2003. *Corrections Digest* 74(3): 4.

Palmer, Richard. 1972. "The Prisoner-Mother and Her Child." *Capitol University Law Review* 1(1): 122–44.

Paloutzian, Raymond F., and Craig W. Ellison. 1982. "Loneliness, Spiritual Well-Being, and the Quality of Life." In *Loneliness: A Sourcebook of Current Theory, Research, and Therapy,* edited by Letitia Anne Peplau and Daniel Perlman (224–37). New York: John Wiley & Sons.

Pennix, Pamela R. 1999. "Analysis of Mothers in the Federal Prison System." *Corrections Compendium* 24(12): 4–6.

Pollock, Joycelyn M. 2002. "Parenting Programs in Women's Prisons." *Women and Criminal Justice* 14(1): 131–54.

Quaker Council for European Affairs, The. 2007. *Mothers in Prison: A Review of the Conditions in Member States of the Council of Europe.* Geneva: Quaker Council for European Affairs.

Quinney, Richard. 1991. "The Way of Peace: On Crime, Suffering, and Service." In *Criminology as Peacemaking,* edited by Harold E. Pepinsky and Richard Quinney (3–13). Bloomington: Indiana University Press.

Radloff, Lenore. 1977. "The CES-D Scale: A Self-Report Depression Scale for Research in the General Population." *Applied Psychological Measurement* 1:385–401.

Radosh, Polly. 1988. "Inmate Mothers: Legislative Solutions to a Difficult Problem." *Crime and Justice* 11(1): 61–77.

———. 2002. "Reflections on Women's Crime and Mothers in Prison: A Peacemaking Approach." *Crime and Delinquency* 48:300–15.

Robertson, Oliver. 2008. *Children Imprisoned by Circumstance.* New York: Quaker United Nations Office.

Rosenberg, Morris. 1964. *Society and the Adolescent Child.* Princeton, NJ: Princeton University Press.

Roulet, Elaine, Patricia O'Rourke, and Mary Reichers. 1993. "The Children's Centre— Bedford Hills Correctional Facility." Paper presented at the fourth North American Conference on the Family and Corrections, Quebec City, October.

Ryder, Edward. 1884. *Elizabeth Fry: Life and Labors of the Eminent Philanthropist, Preacher, and Prison Reformer.* New York: E. Walker's Son.

Schehr, Jill M. 2004. "Reflections from the Outside: The Stories of Three Women Who Lived Together in a Prison Nursery." Ann Arbor, MI: ProQuest.

Sered, Susan, and Maureen Norton-Hawk. 2008. "Disrupted Lives, Fragmented Care: Illness Experiences of Criminalized Women." *Women and Health* 48(1): 43–61.

Shearer, Robert A. 2003. "Identifying the Special Needs of Female Offenders." *Federal Probation* 67(1): 46–51.

Shepard, Dean, and Eugene S. Zemans. 1950. "Prison Babies: A Study of Some Aspects of the Care and Treatment of Pregnant Inmates and Their Infants in Training Schools, Reformatories, and Prisons." Chicago: John Howard Association.

Siefert, Kristine, and Sheryl Pimlott. 2001. "Improving Pregnancy Outcomes during Imprisonment: A Model Residential Care Program." *Social Work* 46(2): 125–34.

Silverman, Susan W. 2005. "When the State Has Custody: The Fragile Bond of Mothers and Their Infants on the Prison Nursery." In *A Handbook of Divorce and Custody: Forensic, Developmental, and Clinical Perspectives,* edited by Linda Gunsberg and Paul Hymowitz (151–60). New York: The Analytic Press/Taylor and Francis Group.

Snell, Tracy L., with Danielle C. Morton. 1994. *Women in Prison: Survey of State Prison Inmates 1991.* NCJ 145321. Washington, DC: U.S. Department of Justice, Bureau of Justice Statistics.

Spitz, René A. 1945. "Hospitalism—An Inquiry into the Genesis of Psychiatric Conditions in Early Childhood." *Psychoanalytic Study of the Child* 1:53–74.

———. 1956. "Childhood Development Phenomena: The Influence of Mother-Child Relationships and Its Disturbances." In *Mental Health and Infant Development,* by Kenneth Soddy. New York: Basic Books.

Spradley, James. 1979. *Ethnographic Interviewing.* New York: John Wiley & Sons.

———. 1980. *Participant Observation.* New York: John Wiley & Sons.

Squires, Jane, LaWanda Potter, and Diane Bricker. 1999. *The ASQ User's Guide.* 2nd ed. Baltimore, MD: Paul H. Brookes Publishing Co.

Sroufe, L. Alan. 2005. "Attachment and Development: A Prospective, Longitudinal Study from Birth to Adulthood." *Attachment & Human Development* 7(4): 349–67.

State of New York Department of Correctional Services. Division of Program Planning, Research, and Evaluations. 2002. "Profile and Three Year Follow-Up of Bedford Hills and Taconic Nursery Program Participants: 1997 and 1998." Albany: State of New York Department of Correctional Services.

United Nations Committee on the Rights of the Child. 2006. *A Guide to General Comment 7: "Implementing Child Rights in Early Childhood."* The Hague, NL: UNICEF/ Bernard van Leer Foundation.

Vainik, Jenni. 2008. "The Reproductive and Parental Rights of Incarcerated Mothers." *Family Court Review* 46(4): 670–94.

Van IJzendoorn, Marinus H., Carlo Schuengel, and Marian J. Bakersman-Kranenburg. 1999. "Disorganized Attachment in Early Childhood: Meta-Analysis of Precursors, Concomitants, and Sequelae." *Development & Psychopathology* 11:225–49.

Vaughan, Roger. 2008. "Innovation!" *American Journal of Public Health* 98(8): 1353.

Ware, John E., Mark Kosinski, and Barbara Gandek. 2000. *SF-36 Health Survey: Manual and Interpretation Guide.* Lincoln, RI: Quality Metric Incorporated.

Weintraub, Judith F. 1987. "Mothers and Children in Prison." *Corrections Compendium* 11(17): 1, 5–12.

West, Stephen G., Naihua Duan, Willo Pequegnant, Paul Gaist, Don C. DesJarlais, David Holtgrave, José Szapocznik, et al. 2008. "Alternatives to the Randomized Controlled Trial." *American Journal of Public Health* 98(8): 1359–66.

Whitehead, Dean. 2006. "The Health Promoting Prison (HPP) and Its Imperative for Nursing." *International Journal of Nursing Studies* 43:123–31.

Women's Prison Association. Institute on Women and Criminal Justice. 2009. *Mothers, Infants, and Imprisonment: A National Look at Prison Nurseries and Community-Based Alternatives.* New York: Women's Prison Association.

Zwerman, Gilda, and Gilbert Gardner. 1986. "Obstacles to Research in a State Prison: Regulated, Segregated, and under Surveillance." *Qualitative Sociology* 9(3): 293–300.

10

Parenting Programs for Prisoners

Ann Booker Loper and Caitlin M. Novero

With the rise in U.S. incarceration rates, the number of incarcerated parents who have minor children has also risen (Glaze and Maruschak 2008). Bolstered by a growing literature focusing on the impact of incarceration on children, as well as the emergence of policies that link improved family relationships with reduced re-offending (such as H.R. 1593, the Second Chance Act of 2007), institutions have begun to provide parenting training programs for their inmates to ameliorate some of the negative effects of parental incarceration (Hughes and Harrison-Thompson 2002). In a survey of key personnel from state correctional departments, Pollock (2003) found 38 of the reporting states had some form of parenting classes for inmate mothers. Hughes and Harrison-Thompson gathered information directly from 315 participating state prisons and learned that approximately half the institutions offered parenting programs.

Although these data indicate that parenting interventions are available in many prisons, the numbers overestimate the percentages of inmates involved in parenting programs. Glaze and Maruschak's (2008) analysis of the Bureau of Justice Statistics survey of incarcerated parents revealed that only 11 percent of the parents in state prison reported participation in parenting or child-rearing classes. Correctional institutions may offer parenting intervention, but access to participation may be limited by, for example, available funding, security restrictions of the institution, waiting lists for enrollment, schedule conflicts, or lack of interest from inmates. As a result, only a minority of inmate parents have the opportunity to bene-fit from supportive programming around parenting issues.

Unique Aspects of Parenting Interventions for Prisoners

A rich body of work focuses on empirically supported approaches to par-enting training for various child behavior problems (e.g., Reid, Patterson, and Snyder 2002; Sanders et al. 2000; Thomas and Zimmer-Gembeck 2007; Webster-Stratton, Reid, and Hammond 2004). However, with few exceptions (e.g., Eddy et al. 2008; Mindel and Hoefer 2006; Palusci et al. 2008), this body of work has largely not been translated into parenting programs for prisoners. More frequently, interventions in prison have drawn from universal parenting programs (Valle et al. 2004) designed to provide broad psycho-educational support for a general population. Although some of these broader community-based programs have been investigated empirically, in general they have not received the intense empirical attention garnered for interventions designed for specific child behavioral problems.

The gap between interventions inside and outside prison reflects the unique aspects of parental incarceration. Outside prison, parents typically seek parenting consultation because of a specific problem with an iden-tified child. Meta-analyses focusing on the impact of parenting interven-tions frequently identify reduction of child disruptive behaviors as a marker of program success (e.g., de Graaf et al. 2008). For parents outside prison the child's problem behavior creates an immediate motivation for participation in treatment with the timing to start as soon as possible. While parents in prison may likewise seek immediate support to deal with child-related problems, the opportunity and timing for entry into classes is dictated by the availability of programs and inmate eligibility for enroll-ment (Arditti, Smock, and Parkman 2005; Holtfreter and Morash 2003). Moreover, the typical skills covered in "outside" parenting interventions may not be applicable to parents "on the inside." Learning how to handle tantrums and other misbehaviors may have a limited shelf life for the inmate parent who has no opportunity for practice.

Likewise, unique skills addressed in prison parenting programs are largely irrelevant in parenting programs for non-incarcerated individuals. Many components often included in parenting interventions for prisoners—instruction in prison-specific communication avenues (e.g., letter writing, phone calls, and personal visits), strategies for better collaboration with at-home caregivers (i.e., co-parenting issues), awareness of legal rights concerning children, and ways to deal with intense emotions regarding separation and incarceration—would not ordinarily have a place in interventions conducted on the outside.

Current Status of Parenting Programs in Prison

In the United States, parenting programs for prisoners fall into one of three categories: programs that have not been evaluated; programs that have been described qualitatively; and programs that have been evaluated quantitatively, with or without a qualitative component. Whereas this chapter focuses on quantitative investigations, these have included only a small portion of prison parenting programs. Most parenting interventions in prison have not been evaluated. The typical quantitative investigation has focused on the effect of a parenting program on inmate participants and has measured constructs of interest just before and just after the intervention was conducted.

Unevaluated Programs

Numerous parenting programs delivered in U.S. prisons have not been evaluated, or their internal evaluations are not made public. Programs may be implemented by prison staff members, members of religious groups or other community organizations, or independent community volunteers. Curricula may comprise informal lectures, discussions led by individuals, or other supportive activities. Content generally depends on the knowledge and preferences of the trainer. Although these classes are usually welcome additions to opportunities for inmates, the wide diversity of offerings, trainers, and content prevent systematic evaluation of their impact.

However, a few such programs have been widely disseminated. For example, the Prison Parents' Education Project (PPEP), developed by the Center for Children and Incarcerated Parents (CCIP), is available throughout the country. PPEP is designed to provide inmates with objective knowledge about child development and parenting topics using standardized methods supported by student and instructor manuals.

The CCIP offers training to individuals who intend to use the program. The program has been distributed widely and is now used in more than two hundred correctional institutions throughout the nation. However, despite its presence in the correctional community and reasoned objectives and methods, it has not been empirically evaluated. CCIP director Denise Johnson commented, "We have never considered parent education as a useful intervention in isolation from the other, more intensive services we provide to our clients."[1] Thus, in some cases, the lack of specific evaluation of parenting intervention effects may reflect a prioritized emphasis on a larger, multipart intervention; in such cases, parenting education may serve as a treatment component but not be considered a stand-alone change agent.

Qualitative Program Evaluations

In the academic literature, many studies qualitatively describe parenting education programs for inmates (e.g., Bruns, King, and Stateler 2003; Kazura 2001; Meek 2007; Robbers 2005) or use qualitative analysis of information collected as part of a program evaluation (Antonio et al. 2009; Bushfield 2004; LaRosa and Rank 2001; National Fatherhood Initiative [NFI] 2008; Skarupski et al. 2003). These studies typically use informal interviews to learn what inmates find useful about the parenting programs offered, what is missing from the program, and ideas for improvements. For example, Meek (2007) collected course feedback through open-ended questions following a one-week intensive parenting class for young offenders (age 18 to 21 years; $N = 75$). When queried regarding the usefulness of various components of treatment, inmates valued general child care issues, such as the correct way to care for a child, and more specific issues related to physical care of children, such as learning how to change diapers. Areas that the inmates felt were absent from the class varied widely depending on the individual. All participants rated the course in the fairly to very useful range.

Qualitative descriptive studies may aid in understanding how inmates view themselves as parents and their attitudes toward parenting in general (Bushfield 2004; Robbers 2003). Robbers (2003) finds that inmates think that the most beneficial aspect of a 10-week program for fathers in prison is an increase in self-esteem and a renewed desire to build relationships with children. Inmates also report an increase in contact with their children as a result of the knowledge and confidence gained through the program. Bushfield (2004) notes that, after parenting training, inmate fathers report re-evaluating their attitudes regarding the importance of involvement in their child's life. Generally, qualitative descriptive studies have demonstrated that parenting education programs are met with approval from inmates. The wide variety of responses regarding optimal components of treatment suggests that inmates find parent programs useful, although the parents have diverse needs.

Quantitative Program Evaluations

Qualitative studies provide a rich source of information affording a body of research that illuminates trends and likely mechanisms for change associated with positive effects. However, these studies do not statistically measure the degree of change, or compare changes to those afforded under other conditions (e.g., alternate treatment, waiting list). Quantitative studies provide additional grounding to the knowledge generated by qualitative research. As is the case with the overall body of knowledge concerning parents in prison, the quantitative empirical body of literature on parenting training for prisoners is small. Table 10.1 summarizes this review of quantitative evaluations of parenting programs. It includes any evaluation located either through searches of PSYCHINFO and National Criminal Justice Reference Service databases, searches on the Internet, and examination of references of studies provided in other articles on prison parenting programs. In addition, the chapter authors contacted key researchers to obtain unpublished reports or other information. In several instances, the results of an evaluation were articulated in state reports or contract summaries rather than academic journals. Thus, to be included here, a report did not have to be published in a peer-reviewed journal.

Table 10.1 includes any located study that had at least a pre-post design, used quantitative measures of performance, and provided descriptive information regarding a specified parenting intervention. It does not include programs that facilitated enhanced visitation experiences (e.g., Block and Potthast 1998; Snyder-Joy and Carlo 1998) unless parenting training was included as a central feature of the intervention. Likewise, it does not include prison nursery programs (e.g., Carlson 1998; Goshin and Byrne 2009), described in chapter 9 of this volume. Twelve studies used pre-post designs but did not include comparison groups, nine studies included nonrandomized comparison groups, and four studies included randomly assigned comparison groups. These design differences

Table 10.1. Summary of Empirically Based Evaluations of Parenting Interventions

Authors	Participants and program	Results
Pre-post only (no comparison group)		
Browne (1989)[a]	29 females in 24-session Education for Parenthood Curriculum	Improved attitudes (corporal punishment and child expectations); increased self-esteem.
Bushfield (2004)[a]	23 fathers in 30-day daily parenting class	Improved attitudes (corporal punishment and child expectations).
Czuba et al. (2006)[a]	76 fathers and 13 mothers in 10-session People Empowering People	Increase in self-assertive efficacy, sense of mastery, parenting satisfaction, and family problem-solving communication.[b]
Gonzalez et al. (2007)[a]	191 mothers in adaptation of Partners in Parenting	No change in communication or parental control; increased parental confidence; decreased parental understanding.
Harm et al. (1998)[a]	104 mothers in 15-session adaptation of Nurturing Parent Program	Improved attitudes (child expectations). For substance-abuse subsample: increased self-esteem and improved attitudes (parent/child roles).
Kennon (2003)	66 mothers in 12-session Moms, Inc.	Improved parenting attitudes, legal knowledge, and self-esteem; no change in frequency of communication.
LaRosa and Rank (2001)[a]	23 fathers in 5-session Real Life Parenting Skills Program	Improved attitudes (child expectations).
Maiorano and Futris (2005)[a]	74 males in 9–17 session Fit 2-B Fathers Program	Improved parenting attitudes; no difference in recidivism rates.
Mindel and Hoefer (2006)[a]	38 parents and 38 children in 10-session Family Strengthening Program for children and parents	Improved family resilience, opportunities for pro-social involvement of children and family bonding.

Study	Findings
NFI (2009)	219 fathers in 12-session InsideOut Dad™	Improved parenting knowledge and attitudes on selected items of author questionnaire; increased phone contact.

Study	Program	Findings
NFI (2009)	219 fathers in 12-session InsideOut Dad™	Improved parenting knowledge and attitudes on selected items of author questionnaire; increased phone contact.
Palusci et al. (2008)[a]	169 women and 324 men (jail) in adaptation of 10-session Nurturing Parent Program	Improved parenting attitudes (child expectations, empathy, corporal punishment, parent/child roles).
Thompson and Harm (2000)[a]	104 mothers in 15-session adaptation of Nurturing Parenting Program	Improved attitudes (child expectations, corporal punishment, and parent/child roles); increased self-esteem (subsample of mothers who received letters).
Nonrandomized comparison group		
Antonio et al. (2009)	79 fathers in 12-session Long Distance Dads (control $n = 84$)	Improved parenting knowledge, attitudes, and behavior on selected items of author questionnaire.
Gat (2000)	16 mothers in 8–10 session Mother/Offspring Life Program (control $n = 4$)	No change in recidivism, pro-social moral reasoning, attachment empathy, or hope.
Moore and Clement (1998)[a]	20 mothers in 9-week Mothers Inside Loving Kids (control $n = 20$) and enhanced visitation	Increased parenting knowledge; no change in parenting attitudes or self-esteem; no difference between groups.
NFI (2008)	89 fathers in 12-session InsideOut Dad™ (control $n = 13$)	Improved parenting knowledge and attitudes on selected items of author questionnaire; no difference in parent behavior.
Robbers (2005)	56 fathers in 10-session parenting education program (control $n = 31$)	Increased contact, improved parenting knowledge and attitudes (select items); no change in relationship with caregiver.
Sandifer (2008)[a]	64 mothers in 24-session adaptation of Rebonding and Rebuilding curriculum with linked visitation (control $n = 26$)	Improved parenting knowledge and attitudes (empathy) toward children.

(continued)

Table 10.1. *(Continued)*

Authors	Participants and program	Results
Showers (1993)[a]	203 mothers in 10-session adaptation of Systemic Training for Effective Parenting (STEP) (control *n* = 275)	Increased knowledge of child behavior management skills.
Skarupski et al. (2003)	84 fathers in 12-session Long Distance Dads (control *n* = 60); 37 caregiver reports	No change in knowledge, skills, or attitudes; increased child contact (findings not corroborated by caregivers).
Wilczak and Markstrom (1999)[a]	21 fathers in 8-session adaptation of STEP (control *n* = 21)	Increased knowledge, internal locus of control, and parent satisfaction.
Randomized comparison group		
Bayse et al. (1991)[a]	27 fathers in 4-session How to Keep Your Family Alive While Serving a Prison Sentence (control *n* = 27)	Reduced narcissism and improved attitudes toward present and ideal family functioning; no change in adaptability.
Harrison (1997)[a]	15 fathers and children in an 18-session parenting class (control *n* = 15)	Improved parenting attitudes; no change in inmate or child self-esteem.
Landreth and Lobaugh (1998)[a]	16 fathers in 10-session filial therapy training class and 16 children (control *n* = 16)	Improved parenting attitudes; decreased parenting stress; improved self-concept among children.
Loper and Tuerk (forthcoming)[a]	60 mothers in 9-session Parenting on the Inside (control *n* = 46)	Improved parenting stress, alliance with caretakers, mental health symptoms, and letter writing; marginal waiting-list-control differences.

[a]Results published in a peer-reviewed journal.

[b]Includes post-intervention follow-up measurement.

temper confidence in the robustness of evaluation results. Pre-post-only comparisons allow estimation of change over the course of treatment but are unable to identify change independent of unmeasured ecological effects (e.g., administration changes during treatment) or error due to lack of measure reliability. Including a comparison group that receives either no treatment or, preferably, an alternate treatment allows more accurate estimation of treatment-specific effects. Random assignment of participants to comparison treatments further reduces error associated with systematic differences in groups and represents a generally stronger research design. Seventeen of the 25 reports were published in peer-reviewed journals.

Intervention Content. The content of interventions varies considerably, making it difficult to portray a standard parenting program. For example, interventions may differ in length. LaRosa and Rank's (2001) Real Life Parenting Skills program met for 90 minutes once a week for five weeks. By contrast, Sandifer (2008) implemented the Rebonding and Rebuilding curriculum (Meyer and Moriarty 1995), which met for three hours a day, twice a week for 12 weeks. Interventions may be specific to fathers (Antonio et al. 2009; Maiorano and Futris 2005; Skarupski et al. 2003), to mothers (Harm, Thompson, and Chambers 1998; Loper and Tuerk forthcoming; Thompson and Harm 2000), or both (Palusci et al. 2008). Some interventions feature inclusion of visitation experiences (e.g., Snyder-Joy and Carlo 1998) as integral to the training. Some interventions are aimed at inmates nearing release (Bushfield 2004; Maiorano and Futris 2005), whereas others include long-term offenders (Loper and Tuerk forthcoming). Because of this diversity, it is difficult to make comparisons based on the content of interventions.

A more fruitful way to understand the big picture in parenting programs in prison is to look at common targeted outcomes. Typical outcomes for parenting interventions (listed by frequency of use in the studies reviewed) include *knowledge and attitudes,* defined as acquisition of information regarding child development and more socially normative beliefs about appropriate child rearing, discipline, and the role of a parent; *mental well-being and parenting stress,* defined as improvement in mood, self-image, and stress levels; and *behavioral changes,* such as frequency of contact and communication with children, recidivism rates, and reductions of negative or harmful behaviors (e.g., substance use). In general, child outcomes have been either not included in prison parenting evaluations or obtained by small-sample auxiliary measures

(Harrison 1997; Landreth and Lobaugh 1998). This is in marked contrast to most parenting interventions for non-incarcerated parents, for which child outcomes are a primary marker, if not the only marker, of program success (e.g., Webster-Stratton and Herman 2008; Webster-Stratton, Reid, and Hammond 2001; Webster-Stratton et al. 2004).

Knowledge and Attitudes. The most widely used benchmark of a successful prison parenting education program has been a significant change in the inmate's attitudes or knowledge about parenting. All studies listed in table 10.1 measure pre-post change in at least one aspect of knowledge or attitudes. While the instrumentation varies widely, several studies used the Adult-Adolescent Parenting Inventory, or AAPI-2 (Bavolek and Keene 2001). The self-report measure was originally introduced in 1979 and has since been used across various settings to assess change in parenting attitudes and knowledge (Family Development Resources 2008). The AAPI-2 yields an overall score and five subscales intended to measure attitudes involving inappropriate parental expectations, empathy toward children, corporal punishment, parent-child role expectations, and child need for power and independence. Whereas these various scores have good reliability, investigations of the validity of the scales have focused on populations at risk for child abuse (Connors et al. 2006), which in some cases include prisoners (Minor, Karr, and Jain 1987). In general, however, the validity of the scales has not yet been established in the prison parent population.

Palusci and his colleagues (2008) used the APPI-2 to measure change in parenting attitudes and knowledge following implementation of a parenting education program in a variety of community settings, including a local jail. The program, Helping Your Child to Succeed (HYCS), is a 10-week program in which the inmates meet weekly with trained counselors and social workers. The curriculum was adapted from a universal parenting education program, the Nurturing Parent Program (Bavolek 1999), described as a family-centered program "proven to help parents and children learn to care for themselves and each other and to replace old, unwanted abusive interactions with newer, more nurturing ones" (Bavolek 2005, 11). The 10 HYCS sessions are devoted to teaching 10 democratic child-rearing topics, such as positive attention and praise, setting appropriate expectations, and developing healthy communication patterns. Inmates from the county jail, in addition to other community members, participated in HYCS as a part of a 10-week substance abuse treatment program (Palusci et al. 2008). Of the 446 jail inmates who participated during a six-year span, 372 completed both pre- and post-test measures of the APPI-2. Palusci and his colleagues (2008) reported that mean scores increased significantly on four of the five constructs (expectations, empathy, corporal punishment, and role reversal).

Other studies presented in table 10.1 used a similar design to Palusci and his colleagues (2008) and employed a version of the AAPI to measure change (Bavolek 1984; Bavolek and Keene 2001). At first glance, this would seem a welcome sign and an opportunity to draw conclusions across programs using meta-analytic approaches. However, methods for the use of the measure vary substantially. For example, Robbers (2005) used only 7 of the 40 items, and Bushfield (2004) only reported the items that resulted in significant changes. Harrison, like Palusci and his colleagues, drew from Bavolek's Nurturing Programs, but only briefly reported on one AAPI score and did not provide full descriptive information (e.g., scale standard deviations). Harm and her colleagues (1998) likewise presented limited descriptive information regarding performance on all subscales. Thus, although there is welcome common measurement across several studies, and general consensus that attitudes improved with intervention, the variations in measurement patterns prelude making statistically based generalizations across studies regarding the impact of parenting interventions on attitudinal change of inmate parents.

A number of the empirical studies have not used standardized measures of attitudes or knowledge and have instead favored researcher-designed surveys. The National Fatherhood Initiative (http://www.fatherhood.org), an organization that develops and evaluates parenting resources and education programs for fathers, has used this method for the internal evaluation of their many programs, including InsideOut Dad™, an NFI program designed specifically for incarcerated fathers (NFI 2005, 2008, 2009). The program consists of 12 one-hour sessions that address such topics as self-awareness, being a man, spirituality, handling emotions, relationships, fathering (both inside and outside prison), parenting, and child development. The Dad program was implemented in several correctional institutions in Maryland and Ohio (NFI 2008, 2009). Participants answered 26 multiple-choice questions before and after the program. A typical question included "Self-worth is a term used to describe (a) How a person feels about himself, (b) What a person thinks about himself, (c) Both the feelings and thoughts a person has about himself, (d) Don't know." Mean scores for parenting knowledge and items on attitudinal questionnaires improved significantly for program graduates.

Other nonstandardized instruments used by some parenting interventions have used broad statements in which the participant self-evaluates his or her own parenting skills. Questions have included, for example, "I know how to talk about my child's feelings and emotions," "I can parent my children effectively from prison," and "I am confident about my parenting skills" (Antonio et al. 2009; Gonzalez, Romero, and Cerbana 2007; Maiorano and Futris 2005). Generally speaking, inmates show increased confidence in their attitudes and knowledge using this type of measurement. However, meta-cognitive assessment of beliefs and knowledge is not the same as direct measurement, and it is unclear whether so-measured change represents true shifts in maladaptive attitudes or a broader confidence that one's attitudes—adaptive or not—are correct. Further, it is unclear whether a change in reported attitudes in the prison population leads to changes in inmate parenting behaviors, let alone changes in child behaviors.

Mental Well-Being and Parenting Stress. Incarcerated men and women are more likely than non-incarcerated men and women to suffer from mental illness (James and Glaze 2006). Women in prison, in particular, tend to report high levels of depression and anxiety, as well as other serious mental health problems (Jordan et al. 1996; Warren et al. 2002). For inmate parents, separation from their children often represents the most excruciating of the pains of prison and is a key source of stress (Arditti et al. 2005; Clarke et al. 2005; Hairston 1991). For these inmates, depression or anxiety can reflect negative affect associated with stress about how to meaningfully connect with and guide children. A large body of evidence in non-incarcerated samples has linked parenting stress, or high levels of concern regarding the roles and responsibilities surrounding parenting, with impaired parenting practice as well as with mental disorders (Ortega, Beauchemin, and Kaniskan 2008; Rodgers 1998; Rodgers-Farmer 1999). A focus on developing methods for controlling stress regarding separation from children and improving general emotional reactivity about child-related issues is appropriate for many parent prisoners.

Loper and Tuerk (forthcoming) developed a program for long-term incarcerated mothers designed to provide parents coping strategies for dealing with the stress of separation and to improve communication with children and caregivers. The program employs an inmate manual that elaborates on each of eight sessions, conducted in small groups.

Where possible, the sessions are structured using computer presentation software, videotaped vignettes of difficult situations, and small group discussions. Central to all sessions is reference to a cognitive-behavioral strategy that inserts conscious evaluation of ongoing assumptions and emotional reactions. Using the acronym MOM-OK, inmates learn to "*m*ellow *o*ut" using brief breathing and relaxation strategies, use their "*m*ind" to identify dysfunctional thoughts, counter negative thoughts with "*o*ther" possibilities, and ask "What is best for my *k*id?" This strategy is infused throughout all eight sessions. For example, during the sessions that focus on dealing with a child's questions about why the mother is in prison, the inmate mother might be urged to replace the thought "Her father put her up to this to shame me" with "She is curious and wants to understand why things are this way."

Loper and Tuerk evaluated the benefits of the program in reducing parenting stress and other mental health difficulties, improving alliances with child caregivers, and changing the frequency of mother-initiated contact through letters (Loper and Tuerk forthcoming). Pre-post intervention comparisons documented improvements in scores on the Parenting Stress Index (Abidin and Brunner 1995), the Parenting Alliance Scale (Abidin and Konold 1999), and the Brief Symptom Inventory (Derogatis 1993), as well as the frequency of letter-writing. When significant pre-post comparisons were reanalyzed controlling for the frequency of using the MOM-OK strategy, previously significant effects were no longer significant, suggesting that the strategy may mediate some positive effects. However, pre-post changes were generally not significant in comparison to a randomly assigned waiting-list group, limiting conclusions regarding the benefits of the program.

Other interventions that have targeted emotional and personal stressors have tended to focus on inmates' personal sense of self-esteem or confidence in their ability to parent. For example, Harm and her colleagues (1998) found improvements in self-esteem among a group of female inmates with substance problems using the Nurturing Parent curriculum (Bavolek and Comstock 1985). Along similar lines, the same authors later found that improvements in self-esteem were more apparent among mothers who had some contact with children, emphasizing the importance of opportunity to practice skills in achieving desired outcomes (Thompson and Harm 2000). In general, interventions that have examined mental health issues have found positive changes in inmate stress and sense of well-being following parenting program participation. The question arises whether such positive changes are then generalized to improved parent-child interactions. The challenge for these interventions, as is the case for interventions designed to improve knowledge and attitudes, is in affording practice opportunities and direct measurement of the acquired skills.

Behavioral Changes. Changes in inmate behaviors, particularly regarding contact and communication with their children, have been examined in several evaluations. Parent and child contact and communication patterns can change abruptly and dramatically when the parent enters prison, especially when the parent has functioned as the child's primary caregiver before imprisonment. Most inmate mothers and a substantial portion of fathers reside with their children before incarceration (Glaze and Maruschak 2008). However, in prison, parent-child contact is typically limited to letter writing, phone calls, and visits. Institutional policies and financial burdens further limit the number of phone and visitation opportunities, and the cooperation of the caretaker and child can alter the success of the contact (Arditti et al. 2005; Meek 2007).

Assessment of change in communication patterns has typically relied upon inmate self-reports regarding frequency of phone calls, letter writing, and visits (Antonio et al. 2009; Harm et al. 1998; Kennon 2003; NFI 2008, 2009). A few studies have also sought to assess change in the quality of communication by asking about the presence of specific behaviors, such as yelling at children or telling them that they are loved (Czuba, Anderson, and Higgins 2006; NFI 2008, 2009). Antonio and his colleagues evaluated behavior changes following the 12-week parenting program Long Distance Dads using inmate responses to 12 self-reports of specific parent behaviors, such as "How often have you talked about events that are currently going on in your child's daily life?" The participants were also asked how often they sent gifts, communicated via phone or letters, or requested visits. Pre- and post-program analysis showed that those who completed the program increased frequency of talking about events in their children's lives, sending gifts, phoning, and assessing their children's physical and emotional needs.

In general, evaluations have reported mixed results concerning changes in contact frequency; some investigations have showed improvement (Antonio et al. 2009; Loper and Tuerk forthcoming; Robbers 2005; Skarupski et al. 2003), whereas others have not detected change (Gonzalez et al. 2007; Kennon 2003). Null results may reflect insufficient focus on this outcome; variations in institutional constraints regarding contact, inmate family resources, and other unmeasured effects; or a lack of program effectiveness regarding changes in parent-child contact.

Mindel and Hoefer (2006) evaluated change in parental behaviors following a family strengthening program offered through a substance abuse treatment facility for inmates who were nearing release or recently released and their children. This was one of the few studies reviewed in this chapter that implemented a curriculum adapted from a universal parenting program that met the criteria as an evidence-based program by the National Registry of Effective Programs and Practices. The 14-week program included separate 60-minute meetings for children and parents followed by a communal meeting to allow parents to practice newly learned skills. Mindel and Hoefer's study is exceptional in its inclusion of measures completed by participating children. Inmate parents as well as their children reported improvements in family bonding and parental involvement, as well as an increase in the opportunities and rewards that accompany pro-social behavior.

A related area of inquiry in a few studies has been examining inmate behavior following release from prison. A primary rationale for educational opportunities in prison rests on the assumption that such intervention reduces the likelihood of dysfunctional behaviors that lead to inmates re-offending after release. Parenting education may reduce conflict and stress with family members and may result in a more successful adjustment during and after prison, which in turn may reduce offending.

Studies have not yet examined the impact of parenting programs on re-offending per se, but several studies have examined one consequence of offending after release, namely recidivism back to prison. Maiorano and Futris (2005) found that the recidivism rates among prisoners who completed the Fit 2-B FATHERS program were comparable to the recidivism rates of the general prison population. Similarly, Gat (2000) found no significant differences in recidivism between parenting program participants and inmates who did not participate in the parenting program. Whereas this objective makes sense in a correctional context, it may be overly optimistic to expect that relatively brief parenting interventions alone will reduce re-offending. Rather, parenting education's success in reducing recidivism may be better estimated when considered within the context of various other forms of inmate and family support during and after incarceration and within the context of inmates' lives following release.

Limitations in Parenting Intervention Research

While relatively few, most publicly available reports regarding quantitative evaluations of parenting programs in prison have been positive. However, several serious limitations appear across these studies. Most studies use pre-post designs that do not involve comparison groups, such as no-treatment control groups. Of the 25 studies presented in table 10.1, only 13 used comparison groups, which in many cases were limited in size and composition.

Further, whereas the generally positive pre-post changes that have been observed are encouraging, it is important to know whether these changes are independent of regression to the mean or unmeasured environmental effects at the prison or following prison release. Seasonal changes, proximity to holidays, large transfers of inmates, and changes in administration are but a few prison-wide agents for changes in inmate attitudes and behaviors. Documentation that positive changes occur irrespective of systemic effects is particularly important for this environment.

Along similar lines, most investigations do not use random assignment, and substantial dropout rates in studies with parent inmates are common. For example, Czuba and her colleagues (2006), Loper and Tuerk, Sandifer (2008), and Skarupski and her colleagues (2003) observed attrition rates of approximately 50 percent of the initial sample. The presumed initial equality of groups that is the objective of random assignment can be lost when huge portions of either group drop out. Moreover, institutional conditions often limit who is allowed to be part of a control group. For example, the control group in Antonio and colleagues' (2009) evaluation of Long Distance Dads mainly comprised men who were ineligible for the training program due to problematic offenses, legal barriers to child contact, and lack of desire for program participation. These problems create substantial difficulties in understanding who is being evaluated and, therefore, to whom the intervention appropriately applies.

Many evaluations have very small sample sizes, sometimes as the result of the high dropout rates described above (Browne 1989; Bushfield 2004; Gat 2000; Harrison 1997; Landreth and Lobaugh 1998; LaRosa and Rank 2001). The small sample sizes are particularly problematic when small waiting list comparison groups are used, as null effects may result from low power rather than lack of intervention. For example, after experiencing a considerable attrition rate, Sandifer's (2008) evaluation of the Rebonding and Rebuilding curriculum was hampered by a small control group ($n = 26$). In several areas, the treatment group showed positive pre-post intervention gains, whereas the control group generally did not change on measured variables. While these results are encouraging, the observed absence of change in this waiting list group may reflect lowered statistical power. Waiting list attrition is a particular problem in prison settings as inmates may be transferred, experience incompatible schedule changes, commit infractions that restrict educational opportunity, or simply lose interest. It is not surprising that many interventions opt for simple pre-post designs rather than deal with the likely difficulties of finding durable control groups.

By and large, most interventions rely exclusively on self-reported measures. In some cases, the measures reflect self-evaluation of a quality rather than a more objective measure of the quality itself. For example, Robbers' (2005) assessment of improved legal knowledge included the item "I know who to call to have my support payments adjusted if my employment status changes" (p. 17) rather than a direct query regarding who the inmate would call. The problems of using self-report are particularly risky with researcher-developed surveys that have not been subjected to psychometric scrutiny. Given these various problems, the body of work focusing on prison-based parenting programs is clearly lacking in scientific rigor, and it is difficult to draw solid conclusions about the impact of prison parenting programs on either inmates or their children.

Why Are Rigorous Studies of Prison-Based Parenting Programs So Hard to Conduct?

The spotlight on the common limitations that so frequently plague prison parenting interventions leads to the question, "Why do so few evaluations satisfy basic conditions for scientific rigor?" The resounding answer: "They are conducted in prisons." Numerous unique logistical, political, and practical considerations in conducting treatment or evaluation in a prison are not apparent in other settings. Some of the most basic needs for consistent programming—dependable locations for training, reliable equipment, availability of materials—can be road-blocked in a prison or jail setting. Delays in twice-daily counts routinely cut into scheduled time. Unexpected transfers of inmates can dramatically change class sizes. Although computer presentations are normative in most educational settings, prisons and jails often have restrictions on the use of computer equipment that preclude such innovation. Simple features such as turning on electric lights, rearranging furniture, and permitting small group discussion can be curtailed depending upon institutional security policies.

While concern for the well-being of the children of incarcerated parents is typically one purpose of education initiatives, few studies conducted in prisons incorporate child outcome measures (Harrison 1997; Landreth and Lobaugh 1998). Access to children is often very difficult in prison settings. Inmate families irregularly visit inmates, and the hospitality of conditions varies widely (Kazura 2001; Laughlin et al. 2008). Many parent inmates receive no visits from children (Glaze and Maruschak 2008). Many institutions have policies that prevent physical contact and limit communication during visitation. For example, inmate parents may be required to sit in a separate chair and refrain from touching their children. Long-distance travel to institutions can be burdensome on financially strapped home caregivers. The various personal activities of the inmate's child—often scheduled on weekends—can interfere with weekend-only visitation hours. These scenarios make it difficult to adequately assess whether inmate parents are using skills targeted by parenting programs.

Political concerns can also influence how parenting interventions are devised and assessed. To implement a program in prison it is sometimes necessary to demonstrate that the program has higher-order social benefits, beyond those for the individual family. For example, Antonio and colleagues' evaluation included goals "to become emotionally, morally, spiritually, psychologically, and financially responsible parents" (2009, 9). Along similar lines, Robbers' intervention included objectives to "promote emotional, moral, spiritual, and financial responsibility for children" (2005, 7). Many of Robbers' and Antonio and colleagues' other goals included objectives for skill development that are more typical in parenting interventions on the outside. However, the inclusion of goals for improved moral behavior would rarely, if ever, occur in interventions with the non-incarcerated.

This type of conceptualization of a prison-based parenting intervention can be crucial in gaining political support to conduct the intervention. For example, in a survey of 200 adults living in Florida, Applegate (2001) found most were skeptical about providing many of the possible services and amenities for inmates. However, nearly all respondents indicated that they would be willing to support such programming if there was a clear link between providing the service and reduced offending. The provision of services in prison can require selling the public on the redemptive value of an intervention in ways that would not be otherwise needed on the outside. Unfortunately, the focus on these objectives may obscure goals for acquisition and measurement of more parenting-specific skills.

Future Directions for Improving Parenting Intervention Scholarship

Despite the common limitations as well as the ubiquitous difficulties of conducting research in prison, the number of published evaluations of parenting interventions has increased, as has the understanding of the value of such approaches. As seen in table 10.1, 17 quantitative evaluations of parenting programs were made publicly available between 2000 and 2009, compared with only 8 such studies between 1989 and 1999. In 2007, the U.S. Congress passed the Second Chance Act, which provides localities with funding for initiatives to reduce prison reentry and specifically prioritizes interventions aimed at improving the family relationships of prisoners. In Applegate's (2001) public opinion survey regarding correctional services, more than 90 percent of respondents indicated support for psychological counseling as well as opportunities for inmate family visits.

Another optimistic sign is the presence of new initiatives that, while still in development, offer promise. For example, Eddy and associates (2008) have developed a multisystemic parenting intervention that provides instruction in communication patterns, effective child management, and opportunities for practice in a therapeutic visitation program. Moreover, the program is implemented in concert with several community agencies that provide support during the entire course of judicial involvement. A randomized controlled longitudinal trial of the prison-based parenting component of this promising intervention is in progress.

The difficulties and limitations of doing interventions in prison will probably not change. However, knowledge can still grow by implementing several simple initiatives that would vastly improve this important and growing body of research.

Maintain High and Consistent Standards for Measurement. In order to investigate the value of parenting interventions, there needs to be a stronger and more unified effort regarding the measurement of effects. More consistent use of established standardized measures, full reporting of descriptive information, and assessment of scale reliability and validity within studies would afford improved evaluation at little additional cost or effort. Further, statistically accounting for such issues as missing data, the clustering of participants in classes, and sample attrition would decrease misinterpretation of the results and strengthen study findings.

Explore Key Components of Change. The treatment components that are presumed to mediate effectiveness also need to be better identified. Most research emphasizes demonstrating that the approach works in improving some skill or belief. However, why is the approach working, and how can the mediating mechanisms be evaluated? Whereas some qualitative studies explore this question by asking inmates about useful program aspects, quantitative investigation of such mechanisms is largely lacking. Loper and Tuerk observed that frequent use of the MOM-OK cognitive-behavioral strategy accounted for some positive change in mothers following a parenting class (Loper and Tuerk forthcoming), supporting the theoretical rationale for the intervention. Attention to understanding the specific program mechanisms for change is needed to continually revise and improve programming.

Include Child Measures. Better documentation of the impact of programming on children is obviously needed. The information collected should be consistent with program goals. For example, if an objective of a program includes teaching parents to be more sensitive to children's feelings and emotions regarding painful separation from parents, it would be useful to gain information about changes in the child's comfort level with the separation. This might be obtained by caregiver ratings, projective examination of child drawings, or self-report in interviews or simple measures. If the objective is to teach better child management techniques to inmate parents that are presumed to directly affect child behavior, child behavior rating scales completed by caregivers or teachers could be useful. Although the quality and type of information collected will likely vary, it makes sense to gather this information for ongoing improvement of the intervention.

Provide Opportunities for Practice. Structured visitation programs that allow for practice of newly learned skills affords the opportunity for better acquisition and measurement of targeted skills. While some interventions include children through planned regular visitation programs (Landreth and Lobaugh 1998; Moore and Clement 1998), logistic and security features of many prisons bar this as common practice. However, in these cases, skills can still be measured directly with a bit of creativity. Examination of letters sent before and after instruction on optimal written communication, for example, can afford objective information for assessment and instruction. Daily checklists in which inmates monitor their use of covered strategies can provide routine information regarding treatment compliance. In-class exercises that call for practice of skills (e.g., role plays, observation and critiques of video vignettes) afford opportunities for "virtual" practice as well as for simple measurement of skill acquisition.

Improve the Documentation of Programs. Efforts to replicate and build upon the existing literature will require better documentation of treatment content. Currently, the level of description provided for interventions varies widely, as does information regarding the training or professional skills of the program facilitators. Inmate manuals or documented guidelines for how to conduct sessions are rarely provided. There are, however, welcome exceptions to this pattern (Antonio et al. 2009; Czuba et al. 2006; Loper and Tuerk forthcoming). Facilitators using the InsideOut Dad™ program received training by creators of the curriculum (NFI 2008, 2009). Some interventions use portions of outside programs that provide documentation of training procedures. For example, Harrison (1997) used a combination of Bavolek and Comstock's (1985) Nurturing Parenting Program and components from Dinkmeyer and McKay's (1989) Systematic Training for Effective Parenting. Specific descriptions of intervention content allows for replication of reported successful interventions and guidelines on important intervention features.

Delineate and Describe Contextual Features. The varying content of interventions likely reflects the various contexts in which intervention is implemented. Better attention to and description of these contexts will improve understanding and cross-fertilization of efforts. While many situations characterize a particular setting or program, two major contextual dimensions can substantially affect the content of programming. The first concerns whether the program is implemented for mothers or fathers. Whereas a few interventions have been used with both men and women, many are specifically designed by gender. This is not surprising; most prisons are gender specific. The needs and stresses of inmate mothers can differ considerably from men because of differences in pre-prison primary caretaker status, length of sentence, connection with caretakers, presence of mental health problems, and many other factors (Loper and Tuerk forthcoming).

Along similar lines, program content may vary depending upon whether reunification is expected within the short or long term. Inmates who will soon be resuming contact with children, as is the case in many jail programs, may benefit from more instruction in behavioral management and awareness of transitional issues that can arise with unification. Inmates who serve longer sentences may need more instruction on using existing communication avenues, growing personally, and collaborating with caregivers. Unlike most empirically supported family interventions that target a particular child issue (e.g., conduct disorder, autism), interventions with the incarcerated may be better summarized by the key contextual features of the prisoner parents.

Policy Implications and Summary

The continued development and improvement of effective parenting programs for prisoners requires considering policies regarding inmates. Foremost is the prioritization of intervention as an institutional objective. Currently, only 27 of the 50 U.S. state prison systems explicitly include inmate treatment, rehabilitation, or educational programming as part of the mission of the correctional system.[2] Under these conditions, the value of treatment is less central to the sense of purpose that guides administrators and officers at the ground level of operations. Many scientific weaknesses identified in this review reflect difficulties carrying out controlled systematic research under adverse conditions or with limited institutional support. A universally embraced understanding of the importance of intervention by institutional personnel can ameliorate these difficulties, enabling the improved scientific work needed to effectively support inmates and their families.

Consistent with policies that prioritize prisoner support and treatment is a need for family contact policies that promote meaningful child-parent communication. More family-friendly visitation policies, such as extended time with children, provision of child-centric materials, and the opportunity to plan child activities, can promote child-parent contact that allows inmates to practice the skills learned during parenting class. Along similar lines, better opportunities for telephone contact between inmates and family are needed. At least two interventions directly address the importance and value of positive and reliable phone contact with children (Kennon 2003; Loper and Tuerk forthcoming; Loper et al. 2009). However, the common prison practice of requiring costly collect-call procedures eliminates this important communication avenue for many inmates.

Just as the child-parent relationship is ongoing and evolving, supportive parenting programs are needed throughout and after an inmate's stay so knowledge and connection developed during incarceration can be bridged with effective practice and application after prison. Eddy and colleagues' (2008) multisystemic intervention provides for in-prison parenting training linked with therapeutic visitation experiences that allow supervised practice; support for these acquired skills is then reiterated by postrelease programming. Institutional and community collaboration throughout and after incarceration can afford needed support for inmate parents and affected family members.

Many prisons, community agencies, and citizens have responded to the increase of incarcerated parents by providing supportive parenting training. Although relatively few U.S. prisoners are enrolled in these efforts, there is a growing awareness of the importance of intervention with this high-risk segment of the population. More and better evaluation of prison parenting programs, tolerance for the unique challenges of doing research and evaluation in prison settings, and reconsideration of policies that can road-block progress is needed. Recent legislative attention to the needs of inmates in the United States is a welcome sign of support for aiding families affected by incarceration. Although this work has its difficulties, there is plenty of room for clinicians, community organizers, correctional professionals, and scholars to create and refine programs on the inside as one step toward making a difference on the outside for inmates, their children, their families, and society at large.

NOTES

1. Denise Johnston, personal communication with the authors, February 16, 2009.

2. About.com, "State Prison Systems," http://crime.about.com/od/state/State_Prison_Systems.htm.

REFERENCES

Abidin, Richard R., and Jack F. Brunner. 1995. "Development of a Parenting Alliance Inventory." *Journal of Clinical Child Psychology* 24:31–40.

Abidin, Richard R., and Timothy Konold. 1999. *Parenting Alliance Measure: Professional Manual.* Odessa, FL: Psychological Assessment Resources, Inc.

Antonio, Michael E., Lisa M. Winegeard, Jacqueline L. Young, and Jesse S. Zortman. 2009. *An Evaluation of Pennsylvania's Department of Corrections Parenting Program: Final Report.* Harrisburg: Pennsylvania Department of Corrections.

Applegate, Brandon K. 2001. "Penal Austerity: Perceived Utility, Desert, and Public Attitudes toward Prison Amenities." *American Journal of Criminal Justice* 25:253–68.

Arditti, Joyce A., Sara A. Smock, and Tiffaney S. Parkman. 2005. " 'It's Been Hard to Be a Father': A Qualitative Exploration of Incarcerated Fatherhood." *Fathering* 3:267–88.

Bavolek, Stephen J. 1984. *Adult-Adolescent Parenting Inventory (AAPI)*. Park City, UT: Family Development Resources.

———. 1999. *Nurturing Parenting: Teaching Empathy, Self-Worth, and Discipline to School-Age Children*. 4th ed. Park City, UT: Family Development Resources.

———. 2005. "Research and Validation Report of the Nurturing Parenting Program." Park City, UT: Family Development Resources.

Bavolek, Stephen J., and Christine Comstock. 1985. *The Nurturing Program*. Eau Claire, WI: Family Development Resources.

Bavolek, Stephen J., and Richard G. Keene. 2001. *Adult-Adolescent Parenting Inventory AAPI-2: Administration and Development Handbook*. Park City, UT: Family Development Resources, Inc.

Bayse, Daniel J., Scott M. Allgood, and Paul H. Van Wyk. 1991. "Family Life Education: An Effective Tool for Prisoner Rehabilitation." *Family Relations* 40:254–57.

Block, Kathleen J., and Margaret J. Potthast. 1998. "Girl Scouts Beyond Bars: Facilitating Parent-Child Contact in Correctional Settings." *Child Welfare* 77:561–78.

Browne, Dorothy H. 1989. "Incarcerated Mothers and Parenting." *Journal of Family Violence* 4:211–21.

Bruns, Deborah A., Terri King, and Teena Stateler. 2003. " 'The Parenting Class . . . Has Helped Me to Better Realize the Parent I Want to Be': The HOPE Program for Female Offenders and Their Children." *NHSA Dialog* 6:289–301.

Bushfield, Suzanne. 2004. "Fathers in Prison: Impact of Parenting Education." *Journal of Correctional Education* 55:104–16.

Carlson, Joseph R. 1998. "Evaluating the Effectiveness of a Live-In Nursery within a Women's Prison." *Journal of Offender Rehabilitation* 27:73–85.

Clarke, Lynda, Margaret O'Brien, Randall D. Day, Hugo Godwin, Jo Connolly, Joanne Hemmings, and Terri Van Leeson. 2005. "Fathering Behind Bars in English Prisons: Imprisoned Fathers' Identity and Contact with Their Children." *Fathering* 3:221–41.

Connors, Nichola A., Leanne Whiteside-Mansell, David Deere, Toni Ledet, and Mark C. Edwards. 2006. "Measuring the Potential for Child Maltreatment: The Reliability and Validity of the Adult Adolescent Parenting Inventory-2." *Child Abuse and Neglect* 30:39–53.

Czuba, Cheryl, Stephen A. Anderson, and Shirley Higgins. 2006. "Evaluation of the People Empowering People Program within a Prison Population." *Journal of Extension* 44(4): article 4RIB4.

de Graaf, Irene, Paula Speetjens, Filip Smit, Mariane de Wolff, and Louis Tavecchio. 2008. "Effectiveness of the Triple P Positive Parenting Program on Behavioral Problems in Children: A Meta-Analysis." *Behavior Modification* 32:714–35.

Derogatis, Leonard. 1993. *Brief Symptom Inventory (BSI): Administration, Scoring, and Procedures Manual*. 3rd ed. Minneapolis, MN: National Computer Systems.

Dinkmeyer, Don, and Gary D. McKay 1989. *The Parent's Handbook: STEP Systematic Training for Effective Parenting*. 3rd ed. Circle Pines, MN: American Guidance Services.

Eddy, J. Mark, Charles R. Martinez, Tracy Schiffmann, Rex Newton, Laura Olin, Leslie Leve, Dana M. Foney, and Joann Wu Shortt. 2008. "Development of a Multisystemic

Parent Management Training Intervention for Incarcerated Parents, Their Children, and Families." *Clinical Psychologist* 12:86–98.

Family Development Resources. 2008. "Nurturing Parenting Program Validation Studies 1983–2008." Park City, UT: Family Development Resources.

Gat, Irit. 2000. "Incarcerated Mothers: Effects of the Mother/Offspring Life Development Program (MOLD) on Recidivism, Prosocial Moral Development, Empathy, Hope, and Parent-Child Attachment." Ph.D. diss., University of Nebraska, Lincoln.

Glaze, Lauren, and Laura Maruschak. 2008. *Parents in Prison and Their Minor Children.* NCJ 222984. Washington, DC: U.S. Department of Justice, Bureau of Justice Statistics.

Gonzalez, Patricia, Tony Romero, and Christine B. Cerbana. 2007. "Parenting Education for Incarcerated Mothers in Colorado." *Journal of Correctional Education* 58:357–73.

Goshin, Lorie S., and Mary W. Byrne. 2009. "Converging Streams of Opportunity for Prison Nursery Programs in the United States." *Journal of Offender Rehabilitation* 48:271–95.

Hairston, Creasie F. 1991. "Mothers in Jail: Parent-Child Separation and Jail Visitation." *Affilia* 6:9–27.

Harm, Nancy J., Patricia J. Thompson, and Helen Chambers. 1998. "The Effectiveness of Parent Education for Substance-Abusing Women Offenders." *Alcoholism Treatment Quarterly* 16:63–77.

Harrison, Kim. 1997. "Parental Training for Incarcerated Fathers: Effects on Attitudes, Self-Esteem, and Children's Self Perceptions." *Journal of Social Psychology* 137:588–93.

Holtfreter, Kristy, and Merry Morash. 2003. "The Needs of Women Offenders." *Women and Criminal Justice* 14:137–60.

Hughes, Margaret, and Jenee Harrison-Thompson. 2002. "Prison Parenting Programs: A National Survey." *Social Policy Journal* 1:57–74.

James, Doris J., and Lauren E. Glaze. 2006. *Mental Health Problems of Prison and Jail Inmates.* NCJ 213600. Washington, DC: U.S. Department of Justice, Bureau of Justice Statistics.

Jordan, B. Kathleen, William E. Schlenger, John A. Fairbank, and Juesta M. Caddell. 1996. "Prevalence of Psychiatric Disorders among Incarcerated Women: Convicted Felons Entering Prison." *Archives of General Psychiatry* 53:513–19.

Kazura, Kerry. 2001. "Family Programming for Incarcerated Parents: A Needs Assessment among Inmates." *Journal of Offender Rehabilitation* 32:67–83.

Kennon, Sue. 2003. "Developing the Parenting Skills of Incarcerated Parents: A Program Evaluation." Master's thesis, Virginia Commonwealth University, Richmond.

Landreth, Garry L., and Alan F. Lobaugh. 1998. "Filial Therapy with Incarcerated Fathers: Effects on Parental Acceptance of Child, Parental Stress, and Child Adjustment." *Journal of Counseling and Development* 76:157–65.

LaRosa, Justin J., and Michael G. Rank. 2001. "Parenting Education and Incarcerated Fathers." *Journal of Family Social Work* 6(3): 15–33.

Laughlin, Jade S., Bruce A. Arrigo, Kristle R. Blevins, and Charisse T. M. Coston. 2008. "Incarcerated Mothers and Child Visitation." *Criminal Justice Policy Review* 19:215–38.

Loper, Ann Booker, and Elena H. Tuerk. Forthcoming. "Improving the Emotional Adjustment and Communication Patterns of Incarcerated Mothers: Effectiveness of a Prison Parenting Intervention." *Journal of Child and Family Studies.*

Loper, Ann Booker, Wrenn Carlson, Lacey Levitt, and Kathryn Scheffel. 2009. "Parenting Stress, Alliance, Child Contact, and Adjustment of Imprisoned Mothers and Fathers." *Journal of Offender Rehabilitation* 48(6): 483–503.

Maiorano, Joseph J., and Ted G. Futris. 2005. "Fit 2-B FATHERS: The Effectiveness of Extension Programming with Incarcerated Fathers." *Journal of Extension* 43(5): article 5FEA6.

Meek, Rosie. 2007. "Parenting Education for Young Fathers in Prison." *Child and Family Social Work* 12:239–47.

Meyer, Doris, and Cathy Moriarty. 1995. *Rebonding and Rebuilding: A Parenting Curriculum.* 4th ed. Los Angeles: Hacienda La Puenta.

Mindel, Charles H., and Richard A. Hoefer. 2006. "An Evaluation of a Family Strengthening Program for Substance Abuse Offenders." *Journal of Social Service Research* 32:23–38.

Minor, Kevin I., Sharon Karr, and Swaran Jain. 1987. "An Examination of the Utility of the MMPI in Predicting Male Prison Inmate Abusive Attitudes." *Psychological Record* 37:429–36.

Moore, Alvin, and Mary J. Clement. 1998. "Effects of Parenting Training for Incarcerated Mothers." *Journal of Offender Rehabilitation* 27:57–72.

National Fatherhood Initiative. 2005. *InsideOut Dad™: A Program for Incarcerated Fathers.* Gaithersburg, MD: National Fatherhood Initiative.

———. 2008. *InsideOut Dad™ Program Evaluation Report.* Gaithersburg, MD: National Fatherhood Initiative.

———. 2009. *InsideOut Dad™ Program in Maryland and Ohio Prisons Evaluation Report.* Gaithersburg, MD: National Fatherhood Initiative.

Ortega, Sandra, Antoine Beauchemin, and Reyhan Burcu Kaniskan. 2008. "Building Resiliency in Families with Young Children Exposed to Violence: The Safe Start Initiative Pilot Study." *Best Practices in Mental Health* 4:48–64.

Palusci, Vincent J., Pat Crum, Rosalynn Bliss, and Stephen J. Bavolek. 2008. "Changes in Parenting Attitudes and Knowledge among Inmates and Other At-Risk Populations after a Family Nurturing Program." *Children and Youth Services Review* 30:79–89.

Pollock, Joycelyn. 2003. "Parenting Programs in Women's Prisons." *Women and Criminal Justice* 14:131–54.

Reid, John B., Gerald R. Patterson, and James Snyder. 2002 *Antisocial Behavior in Children and Adolescents: A Developmental Analysis and Model for Intervention.* Washington, DC: American Psychological Association.

Robbers, Monica L. P. 2003. "Reconnecting, Rebuilding, and Re-Educating: Evaluating a Responsible Fatherhood Program for Incarcerated 'Deadbeat' Dads." *Corrections Compendium* 28(4): 1–4, 29–31.

———. 2005. "Focus on Family and Fatherhood: Lessons from Fairfax County's Responsible Fatherhood Program for Incarcerated Dads." *Justice Policy Journal* 2(1).

Rodgers, Antoinette Y. 1998. "Multiple Sources of Stress and Parenting Behavior." *Children and Youth Services Review* 20:525–46.

Rodgers-Farmer, Antoinette Y. 1999. "Parenting Stress, Depression, and Parenting in Grandmothers Raising Their Grandchildren." *Children and Youth Services Review* 21:377–88.

Sanders, Matthew R., Carol Markie-Dadds, Lucy A. Tully, and William Bor. 2000. "The Triple P Positive Parenting Program: A Comparison of Enhanced, Standard, and Self-Directed Behavioral Family Intervention for Parents of Children with Early Onset Conduct Problems." *Journal of Consulting and Clinical Psychology* 68:624–40.

Sandifer, Jacquelyn L. 2008. "Evaluating the Efficacy of a Parenting Program for Incarcerated Mothers." *The Prison Journal* 8:423–45.

Showers, Jacy. 1993. "Assessing and Remedying Parenting Knowledge among Women Inmates." *Journal of Offender Rehabilitation* 20:35–46.

Skarupski, Kimberly A., Campbell J. Bullock, Chivon Fitch, Amy Linda Johnson, Linda M. Kelso, Erica R. Fox, Brandi Napenas, Marge Dimperio, and Michael J. Drabik. 2003. *Outcomes Evaluation of the Long Distance Dads© Program.* Erie, PA: Center for Organization Research, The Behrend College, Penn State Erie.

Snyder-Joy, Zoann K., and Teresa A. Carlo. 1998. "Parenting through Prison Walls: Incarcerated Mothers and Children's Visitation Programs." In *Crime Control and Women: Feminist Implications of Criminal Justice Policy,* edited by Susan L. Miller (130–50). Thousand Oaks, CA: SAGE Publications.

Thomas, Rae, and Melanie J. Zimmer-Gembeck. 2007. "Behavioral Outcomes of Parent-Child Interaction Therapy and Triple P-Positive Parenting Program: A Review and Meta-Analysis." *Journal of Abnormal Child Psychology* 35:475–95.

Thompson, Patricia J., and Nancy Harm. 2000. "Parenting from Prison: Helping Children and Mothers." *Issues in Comprehensive Pediatric Nursing* 23:35–46.

Valle, Linda A., Daniel J. Whitaker, John R. Lutzker, Jill H. Filene, Jennifer M. Wyatt, Kendall C. Cephas, and D. Michele Hoover. 2004. "Using Evidence-Based Parenting Programs to Advance CDC Efforts in Child Maltreatment Prevention." Research brief. Atlanta, GA: Centers for Disease Control and Prevention.

Warren, Janet I., Susan Hurt, Ann B. Loper, Risha Bale, Roxanne Friend, and Preeti Chauhan. 2002. "Psychiatric Symptoms, History of Victimization, and Violent Behavior among Incarcerated Female Felons: An American Perspective." *International Journal of Law and Psychiatry* 25:129–49.

Webster-Stratton, Carolyn, and Keith C. Herman. 2008. "The Impact of Parent Behavior-Management Training on Child Depressive Symptoms." *Journal of Counseling Psychology* 55:473–84.

Webster-Stratton, Carolyn, M. Jamila Reid, and Mary Hammond. 2001. "Preventing Conduct Problems, Promoting Social Competence: A Parent and Teacher Training Partnership in Head Start." *Journal of Clinical Child Psychology* 30:283–302.

———. 2004. "Treating Children with Early-Conduct Problems: Intervention Outcomes for Parent, Child, and Teacher Training." *Journal of Clinical Child and Adolescent Psychology* 33:105–24.

Wilczak, Ginger L., and Carol A. Markstrom. 1999. "The Effects of Parent Education on Parental Locus of Control and Satisfaction of Incarcerated Fathers." *International Journal of Offender Therapy and Comparative Criminology* 43:90–102.

11

Mentoring Interventions for Children of Incarcerated Parents

Liza Zwiebach, Jean E. Rhodes,
and Catherine Dun Rappaport

The United States has the highest incarceration rate in the world, with more than 1 in 100 adults behind bars (Warren 2008). As of a 2004 survey, between 56 and 62 percent of incarcerated women have children, as do between 51 and 63 percent of incarcerated men (Glaze and Maruschak 2008). Mentoring relationships have been proposed as a strategy to help children with incarcerated parents, potentially providing a measure of stability and support in an otherwise difficult situation (U.S. Department of Health and Human Services 2008). This chapter defines mentoring as "a relationship between an older, more experienced adult and an unrelated, younger protégé—a relationship in which the adult provides ongoing guidance, instruction, and encouragement aimed at developing the competence and character of the protégé" (Rhodes 2002, 3).

The following sections discuss the particular vulnerabilities experienced by many children of prisoners and the ways both natural and assigned mentoring relationships might protect them. Within this context, the chapter considers research findings and the mentoring initiatives currently under way.

Children of Incarcerated Parents

Children of prisoners potentially face a host of difficulties that put them at risk for poor developmental outcomes. When a parent is incarcerated, children may face increased poverty, family instability, and feelings of stigmatization and shame (Gabel 1992; Gaudin and Sutphen 1993). Further, because many families with an imprisoned parent may have already struggled with poverty, discrimination, violence, and limited access to material and social resources before the parent's incarceration (Johnston and Gabel 1995; Murray and Farrington 2005), some children of incarcerated parents are already at increased risk for negative outcomes at the time of separation from their parent. Thus, the incarceration of a parent may exacerbate difficulties that children are already encountering (Nesmith and Ruhland 2008).

The situations and characteristics within this group of children vary widely, and by no means are all individuals at the same extent of risk simply by virtue of having an incarcerated parent. However, research has identified characteristics more likely to occur among such youth compared with the general population. The most common problems that appear to covary with parental incarceration include low self-esteem, anger and depression, emotional withdrawal, feelings of abandonment, eating and sleeping disorders, and academic and behavioral problems (Henriques 1982; Johnston 1995; Jose Kampfner 1995; Travis 2002). In light of such difficulties, some children of prisoners show relatively poor psychological, academic, and behavioral outcomes compared with their peers. For example, Murray and Farrington (2005) find that boys who have experienced the incarceration of a parent are more likely to exhibit a number of antisocial behaviors later in life, including criminal conviction, violence, and drug-taking. The same authors also find that parental incarceration is associated with greater risk of anxiety and depression from adolescence into adulthood (Murray and Farrington 2008). Notably, the comparison group used in these investigations comprised boys who had been separated from parents for reasons besides incarceration, as well as boys who had never been separated from parents, and boys whose parents had been incarcerated only before their children's births.

The Role of Caring Adults

Despite the considerable risks, all children do not experience parental incarceration in the same way. Apart from studies specifically of children of incarcerated parents, researchers have demonstrated that even in the face of significantly adverse circumstances—war, natural disasters, family violence, extreme poverty, parental mental illness, and parental incarceration—some youth thrive (Rutter 1979). Three broad clusters of protective factors have been associated with such resilience (Masten and Coatsworth 1998): characteristics of the individual, such as intelligence, self-confidence, or special talents; characteristics of the family, such as authoritative parenting and socioeconomic advantages; and characteristics of the community outside the family, such as a relationship with a caring adult (e.g., a teacher, a religious leader).

While a substantial body of literature exists on the first two clusters, less is known about the third. But this third cluster has informed youth mentoring. The significance of supportive, nonparental adults in the lives of children was highlighted in the landmark Children of Kauai study, which followed an entire birth cohort across their first 30 years of life (Werner 1989). Many children studied were classified as high risk because they had been born into poverty and were living in conflict-ridden or traumatic family environments; however, a large proportion of the high-risk children reached adulthood as competent, high-functioning individuals. A widespread feature among this group of children was a strong relationship with at least one supportive adult other than a parent. Another identified protective factor was involvement in a religious or other community group (Werner and Johnson 2004).

Subsequent studies have corroborated this finding. Rishel, Sales, and Koeske (2005) associated relationships with nonparental adults with fewer behavioral problems among children and adolescents. Similarly, Klaw, Rhodes, and Fitzgerald (2003) examined academic achievement in a sample of low-income African American adolescent mothers over the course of two years. At the beginning and end of the study period, participants were asked to name an adult who had offered them emotional support. Those who had mentioned the same adult both times were 3.3 times less likely to have dropped out of high school than were those participants who had not named someone at either time (because enduring mentoring relationships were the focus of this study, participants who had nominated different individuals at the two time points were not included in the analysis).

More recently, an epidemiological study demonstrated the salutary effects of supportive, nonparental adults in the lives of youth (DuBois and Silverthorn 2005). Participants in the National Longitudinal Study of Adolescent Health (LSAH) were asked whether an adult other than a parent or stepparent had "made an important positive difference" in their lives since the age of 14. The presence of such a figure was associated with a greater likelihood of completing high school and attending college. For those who were not attending college at the time of assessment, the presence of a supportive adult was associated with an increased likelihood of working regularly. In addition, this type of relationship was associated with decreased risk-taking, violent behavior, and gang involvement. Finally, positive effects were shown with regard to physical activity, regular use of birth control, and psychological health. The presence of a supportive adult also was associated with greater self-esteem and life satisfaction.

Replicating the Kauai findings regarding the importance of non-parental supportive adults in the large, representative LSAH sample is encouraging. DuBois and Silverthorn extended the early work by going on to examine variability in the effects of such adults as a function of adolescents' risk status (i.e., interaction effects). They hypothesized that a supportive relationship would be most beneficial to participants exhibiting high levels of individual risk (e.g., academic difficulties, physical disability) or environmental risk (e.g., low educational attainment of parents, feeling unsafe in one's neighborhood). However, the expected interaction effects were not found, leading DuBois and Silverthorn to conclude that simply having a relationship with a caring adult, while certainly valuable, may not be a sufficiently strong force to offset the negative effects that at-risk children and adolescents face. Of additional concern is that recent changes in the composition of low-income communities (Wilson 1996) and the growing demands on school personnel have made it more difficult for economically disadvantaged youth to connect and develop relationships with "natural" mentors within their communities (Eccles and Gootman 2002; Putnam 2000).

In recent years, a range of organized mentoring programs has emerged to fill this gap. Mentoring has become a popular preventive intervention, with an estimated 3 million children and adolescents participating in these relationships in the United States (Rhodes and DuBois 2008). Most programs match one volunteer mentor with one youth and encourage frequent, regular interaction. They may differ in terms of a specific or general focus. For example, school-based programs are implemented at the mentees' schools, with academic success a primary goal, whereas other programs are less structured and the mentors and mentees have relatively more freedom to define their interactions as they choose (Karcher 2008).

From 2000 to 2010 in particular, mentoring programs tailored for children of incarcerated parents have expanded dramatically. The largest such effort is the federal government's Mentoring Children of Prisoners

Program, which was initiated during President George W. Bush's administration and has received allocations of approximately $50 million or more in funding each year since 2004. Despite much public enthusiasm for mentoring as an intervention with the members of this vulnerable population, the success of such programs is unclear. Little is known about how mentoring relationships actually work for children of prisoners. Although the outcomes for mentored children of prisoners are thought to be comparable to those found in prior evaluations of mentoring with the general youth population, this remains an untested assumption. Given the paucity of information, it is useful to take stock of what we do know about the mentoring of youth in general, and consider how these data may be relevant to the children of incarcerated parents.

Research on the Effectiveness of Youth Mentoring

Regardless of the youth population of interest, most evaluations of mentoring programs have revealed only modest effects. For example, in a randomized controlled trial of community-based mentoring offered by Big Brothers Big Sisters of America (BBBS), the nation's oldest and most well-known mentoring organization, researchers traced the experiences of youth who were given access to the program, as well as youth assigned to a control condition, over time (Grossman and Tierney 1998). Several statistically significant differences in behaviors and academic functioning between the mentored youth and the control group were found 18 months after the initial interview.

While such findings are promising, statistical significance does not imply practical significance. In that regard, standardized effect sizes are considered a more useful metric of evaluation (Flay et al. 2005). In statistical terms, the effect size represents the degree to which two groups differ (in this case, the mentoring group versus the wait-listed control group). Effect size is derived as the difference between the standardized group means, using Cohen's d (Tabachnick and Fidell 2007). Effect sizes using this measure are interpreted as small if $d = 0.2$, medium if $d = 0.5$, and large if $d = 0.8$ (Cohen 1988). An additional way of interpreting Cohen's d is by considering the degree of "nonoverlap" between the distributions of the two groups; for example, a small effect size of 0.2 is equivalent to 14.7 percent nonoverlap.[1] In the Big Brothers Big Sisters study, although mentor-child match quality and the length of mentoring relationships varied considerably, the standardized effect sizes across all matches and outcomes in the study were small ($d = 0.06$) (Herrera et al. 2007). Notably, this effect size indicates less than 7 percent nonoverlap between the mentored and the wait-listed groups.

The same effect sizes emerged in a large randomized controlled evaluation of BBBS's new, school-based mentoring program (Herrera et al. 2007). In school-based mentoring, interactions between youth and mentors typically are confined to the school setting and the one-year minimum commitment of mentors is shortened to the nine-month school year. Because school-based mentoring is linked to the academic calendar, the relationships tend to be less enduring than those forged through community-based mentoring. Indeed, the average length of the relationships in the school-based mentoring evaluation was just 5.3 months, compared with 11.4 months in the community-based mentoring evaluation. In addition, nearly half (48 percent) of the school-based mentoring relationships did not continue into the following school year. The size of the effect varied by outcome: for school-related outcomes (such as proficiency in specific subjects, number of completed assignments, and number of absences), the overall effect size was 0.09, and for non-school-related outcomes (i.e., behavioral and psychosocial outcomes), effect sizes ranged from 0.02 to 0.18. These effects did not persist over time, however, and, when youth were reassessed a few months into the following school year, most differences were no longer statistically significant. A related and more recent evaluation was conducted of the U.S. Department of Education's Student Mentoring Program, which has funded over 300 mentoring programs nationwide to promote academic achievement and advancement, interpersonal relationships and personal responsibility, and reductions in delinquent behavior (Bernstein et al. 2009). It found that the program has not led to statistically significant impacts on mentees across these three outcomes.

Based on a meta-analysis of 55 studies of community-based mentoring, using either a pretest-posttest design or a comparison group (randomly or nonrandomly assigned), DuBois and colleagues (2002) estimated the average effect size for youth mentoring programs using Cohen's d. Similar to the Big Brothers Big Sisters studies, a significant, though modest, aggregate effect was found on various youth outcomes. In addition, the impacts of varied potential moderators of such effects were investigated. Of particular interest here, DuBois and his colleagues (2002) examined the at-risk status of youth as a moderator of mentoring effectiveness. Children were classified as being at environmental risk (i.e., "considered vulnerable by virtue of their present life circumstances but who are not yet demonstrating significant dysfunction," p. 189) or at individual risk (i.e., experienced risk in their individual characteristics, such as failing in school, behavioral problems, or emotional disturbance). Not surprisingly, a subset of youth was classified as being at both environmental and individual risk. Risk status proved a significant moderator, with the group at combined environmental and individual risk benefiting the most from mentoring, and the group with neither risk benefiting less. Interestingly, children at environmental risk alone showed a larger effect than did children not experiencing either type of risk, but children at individual risk alone showed an effect size of near zero, suggesting that, on average, mentoring had little impact on this group.

DuBois and colleagues asserted that the children classified as experiencing individual risk were in fact already exhibiting considerable personal problems. Possibly such youth simply needed more intensive and professional services than could be realistically asked of a volunteer, non-professional mentor. However, investigating their findings more closely, the authors examined whether mentoring program practices might account for the poorer prognosis of youth at individual risk. They developed an index of 11 empirically based best practices, program features identified through previous research as related to positive outcomes for youth (box 11.1). For each program in the meta-analysis, DuBois and

---

Box 11.1. Program Features Comprising Best Practices for Mentoring

Monitoring of program implementation
Screening of prospective mentors
Matching of mentors and youth based on one or more relevant criteria
Prematch training of mentors
Ongoing training of mentors
Supervision of relationship by program staff
Support group for mentors
Structured activities for mentors and youth
Involvement of parents
Expectations for frequency of contact between mentors and youth
Expectations for length of relationships

Source: Adapted from DuBois et al. (2002).

colleagues calculated the number of best practice features used in the program. This best practice index was related to program effect sizes for youth at individual risk. Specifically, positive effects of mentoring for this group were high when programs featured a majority of identified best practices, but effects were negative otherwise, meaning not only a lack of perceivable benefit from mentoring but also a heightened risk of outright problematic outcomes.

These findings converge with those of Grossman and Rhodes (2002), who found that very early termination of the mentoring relationship was associated with decrements in mentee functioning. Thus, it seems that mentoring, if done poorly, could cause harm to more vulnerable youth. Whereas it is always advisable to follow identified best practices when conducting a mentoring program with any youth, it is critical under conditions where youth are experiencing individual difficulties or dysfunction. DuBois and his colleagues make the point that higher-risk children may need multiple intensive services, mentoring being but one, and that the importance of continued and rigorous training and support is paramount when providing mentoring to this population.

Because of results such as these, it is essential to consider the potential risks of providing mentoring services for children of incarcerated parents. In addition to other stressors these children have encountered, many children of incarcerated parents are separated from their primary caregivers, most typically their mothers. Moreover, many such children have gone on to experience recurrent changes in caregivers or living arrangements (Johnston and Gabel 1995). Children of prisoners are particularly likely to experience discontinuity in care by moving from home to home, whether such homes are those of kin or of foster families. A consistent finding in mentoring research has been the positive effect of relationship length on benefits accrued by participating youth (Grossman and Rhodes 2002), where a longer duration of the mentoring match has been associated with greater gains in children's functioning compared with briefer mentoring experiences. In fact, Grossman and Rhodes found that shorter mentoring relationships were associated with decrements in children's functioning, suggesting that a short-lived match may be worse than no match at all. Because many children of incarcerated parents are likely to have a history of transient connections with adults, care must be taken to provide a mentoring match that does not prove to be yet another disruptive relationship, adding further instability to their lives.

Despite this caution, the group differences that have been found in rigorous evaluations of mentoring provide some basis for cautious optimism about the potential viability of mentoring interventions for the children of incarcerated parents. Of particular importance are the findings suggesting that positive effects are greatest among youth from backgrounds of high environmental risk. Preliminary evidence for the benefits of mentoring on high-risk youth, combined with the intuitive appeal of the mentoring approach, makes mentoring programs a promising intervention for the children of incarcerated parents. Mentoring, when carried out sensitively and according to identified best practices, may be construed as promoting resilience among vulnerable children. This is not to say that mentoring should be the only strategy aimed at improving the lives of children of incarcerated parents. Rather, mentoring can be introduced alongside other initiatives targeted at enriching the support systems of non-incarcerated caregivers.

Based on what is known about the children of incarcerated parents, many likely need the social support, guidance, and stability offered by a strong and enduring mentoring relationship. However, although a few small mentoring programs for children of prisoners have been successfully conducted in other countries, including Israel and the Netherlands (e.g., van Nijnatten 1997), such programs have emerged only recently in the United States. To our knowledge, no large-scale evaluation of mentoring initiatives for children of incarcerated parents has been published either in this country or abroad. The remainder of this chapter is devoted to two groundbreaking programs to reach children of incarcerated parents through mentoring relationships in the United States.

Mentoring Programs for Children of Prisoners

Amachi

The first major effort to mentor children of prisoners was a partnership among two nonprofit organizations (Public/Private Ventures and BBBS), the Center for Research on Religion and Urban Civil Society at the University of Pennsylvania, and local churches. The program, named Amachi (a West African word meaning "who knows but what God has brought us through this child"), was launched in Philadelphia in 2000. Volunteers were recruited from local church congregations and matched with identified children of incarcerated parents. By the end of January 2002, 42 churches had joined the partnership and almost 400 children had been matched with mentors (Jucovy 2003).

Amachi implementation depends on systematic efforts to target churches—and children—in the underserved sections of the city. Once a congregation has signed on to the partnership, it is obligated to recruit 10 volunteers from its membership to serve as mentors. A volunteer coordinator is also selected from each congregation to provide regular informal support to its mentors. The infrastructure for the program is handled by BBBS, which oversees Amachi's screening activities, training, and supervision of mentors. In addition, paid positions have been created to liaise between the BBBS case managers and the church volunteer coordinators so as to best support the child-volunteer matches.

In accordance with identified best practices (DuBois et al. 2002), prospective Amachi mentors are interviewed by BBBS staff and undergo a criminal background check. They also are asked to provide several references, including one from their pastor. BBBS staff also holds training sessions for mentors in groups, located at the volunteers' churches (Husock 2003). Throughout the match, mentors are supervised by both their church volunteer coordinator and a BBBS case manager.

Amachi mentors are expected to meet with mentees for one hour each week for one year. Researchers at Public/Private Ventures found that while the total number of hours that Amachi mentors spent with children exceeded requirements (7.3 hours per month on average for a mentor-child pair), the frequency of meetings fell short, averaging only twice a month. Over 50 percent of the matches extended beyond the one-year mark—a vital benchmark for mentoring relationships (Grossman and Rhodes 2002)—and a quarter of matches lasted for more than two years. However, nearly half the matches (46 percent) ended in less than a year. Most of these early terminations were the result of change in the child's life, such as family mobility or caregiver decisions, as opposed to the mentor failing to fulfill the commitment. Still, this high rate of early termination is a cause for concern.

Researchers at Public/Private Ventures conducted descriptive analyses of Amachi's first mentor-child matches (Jucovy 2003). During the first two years of operation, 517 children were matched with mentors. Of these, 47 percent were male. The vast majority of mentees were under the age of 13, with the largest group (34 percent) between ages 10 and 12. Of the 482 mentors, 42 percent were male. The range of mentor ages was broad, with nearly a quarter under 31 and another quarter over 60. Eighty-two percent of mentors were African American mentors, with the rest primarily Latino/a or Caucasian (information on youth's racial/ethnic backgrounds is not publicly available).

How mentors and mentees spent their time together also aligned with identified best practices (DuBois et al. 2002). Most pairs engaged in fun activities (attending sports, movies, concerts, or theatre, or just "hanging out"), and some attended church services or other church activities or completed schoolwork together. After mentors had been meeting with their mentees for one year, they were asked to complete a survey in which they indicated any observed changes in the child's attitudes and behaviors. A similar survey was administered to the mentees' caregivers. Perhaps not surprisingly, most mentors and caregivers felt that the mentee had greater self-confidence and an improved sense of the future as the result of the mentoring relationship.

Several features of the Amachi model suggest that it can promote positive outcomes (Jucovy 2003). The Amachi partnership includes BBBS, which bodes well for program implementation and replication around the United States given the far geographic reach of that organization. Indeed, many BBBS programs across the country already have adopted the Amachi model (Sherman 2005). Further, the involvement of a national mentoring organization partner may be a particularly important part of Amachi's promise. The infrastructure and expertise lent by a program like BBBS could not easily be supplied by the partnering churches. In fact, assuring church leaders that the organizational and supervisory duties of mentoring support would not be their responsibility, but would be provided by BBBS, was likely a key factor for many congregations in deciding to join the Amachi partnership. The congregations are thus free to capitalize on their own strengths, namely access to their communities and to a large number of potential mentors. In addition, Amachi's emphasis on accountability has likely been a strength for the program. Requirements on the minimum number of meetings, hours spent, and duration of mentoring relationship, though not always met, probably help impart a sense of commitment to the volunteers.

Mentoring Children of Prisoners Program

Whereas the origins of Amachi were characterized by a bottom-up, local approach, the Mentoring Children of Prisoners (MCP) initiative represents a broad and sweeping national effort to ameliorate some of the hardships and negative outcomes that can result from parental incarceration. MCP was launched in 2002 by Congress, which initially authorized $67 million to provide mentors for the children of prisoners, with subsequent funding subject to annual allocation. The Family and Youth Services Bureau (FYSB) of the U.S. Department of Health and Human Services used this funding to develop the MCP program, which aims to support the creation and expansion of programs that provide children of prisoners with caring mentors. As of fiscal year 2008, according to federal program staff, the Bureau had awarded approximately $260 million to more than 320 different faith-based and community organizations, state and local governments, and tribes to launch mentoring programs for children of prisoners.[2] Grants are intended to last three years.

MCP grantees are expected to implement programs aligned with identified best practices in mentoring. Programs are expected to screen volunteers, train them before they are matched with children, and provide supervision and support after volunteers are matched. Programs also must require volunteers to commit to spending at least one hour a week with their assigned children for at least one year. MCP grantees include faith- and community-based organizations, which receive referrals for mentoring services from caregivers, schools, social-service agencies, religious congregations, and the courts. Approximately 11 percent of lead grantees (i.e., organizations receiving MCP funding directly from FYSB) were faith-based organizations, with another 40 percent of grantees partnering with at least one faith-based organization.[3]

Beginning in late 2007, the MCP program expanded to include a voucher demonstration program, called Caregiver's Choice. From 2007 to 2010, the program is intended to distribute approximately $25 million through vouchers to organizations that provide mentoring services. Through Caregiver's Choice, individuals who are the primary caregivers to children of prisoners apply to join the program. Once their applications are accepted, they receive a list of approved local mentoring programs and vouchers for their children. Caregivers then can choose whichever mentoring programs best fit their needs and provide the programs they select with vouchers that programs use to support their efforts to provide targeted youth with mentors. For each youth served, mentoring programs receive $1,000. Programs receive most of their payments when they have matched youth and mentors and the pairs have met at least once ($600), and smaller amounts when the matches last three months ($200) and 12 months (another $200). FYSB is working with MENTOR/National Mentoring Partnership (a well-established umbrella organization that provides support and resources to mentoring programs) to develop a list of approved programs for Caregiver's Choice. Criteria for approval include expectations for mentor recruitment, screening, training, and monitoring and evaluation in accordance with identified best practices (DuBois et al. 2002). According to FYSB program staff, more than 3,000 vouchers were redeemed in 2008 through this program.[4]

Youth Characteristics. MCP program grantees target youth age 4 through 18, and a large percentage of youth served are at the younger end of this continuum. As of July 2007, the average age of youth in the program was 11 years, and more than half (52.3 percent) of all youth served were girls (U.S. Department of Health and Human Services 2008). Participant information is being collected through annual assessments of youth age 9 and older as part of an ongoing evaluation study. Similar data have been collected as part of a quasi-experimental study of the MCP program. According to these data, mentees come from diverse racial backgrounds, with the majority (63 percent) identifying as African American, 29 percent identifying as white, and 19 percent as Hispanic.[5] These data do not include information about youth younger than age 9, the minimum age necessary to participate in the aforementioned research. For this reason, little is known about participating children age 4 through 8.

According to this research, youth in the MCP program age 9 and older have experienced more than their share of stressful events. When presented with a list of 12 stressful events over the past six months, respondents indicated the occurrence of, on average, at least 4. Thirty-six percent indicated that they had experienced more than five of the stressful events on the scale. Specifically, more than half the youth who participated in the survey reported that someone they knew well was hurt badly or was very ill over the past six months, and close to half reported that someone they knew well died within that same period. Youth in the evaluation study sample have made several residential transitions, and many have lived away from their primary caregivers for extended periods. Forty-two percent of surveyed youth reported having changed where they lived over the past six months. Likewise, 84 percent reported living away from their birth fathers for more than 12 months, and 30 percent reported living away from their birth mothers for that same amount of time.

This level of stress may not be unusual compared with other children who receive mentoring. For example, the Big Brothers Big Sisters evaluation (Herrera et al. 2007) used a similar list of recent life events, and participants reported having experienced on average between four and five of them. However, the rate of residential transition in this sample was markedly lower than in the MCP study (though at 32 percent it is still considerable, as the authors note).

FYSB staff hypothesize that implementing the program as planned will produce short- and long-term youth outcomes, including improved academic development, lower incidence of risk-taking behaviors, better relationships with others, and increased social and emotional functioning. Key variables monitored through the program include the number of youth matched, the length of matches, and the quality of relationships between youth and mentors. Further, FYSB is sponsoring Abt Associates to conduct a quasi-experimental evaluation of program effects.

Annual Assessments of Program Performance.   One way FYSB staff assess MCP program performance is the number of matches made. As of September 2008, more than 110,800 matches had been created through grantee organizations. In addition, FYSB assesses program performance annually using a validated measure for determining the quality of relationships between youth and mentors: the Relationship Quality Instrument. This questionnaire (which is appropriate only for youth age 9 and older) gauges youths' trust in their mentors and satisfaction with their relationships. This assessment is limited, however, to those participants who have remained in relationships for at least nine months with their mentors.

To date, findings are positive for the matches that continue nine months or longer. More than 95 percent of program participants who completed the assessment in 2008 scored three or higher (on a four-point scale), which indicates a positive assessment of relationship quality (U.S. Department of Health and Human Services 2008). Relationships that did not reach the nine-month milestone (and thus, presumably, those more likely to be troubled than relationships that did) were not included in the analysis. In addition, the response rate among youth eligible to participate in the survey was relatively low. This lack of data on shorter matches may be problematic, particularly given earlier discussions of potential harm to children in more short-lived mentoring relationships (Grossman and Rhodes 2002; Shlafer et al. 2010). A challenge for this assessment of relationship quality is that it would be premature to assess relationship quality in new or very young mentor/mentee relationships. The evaluation of relationship quality must presuppose a minimum level of contact between mentor and mentee.

Quasi-Experimental Evaluation of the MCP Program. FYSB engaged Abt Associates to conduct a quasi-experimental assessment of the MCP program, comparing changes in MCP youths' behavior to changes in a group of youth without incarcerated parents who were assigned to the control group in a 2005 evaluation of school-based mentoring programs (Herrera et al. 2007). Although this study will illustrate the potential for MCP program impact and will provide some descriptive information about the program, this comparison group is less than ideal, given differences in study timing and circumstances. Most notably, the aforementioned environmental and situational characteristics frequently associated with having an incarcerated parent may make a comparison to children without such an incarcerated parent unrealistic, even if the latter sample exhibits other high risks.

In closing, although mentoring has intuitive appeal and impressive strides have been made to establish mentoring programs, data are not yet available that would suggest whether mentoring is a viable intervention for children of prisoners. More rigorous evaluations are needed to obtain not only an understanding of how mentoring programs work for children of prisoners, but whether, with whom, when, and how they make a positive impact. In addition, an in-depth descriptive study could illustrate how these programs differ from other mentoring programs (both in structure and in challenges faced by participating youth), and how they might be improved to better serve this high-risk population. Practitioners and policymakers need to know more about the potential for mentoring to make a positive difference in these children's lives. Indeed, as mentioned previously, some research suggests that youth who have many serious barriers to success may not thrive in mentoring programs, particularly if such programs are not rigorous in their adherence to identified best practices (DuBois et al. 2002). Thus, although proponents assume that Amachi and MCP outcomes are at least comparable to the outcomes demonstrated by BBBS in their earlier evaluation (Cnaan et al. 2006), this assumption must be confirmed through rigorous evaluation.

Policy and Practice Considerations

The findings reviewed in this chapter have several policy implications. As discussed, many mentoring programs for children of prisoners are administered through faith-based organizations. It will be important to remain mindful of the consequences and potential complexities of this relatively new trend in mentoring. One benefit of administering mentoring programs through faith-based organizations is the potential access to a rich pool of volunteers and, in some congregations, children of prisoners. Social policies in general, and mentoring programs in particular, often do not reach or support the most severely disadvantaged youth. Since religious involvement appears to play an important role in lives of many urban youth (Johnson et al. 2000), faith-based organizations are well positioned to connect youth with social programs. Additionally, mentoring relationships that are forged through religious organizations could offer some advantages in mentees' spiritual development. For example, adolescents searching for meaning or attempting to reconcile their own belief system with those of their parents may be guided in these pursuits by their mentors (Chan and Rhodes 2008).

On the other hand, some critics have raised concerns about the role of the federal government in promoting faith-based initiatives. Constitutional separation of church and state mandates that public funds not be used for religious purposes; therefore it is vital to ensure that the mentoring relationship not become a platform for proselytizing. FYSB program staff has continued to issue guidance on religious activities among faith-based grantees to this effect.[6] Some churches in Philadelphia viewed mentoring as an opportunity for religious expression, though Amachi leadership has discouraged preaching of this sort (Bane 2006). Particularly when the mentee is not already a member of a congregation, a religiously motivated mentor might feel compelled to try to share his or her beliefs with the child. Such efforts are not supported by empirical evidence and could ultimately be counterproductive; indeed, previous research has underscored the importance of nonjudgmental approaches so the youth learns to think critically and independently (Styles and Morrow 1992). Another potential problem with the role of religious organizations in these national mentoring initiatives concerns their manifest lack of sociodemographic diversity. African American Christians and white evangelical Christians tend to be the most actively involved in providing faith-based mentoring, whereas people from other backgrounds are poorly represented.

Apart from the role of religious organizations in mentoring children of prisoners, a second broad area of concern relates to unique challenges posed by this special population. It has been estimated that over 17 million young people in the United States may benefit from mentoring (MENTOR 2006). Although other federally funded programs support mentoring of youth besides children of prisoners (i.e., National Guard's Youth Challenge and Senior Corps/Foster Grandparents), a sizable proportion of the government funding for mentoring other children has been concentrated on the children of incarcerated parents, who despite their increased risk are a small subset of vulnerable youth. Although children of prisoners deserve support, federal and state funding is also needed for programs that can address the needs of all vulnerable youth.

Moreover, as generous funding for children of prisoners was dispersed, programs were thrown into competition with each other in recruitment efforts. In the push to recruit large numbers of children of prisoners, programs might be including children who would benefit from more intensive therapeutic or educational services. Mentoring programs may be feeling pressure to stay financially afloat and viable by demonstrating their capacity to recruit large numbers of children of prisoners and volunteers who are willing to work with them. Such demands can potentially eclipse concerns about the appropriateness and readiness of children and volunteers to engage in mentoring relationships. Because most mentoring program staff worked under the tacit assumption that their programs are inherently beneficial to youth, they sometimes put their limited resources into creating new matches, rather than sustaining matches that had already been made. Funding agencies reinforce this tendency, often using the number of new matches with children of prisoners—as opposed to their sustainability—as the measure of a program's success. For example, FYSB set an ambitious, yet very challenging, goal of creating at least 100,000 matches within the first few years. This is not the sole measurement of outcome for FYSB, however, and funding has been allocated to evaluate the quality of mentoring relationships as well as their mere existence.

Conclusion

It would be difficult to imagine a group of children more in need of a connection with a caring adult than those with a parent in prison. The large body of existing research focusing on mentoring within the general population—when implemented according to identified best practices—points to positive long-term effects on participating youth. Generous public support has laid the foundation for new mentoring initiatives devoted specifically to children of incarcerated parents. A deeper understanding of the particular circumstances and needs of these children, combined with high-quality programs and enriched settings with well-designed evaluation components, will better position us to harness the full potential of mentoring for children of prisoners.

NOTES

1. See the conversion table at http://web.uccs.edu/lbecker/Psy590/es.htm.

2. J. E. Hocker, personal communication with the authors, January 26, 2009.

3. J. E. Hocker, personal communication with the authors, January 15, 2009.

4. J. E. Hocker, personal communication with the authors, February 19, 2009.

5. Preliminary data from Abt Associates, Inc.'s 2006–11 study of the MCP program. Used with permission from FYSB.

6. J. E. Hocker, personal communication with the authors, June 12, 2009.

REFERENCES

Bane, Mary Jo. 2006. *Starting Amachi: The Elements and Operation of a Volunteer-Based Social Program.* Cambridge, MA: John F. Kennedy School of Government, Harvard University.

Bernstein, Lawrence, Catherine Dun Rappaport, Lauren Olsho, Dana Hunt, and Marjorie Levin. 2009. *Impact Evaluation of the U.S. Department of Education's Student Mentoring Program.* NCEE 2009-4047. Washington, DC: U.S. Department of Education, Institute of Education Sciences, National Center for Education Evaluation and Regional Assistance.

Chan, Christian, and Jean E. Rhodes. 2008. "Youth Mentoring and Spiritual Development." *New Directions for Youth Development* 2008(118): 85–89.

Cnaan, Ram A., Stephanie C. Boddie, Charlene C. McGrew, and Jennifer Kang. 2006. *The Other Philadelphia Story: How Local Congregations Support Quality of Life in Urban America.* Philadelphia: University of Pennsylvania Press.

Cohen, Jacob. 1988. *Statistical Power Analysis for the Behavioral Sciences.* 2nd ed. Hillsdale, NJ: Lawrence Erlbaum Associates.

DuBois, David L., and Naida Silverthorn. 2005. "Natural Mentoring Relationships and Adolescent Health: Evidence from a National Study." *American Journal of Public Health* 95(3): 518–24.

DuBois, David L., Bruce E. Holloway, Jeffrey C. Valentine, and Harris Cooper. 2002. "Effectiveness of Mentoring Programs for Youth: A Meta-Analytic Review." *American Journal of Community Psychology* 30(2): 157–97.

Eccles, Jacquelynne, and Jennifer A. Gootman. 2002. *Community Programs to Promote Youth Development.* Washington, DC: National Academies Press.

Flay, Brian R., Anthony Biglan, Robert F. Boruch, Felipe G. Castro, Denise Gottfredson, Sheppard Kellam, Eve K. Moscicki, Steven Schinke, Jeffrey C. Valentine, and Peter Ji. 2005. "Standards of Evidence: Criteria for Efficacy, Effectiveness, and Dissemination." *Prevention Science* 6(3): 151–75.

Gabel, Stewart. 1992. "Children of Incarcerated and Criminal Parents: Adjustment, Behavior, and Prognosis." *Bulletin of the American Academy of Psychiatry and the Law* 20(1): 33–45.

Gaudin, James M., and Richard Sutphen. 1993. "Foster Care vs. Extended Family Care for Children of Incarcerated Mothers." *Journal of Offender Rehabilitation* 19(3/4): 129–47.

Glaze, Lauren E., and Laura M. Maruschak. 2008. *Parents in Prison and Their Minor Children.* NCJ 222984. Washington, DC: U.S. Department of Justice, Bureau of Justice Statistics.

Grossman, Jean B., and Jean E. Rhodes. 2002. "The Test of Time: Predictors and Effects of Duration in Youth Mentoring Relationships." *American Journal of Community Psychology* 30(2): 199–219.

Grossman, Jean B., and Joseph P. Tierney. 1998. "Does Mentoring Work? An Impact Study of the Big Brothers Big Sisters Program." *Evaluation Review* 22:403–26.

Henriques, Zelma W. 1982. *Imprisoned Mothers and Their Children: A Descriptive and Analytical Study.* Washington, DC: University Press of America.

Herrera, Carla, Jean B. Grossman, Tina J. Kauh, Amy F. Feldman, and Jennifer McMaken. 2007. *Making a Difference in Schools: The Big Brothers Big Sisters School-Based Mentoring Impact Study.* Philadelphia, PA: Public/Private Ventures.

Husock, Howard. 2003. *Starting Amachi: The Elements and Operation of a Volunteer-Based Social Program.* Cambridge, MA: John F. Kennedy School of Government, Harvard University.

Johnson, Byron R., Sung J. Jang, Spencer D. Li, and David Larson. 2000. "The 'Invisible Institution' and Black Youth Crime: The Church as an Agency of Local Social Control." *Journal of Youth and Adolescence* 29(4): 479–98.

Johnston, Denise. 1995. "The Care and Placement of Prisoners' Children." In *Children of Incarcerated Parents,* edited by Katherine Gabel and Denise Johnston (103–23). New York: Lexington Books.

Johnston, Denise, and Katherine Gabel. 1995. "Incarcerated Parents." In *Children of Incarcerated Parents,* edited by Katherine Gabel and Denise Johnston (3–20). New York: Lexington Books.

Jose Kampfner, Christina. 1995. "Post-Traumatic Stress Reactions in Children of Imprisoned Mothers." In *Children of Incarcerated Parents,* edited by Katherine Gabel and Denise Johnston (89–100). New York: Lexington Books.

Jucovy, Linda. 2003. *Amachi: Mentoring Children of Prisoners in Philadelphia.* Philadelphia, PA: Public/Private Ventures.

Karcher, Michael J. 2008. "The Study of Mentoring in the Learning Environment (SMILE): A Randomized Evaluation of the Effectiveness of School-Based Mentoring." *Prevention Science* 9(2): 99–113.

Klaw, Elene L., Jean E. Rhodes, and Louise F. Fitzgerald. 2003. "Natural Mentors in the Lives of African American Adolescent Mothers: Tracking Relationships Over Time." *Journal of Youth and Adolescence* 32(3): 223–32.

Masten, Ann S., and J. Douglas Coatsworth. 1998. "The Development of Competence in Favorable and Unfavorable Environments: Lessons from Research on Successful Children." *American Psychologist* 53(2): 205–20.

MENTOR. 2006. *Mentoring in America 2005: A Snapshot of the Current State of Mentoring.* Alexandria, VA: MENTOR.

Murray, Joseph, and David P. Farrington. 2005. "Parental Imprisonment: Effects on Boys' Antisocial Behaviour and Delinquency through the Life Course." *Journal of Child Psychology and Psychiatry* 46(12): 1269–78.

———. 2008. "Parental Imprisonment: Long-Lasting Effects on Boys' Internalizing Problems through the Life Course." *Development & Psychopathology* 20:273–90.

Nesmith, Ande, and Ebony Ruhland. 2008. "Children of Incarcerated Parents: Challenges and Resilience, in Their Own Words." *Children and Youth Services Review* 30:1119–30.

Putnam, Robert D. 2000. *Bowling Alone: The Collapse and Revival of American Community.* New York: Simon and Schuster.

Rhodes, Jean E. 2002. *Stand by Me: The Risks and Rewards of Mentoring Today's Youth.* Cambridge, MA: Harvard University Press.

Rhodes, Jean E., and David L. DuBois. 2008. "Mentoring Relationships and Programs for Youth." *Current Directions in Psychological Science* 17(4): 254–58.

Rishel, Carrie, Esther Sales, and Gary F. Koeske. 2005. "Relationships with Non-Parental Adults and Child Behavior." *Child and Adolescent Social Work Journal* 22(1): 19–34.

Rutter, Michael. 1979. "Protective Factors in Children's Responses to Stress and Disadvantage." In *Social Competence in Children,* vol. 3 of *Primary Prevention of Psychopathology,* edited by M. W. Kent and J. E. Rolf (49–74). Hanover, NH: University Press of New England.

Sherman, Alexis. 2005. *Children of Prisoners.* Washington, DC: Center for Research on Children in the U.S. (CROCUS) and Georgetown Public Policy Institute.

Shlafer, Rebecca J., Julie Poehlmann, Brianna Coffino, and Ashley Hanneman. 2010. "Mentoring Children with Incarcerated Parents: Implications for Research, Practice, and Policy." *Family Relations* 58:507–19.

Styles, Melanie, and Kristine Morrow. 1992. *Understanding How Youth and Elders Form Relationships: A Study of Four Linking Lifetimes Programs.* Philadelphia, PA: Public/Private Ventures.

Tabachnick, Barbara G., and Linda S. Fidell. 2007. *Using Multivariate Statistics.* 5th ed. Boston: Pearson Education, Inc.

Travis, Jeremy. 2002. "Invisible Punishment: An Instrument of Social Exclusion." In *Invisible Punishment: The Collateral Consequences of Mass Imprisonment,* edited by Marc Mauer and Meda Chesney-Lind (15–36). New York: The New Press.

U.S. Department of Health and Human Services. 2008. *Mentoring Children of Prisoners: 100,000 Matches Strong and Growing.* Washington, DC: U.S. Department of Health and Human Services.

van Nijnatten, Carolus. 1997. "Children in Front of the Bars." *International Journal of Offender Therapy and Comparative Criminology* 41(1): 45–52.

Warren, Jenifer. 2008. *One in 100: Behind Bars in America 2008.* Washington, DC: Pew Charitable Trusts.

Werner, Emmy E. 1989. "High-Risk Children in Young Adulthood: A Longitudinal Study from Birth to 32 Years." *American Journal of Orthopsychiatry* 59(1): 72–81.

Werner, Emmy E., and Jeannette L. Johnson. 2004. "The Role of Caring Adults in the Lives of Children of Alcoholics." *Substance Use and Misuse* 39(5): 699–720.

Wilson, William Julius. 1996. "When Work Disappears." *Political Science Quarterly* 111(4): 567–95.

12

Theory-Based Multimodal Parenting Intervention for Incarcerated Parents and Their Families

J. Mark Eddy, Jean M. Kjellstrand,
Charles R. Martinez, Jr., and Rex Newton

O ver the past decade, the two interventions most frequently discussed for children of incarcerated parents in the United States are community-based youth mentoring programs (chapter 11, this volume) and prison-based parenting programs (chapter 10, this volume). While keen interest in mentoring for this population is a recent phenomenon and has been driven largely by federal funding initiatives, grassroots interest in prison-based parenting programs has persisted for decades within adult corrections systems throughout the country. Given the established nature and widespread reach of parenting programs, finding ways to maximize their effectiveness might be the best way to directly improve the lives of the children of incarcerated parents in the near future.

Parenting programs have had lasting appeal within corrections for two major reasons. Over the short run, by developing and strengthening the communication skills of inmates, parenting programs are thought to increase the likelihood of positive contact between inmates and their families, which in turn may increase family support after release, increase the probability of prosocial success in the community, and reduce recidivism. Over the long run, by developing and strengthening an array of other parenting skills of inmates relevant to their lives back in the community, parenting programs are thought to decrease the likelihood of transmission of antisocial behavior from inmate to child, and thus decrease the risk of the next generation becoming incarcerated.

Hopes for outcomes such as these have maintained the attention of correctional systems on parenting programs. Increasing positive family contact does appear a worthy intervention target, with limited studies finding that more contact is related both to increased family support (La Vigne et al. 2005) and decreased recidivism (Bales and Mears 2008; Baumer, O'Donnell, and Hughes 2009; Glaser 1969; Holt and Miller 1972; LeClair 1978; Ohlin 1954). Enhancing the parenting skills of inmates also has merit, given that numerous studies have found that the children of incarcerated parents are at heightened risk for engaging in antisocial behavior (chapter 4, this volume), that youth who engage in such behaviors are at risk for engaging in criminal behavior during adulthood (Lipsey and Derzon 1998), and that a key predictor for the development and maintenance of youth antisocial behavior is inept parenting (Reid, Patterson, and Snyder 2002). Unfortunately, few studies have been conducted on the impact of prison-based parenting programs on any of these outcomes (see chapter 10, this volume), and it is still not clear how helpful such programs are for inmates, their children, or their families.

At this point, scientifically rigorous studies, such as randomized controlled trials, are needed to provide policymakers and practitioners with information on whether and under what conditions parenting programs positively influence inmates, their children, and their families. This chapter proposes that such studies would be most beneficial if the conventional notion of what constitutes a parenting program for inmates be broadened to also address the context within which the parenting of the children of incarcerated parents occurs.

The most common definition of a parenting program in prison is a parenting class. The theoretical model guiding such classes is usually not specified, or is limited in scope. An alternative theoretical model, coercion theory (Patterson 1982; Patterson, Reid, and Dishion 1992), describes the development and maintenance of youth antisocial behavior and related problems, and the role that parenting plays in such outcomes. A contextually sensitive, multimodal corrections-based parenting program based on coercion theory seems more likely than parenting classes alone to have a lasting, positive impact on inmates, their children and families, and society at large. Implementing such a program raises research, practice, and policy issues.

For practical reasons, this proposal is built on services provided to an inmate, rather than his or her child or family. The corrections system has the widest access to children of incarcerated parents, and thus has the

potential to foster the greatest public health impact. The inmate is the per- ·
son of interest in corrections. Other social service systems are not designed
to connect with inmate parents, their children, and the caregivers of their
children if the *only* reason for such intervention is that a parent is incarcerated. As discussed by de Haan in chapter 13, however, the child welfare
system does serve a significant number of children of incarcerated parents and their families, and seems like a prime location for certain aspects
of a multimodal intervention.

Current Parenting Programs

By the 1990s, most U.S. jurisdictions offered parenting programs in at least
some of their institutions, but only 1 percent of incarcerated men and
4 percent of incarcerated women reported participating (Morash, Haarr,
and Rucker 1994). The typical program was a group-based parent education class that took place once a week for several months (Clement 1993;
Jeffries, Menghraj, and Hairston 2001). Contemporary prison based
parenting programs remain short term and classroom based (Eddy et al.
2008), but the number of participating parents appears to have increased.
In state prisons today, approximately 11 percent of men and 27 percent of
women who are parents of minor children have attended at least some parenting or childrearing classes since their admission (Glaze and Maruschak
2008). The typical program offers instruction in generic communication
and parenting skills and provides an overview of child development (see
Eddy et al. 2008). While numerous curricula are available on these topics,
standardized curricula developed specifically for incarcerated parents are
lacking, and the typical prison-based class is created and delivered in house
by a local parenting instructor working in relative isolation (Eddy et al.
2008; Jeffries et al. 2001).

 While generally not specified by researchers and practitioners of prison-
based parenting classes, most programs described in the published literature seem grounded in a theoretical model that simply states that inmate
(and former inmate) parenting influences child behavior. Thus, classes are
offered to improve parenting skills, knowledge, and attitudes, which in
turn are hypothesized to increase the effectiveness of parenting behaviors
in shaping positive outcomes for children. Such a model is lacking in two
major respects. It ignores the day-to-day context within which the children
of incarcerated parents are parented, and it fails to attend to differences in

parent and child interactions over the course of child development. A life course theoretical framework (see chapter 14) that attends to these issues is needed to guide prison-based parenting programs.

Coercion Theory

In recent years, research groups from various academic disciplines have converged on a general developmental model of child and adult problem behaviors (including antisocial, aggressive, and violent behaviors) that considers context (e.g., Coie and Jacobs 1993; Dodge 2000; Hawkins and Weis 1985; Kellam and Rebok 1992). Coercion theory is one of the most influential iterations of this model (Reid et al. 2002). At the center of this theory are the daily, moment-to-moment social interactions between a child and his or her parents, caregivers, siblings, teachers, and peers (figure 12.1). Throughout life, social interactions are hypothesized to be a potent force in shaping the behavior of a child toward prosocial or antisocial outcomes.

Surrounding these social interactions is the environmental context, aspects of which also play extremely important roles in child and family development (Bronfenbrenner 1986). Context includes both intrapersonal factors, such as the temperament of a child and the personalities of parents,

Figure 12.1. An Overview of Coercion Theory

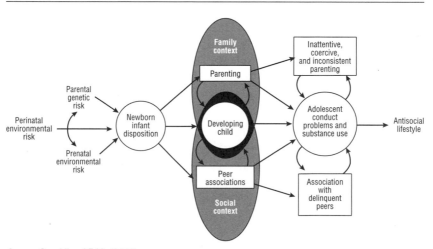

Source: Capaldi and Eddy (2005).

and external factors, such as characteristics of the social and physical environment. In coercion theory, the contextual factors hypothesized to be most closely associated with the development of child antisocial behavior are those that significantly disrupt day-to-day parenting, such as parent substance abuse, criminal behavior, and chronic mental or physical illness, as well as family poverty, housing instability, and neighborhood deviancy.

Child antisocial and other problem behaviors may begin at any point in childhood and adolescence, but children who initiate these behaviors early in life tend to be at highest risk for adjustment difficulties during adulthood (Moffitt 1993). While children may begin to behave problematically for various reasons, the actions of parents and siblings may perpetuate these behaviors. Most notably, when parents back down when faced with aversive child behavior, both parent and child receive encouragement to repeat such a process. The parent feels relieved that the negative behavior of his or her child stops. The child gets at least part of what he or she wanted. As a result, each person is more likely to act the same way the next time a similar situation occurs. These types of coercive family interactions *inadvertently* teach the child and his or her parents and siblings to become increasingly aversive with each other in order to have their needs and desires met.

As these social interaction patterns become more regularized, they may be transported to interactions between the child and his or her peers, as well as between the child and other adults, such as teachers. This can set a dynamic of noncompliance and misbehavior into motion that can lead to a life course dominated by difficult social interactions and their consequences. An accelerator of antisocial development is thought to be social rejection by prosocial peers and adults, which often leads to decreased supervision and engagement by parents, and increased interaction between a child and a deviant peer group. Association with deviant peers, in the presence of decreased adult interaction, provides relatively unfettered opportunity for youth involvement in substance use and abuse, high-risk sexual behaviors, and delinquency (see Reid and Eddy 1997).

A Theory-Based Parenting Program

In coercion theory, parents play a key role in the development of child antisocial behavior because of what they do (e.g., engage in coercive interactions with the child) and what they do not do (e.g., adequately supervise the child). Coercion theory–based clinical interventions, which

may be conducted with individuals or groups, are designed to help parents stop coercive family processes and establish positive, constructive family communication patterns. Coercion theory–based preventive interventions, which are usually group based, are designed to help parents avoid getting caught in coercive social interaction patterns with their children in the first place, and to strengthen and expand established positive family interactions. Both interventions focus primarily on developing, refining, and consistently applying positive involvement and encouragement, supervision and monitoring, appropriate discipline, and family problem solving. These skills empower parents to effectively "manage" social interactions within their family, therefore programs of this type are known as parent management training, or PMT (see Forgatch and Martinez 1999 and Taylor and Biglan 1998).

Child outcomes related to PMT have been rigorously studied, and PMT is one of the only interventions considered a "well established" evidence-based treatment for children and adolescents with serious antisocial behavior problems (Brestan and Eyberg 1998). Various intervention and prevention programs that include PMT, or at least key PMT components, are on numerous national best-practices lists for the intervention and prevention of youth problem behaviors.[1] In short, of all the parenting interventions available, PMT has the strongest evidence base for addressing one specific problem of interest for children of incarcerated parents, the development of youth antisocial behavior (and thus the intergenerational transmission of antisocial behavior). The first large-scale randomized controlled trial of PMT with inmates is currently in progress.[2]

While PMT may hold promise for improving outcomes for children of the incarcerated, many families raising children with incarcerated parents live within a context that presents numerous challenges to effective parenting, and PMT alone does not address these. As discussed throughout this book, for many families, such challenges were present long before a parent was arrested, jailed, tried, and sent to prison, and they often continue or deepen during an incarceration. Given the presence of potentially serious disruptors to parenting in the lives of incarcerated parents, a program intended to positively influence their children over the long run would not only provide parents (inmates and caregivers alike) with opportunities, such as parenting classes, to develop or refine key family interaction skills, but also address pertinent contextual factors that are likely to disrupt parenting after release.

The contextual challenges most commonly faced by incarcerated parents are parental health problems (most notably substance addiction and other mental health problems), inadequate housing, parent unemployment, and parent problem relationships.[3] The impact of these challenges on incarcerated parents and their families and children are described below, followed by an overview of research on interventions that target these challenges in incarcerated populations.

Contextual Challenges

Physical and Behavioral Health Problems. Incarcerated individuals are disproportionately affected by mental health problems, substance abuse, and chronic and infectious diseases (Hammett, Roberts, and Kennedy 2001). Among parents in state prison, 41 percent report medical problems, 57 percent report mental health problems, and 67 percent report substance abuse and dependence problems (Glaze and Maruschak 2008). The rates of these problems in incarcerated individuals exceed general population rates (e.g., Fazel and Danesh 2002; Fazel, Bains, and Doll 2006). Similarly, the prevalence of chronic and infectious diseases, including HIV, hepatitis, and tuberculosis, is significantly higher in incarcerated populations than in the general public (Gaes and Kendig 2003). This is not surprising given that inmates often have histories of poverty, a lack of health care, homelessness, risky sexual practices, and substandard living conditions, each of which is related to increased exposure to these diseases (Conklin, Lincoln, and Tuthill 2000; Petersilia 2001). Although incarcerated individuals have access to basic health care while in prison, once released, they often have difficulty accessing and affording medicine and ongoing care and services. Chronic pre-incarceration problems, which may have subsided or at least been under control while in prison, are likely to return. Serious parental physical and/or mental health problems can disrupt parenting, such as a parent's ability to effectively supervise and monitor his child's whereabouts and friends, and can worsen the parent-child relationship. Further, certain problems, such as substance abuse relapse, can lead to re-incarceration (Mumola and Karberg 2004) and a new bout of parent-child separation. Problems in parent-child relations during childhood are a significant predictor of concurrent and subsequent child antisocial behavior, adolescent delinquency, and adult criminality (Lipsey and Derzon 1998).

Inadequate Housing. Stable housing is associated with decreased recidivism (Bahr et al. 2005; Kjelsberg and Friestad 2008). However, because of lack of money, a poor credit history, and discrimination connected to their felon status as well as other individual characteristics, such as race or ethnicity, many newly released inmates find it difficult to secure and sustain housing unless they have support from family members or friends. Compounding this problem, public housing is often not available for released inmates because federal policies dictate that housing may not be offered to individuals who have been convicted of drug-related and violent crimes or who have engaged in activity deemed threatening to the health and safety of other residents (Legal Action Center 2004). The lack of options may lead to homelessness. While research focusing on ex-offender homelessness is limited, several studies have found that from 20 to 50 percent of newly released inmates do not have housing (Rodriguez and Brown 2003). In contrast, only 9 percent of incarcerated parents report being homeless the year before their arrest (Glaze and Maruschak 2008). The lack of a safe and stable home seriously obstructs parents' reintegration into the community, reunification with their children, and successful parenting. While the homelessness of a former offender does not necessarily mean the homelessness of their children, children who do experience homelessness are at high risk for a myriad of problems, such as antisocial behavior, academic problems, and depression (e.g., Bassuk et al. 1997; Masten et al. 1993; Yu et al. 2008), that in turn are related to such problems as delinquency during adolescence.

Parent Unemployment. Not only do many incarcerated individuals and their families struggle financially before incarceration, but incarceration often worsens the financial situation of inmates' families. This occurs not only through the loss of the income that an inmate had earned before arrest (Reuter, MacCoun, and Murphy 1990) but also through new financial burdens that arise when a family member is incarcerated (Arditti, Lambert-Shute, and Joest 2003; Shinkfield and Graffam 2009). After release, inmates typically face limited employment prospects because of the stigma of a criminal record and the significant gap since their last date of employment in the community. These issues compound the problems that many incarcerated individuals have before incarceration, such as limited education, a lack of basic vocational skills, and a poor work history (Andrews and Bonta 1994; Bushway 1998; Fletcher et al. 2001; Petersilia 2003; Webster-Stratton, Reid, and Hammond 2001). Low family socioeconomic status during childhood is one of the strongest predictors of violent or serious delinquency during late adolescence (Lipsey and Derzon 1998).

Parent Problem Relationships. A number of researchers have described the high frequency of tumultuous relationships in the personal and family histories of inmates, including an unstable and violent home life (e.g., Greenfeld and Snell 1999; James and Glaze 2006; Myers et al. 1999; Poehlmann 2005). Within the home, a significant number of incarcerated mothers and fathers report that they were sexually or physically abused at some point during their lifetimes (Glaze and Maruschak 2008), and ongoing domestic violence may play a role in the genesis and continuation of the criminal behavior of some parents. This seems particularly true for women (e.g., Whaley et al. 2007). Outside the home, before their incarceration, many inmates commonly associated with friends who also were committing criminal behaviors. Returning to or beginning new friendships with criminal peers is one of the strongest predictors of recidivism (Gendreau, Little, and Goggin 1996). In contrast, positive relationships with other adults are associated with positive outcomes for inmates. For example, Bahr and his colleagues (2005) find that close family relationships are associated with lower recidivism; however, as the number of conflictual family relationships increases, so does the likelihood of a parolee recidivating. Thus, the hypothesized relationship between positive family contact and recidivism may be moderated by whether an inmate's family members are involved in antisocial behaviors, including interpersonal aggression. The strongest predictors of serious delinquency and criminal behavior during adolescence and young adulthood relate to associating with deviant peers (Lipsey and Derzon 1998), a problem heightened when parents associate with their own criminal peers and family members.

Interventions Targeting Contextual Challenges

The four contextual challenges detailed above are well known to corrections systems (Gaes and Kendig 2003). Interventions that attempt to address at least some aspects of overcoming each challenge are already delivered within most institutions, with the typical target a reduction in recidivism. For example, in a recent national survey, incarcerated parents were queried about their participation in programs during their sentences (Glaze and Maruschak 2008). The area of highest participation was in programs related to employment, with 67 percent participating in work assignments, 27 percent participating in vocational or job training programs, and 9 percent in employment-related counseling. Next highest was participation in programs related to health problems, with 43 percent of those with alcohol or drug problems participating in substance abuse treatment programs since admission to prison and 31 percent of those with mental health problems participating in relevant treatment programs.

While corrections systems consider these types of interventions important, inmates also perceive that participation in them is vital to postrelease success. In a survey of incarcerated parents who had some parenting role with their children before incarceration,[4] the type of program that was thought the most important in reducing the likelihood that an inmate would return to prison was substance abuse treatment. Not far behind were programs that help an inmate engage in positive behaviors, address parenting issues, assist in preparing for or gaining employment, and help inmates avoid contact with former criminal associates after release. Numerous studies have been conducted on inmate outcomes from programs targeting health, housing, employment, and parent relationships, and the results are summarized in the following sections.

Health Care. Basic health care services are provided to prisoners throughout the United States. However, as noted above, the number of incarcerated parents that receive services for specific health problems varies significantly. Substance abuse treatment has received the most attention by researchers. Only about 11 percent of incarcerated parents who meet the criteria for substance abuse treatment receive residential treatment, either through a separate facility or a special unit within a prison (Glaze and Maruschak 2008). More common interventions are self-help and peer counseling groups, in which 34 percent of incarcerated parents with substance problems participate (Mumola and Karberg 2004).

A recent meta-analysis of 66 studies of institution-based substance abuse treatment programs finds that residential treatment (specifically, intensive "therapeutic community" programs) and counseling tend to decrease postrelease offending, but that their impact on drug use is not significant (Mitchell, Wilson, and MacKenzie 2007; see also Pearson and Lipton 1999). In contrast, research on "aftercare" programs for released inmates who participated in prison-based residential programs suggests that continued support may enhance positive outcomes. In one of the only cost-effectiveness studies of prison-based substance abuse treatment and aftercare, voluntary participation in aftercare decreases the number of subsequent days incarcerated by over 70 percent (McCollister et al. 2003). The longer an inmate participates in prison-based treatment, the more likely he or she is to participate in aftercare services (Burdon, Messina, and Prendergast 2004).

Housing. Planning for postrelease housing is often a part of pre-release programs for incarcerated individuals. Unfortunately, only 31 percent of incarcerated parents receive any pre-release programming, and this varies widely in practical help for housing, from self-help support groups to group-based life skills classes to ongoing assistance and counseling (Glaze and Maruschak 2008). Once an offender is released into the community, few programs address housing assistance; this situation stems largely from a lack of funding, but also from such issues as limited professional expertise with and wariness of working with ex-offenders (Rodriguez and Brown 2003). Few studies have been conducted on housing programs, and their impact is unclear.

Employment. Work and employment-related programs are common in prisons (Glaze and Maruschak 2008; Stephan 1997). In a recent meta-analysis of 33 evaluations of institution-based education, vocation, and work programs, Wilson, Gallagher, and MacKenzie (2000) find that, on average, program participants are more likely to be employed at higher rates, and to recidivate at lower rates, than nonparticipants. However, the scientific quality of the studies Wilson and his colleagues (2000) reviewed is low, and the evidence insufficient to conclude that the programs are related to subsequent employment. In a more recent analysis of community-based employment programs for former offenders, eight high-quality studies find that the programs were mixed in improving employment prospects and did not reduce recidivism (Visher, Winterfield, and Coggeshall 2005).

Adult Relationships. It is unknown how many incarcerated parents participate in programs that have at least some focus on developing and maintaining prosocial adult relationships and avoiding relationships with deviant peers and partners. Certainly, these issues are often discussed during prison-based parenting programs (Eddy et al. 2008), and life skills that foster healthy relationships are sometimes taught as a part of pre-release programs. However, few studies have been conducted on how these interventions affect postrelease adult relationships in the general population of inmates. One subpopulation of interest that has been studied is domestically violent batterers. Results have been mixed from intervention studies designed to decrease subsequent abuse by batterers (e.g., Babcock, Green, and Robie 2004; Feder and Wilson 2005; Gondolf 2003). Probably the most discussed area with inmates relevant to relationships is cognitive training, which focuses on improving interpersonal skills in such areas as monitoring and maintaining self-control, accurately appraising a situation, and solving problems constructively. While participation in cognitive skills programs tends to reduce recidivism (Wilson et al. 2000), it is unclear whether these programs influence the types and qualities of the adult relationships of inmates following release from prison.

Multimodal Intervention

A coercion theory–based parenting program for inmates would address both the development of effective parenting skills and the mitigation of the contextual challenges that are most likely to disrupt parenting. When feasible, it would also target the current caregivers of the child. It would help all parents involved with a child identify his or her strengths and problems, and provide guidance on appropriate actions following such an assessment. This specific proposal for a multimodal parenting program is influenced not only by coercion theory, past intervention research, and the chapter authors' own clinical experience, but also by prior suggestions concerning inmates, families, and the transition period following release from prison (for a review, see Rose and Clear 2003). What follows are examples of components of a coordinated multimodal parenting intervention based within a corrections system. Complementary parenting interventions for caregivers and families that might be sustainable within existing systems of care are also noted.

Family Check-Up. The family check-up is a brief intervention designed by Dishion and colleagues to help motivate parents to make changes that are likely to benefit their family (e.g., Gill et al. 2008). The check-up uses motivational interviewing (Miller and Rollnick 2002) to help engage parents in assessing the unique strengths and problems within their family, create their own plan to address both family and individual family member needs, and develop a reasonable strategy to carry out the plan. The check-up approach provides interventionists the opportunity to consider factors that are often ignored or downplayed during intervention, such as important cultural values and practices in the lives of a particular inmate and family (see chapter 8, this volume). A check-up with inmates would start the entire sequence of interventions, and thus would be conducted near the beginning of a sentence. Ideally, it would involve both inmates and their children's caregivers.

Family Support Coach. After a family check-up, a family support coach would be assigned to an inmate. This person would have the knowledge, skills, and experience needed to appropriately assist, encourage, and advocate for inmates as they deal with parenting and contextual challenges. The family support coach would work with inmates throughout their sentence and after release, and he or she would facilitate communication throughout a sentence and afterward among the key players that are important to postrelease success. This person would be a mentor and role model to the inmate, and would be available to help an inmate and former inmate deal with difficult family situations as they arise. At various points during a sentence, the family support coach would convene "reach in" meetings with the inmates, the caregiver, the inmate's counselor, and other pertinent professionals as they become involved, such as a child welfare caseworker or a probation officer. Participants would discuss progress, make plans, and troubleshoot problems and potential problems. For example, an inmate and his or her family often must make particularly difficult decisions about contact between a parent and a child after release, including if and when this should occur, and how it will be properly negotiated if the relationship between the inmate and the caregiver is strained. Finding solutions to these types of problems takes time and support.

The presence of a person who oversees a particular case from start to finish is important for a number of reasons. Impressive plans can be made by an inmate and prison staff over the course of a sentence, only to collapse a few days after release. At this point, the professional that the inmate may have worked with most closely, the prison counselor, is no longer involved. A parole officer (PO) is now available to assist, but his or her knowledge of the plans is likely limited at best. Further, the caseload of a typical PO is so high that being able to adequately support any one individual is difficult. Decreasing the size of PO caseloads is one solution (e.g., Skeem and Louden 2006), but even then there is a significant advantage to having an additional professional involved who is focused on family issues, who is serving as a supportive advocate, and who is present both during and after prison.

Parent Management Training. Early in a prison sentence, a prison-based version of PMT would be available for inmates who are parents and address not only the skills needed to be an effective parent, but also the skills needed to co-parent with other caregivers (Cecil et al. 2008). Simultaneously, a community-based version of PMT would be available for caregivers and address the unique parenting challenges of a child who has an incarcerated parent. Such a program would include learning how to identify when a child has a problem that requires professional attention, or when a child is in a situation where special support may be helpful. Referrals to appropriate services within the local community would be provided. This and other community-based components for caregivers could be supported through child abuse prevention funding from the child welfare system. Following practice in a wide variety of recent PMT studies (e.g., Reid et al. 1999), both the inmate and caregiver interventions would be delivered in a group-based format. To maximize parent participation, PMT interventions would be offered on a regular, ongoing basis, providing parents with multiple opportunities to participate (e.g., Eddy, Reid, and Fetrow 2000).

Parenting Support Groups. After the completion of PMT, incarcerated parents would be invited to join a parenting support group in prison, and caregivers would be invited to join such a group in the community. These groups would be moderated by a skilled and experienced interventionist. The groups would help parents and caregivers problem solve parenting challenges, provide coaching to parents trying to make cognitive and behavioral changes to improve their parenting, and provide parents and their families with appropriate referrals for dealing with child problems and contextual challenges.

Interventions Targeting Contextual Challenges. Given the importance of helping parents manage contextual challenges so they do not disrupt parenting, additional intervention components would address the unique needs of a particular inmate and his or her family. Key components would focus on identified needs, and particularly those related to the four contextual challenges discussed in this chapter: health (most notably substance abuse and mental health problems), housing, employment, and adult relationships. Ideally, such assistance would be provided to both inmates and their families. For an inmate, specific needs could be determined by the assessment that typically occurs within correction systems during intake, or through a family check-up, and ideally would be reevaluated during subsequent assessments. An intervention plan could be coordinated and monitored by the family support coach or a prison counselor. For caregivers and children, needs also could be determined through a family check-up. The resulting intervention plan could be brokered by and coordinated through an outside entity, such as a nonprofit agency dedicated to working with the families of incarcerated parents (see Eddy et al. 2008).

Booster Parent Management Training Sessions. During the final months of a sentence, a second round of group-based PMT would be provided for inmates and for caregivers to help families anticipate and deal with the challenges that will arise during the transition back into the community. During this class, inmates would review and practice specific skills for parenting on the outside. Once an inmate is released, a third round of group-based PMT, this time offered for both caregivers and former inmates together, would be provided to help a family, regardless of living situation or visitation arrangements, figure out appropriate strategies for parenting together in the community. As part of this component, individual family meetings would be conducted to assist families in solving their unique problems.

Community Mentors. A family support coach or a parole officer can provide certain types of big-picture support to a former inmate. However, unless caseloads are small, the individuals in these roles are not in the position to provide day-to-day support for the numerous issues that need to be solved during reentry. For example, two key challenges that may confront an inmate repeatedly will be whether to return to relationships with old friends who are involved in criminal behavior and whether to return to a domestically violent partner. A trained, supported, and supervised mentor from within the community where the former inmate lives seems ideal to assist on such issues (e.g., Rose, Clear, and Ryder 2001). This mentor would begin to develop a relationship with the inmate during prison, meet the former inmate when he or she gets off the bus from prison, and be available to help throughout the reentry period. A mentor would have to have an exemplary current life in terms of a prosocial lifestyle, regardless of struggles they may have had in the past. Former offenders who have completed their post-prison supervision period and have established and maintained prosocial lives for a long time might be particularly helpful mentors.

Training and Supervision for Interventionists. A central purpose of a multimodal intervention is to provide incarcerated parents and their families with adequate support over a long enough period that change occurs. Ongoing support is also needed for staff members delivering the various intervention components (i.e., parent interventionists, family support coaches, mentors, and staff involved in interventions targeting contextual factors). Support for staff includes providing adequate initial job training as well as ongoing supervision and training. Supervision and support are vital to ensuring the quality and the effectiveness of intervention efforts and for helping to prevent and resolve issues related to staff isolation, discouragement, and burnout.

The Oregon Example. For the past decade, with policymakers and practitioners in the state of Oregon, we have been developing PMT components and supportive infrastructure for a multimodal intervention of the type proposed here (Eddy et al. 2008). This has been accomplished via collaboration among our research team; the Oregon Department of Corrections (DOC); multiple correctional institutions within the DOC, most notably the Coffee Creek Correctional Facility, the Oregon State Correctional Institution, the Santiam Correctional Institution, the Columbia River Correctional Institution, and the Oregon State Penitentiary; a nonprofit service delivery agency, Pathfinders of Oregon; and a nonprofit advocacy group, the Children's Justice Alliance (CJA). To date, the collaboration has been maintained across the tenures of three DOC administrations.

The inmate PMT program, named Parenting Inside Out (Schiffmann, Eddy, and Johnson 2009; Schiffmann et al. 2008a), is supported by the DOC through regular state funding streams. Support for the caregiver PMT program (Schiffmann et al. 2008b) is from the child welfare system through federal funds targeted to the prevention of child abuse. The community-based components of the intervention are delivered by Pathfinders through several CJA-sponsored Centers for Family Success, community outreach centers designed to support families with justice-involved parents (e.g., in prison, on probation or parole). Research is in progress on the effectiveness of components of the multimodal intervention model. Most notably, outcomes of the prison-based PMT component of this multimodal intervention are being investigated in a randomized trial of 359 men and women inmates and their families.[5] Also in progress is the development and pilot testing of PMT booster sessions that focus on the emotional challenges of inmates, their children, and caregivers before and after release.[6] This most recent project combines elements from dialectical behavior therapy (Linehan, Bohus, and Lynch 2007) and an "emotion coaching" intervention (Havighurst, Harley, and Prior 2004). Components are being developed that directly target incarcerated parents, the caregivers of their children, and the children.

Discussion

Successfully loving and supporting a child requires not only that a parent supervise, discipline, encourage, and problem-solve moment to moment, but also that he or she ensures that the basic needs of that child—such as safety, shelter, nutrition, clothing, and health—are met. While most inmates are parents, many had difficulty before their sentence in meeting one or more of these parenthood tasks. Except for a few incarcerated mothers around the country who care for their infants in prison nurseries (see chapter 9, this volume), no inmates are able to meet the day-to-day needs of their children during their sentences. Given the numerous difficulties to overcome, a multimodal parenting program for inmates and their families that strengthens parenting skills and addresses contextual challenges to parenting seems to have greater potential than prison-based parenting classes alone to reduce recidivism and the intergenerational transmission of antisocial behavior. Such a program has implications for research, policy, and practice.

Research Implications

Multimodal efforts that have included some family focus have been undertaken not as parenting programs but as reentry programs (Petersilia 2003; Seiter and Kadela 2003; Travis and Visher 2005). Outcomes from these programs have been mixed, with some prominent efforts leading to worse, rather than improved, outcomes. For example, the two-month institution-based Project Greenlight Reentry Program (Wilson and Davis 2006) focused on improving family relationships, treating substance abuse problems, and gaining postrelease employment just before release. The program attempted to apply evidence-based principles to intervene with each targeted problem. In a quasi-experimental study, Greenlight participants were *more likely* to recidivate than individuals in parole-as-usual conditions. Researchers have offered varied hypotheses for why Project Greenlight may have had an iatrogenic effect, from failing to follow evidence-based correctional practices (Rhine, Mawhorr, and Parks 2006) to following such practices too closely (Marlowe 2006). Key weaknesses were that the program occurred at the very end of a sentence, was relatively brief, and stopped at release. In short, the program did not provide long-term support for change, either inside or outside prison.

Such a study illustrates a central problem in corrections programming. While the desire to build a field driven by evidence-based practices and programs is admirable, information gaps remain significant. The true impacts of many popular programs remain unknown. Thus, while multimodal intervention efforts should be informed by the available research findings, research findings alone are likely to be insufficient. A multimodal program should integrate established knowledge from both research and practice, and be designed and rigorously tested by teams of researchers, practitioners, instructional designers, and administrators (e.g., Eddy et al. 2008; Lipsey and Cullen 2007; Petersilia 2004; Zhang, Roberts, and Callanan 2006). Within such a multidisciplinary collaboration, the best-practices conclusions of researchers such as Gendreau and Ross (1979) and Andrews and Bonta (1994) can be considered in light of the on-the-ground knowledge of workers in the field, and a multimodal intervention can be constructed that should reasonably work for a particular subpopulation of inmates. During this process, such issues as race, ethnicity, and culture cannot be ignored (see chapter 8, this volume). Studies then can be launched to test the effectiveness of the intervention. To help understand the results of such efforts, measured variables need to expand beyond recidivism and address other important constructs that concern not only how an intervention might be effective, but with whom, why, and under what conditions. Multimodal parenting programs are in particular need of investigation.

Policy Implications

The current national economic currents and the high cost of maintaining security within overburdened corrections systems has made it increasingly difficult for corrections systems to afford reform efforts. For example, whereas it once was possible to complete graduate studies in some prisons, community college classes may not even be available. Cutting programs, rather than adding them, is the norm. To meet the dual goals of punishment and reform in the face of limited resources, something needs to change. In this regard, a recent report by the Pew Center for the States (2009) on incarceration in the United States referred to the current budget crisis as a "perhaps unprecedented opportunity" to "retool" the corrections system.

Retooling could be optimized if it were based on rigorous scientific information about which programs do and do not make a difference in important outcomes such as recidivism. To do this, more studies are needed. Fortunately, the opportunities to generate such information are abundant. Petersilia (2004) estimates that over 10,000 reentry programs were operated in corrections systems across the country during the past several decades, but less than 1 percent of these programs were evaluated, and most evaluations used inferior scientific methods. Given the large number of programs in operation, if policymakers across the country began to fund rigorous randomized controlled trials of the most promising programs operating within their jurisdictions, and actively shared the results of such trials with each other, real progress could be made toward solving issues in a relatively short period. Ideally, such efforts would include the investigation of multimodal parenting programs, and they would be coordinated across corrections systems, with specific research problems investigated within a systematic framework that includes the identification of promising candidates for testing; the conduct of randomized controlled trials that include measures of how, why, and when a program might work; and the launch of replication trials of programs that appear effective. Programs that survive repeated testing within a particular population could be legitimately christened "evidence based."

Practice Implications

While researchers continue to seek more information, and policymakers encourage the conduct of more studies and try to make sense of the findings that already exist, practitioners have to do something. Numerous parenting programs have been studied rigorously and have been found to positively affect children and families, including children and families living in high-risk circumstances. These are easily found via the various best-practice lists posted on federal agency and private foundation web sites. Learning more about these programs, and the research behind them, would be a good place to start for practitioners interested in building a multimodal parenting intervention for inmates and their families. These programs were not designed to address the specific needs of children of the incarcerated and thus will require both adaptation and addition to their content, as well as the development of new processes that support these parents, children, and families. We suggest that this work is best done by a multidisciplinary workgroup of professionals.

A parenting class for inmates should be just one facet of a comprehensive parenting program for incarcerated parents and their families. If the primary goals are for inmates to not return to prison and to guide their children on paths that do not lead to prison, a parenting program should address each key task that parents must accomplish for their children and families. These include not only finding housing, getting a job, not returning to substance abuse, and avoiding destructive relationships, but also skillfully parenting moment to moment, day to day. A multimodal parenting program seems more likely than parenting classes alone to help inmates and their children and families thrive.

NOTES

1. Carol Metzler, J. Mark Eddy, David Lichtenstein, Jean Kjellstrand, and Ted Taylor, " 'Best Practices' for Psychosocial Intervention and Prevention with Children and Families: Characteristics of Programs That Top the List," manuscript in preparation, 2010.

2. J. Mark Eddy, "Effects of an Intervention for Incarcerated Parents," NIMH grant award number MH065553, 2003.

3. This list is based on prior analyses of the challenges facing inmates and their families (Travis and Waul 2003) and the authors' collective clinical experience.

4. Jean Kjellstrand and J. Mark Eddy, "Perception of the Service Needs of Offenders before and after Their Release from Prison," manuscript in preparation, 2010.

5. Eddy, "Effects of an Intervention for Incarcerated Parents."

6. Joann W. Shortt, "Emotion-Focused Intervention for Mothers and Children under Stress," NIMH grant award number MH799112, 2008.

REFERENCES

Andrews, Don A., and James Bonta. 1994. *The Psychology of Criminal Conduct.* Cincinnati, OH: Anderson Publishing.

Arditti, Joyce A., Jennifer Lambert-Shute, and Karen Joest. 2003. "Saturday Morning at the Jail: Implications of Incarceration for Families and Children." *Family Relations* 52(3): 195–204.

Babcock, Julia C., Charles E. Green, and Chet Robie. 2004. "Does Batterers' Treatment Work? A Meta-Analytic Review of Domestic Violence Treatment." *Clinical Psychology Review* 23(8): 1023–53.

Bahr, Stephen J., Anita H. Armstrong, Benjamin G. Gibbs, Paul E. Harris, and James K. Fisher. 2005. "The Reentry Process: How Parolees Adjust to Release from Prison." *Fathering* 3(3): 243–65.

Bales, William D., and Daniel P. Mears. 2008. "Inmate Social Ties and the Transition to Society: Does Visitation Reduce Recidivism?" *Journal of Research in Crime and Delinquency* 45(3): 287–321.

Bassuk, Ellen L., John C. Buckner, Linda F. Weinreb, Angela Browne, Shari S. Bassuk, Ree Dawson, and Jennifer N. Perloff. 1997. "Homelessness in Female-Headed Families: Childhood and Adult Risk and Protective Factors." *American Journal of Public Health* 87(2): 241–48.

Baumer, Eric P., Ian O'Donnell, and Nicholas Hughes. 2009. "The Porous Prison: A Note on the Rehabilitative Potential of Visits Home." *The Prison Journal* 89(1): 119–26.

Brestan, Elizabeth V., and Sheila M. Eyberg. 1998. "Effective Psychosocial Treatments of Conduct-Disordered Children and Adolescents: 29 Years, 82 Studies, and 5,272 Kids." *Journal of Clinical Child Psychology* 27:180–89.

Bronfenbrenner, Urie. 1986. "Ecology of the Family as a Context for Human Development: Research Perspectives." *Developmental Psychology* 22:723–42.

Burdon, William M., Nena P. Messina, and Michael L. Prendergast. 2004. "The California Treatment Expansion Initiative: Aftercare Participation, Recidivism, and Predictors of Outcomes." *The Prison Journal* 84(1): 61–80.

Bushway, Shawn D. 1998. "The Impact of an Arrest on the Job Stability of Young White American Men." *Journal of Research in Crime and Delinquency* 35(4): 454–79.

Capaldi, D. M., and J. Mark Eddy. 2005. "Oppositional Defiant Disorder and Conduct Disorder." In *The Handbook of Adolescent Behavioral Problems: Evidence-Based Approaches to Prevention and Treatment,* edited by Thomas P. Gullotta and Gerald R. Adams (283–308). New York: Springer Science+Business Media.

Cecil, Dawn K., James McHale, Anne Strozier, and Joel Pietsch. 2008. "Female Inmates, Family Caregivers, and Young Children's Adjustment: A Research Agenda and Implications for Corrections Programming." *Journal of Criminal Justice* 36:513–21.

Clement, Mary J. 1993. "Parenting in Prison: A National Survey of Programs for Incarcerated Women." *Journal of Offender Rehabilitation* 19(1/2): 89–100.

Coie, John D., and Marlene R. Jacobs. 1993. "The Role of Social Context in the Prevention of Conduct Disorder." *Development & Psychopathology* 5:263–75.

Conklin, Thomas J., Thomas Lincoln, and Robert W. Tuthill. 2000. "Self-Reported Health and Prior Health Behaviors of Newly Admitted Correctional Inmates." *American Journal of Public Health* 90(12): 1939–41.

Dodge, Kenneth A. 2000. "Conduct Disorder." In *Handbook of Developmental Psychopathology,* 2nd ed., edited by Arnold J. Sameroff, Michael Lewis, and Suzanne M. Miller (447–63). New York: Kluwer Academic/Plenum Publishers.

Eddy, J. Mark, John B. Reid, and Rebecca A. Fetrow. 2000. "An Elementary School–Based Prevention Program Targeting Modifiable Antecedents of Youth Delinquency and Violence: Linking the Interests of Families and Teachers (LIFT)." *Journal of Emotional and Behavioral Disorders* 8(3): 165–76.

Eddy, J. Mark, Charles R. Martinez Jr., Tracy Schiffmann, Rex Newton, Laura Olin, Leslie Leve, Dana M. Foney, and Joann W. Shortt. 2008. "Development of a Multisystemic Parent Management Training Intervention for Incarcerated Parents, Their Children, and Families." *Clinical Psychologist* 12(3): 86–98.

Fazel, Seena, and John Danesh. 2002. "Serious Mental Disorder in 23,000 Prisoners: A Systematic Review of 62 Surveys." *The Lancet* 359:545–50.

Fazel, Seena, Parveen Bains, and Helen Doll. 2006. "Substance Abuse and Dependence in Prisoners: A Systematic Review." *Addiction* 101(2): 181–91.

Feder, Lynette, and David B. Wilson. 2005. "A Meta-Analytic Review of Court-Mandated Batterer Intervention Programs: Can Courts Affect Abusers' Behavior?" *Journal of Experimental Criminology* 1(2): 239–62.

Fletcher, Del Roy, Alan Taylor, Stephen Hughes, and Jonathan Breeze. 2001. *Recruiting and Employing Offenders.* York: York Publishing Services for Joseph Rowntree Foundation.

Forgatch, Marion S., and Charles R. Martinez Jr. 1999. "Parent Management Training: A Program Linking Basic Research and Practical Application." *Tidsskrift for Norsk Psykologforening* 36:923–37.

Gaes, Gerald G., and Newton Kendig. 2003. "The Skill Sets and Health Care Needs of Released Offenders." In *Prisoners Once Removed: The Impact of Incarceration and Reentry on Children, Families, and Communities,* edited by Jeremy Travis and Michelle Waul (105–56). Washington, DC: Urban Institute Press.

Gendreau, Paul, and Bob Ross. 1979. "Effective Correctional Treatment: Bibliotherapy for Cynics." *Crime and Delinquency* 25(4): 463–89.

Gendreau, Paul, Tracy Little, and Claire Goggin. 1996. "A Meta-Analysis of the Predictors of Adult Offender Recidivism: What Works?" *Criminology* 34(4): 575–607.

Gill, Anne M., Luke W. Hyde, Daniel S. Shaw, Thomas J. Dishion, and Melvin N. Wilson. 2008. "The Family Check-Up in Early Childhood: A Case Study of Intervention Process and Change." *Journal of Clinical Child and Adolescent Psychology* 37(4): 893–904.

Glaser, Daniel. 1969. *The Effectiveness of a Prison and Parole System.* Abridged ed. Indianapolis, IN: Bobb-Merrill.

Glaze, Lauren E., and Laura M. Maruschak. 2008. *Parents in Prison and Their Minor Children.* NCJ 222984. Washington, DC: U.S. Department of Justice, Bureau of Justice Statistics.

Gondolf, Edward W. 2003. "MCMI Results for Batterers: Gondolf Replies to Dutton's Response." *Journal of Family Violence* 18(6): 387–89.

Greenfeld, Lawrence A., and Tracy L. Snell. 1999. *Women Offenders.* NCJ 175688. Washington, DC: U.S. Department of Justice, Bureau of Justice Statistics.

Hammett, Theodore M., Cheryl Roberts, and Sofia Kennedy. 2001. "Health-Related Issues in Prisoner Reentry." *Crime and Delinquency* 47(3): 390–409.

Havighurst, Sophie S., Ann Harley, and Margot Prior. 2004. "Building Preschool Children's Emotional Competence: A Parenting Program." *Early Education and Development* 15(4): 423–47.

Hawkins, J. David, and Joseph G. Weis. 1985. "The Social Development Model: An Integrated Approach to Delinquency Prevention." *Journal of Primary Prevention* 6(2): 73–95.

Holt, Norman, and Donald Miller. 1972. *Explorations in Inmate-Family Relationships.* No. 46. Sacramento: California Department of Corrections.

James, Doris, J., and Lauren E. Glaze. 2006. *Mental Health Problems of Prison and Jail Inmates.* NCJ 213600. Washington, DC: U.S. Department of Justice, Bureau of Justice Statistics.

Jeffries, John M., Suzanne Menghraj, and Creasie Finney Hairston. 2001. *Serving Incarcerated and Ex-Offender Fathers and Their Families: A Review of the Field.* New York: Vera Institute of Justice.

Kellam, Sheppard G., and George W. Rebok. 1992. "Building Developmental and Etiological Theory through Epidemiologically Based Preventive Intervention Trials." In *Preventing Antisocial Behavior: Interventions from Birth through Adolescence,* edited by Joan McCord and Richard Ernest Tremblay (162–95). New York: Guilford Press.

Kjelsberg, Ellen, and Christine Friestad. 2008. "Social Adversities in First-Time and Repeat Prisoners." *International Journal of Social Psychiatry* 54(6): 514–26.

La Vigne, Nancy G., Rebecca L. Naser, Lisa E. Brooks, and Jennifer L. Castro. 2005. "Examining the Effect of Incarceration and In-Prison Family Contact on Prisoners' Family Relationships." *Journal of Contemporary Criminal Justice* 21(4): 314–35.

LeClair, Daniel P. 1978. "Home Furlough Program Effects on Rates of Recidivism." *Criminal Justice and Behavior* 5(3): 249–58.

Legal Action Center. 2004. *After Prison: Roadblocks to Reentry. A Report on State Legal Barriers Facing People with Criminal Records.* New York: Legal Action Center.

Linehan, Marsha M., Martin Bohus, and Thomas R. Lynch. 2007. "Dialectical Behavior Therapy for Pervasive Emotion Dysregulation." In *Handbook of Emotion Regulation,* edited by James J. Gross (581–605). New York: Guilford.

Lipsey, Mark W., and Francis T. Cullen. 2007. "The Effectiveness of Correctional Rehabilitation: A Review of Systematic Reviews." *Annual Review of Law and Social Science* 3:297–320.

Lipsey, Mark W., and James H. Derzon. 1998. "Predictors of Violent or Serious Delinquency in Adolescence and Early Adulthood: A Synthesis of Longitudinal Research." In *Serious and Violent Juvenile Offenders: Risk Factors and Successful Interventions,* edited by Rolf Loeber and David P. Farrington (86–105). Thousand Oaks, CA: SAGE Publications.

Marlowe, Douglas B. 2006. "When 'What Works' Never Did: Dodging the 'Scarlet M' in Correctional Rehabilitation." *Criminology and Public Policy* 5(2): 339–46.

Masten, Ann S., Donna Miliotis, Sandra A. Graham-Bermann, MaryLouise Ramirez, and Jennifer Neemann. 1993. "Children in Homeless Families: Risks to Mental Health and Development." *Journal of Consulting and Clinical Psychology* 61(2): 335–43.

McCollister, Kathryn E., Michael T. French, Michael Prendergast, Harry Wexler, Stan Sacks, and Elizabeth Hall. 2003. "Is In-Prison Treatment Enough? A Cost-Effectiveness Analysis of Prison-Based Treatment and Aftercare Services for Substance-Abusing Offenders." *Law and Policy* 25(1): 63–82.

Miller, William R., and Stephen Rollnick, eds. 2002. *Motivational Interviewing: Preparing People for Change.* 2nd ed. New York: Guilford Press.

Mitchell, Ojmarrh, David B. Wilson, and Doris L. MacKenzie. 2007. "Does Incarceration-Based Drug Treatment Reduce Recidivism? A Meta-Analytic Synthesis of the Research." *Journal of Experimental Criminology* 3(4): 353–75.

Moffitt, Terrie E. 1993. "Adolescence-Limited and Life-Course-Persistent Antisocial Behavior: A Developmental Taxonomy." *Psychological Review* 100(4): 674–701.

Morash, Merry, Robin N. Haarr, and Lila Rucker. 1994. "A Comparison of Programming for Women and Men in U.S. Prisons in the 1980s." *Crime and Delinquency* 40(2): 197–221.

Mumola, Christopher J., and Jennifer C. Karberg. 2004. *Drug Use and Dependence, State and Federal Prisoners.* NCJ 213530. Washington, DC: U.S. Department of Justice, Bureau of Justice Statistics.

Myers, Barbara J., Tina M. Smarsh, Kristine Amlund-Hagen, and Suzanne Kennon. 1999. "Children of Incarcerated Mothers." *Journal of Child and Family Studies* 8(1): 11–25.

Ohlin, Lloyd E. 1954. "The Stability and Validity of Parole Experience Tables." Ph.D. diss., University of Chicago.

Patterson, Gerald R. 1982. *Coercive Family Process.* Eugene, OR: Castilia.

Patterson, Gerald R., John B. Reid, and Thomas Dishion. 1992. *Antisocial Boys: A Social Interaction Approach.* Vol. 4. Eugene, OR: Castalia.

Pearson, Frank S., and Douglas S. Lipton. 1999. "A Meta-Analytic Review of the Effectiveness of Corrections-Based Treatments for Drug Abuse." *The Prison Journal* 79(4): 384–410.

Petersilia, Joan. 2001. "When Prisoners Return to Communities." *Federal Probation* 65(1): 3–8.

———. 2003. *When Prisoners Come Home.* New York: Oxford University Press.

———. 2004. "What Works in Prisoner Reentry? Reviewing and Questioning the Evidence." *Federal Probation* 68(2): 4–8.

Pew Center for the States. 2009. *One in 31: The Long Reach of American Corrections.* Washington, DC: Pew Charitable Trusts.

Poehlmann, Julie. 2005. "Children's Family Environments and Intellectual Outcomes during Maternal Incarceration." *Journal of Marriage and Family* 67(5): 1275–85.

Reid, John B., and J. Mark Eddy. 1997. "The Prevention of Antisocial Behavior: Some Considerations in the Search for Effective Interventions." In *Handbook of Antisocial Behavior,* edited by David M. Stoff, James Breiling, and Jack D. Maser (343–56). New York: John Wiley & Sons.

Reid, John B., Gerald R. Patterson, and James J. Snyder. 2002. *Antisocial Behavior in Children and Adolescents: A Developmental Analysis and Model for Intervention.* Washington, DC: American Psychological Association.

Reid, John B., J. Mark Eddy, Rebecca A. Fetrow, and Mike Stoolmiller. 1999. "Description and Immediate Impacts of a Preventative Intervention for Conduct Problems." *American Journal of Community Psychology* 24(4): 483–517.

Reuter, Peter, Robert J. MacCoun, and Patrick Murphy. 1990. *Money from Crime: A Study of the Economics of Drug Dealing in Washington, DC.* Santa Monica, CA: RAND Drug Policy Research Center.

Rhine, Edward E., Tina L. Mawhorr, and Evalyn C. Parks. 2006. "Implementation: The Bane of Effective Correctional Programs." *Criminology and Public Policy* 5(2): 347–58.

Rodriguez, Nino, and Brenner Brown. 2003. *Preventing Homelessness among People Leaving Prison.* New York: Vera Institute of Justice.

Rose, Dina R., and Todd R. Clear. 2003. "Interaction, Reentry, and Social Capital: Social Networks in the Balance." In *Prisoners Once Removed: The Impact of Incarceration and Reentry on Children, Families, and Communities,* edited by Jeremy Travis and Michelle Waul (313–42). Washington, DC: Urban Institute Press.

Rose, Dina R., Todd R. Clear, and Judith A. Ryder. 2001. *Drugs, Incarceration, and Neighborhood Life: The Impact of Reintegrating Offenders into the Community.* New York: John Jay College of Criminal Justice.

Schiffmann, Tracy, J. Mark Eddy, and Mary Johnson. 2009. *Parenting Inside Out: Coaches Manual.* Portland: Oregon Social Learning Center and Children's Justice Alliance.

Schiffmann, Tracy, J. Mark Eddy, Charles R. Martinez Jr., Leslie Leve, and Rex Newton. 2008a. *Parenting Inside Out: Parent Management Training for Incarcerated Parents in Prison.* Portland: Oregon Social Learning Center and Children's Justice Alliance.

———. 2008b. *Parenting Inside Out: Parent Management Training for Parents Involved with Community Corrections.* Portland: Oregon Social Learning Center and Children's Justice Alliance.

Seiter, Richard P., and Karen R. Kadela. 2003. "Prisoner Reentry: What Works, What Does Not, and What Is Promising." *Crime and Delinquency* 49(3): 360–88.

Shinkfield, Alison J., and Joe Graffam. 2009. "Community Reintegration of Ex-Prisoners Type and Degree of Change in Variables Influencing Successful Reintegration." *International Journal of Offender Therapy and Comparative Criminology* 53(1): 29–42.

Skeem, Jennifer L., and Jennifer E. Louden. 2006. "Toward Evidence-Based Practice for Probationers and Parolees Mandated to Mental Health Treatment." *Psychiatric Services* 57(3): 333–42.

Stephan, James J. 1997. *Census of State and Federal Correctional Facilities, 1995.* NCJ 164266. Washington, DC: U.S. Department of Justice, Bureau of Justice Statistics.

Taylor, Ted K., and Anthony Biglan. 1998. "Behavioral Family Interventions for Improving Child-Rearing: A Review of the Literature for Clinicians and Policy Makers." *Clinical Child and Family Psychology Review* 1(1): 41–60.

Travis, Jeremy, and Christy A. Visher. 2005. "Prisoner Reentry and the Pathways to Adulthood: Policy Perspectives." In *On Your Own without a Net: The Transition to Adulthood for Vulnerable Populations,* edited by D. Wayne Osgood, E. Michael Foster, Constance Flanagan, and Gretchen R. Ruth (145–77). Chicago: University of Chicago Press.

Travis, Jeremy, and Michelle Waul, eds. 2003. *Prisoners Once Removed: The Impact of Incarceration and Reentry on Children, Families, and Communities.* Washington, DC: Urban Institute Press.

Visher, Christy A., Laura Winterfield, and Mark B. Coggeshall. 2005. "Ex-Offender Employment Programs and Recidivism: A Meta-Analysis." *Journal of Experimental Criminology* 1(3): 295–315.

Webster-Stratton, Carolyn, Jamila Reid, and Mary Hammond. 2001. "Social Skills and Problem-Solving Training for Children with Early-Onset Conduct Problems: Who Benefits?" *Journal of Child Psychology and Psychiatry and Allied Disciplines* 42(7): 943 52.

Whaley, Rachel B., Angela M. Moe, J. Mark Eddy, and Jean Daugherty. 2007. "The Domestic Violence Experiences of Women in Community Corrections." *Women and Criminal Justice* 18(3): 25–45.

Wilson, David B., Catherine A. Gallagher, and Doris L. MacKenzie. 2000. "A Meta-Analysis of Corrections-Based Education, Vocation, and Work Programs for Adult Offenders." *Journal of Research in Crime and Delinquency* 37(4): 347–68.

Wilson, James A., and Robert Davis. 2006. "Hard Realities Meet Good Intentions: An Evaluation of the Project Greenlight Reentry Program." *Criminology and Public Policy* 5(2): 303–38.

Yu, Mansoo, Carol S. North, Patricia D. LaVesser, Victoria A. Osborne, and Edward L. Spitznagel. 2008. "A Comparison Study of Psychiatric and Behavior Disorders and Cognitive Ability among Homeless and Housed Children." *Community Mental Health Journal* 44(1): 1–10.

Zhang, Sheldon X., Robert E. L. Roberts, and Valerie J. Callanan. 2006. "Preventing Parolees from Returning to Prison through Community-Based Reintegration." *Crime and Delinquency* 52(4): 551–71.

PART IV
Implications and Conclusions

13

The Interface between Corrections and Child Welfare for Children of Incarcerated Parents

Benjamin de Haan

Corrections and child welfare professionals recognize that the increased use of incarceration in the United States, and the resulting expansion of the criminal justice system, has led to dramatic, unintended consequences for children and families (Travis and Waul 2003). Recent estimates suggest that on any given day, at least 7 million children have a parent in prison or jail, on parole, or under some other form of community supervision (Mumola 2000; U.S. Department of Health and Human Services 2008). Significant numbers of these children and their families are also involved with the child welfare system. This chapter discusses the interface between these two systems from the author's perspective as a former administrator of the state corrections and the state child welfare systems in Oregon, and more recently as an independent consultant working in both corrections and child welfare systems in Oregon, Washington, and throughout the country.

Most of the more than 2 million Americans behind bars are parents. Using national data, it is estimated that 52 percent of state prisoners and 63 percent of federal inmates are parents (Glaze and Maruschak 2008). However, there are reasons to suspect that these estimates are conservative. In recent years, several states across the country have reported that a much higher percent of their inmates are parents. For example, the state of Washington Department of Corrections (DOC) reports that 82 percent of prisoners are parents (Russell 2006); Rhode Island KIDS COUNT (2007) reports that 74 percent of women sentenced to prison are parents; the Illinois DOC reports that 81 percent of women in the state prison system are parents (Nickel, Garland, and Kane 2009); and the state of California estimates that while 56 percent of its male prisoners are parents, 80 percent of its female prisoners are parents (Simmons 2000). Perhaps the number of parents in prison, and the number of children affected, is even higher than currently thought.

While parents are in prison, their children and other family members are often involved with various other social service systems. According to a recent study in Washington State (2008), 80 percent of young people born to parents who have served time in the state prison system receive some service from the state Department of Social and Health Services. However, little is known about the scope and breadth of services offered to prisoners' families because police departments do not routinely collect information about the children of those they arrest, and correctional agencies request little information about the families of prisoners or the services they receive (Seymour 1998). As a result, the number of families involved with multiple agencies may also be seriously underestimated.

For example, in 2007, the U.S. Department of Justice reported that based on inmate survey data, 11 percent of incarcerated mothers had a child in foster care (chapter 3, this volume). During the same period, the Adoption and Foster Care Analysis and Reporting System (AFCARS 2007) reported that 6 percent of children in foster care had a parent in prison. AFCARS files include only those children who are placed in foster care as a direct result of parental incarceration. Children who enter foster care for other reasons and who also have a parent in prison are not included. If one more broadly considers contact with the criminal justice system (i.e., arrest, conviction, jail time, parole), not just long-term incarceration, criminal justice systems may have intervened in as many as one of every three families served by public child welfare systems across the country (Phillips and Dettlaff 2009).

Although the number of inmates who are parents of minor children increased by 79 percent between 1971 and mid-year 2007 (Glaze and Maruschak 2008), child welfare and corrections agencies have been slow to recognize the needs of this shared population and even slower to modify their policies and practices to reflect the new challenges. In recent years, many child welfare services have been delivered through systems that have not anticipated the complexities of working with family members who are also simultaneously involved with the criminal justice system.

These complexities go beyond the normal requirements of coordinating services. Child welfare services and criminal justice services are largely non-voluntary and stigmatizing, and they combine in ways that can negatively affect or even permanently sever parent-child relationships.

Further, judges, court officials, and child welfare workers all report difficulties involving incarcerated parents in planning sessions and court hearings regarding their children in state custody (Margolies and Kraft-Stolar 2006). Family visitation is also a problem, and face-to-face interactions between children and their incarcerated parents are limited. In an Oregon survey of parents in prison, 90 percent of fathers and 82 percent of mothers had no face-to-face visitation with their children in the preceding three months (Oregon DOC 2000). The same study found large differences between mothers and fathers regarding the frequency of contact with their children. The most frequent form of contact was by telephone, but mothers were far more likely than fathers to contact their children by phone (70 percent versus 47 percent). Recent national data indicate that across the country, imprisoned mothers have more phone and mail contact with their children than fathers, but mothers and fathers have equal amounts of face-to-face contact (Glaze and Maruschak 2008). A number of systemic factors in the child welfare system and in prisons make it difficult for child welfare workers to maintain contact with parents and to coordinate visits between parents and children in prisons and jails (Allard and Lu 2006). Much of the available information on agency collaboration between child welfare and the criminal justice system is anecdotal and highly speculative. Only a few studies have assessed the population shared by these systems, and operational data from public agencies have only recently elucidated the needs of families involved with multiple public agencies.

Children of Incarcerated Parents in Foster Care

The number of U.S. children in nonrelative foster care increased from an estimated 229,600 in 1986 to 337,000 in 1997 (Johnson and Waldfogel 2002). This upward trend has continued, and an estimated 510,000 children are currently in foster care nationwide (AFCARS 2007). Children of incarcerated parents make up a growing number of the foster care population for obvious reasons: many more people who are parents are now in prison, and because of the proliferation of state mandatory sentencing laws, incarcerated individuals are staying in prison longer (Bureau of Justice Statistics 2008). At the same time, federal laws have become more assertive in moving children in foster care toward permanency; as a result, a larger proportion of prisoners, many of who are returning to prison for a second or third time, either already have had their parental rights terminated (Halperin and Harris 2004) or will have such rights terminated during their current sentence. A large percentage of children involved with the foster care system in New York City, for example, have mothers who are either incarcerated or were involved with the criminal justice system at some point in their children's stay in foster care (Ehrensaft et al. 2003).

The state of Oregon, one of the first jurisdictions to track children with parents involved with the criminal justice system, reported that in 2003, over 20,000 children in Oregon had an incarcerated parent (Oregon DOC 2004). At that point, approximately 11,000 families were involved with Oregon's child welfare system, and more than 9,000 children were in Oregon's foster care system.[1] In empirical case reviews conducted by Oregon's child welfare agency during the early 1990s, parental criminal justice involvement was the second most prevalent reason for child removal, with neglect leading to physical harm the most prevalent.[2]

In 2000, 2002, and 2008, researchers at the Oregon Department of Corrections surveyed parents in prison to better understand the needs of incarcerated parents and their children. These surveys suggested that approximately 10 percent of incarcerated mothers and 6 percent of incarcerated fathers had at least one child in foster care.[3] While these estimates were consistent with national findings (e.g., Glaze and Maruschak 2008; Harnhill, Petit, and Woodruff 1998), Oregon DOC researchers believed that the surveys probably underestimated the number of children in foster care for a number of reasons. In general, prisoners are reluctant to discuss their children for fear of jeopardizing their parental rights. Further, many prisoners are concerned about financial penalties related to cost recovery for child welfare services; many male prisoners have never established paternity, and they may not consider themselves the legal parent even though they may have had parental responsibilities.

Subsequently, when in-person interviews were conducted with all women entering the state prison system in Oregon over four months, new findings emerged: for every 100 women incarcerated in the state, approximately 38 children were involved in either temporary shelter care or long-term foster care.[4] In short, whereas the precise extent of overlap between the foster care and corrections systems is unknown (Moses

2006; O'Donnell 1995; Phillips 2008), a significant number of families are clearly affected by both systems.

Agency Practice and Policy

Monitoring Parental Incarceration

Most child welfare agencies do not consistently track parental incarceration. Consequently, little is known about the children in child welfare who have a parent in prison or jail. In an effort to fill this gap, the Child Welfare League of America surveyed state agencies in 1998 (Harnhill et al. 1998). Of the 38 responding states, 35 did not know the number of children with incarcerated parents. Only 5 states were able to estimate the number of children in foster care who had incarcerated parents. Determining during intake whether a child had an incarcerated parent was standard practice in fewer than 11 states, and many of those states did so only conditionally (i.e., when having an incarcerated parent directly affected the child's involvement in foster care). Further contributing to the information gap, many children of incarcerated parents who are admitted into foster care are there for reasons other than parental incarceration (Seymour and Hairston 2001). In these cases, foster care placement may have preceded parental incarceration (Ehrensaft et al. 2003) or the courts may have established jurisdiction based upon child maltreatment, abandonment, threat of harm, or many other reasons unrelated to parental incarceration. Many child welfare systems do not enter information about parental incarceration unless it is the primary reason for placement, making it difficult to track the true number of children with an incarcerated parent who are receiving child welfare services.

Agency Practices

Child welfare agencies and criminal justice agencies do not routinely collaborate to provide services to families involved with both systems. An early documented attempt to assess the need for cross-agency services was a small study conducted in 1955 in California (Zietz 1963). The study revealed an acute need for child welfare service provision inside the California women's correctional institution. Many years later, professionals in the field are still challenged by barriers to collaboration across disciplines. A recent study continues to find very little coordination and communication between law enforcement and child welfare agencies in California (Nieto 2002). Child protective agencies report that they are only notified by law enforcement a quarter of the time when a mother with a minor child is arrested. Further, only a quarter of law enforcement agencies assume responsibility of a child when arresting his or her mother. Of these, approximately half of subsequent placements occur without involving child protective services.

Similar to the findings in California, Harnhill and colleagues' (1998) national survey finds that only two states provide child welfare and law enforcement staff with training focusing on identified areas of need specific to this population. Of these, only one uses a specific curriculum; the other relies on ad hoc workshops and conferences planned by others. Fortunately, however, in recent years a number of states have used legislation to encourage consideration of the children of incarcerated parents, mostly through interagency data-sharing and joint planning. For example, in 2001, the Oregon legislature passed State Bill 133, which directed key agencies to work in concert to better meet the needs of children with incarcerated parents. In Oregon, the Department of Corrections is now required to gather information about inmates' children as a part of the intake process. Other outcomes of State Bill 133 include the development and implementation of statewide arrest protocols, the provision of training for law enforcement officers in child-sensitive interviewing techniques, the provision of training for court personnel on the federal Adoptions and Safe Families Act and its implications for incarcerated parents, the creation of adequate child visitation space, the release of information to inmates at intake to facilitate work with families, and the initiation of collaborative reentry planning.

Washington State pursued a similar approach with the passage of House Bill 1426 in 2005 and State Bill 1422 in 2007. Both bills required a coordinated approach, with an additional emphasis on gathering information about outcomes for children served by multiple agencies. Specifically, the bills require information sharing between the state departments of corrections and health and human services. By linking administrative data, Washington researchers subsequently determined that 80 percent of children who had a parent in prison at some point in their lives ultimately required services from the Department of Social and Health Services (DSHS), ranging from mental health services to child protection services, including foster care; economic services, including food stamps, TANF payments, and subsidized child care; and medical assistance services, alcohol and drug treatment services, and/or juvenile justice services (Washington State DSHS 2008). The greatest use of services occurred among children who experienced the incarceration of both parents; children who had both parents involved with the DOC were 16 times more likely to need DSHS services than children with no parental involvement in the criminal justice system. It should be noted that the approach in Washington did not include children of offenders housed in county jails or on community supervision, the largest criminal justice populations; therefore, the estimates of service use may be conservative.

Other states also have begun to address the interface between adult corrections and human services agencies, including child welfare. For example, the Hawaii state government has strongly encouraged (but does not require by statute) cooperation among the agencies serving children of incarcerated parents. This cooperation requires systematically collecting information about children to help tailor programs as alternatives to incarceration for women convicted of drug crimes. In California, Assembly Bill 2316 directed the California Research Bureau to study women with children in the California prison system. New York focused attention on the need to preserve parent-child contact through structured visitation and transportation programs, and the state of Virginia designated a lead agency in statute to coordinate research and training for key agency personnel in both the corrections and human services agencies. Many of these early state efforts have focused on identifying families served by multiple agencies, setting up structures for sharing information, and identifying opportunities for coordinating services.

Parental Visitation

Frequent visits between foster children and parents are essential to successful reunification (Davis et al. 1996; Howing et al. 1992; Norman 1995). Similarly, maintaining contact between incarcerated parents and their children is considered beneficial, although several studies also have found that some types of prison or jail visitation can be stressful for children.[5] Barriers to parent-child visitation are clearly an issue for children of incarcerated parents, whether or not they are in foster care. Previous national studies have found that face-to-face contact between parents in prison and their children is infrequent (McGowan and Blumenthal 1978; Mumola 2000). Mumola (2000) finds that most mothers (54 percent) and fathers (57 percent) receive no visits from their children, and less than a quarter of mothers (24 percent) and fathers (21 percent) receive monthly visits from their children. An analysis of two Bureau of Justice Statistics surveys indicates that visitation for both mothers and fathers actually decreased significantly from 1991 to 1997 (Johnson and Waldfogel 2002). According to the most recent analysis by the Bureau of Justice Statistics (Glaze and Maruschak 2008), only 42 percent of state and 55 percent of federal prisoners had a face-to-face visit with their children while they were incarcerated.

One of the most pressing problems for parents who are incarcerated and who are also involved with public child welfare systems is the lack of communication with caseworkers (Beckerman 1994; Johnson and Waldfogel 2002). Unfortunately, this is all too common for several reasons: caseworkers tend to have large caseloads; prisons are often located in remote locations; and correctional facilities can be intimidating and unforgiving to those unfamiliar with the rules and stringent security procedures. Further, caseworkers often lack adequate training on the value of visitation with an incarcerated parent, particularly when reunification is the ultimate goal. In addition, prison administrators have traditionally limited their role to operating safe and secure institutions, with little consideration given to issues affecting prisoners' postrelease outcomes. As a result, many prison policies and practices actively discourage contact between incarcerated parents and their families, and some prison administrators view the relationship between incarcerated persons and their families as beyond the scope of their mission.

Professionals in both corrections and social services have questioned whether child-parent contact during incarceration is constructive. Sometimes these concerns are based on preconceived and untested notions of the value of visiting a parent in prison (see Hairston 2003). Sometimes the concerns center around visitation environments that may be stressful to children because they are not child friendly (e.g., visits behind Plexiglas, children being frisked, no-contact visits). These two issues are very different and are worthy of separate consideration.

While some professional opinions about prisoners' increased risk to children result from lack of information and training specific to the needs of children with incarcerated parents (Seymour 1998), class and racial bias also may play a role. In March 2002, a focus group of stakeholders from the New York's child welfare system and the criminal justice system explored this attitude in depth (Women's Prison Association 2003). A common point of discussion was that child welfare workers in

New York were often cynical about the intentions of the mothers (most often the pre-incarceration caregiver, as opposed to fathers), who did "not place their children's needs above their addiction" (p. 14) before incarceration. Consequently, these professionals may have been less motivated to support the parent-child relationship during the mother's incarceration. Participants felt that criminal justice policies and practices put "apprehension, custody, conviction, and punishment of lawbreakers" (Women's Prison Association 2003, 9) foremost in consideration during an individual's incarceration, and that the relationship between offenders and their children was rarely addressed.

Poverty plays a major role in crime and subsequent incarceration (Cadora, Swartz, and Gordon 2003). Prisoners disproportionately return to disadvantaged communities, which also often have high proportions of people of color (Western and Wildeman 2009). Both the criminal justice system and child welfare systems have a great deal of work to do to overcome class and cultural bias that leads to disproportionate numbers of Native American, African American, and Latino individuals in both systems. However, at least two states, Oregon and Washington, are now required by state statute or executive order to report on the status of children affected by parental incarceration. Coincidentally, these two states also are required to report on the effects of race at key decision points in the child welfare system.

Coordinating Law Enforcement and Child Welfare Practices

In most jurisdictions, child welfare and law enforcement agencies are required by statute to coordinate their activities when investigating child maltreatment. Nevertheless, when a parent is arrested for a crime unrelated to the child, the child's needs are often not the highest priority. Smith and Elstein (1994) find that few child welfare agencies have specific policies or guidelines for placing children whose mothers are arrested. Similarly, few states have a written policy guiding law enforcement in meeting the needs of these children (Harnhill et al. 1998). In California, half the child welfare agencies do not have written policies for placing children when their mother is arrested. Likewise, almost two-thirds of law enforcement agencies do not have specific policies dictating how officers are to respond in situations where a small child is present and the offender is the child's primary caregiver (Nieto 2002).

The absence of clear policy is reflected in the practices of child welfare and criminal justice agencies. At the time the Nieto study was conducted, only 7 percent of responding law enforcement agencies in California reported taking responsibility for minor children every time the sole caregiver was arrested, whereas 11 percent reported never taking responsibility for minor children when the sole caretaker was arrested. There is no question that parental incarceration has gained visibility in recent years, but many law enforcement practices may not have kept pace. In a recent survey of women entering Oregon's prison system,[6] a significant number of respondents reported that their children were present during their arrest, and many women also reported that it appeared that their children were left at the scene to make their own living arrangements (including staying with friends, relatives, or alone) while the parent was incarcerated. Witnessing the arrest of a parent can be traumatizing for children (Dallaire and Wilson 2010).

Termination of Parental Rights

The Adoption and Safe Families Act (ASFA) of 1997 was a modification of the Adoption Assistance and Child Welfare Act of 1980. ASFA was intended to improve outcomes for children involved in the foster care system. However, ASFA neglected to accommodate the unique needs of children whose parents are in prison and has potentially increased damage to families affected by parental incarceration. In response to ASFA, at least 25 states have passed statutes for termination of parental rights and/or adoption that pertain specifically to incarcerated parents.

ASFA shifted the focus of child welfare policy in the United States from family preservation to securing permanent placement for children in foster care (Luke 2002). ASFA created many new challenges for those families with an incarcerated parent for whom family preservation may be the best option. The new act mandates developing a permanency plan for a child within 12 months of entering foster care; previous legislation required a permanency plan by 18 months (Beckerman 1998). In addition, ASFA requires the state to file a petition to terminate parental rights when a child has been in nonrelative foster care for 15 of the most recent 22 consecutive months (Johnson and Waldfogel 2002). Because the average sentence length in state prison is 75 months (Glaze and Maruschak 2008), most incarcerated parents face the federally mandated deadline for permanent placement of their children before they are released or immediately following their release (Norman 1995). Since ASFA, the percentage of incarcerated parents whose parental rights have been terminated has increased significantly (Hairston 2001).

Incarcerated parents are frequently not well-educated about their legal rights (Johnson and Waldfogel 2002; Norman 1995; Smith and Elstein 1994). Often this lack of knowledge, coupled with barriers presented by both the foster care and correctional agencies, can lead to circumstances that are considered grounds for termination under state or federal statute. In addition, Smith and Elstein (1994) note that foster care agencies commonly exclude mothers from initial planning, as well as from ongoing assessments of how well the plan is working. Beckerman (1994) finds that almost half of incarcerated mothers receive no correspondence from their children's caseworker, over a quarter are not informed of their child's custody hearing, and two-thirds do not receive a copy of their child's case plan. Much of the available research on this and other related topics is focused on mothers, and there is little information available about the incarcerated father's role in case planning with public agencies.

Recommendations

If current child welfare and criminal justice policies are viewed from the perspective of the families involved with the two systems rather than the procedural requirements of the respective agencies, a number of strategies for improving outcomes for children emerge. These are delineated below.

Create a Structure for Cross-Disciplinary Policy Coordination

As discussed throughout this chapter, child welfare programs, law enforcement agencies, and adult corrections departments have overlapping target populations, yet their policies and activities are poorly coordinated. Recognizing this, many state legislatures have enacted statutes and commissioned reports to encourage or direct local agencies to share information and coordinate their services. An increasing number of states have assigned responsibility for children of incarcerated parents to a single agency in order to establish clear expectations of them in statute.

These high-level policy directives could be more effective if they include the following:

- A planning entity sponsored by the governor or chief executive and legislative leaders charged with defining and organizing services and policies affecting children of incarcerated parents.
- Formal written agreements among child welfare, law enforcement, and corrections agencies that specify service standards for children of incarcerated parents. These standards should emphasize the family's role in offender reentry, as well as address class and racial disparities. More specifically, standards should address the frequency and quality of parent-child visitation, the effectiveness of prison and community-based family programs, and the alignment of parental release plans with child welfare service agreements.
- Statutory requirements defining what information will be collected to guide policy and program development and under what conditions this information can be shared across agencies. These statutes should explicitly require written reports to the governor and legislature regarding outcomes for prisoners' children.

Increase Positive Parent-Child Contact during Incarceration

A number of studies underscore the need to increase opportunities for positive contacts between incarcerated parents and their children in child-friendly settings. The lack of positive interaction leaves parents and their children unprepared for restructuring a relationship upon release (Hairston 2003). While prisoners have the opportunity to contact their children through letters and telephone calls more frequently than in-person visits, these forms of communication have some significant limitations. In most prisons and jails, prisoners can only make collect calls. The rates for those calls are exorbitant. Many families cannot afford this added expense because incarceration results in significant financial hardship. Letters have limitations as well, since many prisoners have limited writing skills and are unable to effectively communicate using this medium. However, letter-writing affords opportunities for reflection that can foster positive communication, and it gives children something tangible to "hold onto" in their parent's absence.

Parental visitation typically is limited by various factors: the geographic location of the prisons, the visitation procedures in a particular facility, whether children are involved with the child welfare agency, and the nature of the relationship between the child's caretaker and the incarcerated parent. Often caregivers, such as grandparents or other relatives, lack the resources or decisionmaking authority to support ongoing visitation with an incarcerated parent (Hairston 2009). In addition, many prisons are not concerned with visitors' situations or needs; a family may travel for an entire day only to be turned away for wearing the wrong clothes (e.g., blue jeans in an institution where, for security reasons, only inmates are allowed to wear jeans), or they may miss the set visitation time as a result of processing or travel delays. Many prisons and jails greatly need child-friendly visitation spaces, private visits between parents and children, and parenting education programs that can help incarcerated parents facilitate positive relationships with their children. Moreover, because of the multiple hardships faced by incarcerated parents and their children, even before incarceration, they may need assistance in learning new ways of relating to one another to facilitate positive family relationships.

One of the most obvious recommendations would be to increase contact between incarcerated parents and their children by locating prisons closer to prisoners' families. In fact, this was a primary consideration for locating Oregon's Coffee Creek Correctional Facility for women in an urban area rather than in one of the proposed rural sites. In reality, prisons are often mechanisms for stimulating rural economies, and even concerns about operational effectiveness are relegated to a lower position in the decisionmaking hierarchy. Unfortunately, concerns about prisoners' families are typically the lowest of all. As a result, most new prisons today are located in rural areas, even though most prisoners come from urban centers. Prison siting is one of the most politically contentious issues facing political leaders today, and given how this process plays out in most jurisdictions, is probably not a viable general strategy for increasing parent-child contact.

However, a great deal can be done to improve visitation facilities, regardless of location, and to make visitation policies and procedures more humane and respectful. Most visitation facilities are chaotic, noisy, and, from the corrections perspective, difficult to control. One way to take pressure off the visitation facilities is to better use video technology to augment, but not replace, face-to-face visits. As new facilities are constructed, they should include dedicated video visiting as well as dedicated space for face-to-face visits. These spaces should include comfortable furniture, items for children to play with, and freedom from intrusion by other visitors. During family visits, prisoners should be allowed to wear civilian clothing, and security should refrain from using shackles and restraints. *Great* sensitivity must be used when children must be searched for contraband, and all family members and prisoners must be treated with the utmost respect at all times.

Security staff assigned to visitation facilities should be carefully screened and well trained in security techniques that are not frightening to children and intimidating to visitors. Not all correctional officers have the temperament and the values necessary for supervising family visits. Visitation normally occurs during the day shift, a desirable work schedule for most correctional officers. In states with collective bargaining agreements, seniority determines shifts, not necessarily an interest in or an aptitude for the specific duties required. Departments of corrections should consider sidebar agreements with unions exempting visitation from the post-bidding process (competition for specific assignments guaranteed by contract); in return, provision of additional training and other incentives could be considered for those opting for visitation duty.

An additional consideration is special family visitation privileges. These can be significant incentives for prisoners who live in an incentive-poor environment. Incarcerated parents who complete parent training or engage in other prosocial, family-oriented activities should be allowed greater access to family visits. Anecdotal information from security staff in Oregon's 14 state correctional facilities suggests that inmates who are engaged actively with their families are less likely to commit disciplinary infractions for fear of losing visitation privileges. While a few studies have examined the relation between family contact and inmate behavior, further rigorous research on this topic is sorely needed.

Provide Support Services for Kinship Care Providers

Many children are cared for by the other parent when one parent goes to prison, although this differs dramatically by gender. According to Glaze and Maruschak (2008), during incarceration, 88 percent of fathers rely on the mother for primary care of the children. On the other hand, only 37 percent of incarcerated mothers rely on fathers as the primary caregivers for the children. Approximately 20 percent of children whose parents are incarcerated reside with relatives, most frequently grandmothers. The frequency of placements with relatives varies for mothers and fathers. According to Glaze and Maruschak, about half of incarcerated mothers rely on grandmothers to provide care, and only a third of incarcerated fathers rely on the child's grandparents. When parents are able to provide care, children placed with relatives as opposed to foster care tend to have better outcomes, including fewer placement disruptions and more regular contact with their parents and siblings (Gleeson 2007). However, kinship providers face other significant challenges that threaten children's placement stability. Most notably, kin caregivers are often older, poor, and single, and they often have unmet medical needs (Ehrle and Geen 2002).

Given this context, there is a real need for the development of formal supports for kinship care providers, including (a) providing guardianship subsidies to related caregivers regardless of financial eligibility (some states provide guardianship subsidies only to those kinship providers who are eligible for federal Title IV-E reimbursement); (b) funding kinship "navigator" programs to help kinship providers better access services and better understand the complexities of working within multiple systems when a parent is incarcerated; (c) requiring notification of family members when a related child enters foster care; (d) funding community-based support services geared to meeting the needs of kinship providers caring for a relative whose parents are in prison; (e) requiring that when a child welfare agency is involved, kinship providers be involved in every aspect of case planning; (f) requiring that kinship providers be involved in release planning by the department of corrections; and (g) revising statutes to allow kinship providers to enroll children in school and to authorize medical care. In terms of the latter recommendation, the Children's Health Insurance Program and Medicaid are two federally funded medical programs that are based upon the child's eligibility rather than the parent's eligibility. In theory, these programs would be readily available to children of incarcerated parents; in actuality, many kinship care providers face obstacles in registering children for whom they may not have legal custody.

Revise Policies That Reduce Postrelease Parental Success

In addition to the constraints imposed on noncustodial parents by ASFA, other restrictions have their roots in federal policy but are subject to interpretation at the state level. For example, the Personal Responsibility and Work Opportunity Reconciliation Act bans people with parole violations from receiving food stamps. The same law bans people with certain drug offenses from receiving Temporary Assistance for Needy Families benefits for life. Many parents are banned from public housing because of drug convictions, and many relatives cannot provide kinship care (or cannot receive financial support for providing kinship care) because of previous criminal convictions that do not relate to child safety. In many instances, local jurisdictions have the authority to choose a different policy or eliminate state-level statutory bans, although federal funding restrictions may result. These policies need to be reconsidered carefully within the context of parental incarceration. They may have the unintended and undesirable side effect of increasing recidivism, for example.

Provide Additional Statutory Guidance Regarding ASFA

The federal guidelines for implementing ASFA provide little procedural direction regarding "reasonable efforts" and termination of parental rights when the parent is incarcerated. The federal guidelines encourage states to consider terminating parental rights within the context of sentence length and the age of the child. Some states have circumvented the reasonable efforts requirements by passing statutes that make incarceration alone statutory grounds for terminating parental rights (Halperin and Harris 2004).

Emphasize the Family's Role in Prisoner Reentry

Each day across our nation, hundreds of prisoners who have children are released from jails and prisons. The majority will, at some point, resume or assume the role of parent, regardless of their skill, mental condition, problems, or attitude at the time (Travis and Waul 2003). Without a doubt, some of these parents represent a serious threat to the welfare of their children, and great care should be taken when considering reunification. However, for most families, parental reunification with appropriate supports is the most constructive approach. Maintaining strong family ties during and after incarceration is critical for successfully reintegrating the offender and better in the long run for children.

When appropriate, family members should be included in planning for the release of an incarcerated parent. Including families in transition planning can alleviate family members' and prisoners' fears and concerns, correct unrealistic expectations, and prepare children and parents for new roles. Although prisons are absolutely necessary to protect the public from dangerous individuals, they are the bluntest of social instruments, and their use often has serious side effects. To mitigate these effects, reentry efforts must focus on the needs of the entire family.

Expand Prison-Based Parenting Programs

Fortunately, improving opportunities for family contact is one of the most inexpensive services institutions can provide incarcerated persons and their families. Programs such as prison-based Early Head Start, therapeutic visitation, Girl Scouts Beyond Bars, and structured crafts and play times can enhance parents' interactions with their children and parental skills. In Oregon, researchers and corrections administrators collaborated to design and implement a research-informed, prison-based parenting program currently under evaluation (Eddy et al. 2008), and more such research collaborations are needed. Funding parenting programs over the long run requires ongoing and creative efforts from administrative staff and the members of the legislative and executive branches. For example, a large portion of the funding for prison-based parent programs in Oregon, as well as for a similar community-based approach for prisoners who have returned to the community, comes through the Title IV-E portion of the Social Security Act that is normally reserved for supporting children who have been placed in foster care and over whom the courts have established jurisdiction. In this example, federal funding was made available through an IV-E waiver program designed to prevent children from entering the foster care system.

Coordinate Child Welfare Case Plans with Institutional Release Planning

When a child is involved with the child welfare system, the frequency of contact with an incarcerated parent is often dramatically reduced. This effect may be mitigated with enhanced training and supervision of child welfare workers related to cases that involve the children of incarcerated parents. Key training issues include (a) how to use model service agreements that take into account the unique aspects faced by parents in prison, (b) how to help families overcome the difficulties associated with prison visitation protocols, and (c) how to use prison visitation to help families successfully meet their goals during family reunification. Oregon has used IV-E waiver funds to support family-based transition services beginning during incarceration and continuing in the community after release.

Improve Outcomes for Children, Beginning at Arrest

For many children with incarcerated parents, watching the arrest of family members is their first exposure to the criminal justice system. Children often exhibit various long-term effects after the arrest of a parent, including emotional and behavioral problems, depression, and delinquency (Nieto 2002). Because law enforcement officers are poorly equipped to deal with children whose custodial parents are arrested, children are often left alone, and they may subsequently enter inappropriate living arrangements. Most law enforcement agencies have no formal protocols for how officers should respond to children who have contact with police. Given this, state and local law enforcement and child welfare jurisdictions should consider implementing joint training protocols for law enforcement officers and child welfare workers regarding the impact of arrest on children and child-sensitive arrest procedures; developing written working agreements between law enforcement and child welfare agencies that adopt a standard policy about placement and disposition of the case when a child is involved; and including material regarding the children of incarcerated parents in pre-service training curricula at police academies and IV-E-funded, university-based social work programs and related training activities.

Conclusion

Our understanding of the effects of American criminal justice policies on children and families is in its early stages. In the past two decades, the number of children in foster care has increased dramatically, and the number of parents behind bars even more so. The soaring number of people in American prisons is no mystery; they are there as a result of major changes in sentencing policies. But the increase in foster care is poorly understood.

As states struggle to learn how child welfare and criminal justice policies combine to affect families, particularly families of color, a number of questions remain unanswered. Do children enter foster care as a result of parental incarceration or are child foster care placement and parental incarceration simply two discrete results of such issues as poverty and substance abuse? How does parental incarceration affect intergenerational patterns of crime? What are the best strategies for increasing parental success after release? While the answers to these questions are not immediately at hand, a new level of collaboration will clearly be necessary. The correctional officer in the cell block will need to think about the prisoner's return to being a parent; the police officer will need to think about who will care for a child left behind after the parent's arrest; and the child's social worker will have to think about how to maintain visits with an incarcerated mother, rather than filing a petition to terminate parental rights. This new level of collaboration will also require more research about the effectiveness of policies designed to punish offenders, especially if the end result is homelessness, medical neglect, and family disintegration. Finally, this new level of collaboration will happen only when our elected officials require a new approach, one that is truly in the best interests of the child.

NOTES

1. From Oregon Department of Health and Human Services, "Children in Foster Care in Oregon," unpublished raw data, 2009.

2. Benjamin de Haan, Paul Bellaty, J. Mark Eddy, and Jean Kjellstrand, "Interconnections between Child Welfare and Corrections and the Impact on Children and Families," manuscript submitted for publication, 2010.

3. De Haan et al., "Interconnections."

4. De Haan et al., "Interconnections."

5. For a review, see Poehlmann et al. (2010).

6. De Haan et al., "Interconnections."

REFERENCES

AFCARS. 2007. "Adoptions and Foster Care Analysis Reporting System Users Guide. Foster Care File, Annual Supplement." Ithaca, NY: Cornell University, National Data Archive on Child Abuse and Neglect.

Allard, Patricia E., and Lynn D. Lu. 2006. *Rebuilding Families, Reclaiming Lives: State Obligations to Children in Foster Care and Their Incarcerated Parents.* New York: Brennan Center for Justice.

Beckerman, Adela. 1994. "Mothers in Prison: Meeting the Prerequisite Conditions for Permanency Planning." *Social Work* 39(1): 9–14.

———. 1998. "Charting a Course: Meeting the Challenge of Permanency Planning for Children with Incarcerated Mothers." *Child Welfare* 77(5): 513–29.

Cadora, Eric, Charles Swartz, and Mannix Gordon. 2003. "Criminal Justice and Health and Human Services: An Exploration of Overlapping Needs, Resources, and

Interests in Brooklyn Neighborhoods." In *Prisoners Once Removed: The Impact of Incarceration and Reentry on Children, Families, and Communities,* edited by Jeremy Travis and Michelle Waul (285–312). Washington, DC: Urban Institute Press.

Dallaire, Danielle H., and Laura C. Wilson. 2010. "The Impact of Exposure to Parental Criminal Activity, Arrest, and Sentencing on Children's Academic Competence and Externalizing Behavior." *Journal of Child and Family Studies* 19:404–18.

Davis, Inger P., John Landsverk, Rae Newton, and William Ganger. 1996. "Parental Visiting and Foster Care Reunification." *Children and Youth Services Review* 18(4/5): 363–82.

Eddy, J. Mark, Charles R. Martinez Jr., Tracy Schiffmann, Rex Newton, Laura Olin, Leslie Leve, Dana M. Foney, and Joann Wu Shortt. 2008. "Development of a Multisystemic Parent Management Training Intervention for Incarcerated Parents, Their Children, and Families." *Clinical Psychologist* 12(3): 86–98.

Ehrensaft, Miriam K., Ajay Khashu, Timothy Ross, and Mark Wamsley. 2003. *Patterns of Criminal Conviction and Incarceration among Mothers of Children in Foster Care in New York City.* New York: Vera Institute of Justice and Administration for Children's Services.

Ehrle, Jennifer, and Rob Geen. 2002. "Kin and Nonkin Foster Care: Findings from a National Survey." *Children and Youth Services Review* 24(1/2): 15–35.

Glaze, Lauren E., and Laura M. Maruschak. 2008. *Parents in Prison and Their Minor Children.* NCJ 222984. Washington, DC: U.S. Department of Justice, Bureau of Justice Statistics.

Gleeson, James P. 2007. "Kinship Care Research and Literature: Lessons Learned and Directions for Future Research." *Kinship Reporter* 1(2): 1, 8–11.

Hairston, Creasie Finney. 2001. "Fathers in Prison." *Marriage and Family Review* 32(3/4): 31–40.

———. 2003. "Prisoners and Their Families: Parenting Issues during Incarceration." In *Prisoners Once Removed: The Impact of Incarceration and Reentry on Children, Families, and Communities,* edited by Jeremy Travis and Michelle Waul (259–84). Washington, DC: Urban Institute Press.

———. 2009. "Kinship Care when Parents Are Incarcerated: What We Know, What We Can Do." Baltimore, MD: Annie E. Casey Foundation.

Halperin, Ronnie, and Jennifer L. Harris. 2004. "Parental Rights of Incarcerated Mothers with Children in Foster Care: A Policy Vacuum." *Feminist Studies* 30(2): 339–52.

Harnhill, Sandra, Michael Petit, and Kristen Woodruff. 1998. *State Agency Survey on Children with Incarcerated Parents.* Washington, DC: Child Welfare League of America.

Howing, Phyllis T., Sheldon Kohn, James M. Gaudin, P. David Kurtz, et al. 1992. "Current Research Issues in Child Welfare." *Social Work Research and Abstracts* 28(1): 5–12.

Johnson, Elizabeth I., and Jane Waldfogel. 2002. "Parental Incarceration: Recent Trends and Implications for Child Welfare." *Social Service Review* 76(3): 460–79.

Luke, Katherine P. 2002. "Mitigating the Ill Effects of Maternal Incarceration on Women in Prison and Their Children." *Child Welfare* 81(6): 929–48.

Margolies, Julie Kowitz, and Tamar Kraft-Stolar. 2006. *When "Free" Means Losing Your Mother: The Collision of Child Welfare and the Incarceration of Women in New York State.* New York: Correctional Association of New York.

McGowan, Brenda G., and Karen L. Blumenthal. 1978. *Why Punish the Children? A Study of Children of Women Prisoners.* Hackensack, NJ: National Council on Crime and Deiinquency.

Moses, Marilyn C. 2006. "Does Parental Incarceration Increase a Child's Risk for Foster Care Placement?" *NIJ Journal* 255:12–14.

Mumola, Christopher J. 2000. *Incarcerated Parents and Their Children.* NCJ 182335. Washington, DC: U.S. Department of Justice, Bureau of Justice Statistics.

Nickel, Jessica, Crystal Garland, and Leah Kane. 2009. *Children of Incarcerated Parents: An Action Plan for Federal Policymakers.* New York: Council of State Governments Justice Center.

Nieto, Marcus. 2002. *In Danger of Falling through the Cracks: Children of Arrested Parents.* Sacramento: California State Library, California Research Bureau.

Norman, Julie A. 1995. "Children of Prisoners in Foster Care." In *Children of Incarcerated Parents,* edited by Katherine Gabel and Denise Johnston (124–34). New York: Lexington Books.

O'Donnell, John M. 1995. "Casework Practice with Fathers in Kinship Foster Care." Ph.D. diss., University of Illinois.

Oregon Department of Corrections. 2004. "Quick Facts." Salem: Oregon Department of Corrections.

Phillips, Susan D. 2008. "Parents Involvement in the Criminal Justice System and Children's Entry into Foster Care: Findings and Implications for 2 Studies." *CW360°: A Comprehensive Look at a Prevalent Child Welfare Issue* (spring): 8–9.

Phillips, Susan D., and Alan J. Dettlaff. 2009. "More Than Parents in Prison: The Broader Overlap between the Criminal Justice and Child Welfare Systems." *Journal of Public Child Welfare* 3:3–22.

Poehlmann, Julie, Danielle Dallaire, Ann B. Loper, and Leslie Shear. 2010. "Children's Contact with Their Incarcerated Parents: Research Findings and Recommendations." *American Psychologist* 65:575–98.

Rhode Island KIDS COUNT. 2007. *2007 Rhode Island KIDS COUNT Factbook.* Providence: Rhode Island KIDS COUNT.

Russell, Kathleen. 2006. *Report to the Washington State Legislature Regarding the Children of Incarcerated Parents.* Olympia: State of Washington.

Seymour, Cynthia. 1998. "Children with Parents in Prison: Child Welfare Policy, Program, and Practice Issues." *Child Welfare* 77(5): 469–93.

Seymour, Cynthia, and Creasie Finney Hairston. 2001. *Children with Parents in Prison: Child Welfare Policy, Program, and Practice Issues.* New Brunswick, NJ: Transaction Publishers.

Simmons, Charlene W. 2000. "Children of Incarcerated Parents." Note Vol. 7, No. 2. Sacramento: California Research Bureau.

Smith, Barbara E., and Sharon G. Elstein. 1994. *Children on Hold: Improving the Response to Children Whose Parents Are Arrested and Incarcerated.* Washington, DC: American Bar Association, Center for Children and the Law.

Travis, Jeremy, and Michelle Waul, eds. 2003. *Prisoners Once Removed: The Impact of Incarceration and Reentry on Children, Families, and Communities.* Washington, DC: Urban Institute Press.

U.S. Department of Health and Human Services. 2008. *Incarceration and the Family: A Review of Research and Promising Approaches for Serving Fathers and Families.* Triangle Park, NC: RTI International.

Washington State Department of Social and Health Services. 2008. "Briefing for the Children and Families of Incarcerated Parents Advisory Committee of the Planning, Performance, and Accountability Administration." Olympia: State of Washington.

Western, Bruce, and Christopher Wildeman. 2009. "The Black Family and Mass Incarceration." *Annals of the American Academy of Political and Social Science* 621:221–42.

Women's Prison Association. 2003. *Partnerships between Corrections and Child Welfare: Collaboration for Change (Part Two).* New York: Women's Prison Association.

Zietz, Dorothy. 1963. "Child Welfare Services in a Women's Correctional Institution." *Child Welfare* 42(4): 185–90.

14

Research with Incarcerated Parents, Their Children, and Their Families

Elizabeth B. Robertson and Eve E. Reider

C hildren of incarcerated parents constitute a relatively small but growing population of highly vulnerable children who are often overlooked by both researchers and policymakers. This chapter discusses the perspective of researchers within the National Institute on Drug Abuse toward funding research on the epidemiology, etiology, and prevention of problem behaviors, disorders, and diseases among at-risk populations, such as children with parents in prison. The chapter addresses the state of the research knowledge and implications of findings for future research with this population.

The National Institutes of Health (NIH) fund research on the biological, psychological, and social factors that have been identified as predictive of problem behaviors and that can lead to subsequent physical and mental diseases and disorders. Building on the knowledge derived from that research, the NIH also funds studies of theory-based interventions designed to prevent the onset or progression of behaviorally based diseases and disorders. Unfortunately, this body of research often overlooks small but highly vulnerable populations, such as the children of incarcerated parents. Since the NIH is a primary funder of scientifically rigorous research in the United States, this tendency has left the accumulated literature pertaining to these children underdeveloped, with many unanswered research questions.

The National Institute on Drug Abuse (NIDA), part of the NIH, funds research focusing on the epidemiology, etiology, and prevention of drug abuse and addiction. NIDA's epidemiology studies assess the incidence, prevalence, patterns, and trends of drug use and abuse and the associated behavioral, social, and health problems and consequences; etiology studies focus on the origins and pathways to drug use and abuse. Prevention intervention researchers use these data to develop, test, and translate programs and policies that target the initiation of drug use, the progression to abuse and dependence, the transmission of drug-related HIV infection, and associated problem behaviors among diverse populations and settings. Most of this work is housed within one funding unit, which uses a life course developmental perspective (e.g., Bronfenbrenner 2005; Elder 1998; Kellam and Rebok 1992) to manage this large body of research grants. The accrued findings from this research portfolio form the conceptual basis for creating initiatives and for funding meritorious researcher-initiated grant applications.

The Life Course Developmental Perspective

The life course developmental perspective proposes that individual and environmental factors interact and, over time, increase or reduce vulnerability to problem behaviors that can lead to physical and mental diseases and disorders. Timing is a critical consideration, as a child's age is inextricably linked to his or her biological, psychological, and social development and associated developmental tasks. For example, a child's cognitive abilities and skills will differ depending on his or her age and social context (O'Connell, Boat, and Warner 2009). Vulnerability can occur at many points in development but generally peaks at critical biological, normative, social, and traumatic life transitions.[1]

Researchers often plan data collection or preventive interventions to coincide with important developmental periods and transitions in order to optimize the potential for data that will elucidate new risk and protective factors or to maximize the effect of the intervention under study. Thus, surveys and interventions could be timed to capture youth at puberty (biological transition), moving from elementary to middle or junior high school (normative transition), dating and obtaining a driver's license (social transition), or the incarceration or release of a parent (traumatic transition). These transitions do not occur in isolation; thus, vulnerability also involves dynamic intrapersonal (e.g., temperament), interpersonal (e.g., family and peer interactions), and environmental (e.g., school environment and neighborhood) influences (Bronfenbrenner 1979). As a consequence, researchers must be aware of interactions between individuals and social systems across the life span when explicating risk and protective factors or assessing new interventions.

Epidemiology/Etiology

Children of parents in the criminal justice system are thought to be highly vulnerable (Travis 2005); however, very little is known about this population, and most research to date has been epidemiologic. For example, in 2007, approximately 52 percent of state and 63 percent of federal inmates were parents, and over 1.7 million children had parents in prison (Glaze and Maruschak 2008). Proportionately more inmates were persons of color than white, and thus black and Hispanic children were much more likely to have an incarcerated parent than white children (eight and three times, respectively). Families with an incarcerated parent experienced various problems including homelessness (9 percent), physical or sexual abuse (20 percent), medical problems (41 percent), mental health problems (57 percent), and substance abuse (67 percent). Despite these problems, just before arrest or incarceration, approximately two-thirds of mothers and half of fathers reported living with their minor children and about half of both fathers and mothers reported being the primary source of support for those children. During incarceration, 85 percent of mothers and 78 percent of fathers reported contact with a child. In addition, 57 percent of parents reported taking a self-help or improvement class, with 27 percent of mothers and 11 percent of fathers reporting attending parenting or child rearing classes while in a state prison.

These data demonstrate the multiple challenges encountered by this population, as well as the involvement of and desire among incarcerated parents to improve their relationships with their children. With further research, data of this type could help identify population-specific risk factors that may be ameliorated through preventive interventions; however, the research would need to move toward examining the process and mechanisms underlying vulnerability. Anecdotal and observational data indicate that the family contexts of these children include experiences around the arrest, entry into the criminal justice system, incarceration, and release of a parent, all stressful events and transitions for both children and their parents (Hairston 2002; Parke and Clarke-Stewart 2002; Travis 2005).

Moreover, these events and transitions occur in the context of child characteristics, possible parental drug abuse and mental health problems, and other family-specific social, emotional, and economic challenges, such as placing children in kin or foster care, social isolation and stigma, poverty, and navigating family reunification (Hairston 2002; Travis 2005).

For these children, exposure to multiple risk factors can increase the probability of problem behaviors. For example, boys whose parents were imprisoned before they were 11 years old had significantly more (5.4) risk factors than boys whose parents had no history of imprisonment or separation (2.3) (Murray and Farrington 2005). In addition, a recent meta-analysis concluded that children of prisoners have about twice the risk for antisocial outcomes and poor mental health problems than their peers (Murray et al. 2009). These data are consistent with the multiple problem perspective, which suggests that children who experience multiple risk factors are more likely to exhibit problem behaviors and that certain types of problem behaviors (e.g., academic failure, delinquency, violence, drug use) tend to cluster in youth at risk (Biglan et al. 2004).

The number of children in the United States who experience parental incarceration has been increasing (Clopton and East 2008). These circumstances could foster an increasingly large, chronic, intergenerational national problem that is challenging to multiple state and federal systems, including criminal justice and public health. Thus, it is critical that epidemiologic and etiologic research focus on understanding characteristics of this population as well as other associated factors, processes, and mechanisms pertinent to developing, adapting, and testing relevant prevention intervention and strategies. NIDA-funded prevention research focuses on the onset and progression of drug use and co-occurring problem behaviors, diseases, and disorders. Considering the complexity of the family situations and problems experienced by this population, NIDA's multiple problem perspective (Biglan et al. 2004) and the interventions supported through NIDA-funded research have much to offer in preventing problems among children of parents in the criminal justice system.

Preventive Interventions

Prevention science has made significant strides in the past 25 years, with the accumulated research findings being replicated across multiple cohorts and subpopulations of youth, over time and across studies. Careful examination of the body of findings reveals some areas for generalization. Some of these generalizations have relevance to children of incarcerated parents and their families and are discussed in the subsequent section. The overarching theme of this section draws from prior etiologic and prevention research, which emphasized context as important in conceptualizing and designing prevention interventions.

Family is the earliest and most important context in a child's life (e.g., Bronfenbrenner 1979; Kellam and Rebok 1992; Weisz et al. 2005), and it continues to play an important role as children mature, even into adulthood (Brody et al. 2009). Throughout childhood, parenting appears to mediate the negative effects of high-risk situations, such as living in poverty, experiencing parental divorce or death, and having a parent with mental illness (O'Connell et al. 2009). Many interventions have been developed to strengthen parenting practices and skills and improve child outcomes when one or more of these situations exist (Ashery, Robertson, and Kumpfer 1998; Forgatch and DeGarmo 1999; Wolchik et al. 2007). Many of these interventions may meet the intervention needs of families of children with incarcerated parents.

High-risk populations tend to benefit the most from universal interventions, perhaps because they have the potential to make more improvements than populations at lower levels of risk. Universal interventions have the added benefit of not grouping or otherwise identifying high-risk individuals, thus avoiding an environment in which those at elevated risk are set apart or stigmatized by their status. Children of incarcerated parents and their families would likely benefit from universal interventions. Moreover, many selective, indicated, and tiered interventions more directly address the problems that this population is likely to encounter; these interventions carefully consider such issues as stigma and the risks and benefits of grouping individuals from a subpopulation that shares similar risk factors (Dodge, Dishion, and Lansford 2006). Children in foster care are an example of an at-risk population with many problems. Research has demonstrated that these youth benefit from selective and indicated parenting interventions (e.g., Fisher, Burraston, and Pears 2005; Price et al. 2008). Children with parents in the criminal justice system also experience many problems related to their life circumstances. The positive evidence for interventions with the foster care population suggests potential positive results for the criminal justice population.

Developmental problems usually begin in early childhood, especially for at-risk children and their families (e.g., Caspi et al. 1996). Fortunately, parenting interventions for very young children have demonstrated positive impacts and improvements in many intra- and interpersonal areas of development. For example, preschoolers identified as having experienced extreme neglect or maltreatment showed increases in secure attachment behaviors (Fisher and Kim 2007) after completing the Early Intervention Foster Care (EIFC) program. Evidence included improvements in disrupted cortisol activity (an intrapersonal factor) for participants, compared with children who did not participate (Fisher and Kim 2007). Further, direct observation of the preschoolers' behaviors demonstrates normalization of their relational and interpersonal skills with caregivers (an interpersonal factor). Thus, the impact of this type of early intervention is evident in changes at the most fundamental level of functioning; moreover, long-term data related to these changes indicate that they may endure throughout the life course.

Other interventions for early childhood populations show similar positive results and support the idea that intervening early can result in life-long positive effects. For example, the family check-up (FCU) and the nurse-family partnership (NFP) programs have shown improvements in both child development and maternal functioning outcomes in at-risk populations (Connell et al. 2008; Olds et al. 2007; Shaw et al. 2009). Given the similarities between the children of incarcerated parents and the members of these populations, it is possible that they too could benefit from efficacious parenting interventions. Moreover, these interventions can be adapted and tested for different living situations, such as prison nurseries, families experiencing reentry after prison or military service, or families in kinship and foster care contexts. Successful adaptations could then be tested to establish efficacy.

A common risk factor underlying many problem behaviors experienced by children is poor academic achievement. As a proximal measure of intervention effectiveness, it is often one of the first indicators of intervention success. Thus, many studies have begun to assess children's academic achievement. Interestingly, the data indicate that academic achievement is positively related to parental involvement in efficacious parenting skills-building programs. When examining the literature as a whole, there are many findings of positive intervention effects on academic achievement. In addition, several studies are reporting positive long-term effects. These positive findings have been found at varying levels of intervention risk (e.g., universal, selective, indicated, and tiered), in multicomponent programs (e.g., combined parent and school programs), and for different development stages (from preschool through high school). For example, the children of at-risk pregnant African American mothers who received the NFP program during pregnancy and through the second year of the child's life had better grade-point averages and achievement test scores in math and reading in grades 1 through 3 than those who did not participate (Olds et al. 2007). Girls in the juvenile justice system who were placed in out-of-home care attended school more regularly, and spent more time on homework after completing the multidimensional treatment foster care (MTFC) program than girls in the services-as-usual group care condition (Leve and Chamberlain 2007). These positive academic findings have strong implications for the opportunities and life chances of these very high risk young people who participated in those interventions.

Prevention science has benefited from being able to follow subjects who participated in prevention research protocols over long periods. Several long-term follow-up studies have focused on parenting interventions (Forgatch et al. 2009; Haggerty et al. 2008; Olds et al. 1998; Wolchik et al. 2002). Results from these studies have shown positive effects on an array of child outcomes over the course of development (including internalizing and externalizing behaviors, academic achievement, drug abuse, mental health, and health-risking sexual behaviors) as well as on parent outcomes (e.g., parenting skills, such as monitoring, rule-setting, support, and warmth, and maternal characteristics, such as depression, education attainment, and employment). These positive findings have been documented for interventions delivered to families with children at different ages (e.g., infancy, middle school) and at different levels of family risk (e.g., universal, selective, indicated, tiered). Selective, indicated, and tiered programs may be most appropriate for adapting to the needs of incarcerated families as they recognize and include components related to stress and coping. Examples of efficacious parenting interventions at those levels of risk include programs for young at-risk mothers, families and children experiencing situational emotional stress (e.g., divorce, bereavement), and children in the child welfare and juvenile justice systems (e.g., Forgatch et al. 2009; Olds et al. 1998; Price et al. 2008).

These long-term follow-up studies have also demonstrated positive effects on outcomes that were not the original target of the intervention; we referred to these unintended positive effects as "crossover" effects. For example, African American 5th graders who completed the universal family-based alcohol abuse prevention program Strong African American Families had less conduct disorder and alcohol use than children who did not participate (Brody et al. 2008). The focus of the intervention was the prevention of alcohol use; the findings on conduct disorder are illustrative of a positive crossover effect.

Another example comes from the Seattle Social Development Project and involved children who participated in a multicomponent school- and family-based intervention. Intervention-involved and control-group subjects were followed over time. Results of the follow-up at age 21 indicated that the participant group reported fewer sexual partners than the control group (Lonczak et al. 2002). Sexual behaviors were not a focus of this intervention, and data on sexual behaviors were not collected until well after the intervention ended. However, this is an area of great interest in prevention given the emergence of HIV and other STD epidemics among youth during the lifetime of these young people. These circumstances make this important crossover finding even more compelling. The epidemiologic data on children of incarcerated parents indicates that this sub-population is at risk for multiple problems in multiple areas, including mental health, substance abuse, and HIV. Thus, the potential for these youth to benefit from programs that have both long-term and crossover effects on many areas of behavior makes them likely targets for intervention adaptation and testing.

Racial and ethnic minority populations are overrepresented in the criminal justice population; thus, culturally appropriate interventions are important to consider. Several efficacious parenting interventions have been developed for, adapted for, and tested with minority populations (e.g., Brody et al. 2008; Martinez and Eddy 2005; Prado et al. 2007). Findings from one such program, Familial Unidas, indicate that Hispanic adolescents had lower levels of drug use and unsafe sexual behaviors after completing this Hispanic-specific, parent-centered intervention when it was paired with Parent-Preadolescent Training for HIV Prevention compared with those who did not participate (Prado et al. 2007). Another example of the positive effects of culturally tailoring programs is from an adapted version of the effective parent management training program called Nuestras Familias. Middle school–age children in Spanish-speaking families exposed to the program showed fewer externalizing behaviors upon completion than the non-exposed control group (Martinez and Eddy 2005). Nuestras Familias is an example of an effective parenting intervention that has been adapted for use with minority families. Previously described positive findings of the NFP program with African American children and their mothers (Olds et al. 2007) is another example of a parenting program that was adapted, tested, and found efficacious with a minority population.

Despite these positive findings on the efficacy and effectiveness of prevention interventions, a major challenge for the prevention field has been disseminating, implementing, and sustaining interventions in real-world settings. It is hypothesized that interventions are more likely to be sustainable if they are delivered within current infrastructures (e.g., educational, health, mental health, child welfare, or juvenile justice systems). The FCU is a brief family-centered intervention focused on family management practices. It is currently being implemented in a multisite randomized control trial administered through the Women Infants and Children (WIC) nutrition program for young children (Dishion et al. 2008). Prior testing of the intervention occurred in a school system with older children (e.g., Dishion, Nelson, and Kavanagh 2003). Both these trials have demonstrated that the program is effective; however, sustainability has not been documented.

An example of an intervention being implemented and evaluated on a larger scale in a service delivery system is the randomized trial of two methods of implementing MTFC in 40 California counties (Chamberlain et al. 2008). This study is an example of a very large scale implementation of an evidence-based parenting intervention for highly vulnerable youth and their caregivers. While the study is still under way and there are no findings related to the dissemination, implementation and sustainability of this efficacious intervention within California or within child welfare systems in other states, it is worth mentioning because it is an attempt to address the needs of highly vulnerable youth who are both involved in and affected by a government system designed to address youth and families at risk. As the results of these and other studies of this type unfold, there will be findings broadly applicable to children of incarcerated parents and their families. Over time, it is hoped that these studies will affect policy and practice, resulting in the increased availability of efficacious parenting interventions.

Considerations for Children of Incarcerated Parents

Interventions like these that have been demonstrated to positively affect children and families are a rich starting place for intervening with the children of incarcerated parents. Generalization from this body of research could be applied to the criminal justice involved population, keeping in mind the special circumstances, needs, and challenges of this subpopulation. For example, almost all family-based interventions assume that parents and children are interacting with each other regularly, if not daily. This is usually not the case for families with an incarcerated parent. Often incarcerated parents live away from the rest of the family and may only be able to talk with their children over the telephone or from behind a Plexiglas window. In addition to the numerous challenges of involving incarcerated parents in an intervention, there are challenges associated with working with the current and sometimes temporary child caregivers of those children. For example, caregivers may be difficult to access or may not be interested in communicating with the incarcerated parents, let alone researchers and prevention providers. In addition, they may have issues related to their own advancing age or other extended family problems (e.g., intergenerational criminality or foster care involvement) that are not typically considered in family-based interventions. Thus, as with any intervention adaptation, it is not a simple process to apply existing evidence-based interventions to a new population. However, work with this vulnerable population, while still in its infancy, has a research and practice base from which to draw.

In sum, a large body of research on the characteristics of this population and on family-based prevention interventions has been developed. The accrued knowledge can be synthesized and integrated in ways that could better understand the needs of and ways to intervene with these vulnerable youth and their families, despite the fact that there are large gaps in the epidemiologic, etiologic, and prevention research regarding this population.

Implications and Recommendations for Research and Intervention

To make a strong, positive, public health impact on children of incarcerated parents and their families, critical gaps in our current knowledge need to be filled. A well-considered approach to filling these gaps, while building on prior research, would benefit these children through correctly identifying who they are; where they and their families are physically located and the environmental risks and protections they are exposed to; at what points in the incarceration process and critical periods of child development they need interventions and services; what those intervention services and needs would be; and how best they could be delivered. Research funding institutions could also benefit from taking a well-considered approach as they would have greater precision in determining how to apply their limited resources to maximize the potential public health impact. Research specific to this population could improve our understanding of its needs and our potential to develop and deliver interventions reconfigured and augmented to meet those needs. Given the paucity of research on children of incarcerated parents and their families, the next section stimulates further research through providing examples of areas suitable for further research. Thus, this section should not be viewed as a research agenda on children of incarcerated parents. This section is divided into the two areas examined: epidemiology and etiology research, and prevention research.

Epidemiology and Etiology

- Survey research that accurately estimates the incidence and prevalence of children experiencing parental incarceration at specific times and in the various penal systems operating within the United States.
- Cross-sectional research studies of representative samples that compare children of incarcerated parents with children of other vulnerable populations (e.g., children in the child welfare system) and with the general population across the course of child development.
- Replication of studies with established associations between parental incarceration and child outcomes to confirm consistency of findings.
- Secondary analysis studies of longitudinal data to examine links between risk and protective factors (e.g., poverty, homelessness, community policing, after-school programming), parental incarceration, and child behaviors (e.g., aggression, academic problems).
- Longitudinal studies that systematically examine interactions between characteristics of the parental arrest and imprisonment and child characteristic (e.g., arrest circumstances; length of incarceration; maternal versus paternal incarceration by child's race, age, gender, and personality characteristics) and long-term child outcomes (e.g., initiation of drug use, health-risking sexual behaviors).
- Research studies of theoretically or empirically based hypotheses of processes and mechanisms that contribute to adjustment or problem behaviors among children using rigorous research designs, such as randomized control trials (e.g., randomization of incarcerated

parents to two or more incarceration paradigms, such as prison as usual, work-camp with weekend furloughs, or community service) or multiple baseline designs (e.g., measuring child functioning at arrest, following sentencing, at the time of incarceration, at intervals throughout incarceration, at release, and at intervals after release).

- Research studies that use longitudinal data to detect common patterns or developmental trajectories among children of incarcerated parents that have implications for prevention research.

Prevention

- Studies that examine the impact of naturally occurring incarceration-specific visitation and communication conditions on child (e.g., academic achievement, peer relations) and family (e.g., ease vs. difficulty of reunification) functioning to promote the development of intervention components and public policy.
- Studies that examine the efficacy or effectiveness of interventions (e.g., parent skill training, social skills development, refusal skills) developed or adapted for criminal justice–involved populations of children and families to prevent development-specific problems (e.g., early aggressive behaviors, externalizing behaviors, academic failure) and their sequelae.
- Studies that adapt theory-based interventions developed for and tested with other highly vulnerable children and families (e.g., foster care, bereavement, divorce) for criminal justice–involved families.
- Studies to develop and test intervention components or boosters specific to the criminal justice population that have been suggested by findings from epidemiology and etiology studies.
- Studies that examine intervention recruitment and retention strategies specific to prisoner and other criminal justice–involved populations, affected families and caregivers, and children placed outside the family.
- Studies that develop and test interventions for children experiencing the arrest of a parent to reduce immediate stress reactions and foster improved coping.
- Studies that vary strategies for coupling access to and delivery of services (e.g., Medicaid, food stamps, WIC) to these highly vulnerable families to determine if and what coordination strategies are most effective.

- Studies to develop and test new interventions and adapt existing effective interventions for minority criminal justice–involved populations.
- Intervention studies, including long-term follow-up studies of interventions, that include the measures necessary to examine the factors associated with intervention success (e.g., child age, gender, and race; maternal versus paternal incarceration; length of incarceration; poverty; neighborhoods).

Conclusion

The children of incarcerated parents are a vulnerable population in need of many educational, health, mental health, and social services interventions. However, little information is available regarding these children and their families. Over the past 30 years, the application of methods from prevention science has led to significant gains in knowledge about, and the development of efficacious prevention interventions for, other vulnerable populations. Applying variants of these interventions to this population would likely help prevent the development of problem behaviors and the consequences of those behaviors. However, further research is clearly needed to better understand the needs of these children and the best way to intervene with them and their families across the developmental spectrum.

NOTES

The views and opinions expressed in this chapter are those of the authors and should not be construed to represent the views of the National Institute on Drug Abuse, National Institutes of Health, U.S. Department of Health and Human Services, or the U.S. government.

1. U.S. Department of Health and Human Services, National Institutes of Health, National Institute on Drug Abuse, "Drug Abuse Prevention Intervention Research. Program Announcement Number: PA-08-217," http://grants.nih.gov/grants/guide/pa-files/PA-08-217.html.

REFERENCES

Ashery, Rebecca S., Elizabeth B. Robertson, and Karol L. Kumpfer, eds. 1998. *Drug Abuse Prevention through Family Interventions.* NIDA Monograph 177. Rockville, MD: National Institutes of Health, National Institute on Drug Abuse.

Biglan, Anthony, Patricia A. Brennan, Sharon L. Foster, and Harold D. Holder. 2004. *Helping Children at Risk: Prevention of Multiple Problem Behaviors.* New York: Guilford Press.

Brody, Gene H., Steven M. Kogan, Yi-fu Chen, and Velma M. Murry. 2008. "Long-Term Effects of the Strong African American Families Program on Youths' Conduct Problems." *Journal of Adolescent Health* 43(5): 474–81.

Brody, Gene H., Yi-fu Chen, Steven R. H. Beach, Robert A. Philibert, and Steven M. Kogan. 2009. "Participation in a Family-Centered Prevention Program Decreases Genetic Risk for Adolescents' Risky Behaviors." *Pediatrics* 124:911–17.

Bronfenbrenner, Urie. 1979. "Contexts of Child Rearing: Problems and Prospects." *American Psychologist* 34(10): 844–50.

———. 2005. "Ecological Systems Theory." In *Making Human Beings Human: Bio-ecological Perspectives on Human Development,* edited by Urie Bronfenbrenner (106–73). Thousand Oaks, CA: SAGE Publications.

Caspi, Avshalom, Terrie E. Moffitt, Denise L. Newman, and Phil A. Silva. 1996. "Behavioral Observations at Age 3 Years Predict Adult Psychiatric Disorders: Longitudinal Evidence from a Birth Cohort." *Archives of General Psychiatry* 53(11): 1033–39.

Chamberlain, Patricia, C. Hendricks Brown, Lisa Saldana, John Reid, Wei Wang, Lynne Marsenich, Todd Sosna, Courtenay Padgett, and Gerard Bouwman. 2008. "Engaging and Recruiting Counties in an Experiment on Implementing Evidence-Based Practice in California." *Administration and Policy in Mental Health and Mental Health Services Research* 35(4): 250–60.

Clopton, Kerri L., and Katheryn K. East. 2008. " 'Are There Other Kids Like Me?' Children with a Parent in Prison." *Early Childhood Education Journal* 36(2): 195–98.

Connell, Arin, Bernadette M. Bullock, Thomas J. Dishion, Daniel Shaw, Melvin Wilson, and Frances Gardner. 2008. "Family Intervention Effects on Co-Occurring Early Childhood Behavioral and Emotional Problems: A Latent Transition Analysis Approach." *Journal of Abnormal Child Psychology* 36(8): 1211–25.

Dishion, Thomas J., Sarah E. Nelson, and Kathryn Kavanagh. 2003. "The Family Check-Up with High-Risk Young Adolescents: Preventing Early-Onset Substance Use by Parent Monitoring." *Behavior Therapy* 34(4): 553–71.

Dishion, Thomas J., Daniel Shaw, Arin Connell, Frances Gardner, Chelsea Weaver, and Melvin Wilson. 2008. "The Family Check-Up with High-Risk Indigent Families: Preventing Problem Behavior by Increasing Parents' Positive Behavior Support in Early Childhood." *Child Development* 79(5): 1395–1414.

Dodge, Kenneth A., Thomas J. Dishion, and Jennifer E. Lansford. 2006. *Deviant Peer Influences in Programs for Youth: Problems and Solutions.* New York: Guilford Press.

Elder, Glen H. 1998. "The Life Course as Developmental Theory." *Child Development* 69(1): 1–12.

Fisher, Philip A., and Hyoun K. Kim. 2007. "Intervention Effects on Foster Preschoolers' Attachment-Related Behaviors from a Randomized Trial." *Prevention Science* 8(2): 161–70.

Fisher, Philip A., Bert Burraston, and Katherine Pears. 2005. "The Early Intervention Foster Care Program: Permanent Placement Outcomes from a Randomized Trial." *Child Maltreatment* 10(1): 61–171.

Forgatch, Marion S., and David S. DeGarmo. 1999. "Parenting through Change: An Effective Prevention Program for Single Mothers." *Journal of Consulting and Clinical Psychology* 67:711–24.

Forgatch, Marion S., Gerald R. Patterson, David S. DeGarmo, and Zintars G. Beldavs. 2009. "Testing the Oregon Delinquency Model with 9-Year Follow-Up of the Oregon Divorce Study." *Development & Psychopathology* 21(2): 637–60.

Glaze, Lauren E., and Laura M. Maruschak. 2008. *Parents in Prison and Their Minor Children.* NCJ 222984. Washington, DC: U.S. Department of Justice, Bureau of Justice Statistics.

Haggerty, Kevin P., Martie Skinner, Charles B. Fleming, Randy R. Gainey, and Richard F. Catalano. 2008. "Long-Term Effects of the Focus on Families Project on Substance Use Disorders among Children of Parents in Methadone Treatment." *Addiction* 103(12): 2008–16.

Hairston, Creasie Finney. 2002. "Prisoners and Families: Parenting Issues during Incarceration." Washington, DC: The Urban Institute.

Kellam, Sheppard G., and George W. Rebok. 1992. "Building Developmental and Etiological Theory through Epidemiologically Based Prevention Intervention Trials." In *Preventing Antisocial Behavior: Interventions from Birth through Adolescence,* edited by Joan McCord and Robert E. Tremblay (162–95). New York: Guilford Press.

Leve, Leslie D., and Patricia Chamberlain. 2007. "A Randomized Evaluation of Multidimensional Treatment Foster Care: Effects on School Attendance and Homework Completion in Juvenile Justice Girls." *Research on Social Work Practice* 17(6): 657–63.

Lonczak, Heather S., Robert D. Abbott, J. David Hawkins, Rick Kosterman, and Richard F. Catalano. 2002. "Effects of the Seattle Social Development Project on Sexual Behavior, Pregnancy, Birth, and Sexually Transmitted Disease Outcomes by Age 21 Years." *Archives of Pediatrics and Adolescent Medicine* 156(5): 438–47.

Martinez, Charles R. Jr., and J. Mark Eddy. 2005. "Effects of Culturally Adapted Parent Management Training on Latino Youth Behavioral Health Outcomes." *Journal of Consulting and Clinical Psychology* 73(5): 841–51.

Murray, Joseph, and David P. Farrington. 2005. "Parental Imprisonment: Effects on Boys' Antisocial Behaviour and Delinquency through the Life Course." *Journal of Child Psychology and Psychiatry* 46:1269–78.

Murray, Joseph, David P. Farrington, Ivana Sekol, and Rikke F. Olsen. 2009. "Effects of Parental Imprisonment on Child Antisocial Behavior and Mental Health: A Systematic Review." *Campbell Systematic Reviews* 4:1–105. Oslo, Norway: Campbell Collaboration.

O'Connell, Mary Ellen, Thomas Boat, and Kenneth E. Warner, eds. 2009. *Preventing Mental, Emotional, and Behavioral Disorders among Young People: Progress and Possibilities.* Washington DC: National Academies Press.

Olds, David, Charles R. Henderson, Robert Cole, John Eckenrode, Harriet Kitzman, Dennis Luckey, Lisa Pettitt, Kimberly Sidora, Pamela Morris, and Jane Powers. 1998. "Long-Term Effects of Nurse Home Visitation on Children's Criminal and Antisocial Behavior: 15-Year Follow-Up of a Randomized Controlled Trial." *Journal of the American Medical Association* 280(14): 1238–44.

Olds, David L., Harriet Kitzman, Carole Hanks, Robert Cole, Elizabeth L. Anson, Kimberly Sidora-Arcoleo, Dennis W. Luckey, et al. 2007. "Effects of Nurse Home Visiting on

Maternal and Child Functioning: Age-9 Follow-Up of a Randomized Trial." *Pediatrics* 120(4): e832–45.

Parke, Ross D., and K. Alison Clarke-Stewart. 2002. "Effects of Parental Incarceration on Young Children." Washington, DC: The Urban Institute.

Prado, Guillermo, Hilda Pantin, Ervin Briones, Seth J. Schwartz, Daniel Feaster, Shi Huang, Summer Sullivan, et al. 2007. "A Randomized Controlled Trial of a Parent-Centered Intervention in Preventing Substance Use and HIV Risk Behaviors in Hispanic Adolescents." *Journal of Consulting and Clinical Psychology* 75(6): 914–26.

Price, Joseph M., Patricia Chamberlain, John Landsverk, John B. Reid, Leslie D. Leve, and Heidermarie Laurent. 2008. "Effects of a Foster Parent Training Intervention on Placement Changes of Children in Foster Care." *Child Maltreatment* 13(1): 64–75.

Shaw, Daniel S., Arin Connell, Thomas J. Dishion, Melvin N. Wilson, and Frances Gardner. 2009. "Improvements in Maternal Depression as a Mediator of Intervention Effects on Early Childhood Problem Behavior." *Development & Psychopathology* 21(2): 417–39.

Travis, Jeremy. 2005. "Families and Children." *Federal Probation* 69(1): 31–42.

Weisz, John R., Irwin N. Sandler, Joseph A. Durlak, and Barry S. Anton. 2005. "Promoting and Protecting Youth Mental Health through Evidence-Based Prevention and Treatment." *American Psychologist* 60(6): 628–48.

Wolchik, Sharlene A., Irwin N. Sandler, Lillie Weiss, and Emily B. Winslow. 2007. "New Beginnings: An Empirically Based Program to Help Divorced Mothers Promote Resilience in Their Children." In *Handbook of Parent Training: Helping Parents Prevent and Solve Problem Behaviors,* edited by James M. Briesmeister and Charles E. Schaefer (25–62). New York: John Wiley & Sons.

Wolchik, Sharlene A., Irwin N. Sandler, Roger E. Millsap, Brett A. Plummer, Shannon M. Greene, Edward R. Anderson, Spring R. Dawson-McClure, Kathleen Hipke, and Rachel A. Haine. 2002. "Six-Year Follow-Up of Preventive Interventions for Children of Divorce: A Randomized Controlled Trial." *Journal of the American Medical Association* 288(15): 1874–81.

15

Mass Parental Imprisonment, Social Policy, and the Future of Inequality in America

Christopher Wildeman

For the bulk of American history, imprisonment was an incredibly rare punishment reserved for the most heinous criminals, the most marginalized, and the most unlucky. On any given day, less than 1 in 1,000 individuals in the population could expect to be imprisoned. In addition to being uncommon, the scope and scale of penal confinement fluctuated little between the mid-1920s and the mid-1970s. During these years, the American imprisonment rate rarely went much below or above 100 per 100,000 (Blumstein and Cohen 1973). Before the mid-1970s, the American imprisonment rate also fell in line with those of the other long-standing democracies of the West, even if it was slightly higher. Amazing as it may seem now, the American and Swiss imprisonment rates were comparable until the mid-1970s (Kuhn 1996).

Starting in the mid-1970s, however, American imprisonment began an ascent from which it has yet to relent. By 2008, the American imprisonment rate was 504 per 100,000—five times what it had been 35 years earlier. Although the rate has stabilized in recent years, it has not greatly diminished, even in the face of a recession that has caused state and federal governments alike to look for ways to cut costs. And while the American imprisonment rate once fell roughly in line with other western democracies, it is now an extreme outlier. For example, the United Kingdom, the long-standing democracy of the West with the second-highest incarceration rate, incarcerates at only 20 percent the American rate.

Table 15.1. Cumulative Risk of Imprisonment by Age 30–34 by Race and Education for Men Born 1945–49 to 1975–79

	Birth Cohort						
	1945–49	'50–54	'55–59	'60–64	'65–69	'70–74	'75–79
White men							
High school dropouts	4.2	7.2	8.0	8.0	10.5	14.8	15.3
High school only	0.7	2.0	2.1	2.5	4.0	3.8	4.1
All noncollege	1.8	2.9	3.2	3.7	5.1	5.1	6.3
Some college	0.7	0.7	0.6	0.8	0.7	0.9	1.2
All	1.2	1.9	2.0	2.2	2.8	2.8	3.3
African American men							
High school dropouts	14.7	19.6	27.6	41.6	57.0	62.5	69.0
High school only	10.2	11.3	9.4	12.4	16.8	20.3	18.0
All noncollege	12.1	14.1	14.7	19.9	26.7	30.9	35.7
Some college	4.9	3.5	4.3	5.5	6.8	8.5	7.6
All	9.0	10.6	11.5	15.2	20.3	22.8	20.7

Source: Western and Wildeman (2009a, 231).

Even compared with the other most-incarcerating nations—South Africa, Malta, and some former Soviet republics—America's incarceration rate is extreme (Mauer 1999; Western 2006).

Not surprisingly, the risk of imprisonment is concentrated among young, marginalized men. While 7 of every 1,000 Americans could expect to be incarcerated on any given day at the turn of the millennium, nearly 1 in 3 young black men who did not complete high school were locked up (Western 2006; see also Tonry 1995). The risk for comparable white men was much smaller; less than 7 percent of them could expect to be imprisoned on any given day. For men who were both white and attended college, the risk of being imprisoned was negligible. The importance of these disparities in the risk of imprisonment becomes clear when considering how these daily risks (also known as point-in-time risks) accumulate over a lifetime. As table 15.1 shows, the share of African American men and men who dropped out of high school who have ever been imprisoned by age 30–34 suggests larger disparities than point-in-time estimates do.

What caused the prison boom? Debates about its causes continue, but most agree that this sea change in confinement had both political and economic roots (Western and Wildeman 2009a, b). Especially important to remember is that the groundwork for the prison boom was laid not in the late 1970s, when the imprisonment rate started to grow, but 15 years earlier. Politically, the unsuccessful presidential campaign of Barry Goldwater was a turning point. By drawing veiled connections between political unrest, rising crime rates, and black criminality, Goldwater laid the groundwork for a law-and-order political message that would be used by conservatives to suggest harsh punishments for years to come (Beckett 1997).

Despite their symbolic importance, these punitive laws would have had only a minimal impact on the American imprisonment rate had several other changes not taken place. When these laws combined with widespread manufacturing decline, the flight of the middle class from cities, and a booming drug trade, however, their effects on the imprisonment rate were acute. Living in devastated urban neighborhoods devoid of economic opportunities, many young, poorly educated, African American men became involved in the drug trade. Given changes in the severity of sentences for involvement in the drug trade and abusing drugs, the imprisonment rate and absolute inequality in the risk of imprisonment began to swell (Western 2006).

Against the backdrop of spiraling imprisonment rates and vast disparities in the risk of imprisonment, scholars from many disciplines became interested in the consequences of mass imprisonment (Comfort 2007; Hagan and Dinovitzer 1999; Pattillo, Weiman, and Western 2004). Research in this area tends to consider the corrosive effects of incarceration on individuals, families, and communities. For those who go to prison, research shows negative effects not only on the labor market (Pager 2003; Western 2002, 2006), but also on health (Massoglia 2008a, 2008b; Schnittker and John 2007) and a host of other areas of social life. For women with imprisoned partners, research shows increased risks of hopelessness, depression, and isolation (Braman 2004). Having a partner imprisoned also elevates the risk of divorce and separation (Lopoo and Western 2005). When elevated risks of divorce and separation are combined with lower earnings and the high cost of maintaining contact with a prisoner (Comfort 2008), the children of ever-imprisoned fathers likely have fewer financial resources available to them than do other children (Geller, Garfinkel, and Western forthcoming). High levels of imprisonment also have negative effects on neighborhoods (Clear 2007), so even those who never experience imprisonment are likely harmed by mass imprisonment if they live in poor communities.

Of the consequences of imprisonment, in recent years, much public attention has been paid to the children of incarcerated parents (e.g., Murray and Farrington 2008; Parke and Clarke-Stewart 2003). Despite great interest in this area, and a growing research base, no edited volume has considered this topic since the mid-1990s. This volume contributes to the study of the collateral consequences of incarceration on children using an interdisciplinary perspective, a logical choice since scholars from many fields have participated in these discussions. The sections in this volume lay the groundwork for considering the roots of mass imprisonment, the effects of having a parent imprisoned on children, and the social policies that may alter these effects. Although this volume is interdisciplinary, many chapters in it use a developmental perspective. This perspective is well suited for considering the effects of parental imprisonment on individual children, as the fine chapters in this volume illustrate.

A demographic perspective provides a different, but no less useful, lens through which to view the effects of mass imprisonment on children. A simple demographic technique—the life table—can be used to demonstrate what share of children can expect to experience imprisonment over their childhood. Since knowing the total number of children ever experiencing parental imprisonment is vital for knowing the effects of mass imprisonment on inequality, this exercise is not just a statistical one. Rather, it is essential for understanding the total costs of mass imprisonment as relates to social inequality—defined broadly as unequal outcomes among different groups, such as whites and African Americans or people who did and did not finish high school.

Skepticism about demonstrating causal relationships with observational data should encourage researchers working in this field to find better data and use more rigorous analytic techniques. Further, if one of the main reasons mass imprisonment is important is because it may exacerbate inequality, researchers must push beyond the micro level to consider the macro-level consequences of mass imprisonment. Moving to higher levels of aggregation may be uncomfortable for those from a developmental tradition, but this move is essential for considering the effects of mass imprisonment on inequality among American children.

Certain social policies might remedy some of the problems exacerbated by mass imprisonment. Few of these suggested policies are novel—indeed, some of them were suggested before the prison boom started—and they are informed only in part by the demographic perspective advanced in this chapter. Nonetheless, a host of social and criminal justice policies appear to be called for in light of the incredibly high risks of parental imprisonment.

The Scope and Scale of Mass Parental Imprisonment

One reason that scholars have become so interested in parental imprisonment is because it is so common, especially for African American children and children whose parents have little formal education. Many of the best efforts to document the scope and scale of parental imprisonment have come from Bureau of Justice Statistics statisticians (Mumola 2000), as chapter 3 in this volume illustrates. These papers tend to quantify the number and percentage of children with a parent imprisoned. Their findings suggest that around 2 percent of American children currently have a parent imprisoned and that the risk is higher for African American than white or Hispanic children.

A demographic perspective suggests that it would be interesting to know not only what share of children has a mother or father imprisoned at any point in time, but also what share of children could expect to ever experience this event and how this risk varies not only by race, but also by class—generally as measured by education. There are various reasons to be interested in knowing how many children experience parental imprisonment over the course of their lifetime. On the most basic level, knowing what percentage of children ever experience this event is important because it is certainly greater than the number experiencing it on any given day. Second, as estimates of the cumulative risk of imprisonment for adult men indicate, *absolute* black-white inequality in the cumulative risk of imprisonment is not only growing but is much larger than are racial disparities in the point-in-time risk of being imprisoned (Pettit and Western 2004; Western and Wildeman 2009a). Finally, without knowing what share of children is ever exposed to parental imprisonment and how that risk is patterned, researchers gain only limited insight into the macro-level consequences of mass imprisonment for social inequality.

To demonstrate how a demographic perspective can lend insight into the effects of mass imprisonment, consider the following estimates of the risks of paternal and maternal imprisonment for black and white children born in 1990 (for a description, see Wildeman 2009b). Since class inequality in the risk of parental imprisonment is likely substantial, the data are differentiated between children whose parents dropped out of high school,

Table 15.2. Cumulative Risk of Paternal and Maternal Imprisonment by Age 14 for Children Born in 1978 and 1990 by Child's Race and Parental Education (percent)

	White Children				African American Children			
	Paternal		Maternal		Paternal		Maternal	
	1978	1990	1978	1990	1978	1990	1978	1990
All children	2.2	3.6	0.2	0.6	13.8	25.1	1.4	3.3
All noncollege	2.9	5.6	0.2	0.8	15.6	30.2	1.5	3.6
High school dropout	4.1	7.2	0.2	1.0	22.0	50.5	1.9	5.0
High school only	2.0	4.8	0.2	0.7	10.2	20.4	0.9	2.6
Some college	1.4	1.7	0.2	0.3	7.1	13.4	1.2	2.6

Source: Wildeman (2009b, 271, 273).

completed only high school, and completed some college. The high school dropout and high school–only categories are combined to make a noncollege category. As can be seen in table 15.2, a demographic perspective provides new insight into the scale and scope of parental imprisonment. Point-in-time estimates of the risk of paternal imprisonment suggest that around 7 percent of black children can expect to have a parent imprisoned on any given day (Mumola 2000), yet the estimates presented here suggest that fully 25 percent of African American children born in 1990 had a parent imprisoned at some point. For comparable children born only 12 years earlier, the risk was slightly more than half that.

Results from table 15.2 also show that for black children born in 1990 to fathers who did not complete high school, paternal imprisonment was modal. For these children, having a father imprisoned has become a normal part of life. Although the risk of having a father go to prison was also high for comparable children born in 1978, it was much lower. The demographic perspective sheds light not only on how common parental—especially paternal—imprisonment is for African American children but also on the magnitude of racial inequality in this risk. Although many components of table 15.2 suggest substantial racial disparities, the fact that the risk of maternal imprisonment for black children born in 1990 (3.3 percent) is comparable to the risk of paternal imprisonment for white children (3.6 percent) born in the same year provides a stark reminder of how large racial disparities in the risk of parental imprisonment are.

Results from table 15.2 demonstrate how applying a demographic perspective to the descriptive study of the children of the incarcerated provides insight into how large the macro-level effects on childhood inequality may be. Given that fully 1 in 4 African American children can now expect to experience parental imprisonment at some point while only about 1 in 30 white children can expect to experience it, consequences of mass imprisonment for inequality among children may be substantial. And since negative effects on childhood inequality have consequences for inequality in the future, to the degree that mass imprisonment exacerbates childhood inequality, it likely does the same for adult inequality.

Questioning Causality and Asking New Questions

For mass parental imprisonment to exacerbate childhood inequality, however, it must not only disproportionately touch the lives of marginalized children, but harm them. For the most part, the chapters in this volume suggest that parental imprisonment negatively affects children. This chapter, however, suggests that researchers and interventionists must be more skeptical of whether the associations considered here are causal. In order to know whether mass imprisonment negatively affects childhood inequality—a fundamentally macro-level question—researchers must use macro-level data. A demographic perspective calls researchers both to be skeptical about causality and to answer macro-level questions using macro-level data.

In his review of longitudinal studies on the effects of parental incarceration on children, Joseph Murray (chapter 4, this volume) suggests that virtually all available evidence points toward parental incarceration negatively affecting children. He also suggests—quite rightly—that the lack of repeated measures of *both* parental contact with the criminal justice system *and* behavioral problems is an impediment to deciphering whether these relationships are causal. While some use propensity score models to estimate effects of parental incarceration on children using such data (Foster and Hagan 2009), repeated measures are preferred because they control for stable (yet generally unobserved) characteristics of individuals—such as self-control, which is rarely observed but correlated with both the risk of parental imprisonment and child well-being. Given that prisoners likely differ from the general population in many stable yet unobserved traits, controlling for these unobserved characteristics is vital for making causal claims. Although not yet in print, some studies apply these models to longitudinal data, providing comparable results to most published findings (Wakefield 2009; Wildeman forthcoming). Thus, early results suggest that stable but unobserved traits (such as self-control) are unlikely to be driving the association between parental incarceration and poor outcomes for children.

Unfortunately, these dynamic models are also limited in a host of ways, only one of which is mentioned here. Fixed-effects models control for fixed characteristics of individuals, but they cannot account for unobserved changes in parents that happen around the same time as parental incarceration and may be the true causes of the change in child behavior. An example may be helpful here. Since researchers might expect incarceration to coincide with a period of elevated drug use, but most data do not measure change in drug use, there is no way to rule out the possibility that the increased drug use caused *both* the incarceration and the child behavioral problems—that incarceration and child behavioral problems are spuriously related.

Thus, even complex models and longitudinal data are limited in what they can tell us about whether parental incarceration harms children. Although several chapters in this volume have pointed out the difficulty of randomization in the criminal justice setting, the difficulties with the current state of the art in this research area suggest that researchers must branch out to using more experimental and quasi-experimental data. Some of these data may be truly experimental—including a control group and a treatment group—but it is also possible to rely on natural variation in penal policy to estimate the effects of policies on child well-being. Although these data are often difficult to find, the limitations inherent in survey data—even longitudinal survey data—suggest a need for future research to move in this direction.

Being more skeptical of what constitutes causality will take us only part of the way, however. Scholars interested in the children of incarcerated parents must also consider asking different questions. In considering the consequences of mass imprisonment for childhood inequality, researchers must consider both variations in the effects of parental imprisonment on children and the macro-level effects of imprisonment on childhood inequality. In thinking about the effects of mass imprisonment on childhood inequality, it is vital to understand whether effects are concentrated among those most (or least) likely to experience the event. If effects are concentrated among white children and children of high-education parents, then mass parental imprisonment has *smaller* effects on childhood inequality than it would if effects were equally negative for all groups. Yet if effects are concentrated among African American (and Hispanic) children and children of low-education parents, then mass parental imprisonment has *larger* effects on childhood inequality than it would were parental imprisonment equally negative for all groups. Considering these race- and class-specific effects provides an important first step into uncovering the consequences of mass imprisonment for childhood social inequality.

For scholars coming from a developmental tradition, looking for variation in effects by parental or child characteristics makes good sense. Yet to better understand how mass parental imprisonment influences childhood inequality, scholars should also consider research questions at higher levels of aggregation. This is necessary for two reasons. First, many of the outcomes researchers are most interested in are uncommon enough that it may be difficult to consider them using traditional survey data (Wildeman 2009a). Researchers have long been interested in whether parental imprisonment leads to foster care placement, for instance, yet the most convincing study in that area comes not from the individual level, but the state level (Swann and Sylvester 2006; see Johnson and Raphael 2009 for a relevant example). Although clinical or other high-risk samples may also provide insight into these processes, they are not population representative, which diminishes the understanding of whether parental incarceration has broad or narrow effects. Researchers should also consider macro-level consequences because imprisonment may have both direct and indirect effects. Since imprisonment has negative consequences not only for the individuals most directly connected to the event, but also for their wider social network and communities (Clear 2007), considering only the individual effects of parental imprisonment on children may lead researchers to underestimate the effects of mass imprisonment on childhood inequality. Thus, while more rigorous individual-level estimates of the effects of parental imprisonment on children are necessary, future research must extend these analyses to consider effects of imprisonment on macro-level inequality among children as well.

Policy Proscriptions

Thus far, this chapter has suggested that a demographic perspective improves researchers' understanding of the social patterning of the risk of parental imprisonment, explains why researchers must be skeptical of causal claims, and suggests what new questions researchers must ask to decipher the macro-level effects of mass parental imprisonment on social inequality. Since mass imprisonment's effects on inequality are largest if imprisonment affects not only the generation entering prison but also its children, it is crucial to understand the effects of parental imprisonment on children if society is to understand the long-term effects of mass imprisonment on social inequality. Step back, however, and assume that having a parent imprisoned harms children and that mass parental imprisonment exacerbates inequality. In making this suggestion, it may sound as though I am disregarding the section of this chapter where I called for more caution in interpreting causal effects. That is not the case. In fact, deciphering whether the effects of parental imprisonment are causal—and the mechanisms and moderators of this relationship—should still be the first goal of researchers working in this area where establishing causality is especially difficult. Yet given that one in four African American children now has a parent go to prison at some point in their childhood, it may be time to make broad policy suggestions even though the evidence only tentatively suggests that having a parent go to prison harms children or mass imprisonment grows inequality among children. Since we do not know that these are the case, however, broader programs should help all members of the communities in which crime and incarceration are endemic rather than just prisoners and their children.

Specifically, I suggest three types of policy interventions. Few of these suggestions are novel, but given the important new finding that 25 percent of African American children has a parent go to prison, this seems a good time to suggest them again. I list them in order of descending importance from a social inequality perspective, although this is not to suggest that any of them are unimportant. The first of these policies focuses on *keeping people out of prison*. Some attention for these policies is paid to changes in laws that may diminish the imprisonment rate, but more emphasis is placed on broad social programs that enhance the well-being of the most marginalized. The second of these policies focuses on *successfully reintegrating prisoners*. Although many of these programs fall under the umbrella of prisoner reentry, others extend beyond programs grouped under that umbrella. The final set of programs focuses on *helping children with incarcerated parents*. Many of these programs fall into the categories suggested earlier in this book, so they are not reviewed at great length. In suggesting both broad social programs that seek to *prevent parental imprisonment* and focused interventions that seek to *minimize the effects of parental imprisonment* on children having already experienced this event, I fall in line with others who suggest that interventions that focus solely on the children of imprisoned parents risk neglecting the broader social ills that affect them (chapter 2, this volume).

In terms of diminishing the macro-level effects of mass parental imprisonment on children, the social policies that hold the most promise are those that keep people out of prison in the first place. In thinking about what sorts of policies might keep people out of prison, I suggest we return to the introduction to this chapter, where I hastily sketched out the roots of mass imprisonment. There I suggested that the proximate determinants of mass imprisonment were a large pool of chronically idle men with few employment prospects and a booming drug trade. Rather than start with criminal justice policies or the booming drug trade that offered these men economic opportunities unavailable elsewhere, we should start with these chronically idle men. As suggested elsewhere (Western and Wildeman 2009b), the idleness of disadvantaged urban men in the wake of deindustrialization is a problem better solved by social welfare policies than by criminal justice ones. To diminish the percentage of marginal men entering prisons anew each year, social policies that help these men increase their human capital—by decreasing high school dropout rates in the most disadvantaged areas and improving the quality of education received in poor urban centers—and match them with employers show the most promise. What programs exactly will work best remains to be seen. However, one thing is clear. If marginal urban men continue to have few skills that make them employable in the primary labor market, whether imprisonment rates continue to grow or not, the problems endemic to poor urban neighborhoods will not diminish. Programs that invest in the urban centers left behind in the wake of the deindustrialization and the flight of whites (and wealthy blacks) also hold great promise, although these programs must be tested to see what works and what does not.

Thus, social investment in the poor urban neighborhoods that have been left behind and the young men and women who inhabit them may hold the most promise for diminishing future prison admissions. Yet these programs alone seem unlikely to drastically reduce prison admission rates in the short term since they will take some time to take hold. Again harkening back to the roots of mass imprisonment, changes in the punitiveness of drug laws played a key role in prison growth. Thus, making these laws less punitive seems a reasonable way to decrease the imprisonment rate.

From a criminal justice policy perspective, the most important changes may be for those who are addicted to drugs and alcohol rather than dealing drugs. For these individuals, drug or alcohol treatment—possibly with probation—should be used instead of prison sentences whenever possible. In suggesting this change, I suggest (as many others have) that addiction is a *social welfare* problem rather than a *criminal justice* one. It bears mentioning, however, that policies that do not place excellent treatment at their core have the potential to place families at great risk. Changes in the sentences imposed for those addicted to drugs and alcohol, while important, are only some of the changes needed to diminish the risk of being imprisoned for those residing in neighborhoods of concentrated disadvantage, however. Policies that mandate shorter sentences for the distribution and sale of drugs—especially small amounts of the least harmful drugs—could also reduce imprisonment rates in the future.

Social policies that diminish the percentage of the population ever entering prison hold the most promise for diminishing the effects of mass imprisonment on social inequality. Yet given that huge numbers of individuals have already entered the prison walls at some point, policies that reintegrate these men (and women) to society also hold much promise. A few areas of policy change could help children of formerly incarcerated parents by making their returning parents more prepared to deal with the challenges of life after prison. First, the structure and function of prisons should be made less criminogenic. As long ago as the middle of the last century, researchers expressed concern about how prisons made those entering their walls worse (Clemmer 1940; Sykes 1958). To diminish the criminogenic effects of imprisonment, prisons should reinstitute the educational and vocational training programs that once were common. Rather than training prisoners for a life of further crime or idleness, prisons should be used to help prisoners find their niche in the labor market and develop skills. Likewise, prisons should introduce classes and programs (like those mentioned earlier in this volume) that prepare men for their family lives when they leave prison. Some research suggests that many prisoners were abusive toward their partners before entering prison (Wildeman 2009a), so programs that focus on dispute resolution are especially important (chapter 12, this volume).

As men and women make the transition from imprisoned to formerly imprisoned, two policy changes may be key. On the most basic level, many obstacles to the reintegration of family members could be removed. Chief among these are bans on ex-felons residing in public housing, voting, or receiving welfare. Since recently released prisoners may be especially vulnerable, social policies should be implemented that help them avoid criminal activity rather than leaving them with few other options. Prisoners and former prisoners often talk about how small some of the offenses they have had their parole revoked for were (Goffman 2009). Thus, it is also crucial that parole revocation be used not for minor infractions but reserved only for major new crimes that demonstrate that an individual poses a serious threat to society.

Although interventions focused on the children of imprisoned parents may not hold the most promise for diminishing the effects of mass imprisonment on social inequality, they are still important. Children of imprisoned parents were likely at elevated risk of experiencing negative outcomes before having a parent go to prison, so interventions that help these children are much needed. Whether programs that focus on parents, families, children, or some combination of the three help offset the negative effects of parental imprisonment on children is an empirical question, but a broad range of interventions seem likely to help these disadvantaged children.

This section suggests three types of social policies that may diminish the effects of mass imprisonment on inequality in America. None of them is a panacea, and researchers lack convincing evidence that having a parent go to prison harms children, but broad social welfare programs will likely diminish social inequality even if their effects on prisoners and their families are small. Although these broad *prevention* programs hold the most promise for diminishing inequality, *intervention* programs for children of incarcerated parents are also needed. By implementing both types of programs, the United States may not only minimize the effects of mass imprisonment on inequality now by helping the children of the prison boom but also lay the groundwork for diminished imprisonment rates in the future. Thus, using these two types of programs together holds the most promise for shrinking future inequality in America. Despite the likely benefits of these programs, it is important to remember that the empirical basis for making such policy recommendations is weak. Thus, while life table estimates derived from a demographic perspective suggest the need for bold policy proscriptions now, skepticism about isolating causal relationships derived from a demographic perspective suggests the need for more research to test whether parental imprisonment harms children and mass imprisonment grows inequality.

REFERENCES

Beckett, Katherine. 1997. *Making Crime Pay: Law and Order in Contemporary American Politics.* New York: Oxford University Press.

Blumstein, A., and Jacqueline Cohen. 1973. "A Theory of the Stability of Punishment." *Journal of Criminal Law and Criminology* 64:198–207.

Braman, Donald. 2004. *Doing Time on the Outside: Incarceration and Family Life in Urban America.* Ann Arbor: University of Michigan Press.

Clear, Todd R. 2007. *Imprisoning Communities: How Mass Incarceration Makes Disadvantaged Neighborhoods Worse.* New York: Oxford University Press.

Clemmer, Donald. 1940. *The Prison Community.* Boston: The Christopher Publishing House.

Comfort, Megan. 2007. "Punishment beyond the Legal Offender." *Annual Review of Law and Social Science* 3:271–96.

———. 2008. *Doing Time Together: Love and Family in the Shadow of the Prison.* Chicago: University of Chicago Press.

Foster, Holly, and John Hagan. 2009. "The Mass Incarceration of Parents in America: Issues of Race/Ethnicity, Collateral Damage to Children, and Prisoner Reentry." *Annals of the American Academy of Political and Social Science* 623:179–94.

Geller, Amanda, Irwin Garfinkel, and Bruce Western. Forthcoming. "Incarceration and Support for Children in Fragile Families." *Demography.*

Goffman, Alice. 2009. "On the Run: Wanted Men in a Philadelphia Ghetto." *American Sociological Review* 74:339–57.

Hagan, John, and Ronit Dinovitzer. 1999. "Collateral Consequences of Imprisonment for Children, Communities, and Prisoners." *Crime and Justice* 26:121–62.

Johnson, Rucker C., and Stephen Raphael. 2009. "The Effects of Male Incarceration Dynamics on Acquired Immune Deficiency Syndrome Infection Rates among African American Women and Men." *Journal of Law and Economics* 52:251–93.

Kuhn, André. 1996. "Incarceration Rates: Europe versus USA." *European Journal of Criminal Policy and Research* 4:46–73.

Lopoo, Leonard, and Bruce Western. 2005. "Incarceration and the Formation and Stability of Marital Unions." *Journal of Marriage and the Family* 67:721–34.

Massoglia, Michael. 2008a. "Incarceration as Exposure: The Prison, Infectious Disease, and Other Stress-Related Illnesses." *Journal of Health and Social Behavior* 49:56–71.

———. 2008b. "Incarceration, Health, and Racial Disparities in Health." *Law and Society Review* 42:275–306.

Mauer, Marc. 1999. *Race to Incarcerate.* New York: The Free Press.

Mumola, Christopher J. 2000. *Incarcerated Parents and Their Children.* NCJ 182335. Washington, DC: U.S. Department of Justice, Bureau of Justice Statistics.

Murray, Joseph, and David Farrington. 2008. "Effects of Parental Imprisonment on Children." *Crime and Justice* 37:133–206.

Pager, Devah. 2003. "The Mark of a Criminal Record." *American Journal of Sociology* 108:937–75.

Parke, Ross D., and Kimberly A. Clarke-Stewart. 2003. "The Effects of Parental Incarceration on Children: Perspective, Promises, and Policies." In *Prisoners Once Removed: The Impact of Incarceration and Reentry on Children, Families, and Communities,* edited by Jeremy Travis and Michelle Waul (189–232). Washington, DC: Urban Institute Press.

Pattillo, Mary, David Weiman, and Bruce Western, eds. 2004. *Imprisoning America: The Social Effects of Mass Incarceration.* New York: Russell Sage Foundation.

Pettit, Becky, and Bruce Western. 2004. "Mass Imprisonment and the Life Course: Race and Class Inequality in U.S. Incarceration." *American Sociological Review* 69:151–69.

Schnittker, Jason, and Andrea John. 2007. "Enduring Stigma: The Long-Term Effects of Incarceration on Health." *Journal of Health and Social Behavior* 48:115–30.

Swann, Christopher, and Michelle Sheran Sylvester. 2006. "The Foster Care Crisis: What Caused Caseloads to Grow?" *Demography* 43(2): 309–35.

Sykes, Gresham M. 1958. *The Society of Captives: A Study of a Maximum Security Prison.* Princeton, NJ: Princeton University Press.

Tonry, Michael. 1995. *Malign Neglect: Race, Crime, and Punishment in America.* New York: Oxford University Press.

Wakefield, Sara. 2009. "Parental Disruption of Another Sort? Bringing Parental Imprisonment into a Model of Children's Mental Health and Well-Being." Paper presented at the 5th annual workshop on crime and population dynamics, Baltimore, Md., June 1–2.

Western, Bruce. 2002. "The Impact of Incarceration on Wage Mobility and Inequality." *American Sociological Review* 67:526–46.

———. 2006. *Punishment and Inequality in America.* New York: Russell Sage Foundation.

Western, Bruce, and Christopher Wildeman. 2009a. "The Black Family and Mass Incarceration." *Annals of the American Academy of Political and Social Science* 621:221–42.

———. 2009b. "Punishment, Inequality, and the Future of Mass Incarceration." *Kansas Law Review* 57:851–77.

Wildeman, Christopher. 2009a. "Imprisonment and Infant Mortality." Research Report 09-692. Ann Arbor: University of Michigan Population Studies Center.

———. 2009b. "Parental Imprisonment, the Prison Boom, and the Concentration of Childhood Disadvantage." *Demography* 46(2): 265–80.

———. Forthcoming. "Parental Incarceration and Children's Physically Aggressive Behaviors: Evidence from the Fragile Families and Child Wellbeing Study." *Social Forces.*

16

A Research and Intervention Agenda for Children of Incarcerated Parents

Julie Poehlmann and J. Mark Eddy

O ver the past decade, an increasing number of studies have focused on children of incarcerated parents and their families. Because of the complexity of the issues and the numerous social service systems involved when parents go to jail or prison, research focusing on children of incarcerated parents has been conducted by scholars from a wide variety of disciplines, including criminology, sociology, social work, nursing, psychiatry, law, public policy, family studies, and developmental, social, and clinical psychology. One result of not having one disciplinary "home" for this area of scholarship is that researchers have tended to work in isolation from one another, and the integration of findings across disciplines has been rare. A key consequence is that accessing this literature has been difficult not only for newcomers to the field, but also for those who need the information the most: the policymakers and practitioners who must make decisions of practical consequence related to this population. Yet because of the complexity of the issues involved, there is a pressing need for an integrated multidisciplinary approach to research and intervention with children whose parents are incarcerated. This need is reflected in the many significant gaps that remain in our knowledge base about this population and our lack of understanding regarding how to most effectively help affected children and families.

One goal of this volume is to stimulate high-quality, collaborative, multidisciplinary research that will generate the information needed by families, practitioners, and policymakers to prevent the development of problem behaviors and promote the health and well-being of the children of incarcerated parents, their families, and their communities. With this goal in mind, this chapter ties together and elaborates upon the suggestions for research, practice, and policy that have emerged in the preceding chapters. It is our hope that this summary will enhance the ability of researchers, practitioners, and policymakers to engage in more successful and comprehensive collaborative research that will ultimately improve the lives of children and families affected by parental incarceration. The chapter then presents an agenda for future research around three conceptual issues—the importance of a developmental perspective for research and intervention, a need for scholarship focusing on resilience processes, and the critical role played by contextual factors—and suggests approaches to various challenges that arise in research, practice, and policy when working with this population that must be faced in future studies. Multidisciplinary collaborations are important for moving the field forward.

A Developmental Perspective

Because of the dramatically different needs and capacities of individuals across the lifespan, a developmental perspective is essential to adequately understand children with incarcerated parents and their families. Whereas peer relationships and involvement in the community may directly relate to the well-being of an adolescent whose parent is in prison or jail, these factors are less likely to have direct associations with the well-being of an infant or young child with an incarcerated parent. Visitation and other forms of contact with incarcerated parents may have different meanings for and impacts on children depending on their ages and developmental capacities (Poehlmann et al. 2010). What is more, an intervention strategy, such as mentoring, may be effective and relevant for a 10-year-old but hold little meaning for a 3-year-old. Thus, it is critical that researchers and interventionists understand developmental processes and the typical range of development for children ranging in age from infancy to early adulthood. Awareness of normative development can contribute to understanding risk and resilience processes in children of incarcerated parents and their families (Sroufe 1991).

A developmental approach also highlights the importance of longitudinal research—that is, studies that follow the same group of children with incarcerated parents across time. Such research should include conceptualization and measurement strategies that are appropriate for children at the different ages they are studied. For example, infants do not exhibit delinquent behavior or substance abuse, whereas these variables may be crucial for children in middle and high school. Parental supervision has a different meaning for teens relative to toddlers. Attachment relationships are critical across the lifespan, although they are expressed and assessed in different ways depending on the age of the individual (see chapter 5, this volume). The effects of proximal processes and contexts of development may differ depending on a child's age, so measurement of home environment quality is crucial for infants, toddlers, and preschoolers, whereas measurement of school contexts and peer relationships is crucial once a child enters school.

Cross-sectional studies with children of incarcerated parents are also needed. Most notably, a better understanding of children's developmental competencies and challenges in cognitive, language, and social-emotional development; motor skills; literacy; and academic skills relative to their same-age peers is important for children of incarcerated parents. Several studies have documented delays in cognitive development and academic achievement in some children affected by parental incarceration (e.g., Poehlmann 2005a; Hanlon et al. 2005). Because of the overwhelming likelihood of past substance abuse in mothers who are incarcerated (James and Glaze 2006), their children are at risk for prenatal substance exposures (Poehlmann 2005a), which may affect their developmental outcomes. In addition, impoverished environments are associated with lags in development and academic achievement. Because of these factors, many children of incarcerated parents may lag behind their peers in attaining developmental milestones. These challenges should be kept in mind when designing research and interventions with this population.

Resilience Processes

Based on the body of work summarized in this book, it is clear that the children of incarcerated parents are at risk for a variety of serious negative outcomes, including alcohol and substance abuse, behavior problems, depressive symptoms, attachment insecurity, cognitive delays, academic failure, truancy, criminal activity, and adult conviction and incarceration. Yet not all children affected by parental incarceration develop such negative outcomes. Indeed, across many risk experiences, children do not exhibit uniform responses to adversity (Cicchetti, Rogosch, and Toth 1998; Werner 2000). To complicate matters further, for some children and families, parental incarceration provides respite from clear danger, such as ongoing domestic violence, and may facilitate, rather than inhibit, resilience. However, researchers know little about the factors and processes that, over time, promote positive adaptation in the presence of risk (i.e., resilience; see Masten 2001) in children affected by parental incarceration.

The next generation of research should identify factors and processes that foster resilience processes in children of incarcerated parents, including proximal factors (e.g., individual characteristics or skills, dyadic interaction patterns, quality of the home environment) and more distal factors (e.g., quality of family supports and resources, characteristics of extended family, friends, and neighborhoods, school quality). Both protective and promotive factors should be identified for children of incarcerated parents. Protective factors have a positive effect under stressful conditions, similar to a seat belt that is activated during a car's sudden stop or impact, and they are often conceptualized in research as moderators, statistical interactions, or indirect effects. In contrast, promotive factors have consistently positive effects on development, even under nonstressful conditions, and they are often detected as main or direct effects on children's outcomes or as mediators. Promotive and protective factors at different contextual levels may work together to foster resilience in children. In addition, interventions can target such factors once they are identified.

When conceptualizing potential resilience processes in children affected by parental incarceration, previous resilience-focused research conducted with other high-risk children should serve as a guide, in addition to relevant theoretical models. For example, attachment theory suggests that establishing trusting and supportive relationships with alternative caregivers can ameliorate the negative effects of disrupted attachments for children (e.g., Poehlmann 2003). Although secure attachments alone are not sufficient to protect children under conditions of multiple risks, security is an important component of resilience, as Poehlmann discusses in chapter 5. Studies are needed that focus on how well such relationships can modify the impacts of parental incarceration on children.

Given the popularity of youth mentoring as an intervention for children of incarcerated parents, of particular interest is whether, when, and how mentoring relationships influence this population. Alternatively, previous research has found that social support, positive school experiences, and adequate supervision and disciplinary practices in the home are associated with resilience in children (Masten and Coatsworth 1998). Studies focusing on these factors in the lives of children with incarcerated parents are needed, including how the absence of a parent due to incarceration may uniquely affect children in the home, school, or community domains. As discussed by Robertson and Reider in chapter 14, identifying promotive and protective factors for the development of children affected by parental incarceration is crucial for the design of innovative and effective interventions, including preventive interventions. In turn, the results from experimental research on interventions provide necessary information for improving understanding of development and resilience processes; these results can also point to knowledge gaps that can then be addressed in further developmental epidemiological work.

For children of incarcerated parents, the next generation of research should consider how risks, promotive and protective factors, and other variables facilitate resilience processes at different points in child development. When studying infants and toddlers affected by parental incarceration, researchers may want to examine processes that lead to secure attachment with one or more caregivers, the attainment of normative developmental milestones, and the consolidation of healthy sleep patterns as examples of positive outcomes in the context of risk. Particularly relevant protective and promotive factors for infants and toddlers include sensitive caregiving, stimulating and supportive home environments, and positive relationships between caregivers and incarcerated parents. Potent risks for poor infant or toddler outcomes may include lack of stability in the caregiving situation (Poehlmann 2005b), challenges related to living in poverty (Poehlmann 2005a), and prenatal substance exposures.

Figure 16.1 depicts examples of relations of interest that could be examined. In this illustrative model, the presence of one or more risk factors, such as poverty, is hypothesized to decrease the chance of positive outcomes for a child, with higher levels of risk related to more problematic outcomes. Certain protective or promotive factors, such as caregiver sensitivity, are hypothesized to mediate (or, in some cases, moderate) the influence of risk factors on children's outcomes. If sufficient protection is present, the impact of risk on child outcomes is likely to decrease substantially. The relations between risk, protective and promotive processes, and positive outcomes are hypothesized to differ in the presence of key

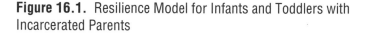

Figure 16.1. Resilience Model for Infants and Toddlers with Incarcerated Parents

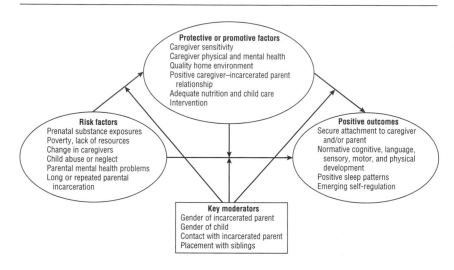

moderating factors, such as certain characteristics of the child, his or her parents and caregivers, and his or her environment.

As children reach school age, variables that are viewed as positive outcomes for infants and toddlers may be conceptualized as different components of the developmental process (figure 16.2). For example, a secure attachment to a caregiver may be viewed as a positive outcome for an infant; however, a secure attachment may be viewed as a promotive factor for school-age children because of its likely association with other important developmental competencies (e.g., academic achievement, positive peer relations, prosocial behaviors, conscience development; see Masten and Coatsworth 1998). Because of children's normative gains in cognitive, language, and social skills and regular exposure to environments outside the family context, additional risks may be present for school-age children whose parents are in jail or prison, such as exposure to social stigma (Shlafer and Poehlmann 2010), witnessing the parent's crime or arrest (chapter 6, this volume), or violence or drug dealing in the neighborhood. Additional protective factors that emerge with increasing age include specific parenting practices, such as supervision, monitoring, and discipline (chapter 12, this volume); nonparental social supports originating from within or outside the extended family; cultural strengths and

Figure 16.2. Resilience Model for School-Age Children with Incarcerated Parents

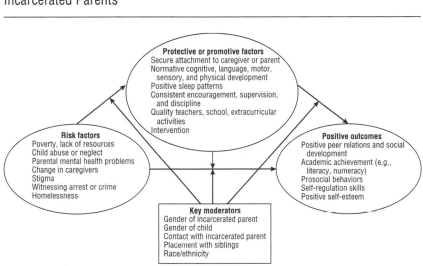

practices (see chapter 8, this volume); and a range of emerging coping strategies.

During adolescence, the interaction between parenting and peers becomes even more important. Deviant peer association becomes one of the strongest risk factors for poor adolescent adjustment and problem behaviors (see chapter 7, this volume). These relations are depicted in figure 16.3. Empirical examinations of conceptual models such as these are needed to enhance understanding of how the various factors in children's lives interact. Information is sorely needed on both the moderators and mediators of the behavioral, affective, and cognitive changes of children with incarcerated parents over time, not only across the course of development, but also over the course of child- and family-focused interventions.

Contextual Factors

Multiple contexts play a role in the development of children affected by parental incarceration. As for all children, family, school, and community contexts are important; however, judicial processes, corrections systems,

Figure 16.3. Resilience Model for Adolescents with Incarcerated Parents

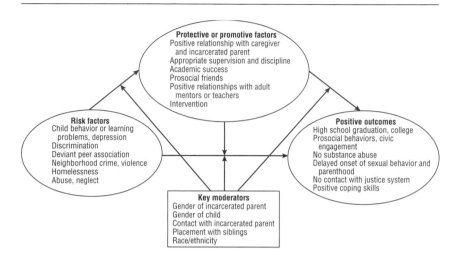

and social policies are also significant, as is the child welfare system for some children (chapter 13, this volume). These contexts may directly and indirectly affect children when their parents are incarcerated, both positively and negatively. More research is needed that documents the effects of these contextual factors on children's development over time. Moreover, interventions are needed that address the multiple contextual challenges that may disrupt the parenting of children with incarcerated parents (chapter 12, this volume).

Sadly, social policies designed to fight crime or strengthen families may have unintended negative consequences for children of incarcerated parents. As Susan D. Phillips discusses in chapter 3, the U.S. drug policies initiated in the 1980s that sent large numbers of people to prison may have perpetuated drug use and criminal behaviors rather than curbing them, affecting large numbers of children in the process. The Adoption and Safe Families Act of 1997 created strict time frames for how long children should remain in foster care before termination of parental rights and moving toward adoption. This policy had negative effects on some families affected by parental incarceration (Lee, Genty, and Laver 2005) but perhaps positive effects on others. Later, the Promoting Safe and Stable Families Act Amendment of 2001 contained legislation authorizing funds for mentoring programs as a preventive intervention for children of incarcerated parents. Whereas this legislation may have produced positive outcomes for children who developed a trusting and long-term mentoring relationship, it may have harmed others whose mentoring relationships failed (see chapter 11, this volume). Most recently, Congress's 2008 Second Chance Act may result in more rapid and well-supported reentry into the community for former offenders, including reunification with family members. Research is needed on how these and other related policy decisions influence children and families, and how the negative effects of such policies can be diminished and the positive effects enhanced.

Future developmental and intervention research should consider broader contextual factors such as these in tandem with questions focusing on children's development and the efficacy and effectiveness of intervention efforts. A better understanding of the wide-reaching consequences of poverty for children; the importance of contexts of race, ethnicity, and culture, including discrimination and racism; and the meaning of intergenerational cycles of insecure attachment, violence, substance abuse, and criminal behavior is needed as they apply to children of incarcerated parents and their families. Moreover, as Wildeman points out in chapter 15, the population of incarcerated individuals has changed over time, resulting in a gross overrepresentation of black children and families affected by parental incarceration, and especially those families affected by poverty and limited educational opportunities (see also chapter 3, this volume). Because of the wide range and complexity of the contextual issues involved and how they have changed over time, multidisciplinary scholarship is sorely needed.

Meeting Challenges

Research

Some of the most methodologically rigorous studies focusing on children of incarcerated parents published in the past decade have relied on secondary analysis of large, longitudinal datasets collected in the United States, the United Kingdom, and other countries (e.g., Murray and Farrington 2005; Huebner and Gustafson 2007). These studies have moved the field forward and addressed important and long-standing questions, such as whether children with parents who are or were incarcerated experience increased risk for negative outcomes as they grow older, or whether such outcomes are related to incarceration or other risks. However, because these studies were not designed to focus on children and families affected by parental incarceration, they tell researchers and interventionists little or nothing about the specific processes and experiences linking parental arrest and incarceration with children's outcomes (e.g., children witnessing the parent's crime or arrest, issues related to visitation and other contact with the incarcerated parent, social stigma that may occur as the result of the parent's criminal behavior or incarceration, changes in caregiving that occur over time because of the parent's incarceration). Smaller-scale studies that have purposively sampled incarcerated parents, their children, and their children's caregivers have begun to shed light on some of these processes, although many methodological limitations are often present. A number of intervention studies have been conducted, but many of these also have suffered from various design problems.

The most pressing need in the field at this point in time is high-quality studies at all levels of inquiry. Researchers simply do not know the answer to certain key questions, such as how does visitation and other contact with incarcerated parents affect children of various ages? What family processes are important in facilitating resilience in infants, children, and adolescents with parents in prison or jail? Does the traumatization or modeling that occurs as the result of children witnessing parental crime or arrest affect children's long-term development? What interventions are most effective for children and families with incarcerated parents? Answering these and many other important questions will require rigorous and numerous longitudinal and cross-sectional studies. Both large-scale and small-scale studies are needed to adequately understand resilience and vulnerability, and how developmental and familial processes may link parental incarceration with children's outcomes. The next four sections offer suggestions for research design, sampling, measurement, and analysis that can be achieved through collaborative multidisciplinary efforts and that can move the field forward during the next decade.

Design. Studies using prospective longitudinal designs are needed to understand the developmental trajectories of children with incarcerated parents. Previous studies have been unable to examine children's development and relationships before parental arrest or incarceration. This would be most feasible if well-funded, large-scale prospective longitudinal studies focused on children living in neighborhoods with high rates of adult incarceration (see chapter 4, this volume). To achieve this end, researchers may need to connect with an ongoing study designed to follow children prenatally to adulthood, such as the National Children's Study in the U.S. (National Children's Study Interagency Coordinating Committee 2003). Within the context of a prospective study, multiple key transitions experienced by children and families affected by parental incarceration could be examined, including the events surrounding the parent's arrest, sentencing, incarceration, release into the community, and reunification with family members. Adequately assessing the impacts of these transitions on children would likely require ongoing brief assessments of the occurrence of such events, followed by additional assessments conducted soon after an event was detected. The same type of strategy could be used within the context of smaller-scale, short-term longitudinal studies.

Longitudinal studies are sorely needed, but they will be challenging to conduct; even short-term longitudinal research with this population can be difficult (e.g., B. A. Eddy et al. 2001). Families affected by incarceration tend to move frequently and often have disconnected phones (Shlafer and Poehlmann 2010). A wide variety of strategies are needed to keep close track of the children of incarcerated parents, such as giving families phone cards or cell phones to call researchers, attempting frequent contacts with families, offering prorated compensation to families based on the number of contacts completed over time, and implementing culturally sensitive practices.

A limited number of intervention studies have been conducted with children of incarcerated parents and their families, and most have used designs that are poorly suited for determining program effectiveness. The majority have examined pre-intervention to post-intervention changes only in a sample that received an intervention of interest, or have compared an intervention group to a non-randomized comparison group. These studies tend to overestimate treatment effects (Shadish, Cook, and Campbell 2002). Rather than more of these studies, new intervention studies should employ designs that minimize bias and control for threats to the validity of the findings.

In particular, randomized controlled trials, where participants are assigned to two or more groups, such as an intervention and a "services as usual" group, and then followed over time, are very much needed. Randomized trials can be challenging to conduct within corrections settings, but they are facilitated when time is taken to develop close collaborations not only with corrections departments and specific institutions but with service delivery partners with experience and skill working within the system (e.g., J. M. Eddy et al. 2008). Such trials are also needed within community settings, as caregiving contexts and schools function as children's proximal environments during a parent's incarceration.

Small-scale cross-sectional studies have been the norm in research with this population and will likely continue to be so. These types of studies provide valuable information to the field, and they offer an opportunity to develop hypotheses that can be examined in the context of longitudinal and intervention studies. However, key in the future conduct of these studies is a new rigor in sampling and a reconsideration of issues related to measurement and analyses.

Sampling. In many previous studies focusing on children of incarcerated parents, small convenience samples have been the norm. This has often resulted from limited funding, difficulties in overcoming challenges in accessing the population (including collaborating with corrections systems), and the difficulty in overcoming challenges inherent in working with high-risk families and their children (e.g., frequent moves, disconnected phones). Samples must be large enough to establish adequate statistical power, especially when examining moderating factors (i.e., statistical interactions), mediating variables, or complex conceptual models. Further, samples must relate back to a population of interest. Although probability sampling is ideal, purposive sampling strategies are also important to consider. The latter approach is characterized by deliberate efforts to include presumably typical groups in the sample if probability sampling is not possible. The goal of these sampling strategies is to create representative samples in order to enhance the generalizability and relevance of the findings that emerge.

With any sampling strategy, thought should be given to the ages of the children sampled and what age is appropriate for the research question under consideration. Collaborating with systems that allow and encourage access to incarcerated parents, children, and children's caregivers are important as well, including corrections departments, jails, schools, hospitals, child welfare systems, extension and community programs, and relevant intervention programs. Indeed, a key problem plaguing much of the research focusing on children of incarcerated parents is how to identify them. Schools, corrections systems, and other institutions do not routinely keep a record of these children, causing various scholars over the years to refer to children of incarcerated parents as an "invisible" population. Of course, a sampling strategy is only one part of the problem; the other is having a recruitment strategy that successfully enrolls participants, and a retention strategy that yields high participation rates over time. Strategies developed over the past several decades in work with other at-risk and high-risk populations should be helpful in this regard (Capaldi and Patterson 1987).

A key consideration for samples in future studies is the inclusion of both incarcerated mothers and fathers and their children. About 10 times more men are incarcerated than women in the United States (Glaze and Maruschak 2008), and therefore children are much more likely to experience the incarceration of their fathers than their mothers. However, it is important to include children affected by maternal incarceration because they are more likely to experience changes in caregivers, poverty, and other risk factors than children of incarcerated fathers (e.g., Murray and Farrington 2008). Previous research has often combined data from children of incarcerated mothers and fathers (e.g., Murray and Farrington 2005) or only focused on one group (e.g., Hanlon et al. 2005). Although no large-scale definitive studies examine differences between children with incarcerated mothers and fathers, there are several reasons that one might expect such differences (e.g., Dallaire 2007; Murray and Murray 2010), and careful work is needed to understand processes and outcomes within families affected by paternal incarceration, maternal incarceration, and the incarceration of both parents.

Past studies have often combined data from samples of children of jailed and imprisoned parents, even though these populations may differ in a number of important ways (e.g., length of separation, severity of crime, family contact with the jailed individual, involvement of alcohol and other substances). Careful specification is needed in future studies regarding the details of parental incarceration. Differences and similarities between children who have parents who are locked up for brief or lengthy jail stays, or shorter versus longer prison stays, for example, need to be delineated. Issues unique to these contexts are important to consider and should not be ignored.

For example, some inmates spend repeated, short stays in jail, followed by rapid reunification with families and communities. Within this context, there may be more reciprocity and overlap in the social networks of these inmates, affected children, and children's caregivers compared with individuals who serve longer jail or prison sentences. Further, such an individual's behaviors might be more likely to place a child at greater risk for harm and might more strongly influence the child's subsequent behaviors (e.g., through increased exposure at home to illegal substances, substance abuse, and deviant associates).

A large proportion of convicted felons who spend time in prison have a history of prior arrest and jail time. Thus, accessing children and families during a parent's jail stay may provide the opportunity to intervene early in a process that may eventually result in longer-term parental incarceration. Further, because jails tend to be locally operated and located, they may be more accessible for community prevention efforts than prisons, which are often located far from affected families and may have more restrictive policies regarding contact with family members.

Measurement. Is it important that the perspectives of children, incarcerated parents, caregivers, and staff members within the various relevant systems (e.g., schools, child welfare, corrections) are assessed, depending on the research questions at hand. For example, parenting interventions for incarcerated parents should measure parenting behaviors and child outcomes as primary indications of success, rather than continuing to focus mostly on changes in parental attitudes (chapter 10, this volume). In such studies, researchers also should assess key process-related variables relevant to intervention efforts, such as caregiver-child interaction patterns and ongoing contact with incarcerated parents, in addition to static factors, such as the parent's pre-incarceration socioeconomic status or gender. The use of multiple methods (interviews, questionnaires, direct observations, standardized assessments) and multiple informants (caregivers, parents, children, teachers) is important to minimize the chance of obtaining spurious significant findings because of within-method or within-respondent shared variance and to obtain the perspectives of as many relevant people to the child and family as possible.

Observational approaches have been underused in previous research focusing on children affected by parental incarceration but are important for the examination of key proximal processes that may be associated with resilience as well as maladjustment (Snyder et al. 2006). When using interviews and observational approaches, application of both quantitative and qualitative coding schemes is possible, depending on the goals of the study. Qualitative data have enriched researchers' understanding of the hardships families face following parental incarceration, including challenging experiences with jail visits (e.g., Arditti 2003) and children's behavioral and emotional reactions to the loss of their imprisoned mothers (e.g., Poehlmann 2005b). In turn, such findings have contributed to theory-building. In the future, mixed-method approaches that combine qualitative and quantitative analyses will be useful, especially as the field begins to test the theories that have been developed.

The reliable and valid measurement of parenting, visitation quality, and other family processes is vital to quantitative analysis in studies related to the children of incarcerated parents, but little work has been done in this area that is particular to the unique issues in this population. Most notably, it is unclear how parenting should be measured for parents behind bars. Typical parenting questionnaires are generally inappropriate because they are intended to provide summary information about the day-to-day, in-person interactions that occur between a parent and child. Except in the case of prison nurseries (chapter 9, this volume) or other unique contact visit experiences, such interactions do not occur. Basic measurement development work is needed on questionnaires that are relevant to the type of parenting that does happen from behind bars.

Another option for measuring that is used in community-based research is observed parent-child interaction (Reid, Patterson, and Snyder 2002). Such interactions are usually videotaped. While it is possible to conduct this type of assessment within a prison or jail, even within the best of collaborations between researchers and correction systems, it is difficult. Further, it is unclear how behaviors during such interactions, which are indexing something that generally occurs infrequently under unusual conditions, would compare with parent-child interactions on the outside. Again, basic measurement development work is needed.

Finally, another option would be to either describe or show a videotaped scenario to parents and ask how they would respond (e.g., Conduct Problems Prevention Research Group 2002). The difficulty here again is that these measures have not been developed for use with this population, and more information is needed. This is just one example of how reliable and valid measures of key constructs are not yet available for important research relevant to children of incarcerated parents, and need to be developed.

In addition to measuring parenting from behind bars and quality of visitation with incarcerated parents, it is crucial to assess children's caregiving environments in the community. Caregivers are the adults responsible for day-to-day interactions with children, including supporting children's growth and development at home, school, and in the community; providing supervision and discipline; and often regulating contact between children and incarcerated parents (see chapter 7, this volume). The nature of the co-parenting system that often arises between caregivers and incarcerated parents is an important consideration (Baker et al. 2010; Cecil et al. 2008), as is the reliable and valid assessment of the caregiver's parenting.

A highly valued outcome for corrections systems is to reduce inmate recidivism, and this is of particular interest in studies of parenting programs as well as more comprehensive multimodal programs that target incarcerated parents and their families. Whereas the impact of programs on recidivism and related variables such as self-reported criminal behavior, official arrest, and lock-up in jail are important to examine, the most important outcome variable is whether intervention programs influence the proximal, more immediate targets that they are supposed to be changing. If this variable is not measured and recidivism is affected, it is unclear why; information about why change happens, not just whether it happens, is needed.

Information is also needed on the mechanism of change within the intervention process for incarcerated parents, their children, and children's caregivers. In this regard, intervention studies related to the children of incarcerated parents often have not described the intended content and process of the intervention well enough to enable replication; further, the studies have rarely reported on whether the actual intervention delivered met the stated standard (i.e., that there was fidelity to the model). Studies on these types of variables are needed to build a science of intervention.

Analysis. Data should be analyzed with appropriately sophisticated techniques designed to address the key questions of interest (MacKinnon and Lockwood 2004). Causal modeling strategies, such as longitudinal growth modeling or structural equation modeling, in particular, may help identify underlying developmental processes. Various multilevel modeling techniques could be used to examine such questions as whether children's behavior problems covary with visitation of incarcerated parents over time (including the examination of intra-individual differences in these patterns), or to examine the development of siblings nested within families affected by parental incarceration, or to determine whether certain contextual variables predict children's increasing or decreasing problem behavior or prosocial behavior trajectories over time. Techniques such as event history analysis, which allows joint examination of the occurrence of an event and the time to that event, should be employed when appropriate. Clustering in the data, such as when parents, families, or children are brought together in groups for treatment, or when incarcerated parents reside together in a prison or treatment unit, should be accounted for in the analyses.

Missing data should no longer be ignored (e.g., such as occurs when listwise deletion is employed). One of the many techniques now available to deal with missing data should be used instead, such as full maximum information likelihood estimation or multiple imputation (Abraham and Russell 2004). It will be important for future research efforts to move beyond mere group comparisons designed to determine children's risk level or document children's outcomes relative to other groups. Rather, the focus should be on identifying developmental, familial, and contextual processes in relation to children's outcomes and trajectories. To do this, larger, more rigorous studies need to be conducted, and data need to be analyzed using more advanced methods.

Practice

The information available for practitioners working in this area is limited, particularly when working individually with the children of incarcerated parents, or when working with incarcerated parents themselves. However, a wealth of knowledge is available on interventions appropriate for caregivers in the community (although it is not specific to issues regarding parental incarceration). The parenting skills and support provided in the evidence-based family interventions that are available (e.g., Webster-Stratton and Hammond 1997, 1998) are likely to be just as relevant and useful for the caregivers of the children of incarcerated parents as to the caregivers of other children. Because these interventions generally do not address issues of special relevance to families with incarcerated parents, such as co-parenting from a distance, visitation issues, or cultural factors in parenting, supplementing these interventions with additional group or individual sessions with clinicians knowledgeable in these areas should be considered.

Practitioners can play a key role in pushing the field forward by joining with researchers to conduct the studies needed to adequately inform practice. Intervention research uniquely relevant to the children of incarcerated parents and their families is only just beginning. Most existing studies have been conducted on institution-based parenting programs, yet only four of the studies on this topic reviewed by Loper and Novero in chapter 10 employed a rigorous randomized comparison group design. Only a few studies of varying quality have been conducted on the other interventions (i.e., youth mentoring, prison nurseries) discussed in this volume. Clearly, further high-quality research focusing on each general type of intervention is needed. Studies of current innovative programs are needed. A new, second generation of interventions is also needed, followed by rigorous studies of such interventions. The multimodal intervention approach discussed by Eddy, Kjellstrand, Martinez, and Newton in chapter 12 is an example of the type of more comprehensive intervention that seems worthy of consideration. Such interventions do not just attempt to work with inmates or with children alone; rather, they bring families, including children's current caregivers, into the process, and thus try to effect change at the family systems level. Through partnerships with researchers, practitioners can play important roles in initiating and conducting each of these types of studies.

Policy

For policymakers and practitioners alike, the sheer lack of developmental and intervention studies in this area is frustrating. Policymakers need to know what interventions are truly "evidence based" and relevant to the children of incarcerated parents, and thus which interventions are particularly worthy of funding. Advocates need answers that will help them engage community interest and action. Practitioners need access to interventions that work. The pressures generated by these needs can lead to the proliferation of unproven anecdotes, such as the myth that children of incarcerated parents are six times more likely to be incarcerated than their peers. For interventions, the most common myths today revolve around whether particular programs are evidence based. This label is often applied inappropriately, at least from the perspective of the scientific community.

To illustrate the problem, a colleague recently was searching for programs relevant to the children of incarcerated parents and their families and asked a group of program developers whether their program was "evidence based." They replied "yes" because the program had addressed individual and family factors that were considered important in reducing recidivism, and a third-party evaluator had examined outcomes for a group of people who had participated in the program. For most researchers, this level of evidence would be considered insufficient for the program to be labeled as evidence based. If policymakers desire to have research shape practice, clear, consistent and meaningful standards must be generated for what is, and what is not, evidence-based practice.

Fortunately, various professional organizations, governmental agencies, and research groups have developed clear definitions of what evidence-based means; in all cases, a fundamental part of the definition is that positive outcomes have been found in a study that used at least one of the more rigorous comparison-group designs, such as randomized controlled trials (e.g., Flay et al. 2005). Most frequently, the results of these studies must have been published in peer-reviewed journals, and thus submitted to close inspection by knowledgeable colleagues who have agreed that the study appears to have been theoretically based, that it appears to have been well conducted, and that the findings have some validity. Many groups require that at least two such studies have been conducted and published, and some go an additional step and require that at least one study be conducted by researchers who do not have an inherent conflict of interest in finding positive results (such as a program developer seeking to market the program). Consistency in definitions such as "evidence-based practice" is needed across research, policy, and practice.

Given the research available to date, policymakers could take three key steps that are directly relevant to the children of incarcerated parents. The first step is to formally recognize that most incarcerated parents have children. Policies and practices that lead to higher incarceration rates will affect children and families, and may disproportionately affect impoverished, minority communities (chapter 15, this volume). The potential impacts on children and on specific populations should be documented and discussed as a matter of course as new legislation, policies, and practices are developed. The second step is to find ways to ensure that the children of incarcerated parents are safe and protected. Policies and practices should be designed to minimize the potential for further trauma to these children. To do this requires carefully considering the context of each event and setting a child may experience during a parental incarceration, from parental arrest, to spending time in foster care, to visiting a parent in prison. The third step is to foster resilience processes in children and families. Policies, practices, and interventions that clearly strengthen families and foster positive developmental outcomes, as demonstrated through rigorous science, should be favored. Current standards for how things are done should be reevaluated with child development and context in mind. Not only should the potential for child harm be reduced, but the probability for child success should be increased.

Closing Thoughts

It is a national tragedy that so many children have a parent in jail or prison in the United States and that many more children have experienced this in the past or soon will in the future. In this volume, we have brought together key scholars from various disciplines who are experts regarding children, parents, caregivers, and systems associated with parental incarceration. The current empirical base relevant to the children of incarcerated parents is summarized here, and there are clearly many gaps in our knowledge, both at the developmental science level and at the intervention science level. These gaps limit our ability to effectively intervene with these children and families. More studies are needed, and thus funding for such work is greatly needed (see chapter 14, this volume).

Because of the complexities involved in the lives of people affected by criminality and incarceration, further studies in this area would be most revealing if conducted in the context of collaborative, multidisciplinary teams that pool their skills, knowledge, and experience. While researchers from multiple academic fields are an important component of such teams, so are corrections administrators, practitioners, and policymakers. Each profession has much to bring to this work, and including their voices, as well as the voices of the children and families involved, is important in moving the field forward.

Perusal of this volume indicates a pressing need for policy changes so, in the future, fewer children will have parents in jail or prison, and those who do will get the support they need to be safe and to thrive. In the meantime, however, we need to act to help vulnerable children and their families, schools, and the other systems that work with them (e.g., child welfare) cope with the consequences of our nation's reliance on incarceration at historically unprecedented levels. The best approaches for such work are evidence-based interventions that are sensitive to context and development and that promote child and family resilience. Continued rigorous developmental and intervention research is needed to broaden the evidence base, and to provide guidance to parents, practitioners, and policymakers so children of incarcerated parents are given the opportunity to succeed in a civil society.

REFERENCES

Abraham, W. Todd, and Daniel W. Russell. 2004. "Missing Data: A Review of Current Methods and Applications in Epidemiological Research." *Current Opinion in Psychiatry* 17:315–21.

Arditti, Joyce A. 2003. "Locked Doors and Glass Walls: Family Visiting at a Local Jail." *Journal of Loss and Trauma* 8:115–38.

Baker, Jason, James McHale, Anne Strozier, and Dawn Cecil. 2010. "Mother-Grandmother Coparenting Relationships in Families with Incarcerated Mothers: A Pilot Investigation." *Family Process* 49:165–84.

Capaldi, Deborah M., and Gerald R. Patterson. 1987. "An Approach to the Problem of Recruitment and Retention Rates for Longitudinal Research." *Behavioral Assessment* 9:169–77.

Cecil, Dawn K., James McHale, Anne Strozier, and Joel Pietsch. 2008. "Female Inmates, Family Caregivers, and Young Children's Adjustment: A Research Agenda and Implications for Corrections Programming." *Journal of Criminal Justice* 36:513–21.

Cicchetti, Dante, Fred A. Rogosch, and Sheree L. Toth. 1998. "Maternal Depressive Disorder and Contextual Risk: Contributions to the Development of Attachment Insecurity and Behavior Problems in Toddlerhood." *Development & Psychopathology* 10:283–300.

Conduct Problems Prevention Research Group. 2002. "The Implementation of the Fast Track Program: An Example of a Large-Scale Prevention Science Efficacy Trial." *Journal of Abnormal and Child Psychology* 30:1–17.

Dallaire, Danielle H. 2007. "Children with Incarcerated Mothers: Developmental Outcomes, Special Challenges, and Recommendations." *Journal of Applied Developmental Psychology* 28:15–24.

Eddy, Bruce A., Melissa J. Powell, Margaret H. Szuba, Maura L. McCool, and Susan Kuntz. 2001. "Challenges in Research with Incarcerated Parents and Importance in Violence Prevention." *American Journal of Preventive Medicine* 20(Suppl. 1): 56–62.

Eddy, J. Mark, Charles R. Martinez Jr., Tracy Schiffmann, Rex Newton, Laura Olin, Leslie Leve, and Joann W. Shortt. 2008. "Development of a Multisystemic Parent Management Training Intervention for Incarcerated Parents, Their Children, and Families." *Clinical Psychologist* 12:86–98.

Flay, Brian R., Anthony Biglan, Robert F. Boruch, Felipe González Castro, Denise Gottfredson, Sheppard Kellam, Eve K. Mościcki, Steven Schinke, Jeffrey C. Valentine, and Peter Ji. 2005. "Standards of Evidence: Criteria for Efficacy, Effectiveness, and Dissemination." *Prevention Science* 6:151–75.

Glaze, Lauren E., and Laura M. Maruschak. 2008. *Parents in Prison and Their Minor Children.* NCJ 222984. Washington, DC: U.S. Department of Justice, Bureau of Justice Statistics.

Hanlon, Thomas E., Robert J. Blatchley, Terry Bennett-Sears, Kevin E. O'Grady, Mark Rose, and Jason M. Callaman. 2005. "Vulnerability of Children of Incarcerated Addict Mothers: Implications for Preventive Interventions." *Children and Youth Services Review* 27:67–84.

Huebner, Beth M., and Regan Gustafson. 2007. "The Effect of Maternal Incarceration on Adult Offspring Involvement in the Criminal Justice System." *Journal of Criminal Justice* 35:283–96.

James, Doris, and Lauren Glaze. 2006. *Mental Health Problems of Prison and Jail Inmates.* NCJ 213600. Washington, DC: U.S. Department of Justice, Bureau of Justice Statistics.

Lee, Arlene F., Philip M. Genty, and Mimi Laver. 2005. *The Impact of the Adoption and Safe Families Act on Children of Incarcerated Parents.* Washington, DC: Child Welfare League of America.

MacKinnon, David P., and Chondra M. Lockwood. 2004. "Advances in Statistical Methods for Substance Abuse Prevention Research." *Prevention Science* 4:155–71.

Masten, Ann S. 2001. "Ordinary Magic: Resilience Processes in Development." *American Psychologist* 56:227–38.

Masten, Ann S., and J. Douglas Coatsworth. 1998. "The Development of Competence in Favorable and Unfavorable Environments: Lessons from Research on Successful Children." *American Psychologist* 53:205–20.

Murray, Joseph, and David P. Farrington. 2005. "Parental Imprisonment: Effects on Boys' Antisocial Behaviour and Delinquency through the Life Course." *Journal of Child Psychology and Psychiatry* 46:1269–78.

———. 2008. "The Effects of Parental Imprisonment on Children." In *Crime and Justice: A Review of Research,* vol. 37, edited by Michael Tonry (133–206). Chicago: University of Chicago Press.

Murray, Joseph, and Lynne Murray. 2010. "Parental Incarceration, Attachment, and Child Psychopathology." *Attachment & Human Development* 12(4): 289–309.

National Children's Study Interagency Coordinating Committee, The. 2003. "The National Children's Study of Environmental Effects on Child Health and Development." *Environmental Health Perspectives* 111:642–46.

Poehlmann, Julie. 2003. "An Attachment Perspective on Grandparents Raising Their Very Young Grandchildren: Implications for Intervention and Research." *Infant Mental Health Journal* 24:149–73.

———. 2005a. "Incarcerated Mothers' Contact with Children, Perceived Family Relationships, and Depressive Symptoms." *Journal of Family Psychology* 19:350–57.

———. 2005b. "Representations of Attachment Relationships in Children of Incarcerated Mothers." *Child Development* 76:679–96.

Poehlmann, Julie, Danielle Dallaire, Ann B. Loper, and Leslie Shear. 2010. "Children's Contact with Their Incarcerated Parents: Research Findings and Recommendations." *American Psychologist* 65:575–98.

Reid, John B., Gerald Patterson, and James Snyder, eds. 2002. *Antisocial Behavior in Children and Adolescents: A Developmental Analysis and Model for Intervention.* Washington, DC: American Psychological Association.

Shadish, William R., Thomas D. Cook, and Donald T. Campbell. 2002. *Experimental and Quasi-Experimental Designs for Generalized Causal Inference.* Boston: Houghton-Mifflin.

Shlafer, Rebecca J., and Julie Poehlmann. 2010. "Attachment and Caregiving Relationships in Families Affected by Parental Incarceration." *Attachment & Human Development* 12:395–415.

Snyder, James, John B. Reid, Mike Stoolmiller, George Howe, Hendricks Brown, Getachew Dagne, and Wendi Cross. 2006. "The Role of Behavior Observation in Measurement Systems for Randomized Prevention Trials." *Prevention Science* 7:43–56.

Sroufe, L. Alan. 1991. "Considering Normal and Abnormal Together: The Essence of Developmental Psychopathology." *Development & Psychopathology* 2:335–47.

Webster-Stratton, Carolyn, and Mary A. Hammond. 1997. "Treating Children with Early Onset Conduct Problems: A Comparison of Child and Parent Training Interventions." *Journal of Consulting and Clinical Psychology* 65:93–109.

———. 1998. "Preventing Conduct Problems in Head Start Children: Strengthening Parenting Competencies." *Journal of Consulting and Clinical Psychology* 66:715–30.

Werner, Emme E. 2000. "Protective Factors and Individual Resilience." In *Handbook of Early Childhood Intervention,* 2nd ed., edited by Jack P. Shonkoff and Samuel J. Meisels (115–32). New York: Cambridge University Press.

About the Editors

J. Mark Eddy is a senior scientist and licensed psychologist at the non-profit Oregon Social Learning Center in Eugene. His work focuses on the development of research-based interventions designed to prevent childhood conduct disorder and related problem behaviors. He is the principal investigator on several long-term randomized controlled trials of interventions conducted within the juvenile justice, criminal justice, and school systems. For the past 10 years, Dr. Eddy has worked closely with the Oregon Department of Corrections and nonprofit service delivery agencies on the design and testing of a multisystemic parenting program for incarcerated fathers and mothers and their children and families.

Julie Poehlmann is a professor of human development and family studies in the School of Human Ecology at the University of Wisconsin–Madison, an investigator at the Waisman Center, and a licensed psychologist in Wisconsin and New York. Her research focuses on the role of family relationships in the development of resilience in high risk infants and young children. Dr. Poehlmann's research focusing on children of incarcerated parents has been funded by the National Institute of Mental Health and the U.S. Department of Health and Human Services. Through numerous publications in psychological, developmental, and family journals and mentoring of new scholars, she has brought attention to the issue of parental incarceration.

About the Contributors

Lauren Aaron is a doctoral student in developmental psychology at the University of California, Riverside. Her research interests include the influence of adversity on children's social functioning broadly. More generally, she is interested in how various risk experiences (e.g., poverty, parental incarceration, child abuse, and so on) influence children's prosocial behavior in early and middle childhood.

Harold E. Briggs is a professor at Portland State University School of Social Work. He has written extensively in the areas of mental health, substance abuse treatment, and child welfare systems to help service providers use evidence to improve child, adult, and family well-being. Dr. Briggs has conducted studies on the fear of AIDS, homophobia, and perception of the African American experience. Throughout his career, Dr. Briggs has trained community members to lead and facilitate community change efforts in an effort to promote community self-governance and transformation. He has also been involved in community and system change efforts that have benefited community-based organizations of color.

Mary Byrne is the Stone Foundation and Elise D. Fish Professor of Health Care for the Underserved at Columbia University. Her program of research focuses on family-centered assessment and intervention for young children at risk. National Institutes of Health and other funding sources have supported her research with children with HIV sero-reversion, infants raised in prison, children receiving primary care in low-income neighborhoods, and seriously ill children. Dr. Byrne's honors include charter membership in the Columbia University Medical Center Garvey Teaching Academy, Fellow in the American Academy of Nursing, the inaugural Emily Fenichel Zero-to-Three Leadership award, the New York State Distinguished Nurse Researcher Award, and the international Audrey Hepburn Award for Contributions to the Health and Welfare of Children.

Danielle H. Dallaire is an assistant professor in the psychology department of The College of William & Mary. Her research interests include children's social and emotional development and promoting resilience in children and families in high-risk environments, particularly children and families dealing with parental incarceration.

Benjamin de Haan is executive director of Partners for Our Children in Seattle, a collaboration of the Washington State Department of Social and Health Services, the University of Washington School of Social Work, and private-sector funders. He has held a number of leadership positions in public agencies, academia, and private philanthropy. He previously served as the managing director of state strategy for Casey Family Programs, where he focused on child welfare policy and practice. Before joining Casey, Dr. de Haan was an associate professor and director of the Criminal Justice Policy Research Institute in the Hatfield School of Government at Portland State University. He also served as the deputy director and interim director of the Oregon Department of Corrections from 1995 to 2003. Earlier in his career, Dr. de Haan was in charge of child welfare services for the State of Oregon and was the founding director of the Child Welfare Partnership, a university-based research and training center at the Graduate School of Social Work at Portland State University.

Catherine Dun Rappaport is an associate at Abt Associates, a public policy research firm. Ms. Dun Rappaport specializes in assessing and supporting programs that serve economically disadvantaged youth and families. She is an expert in evaluation and uses both qualitative and quantitative methodologies in her work. Before her tenure at Abt, she was the executive director of a mentoring organization.

Eleanor Gil-Kashiwabara is a licensed psychologist and research assistant professor at Portland State University, Regional Research Institute for

Human Services. She is currently the lead evaluator for the Nak-Nu-Wit Systems of Care Program, which is implementing culturally appropriate mental health services for American Indian/Alaska Native children, youth, and families in the greater Portland metropolitan area. Dr. Gil-Kashiwabara has also been principal investigator on numerous projects addressing American Indian/Alaska Native children's mental health, transition planning for Latinas with disabilities, and gender issues as they relate to transition planning. Her clinical interests include child/family psychotherapy and psychological evaluations with Spanish-speaking children who are in protective custody.

Lauren E. Glaze is a statistician in the Corrections Statistics Unit of the Bureau of Justice Statistics (BJS). During her 11 years at BJS, Ms. Glaze's work has focused primarily on the community corrections population. Since 1998, she has written or co-written BJS's annual report on probation and parole. In recent years, her research has focused on other topics and special populations, such as inmates who have mental health problems and incarcerated parents. Currently, she is working with other BJS colleagues and mental health experts to enhance the measurement of mental health problems in BJS surveys of prison and jail inmates. One goal of this project is to develop a validated instrument to measure serious mental illness among the incarcerated. Ms. Glaze is also involved in redesigning the next iteration of the BJS national omnibus surveys of prison and jail inmates.

Schnavia Smith Hatcher is an assistant professor in the School of Social Work at the University of Georgia. Dr. Hatcher's research has concentrated on identifying psychosocial determinants and pathways to the criminal justice system for youth and adults and facilitating the development of proper protocol to respond to health issues within the system, such as suicide prevention, mental health and substance abuse treatment, HIV prevention, and continuity of care within the community. Dr. Hatcher also focuses on developing and implementing health promotion programs in collaboration with faith-based organizations for the community. She is currently a postdoctoral fellow with the Mental Health and Substance Abuse in Corrections Clinical Research Scholars Program, a fellowship program funded by the National Institute of Mental Health and organized by Morehouse School of Medicine. In addition to being a social behavioral scientist, Dr. Hatcher is a licensed clinical social worker in Georgia and Maryland, with her professional training focused on addressing health disparities in the community and correctional settings by improving policy, treatment, and service delivery practices.

Jean M. Kjellstrand is a research associate at the nonprofit Oregon Social Learning Center and the nonprofit Oregon Research Institute, both based in Eugene. She has been a licensed social worker for 20 years and has worked with children and families in high-risk circumstances as a clinician as well as with general populations conducting community-level preventive interventions. She recently completed her doctorate in social work at Portland State University, where her research focused on longitudinal outcomes for children with incarcerated parents.

Ann B. Loper is a clinical psychologist and professor at the University of Virginia's Curry School of Education. Her research focuses on mental health and adjustment of prisoners, with a particular interest in understanding the experiences of incarcerated parents and their families. Dr. Loper has collaborated with prison, jail, and community partners in developing a parenting program for incarcerated mothers, and is currently evaluating jail transitional programming. Dr. Loper has also conducted research concerning the needs and characteristics of female juvenile offenders.

Charles R. Martinez, Jr., is a clinical psychologist and senior scientist at the Oregon Social Learning Center (OSLC) in Eugene and directs the OSLC Latino research team. He also serves as the Vice President for Institutional Equity and Diversity at the University of Oregon. He is the principal investigator on National Institutes of Health–funded research projects designed to examine risk and protective factors involved in linking acculturation to behavioral health outcomes for Latino families and to develop and test culturally specific interventions for Latino families at risk of behavioral health problems. Dr. Martinez's work centers on identifying factors that promote healthy adjustment for children and parents following stressful life events, taking into consideration the cultural contexts of families and communities.

Laura M. Maruschak is a statistician with the Corrections Statistics Unit of the Bureau of Justice Statistics (BJS) and has worked at BJS for 14 years. Her research has focused primarily on health-related issues among the correctional population. She has written the annual bulletin on HIV infection each year since 1997, along with numerous other reports on medical problems and treatment of inmates. She has been responsible for the analysis and publication of reports on other topics and special populations, such as mental health treatment in state prisons, DWI offenders, and incarcerated parents. Mrs. Maruschak is currently working on several projects to enhance data that BJS collects on the physical and mental health of inmates. This work includes enhancing the measurement of mental health problems in BJS surveys of prison and jail inmates and designing surveys to measure chronic and infectious diseases, as well as medical services and treatment among the inmate population. Mrs. Maruschak is also involved in efforts to redesign the next iteration of the BJS national omnibus surveys of prison and jail inmates.

Keva M. Miller is an assistant professor at Portland State University School of Social Work and a licensed clinical social worker. Her research focuses on children of criminal justice–involved parents; child welfare; risk, protection, and resilience; social injustices and racial inequalities; and criminal justice practices and policies that affect children and families. As the principal investigator on the Decision Point Analysis research project, Dr. Miller examined multilevel decisionmaking processes that contribute to the disproportionate and disparate representation of black and American Indian children in Oregon's child welfare system. She has also collaborated with research scientists from the Oregon Social Learning Center on a National Institute of Mental Health–funded pilot project, Emotion-Focused Intervention for Mothers and Children under Stress.

Christopher J. Mumola, now with the U.S. Department of State, worked as a policy analyst in the Corrections Statistics Unit of the Bureau of Justice Statistics (BJS) for 13 years. Between 2000 and 2010, he was responsible for developing BJS data collections pursuant to the *Deaths in Custody Reporting Act.* From that series, he wrote several BJS publications on mortality in the criminal justice system. Mr. Mumola managed the Former Prisoner Survey, the first national BJS survey of offenders under parole supervision. He also wrote BJS special reports on such topics as incarcerated veterans, incarcerated parents, and three previous studies on the substance abuse and treatment histories of criminal offenders. Mr. Mumola served as a liaison to the Office of National Drug Control Policy on drug policy data matters, and he oversaw BJS data collections on special correctional populations, such as military correctional facilities, U.S. territorial prisons, and persons under Immigration and Customs Enforcement detention.

Joseph Murray is a senior research associate at the Institute of Criminology and a research fellow at Darwin College, University of Cambridge. His ground-breaking research has focused on epidemiological and longitudinal research with children of incarcerated parents. Dr. Murray was awarded the 2002 Manuel Lopez-Rey Graduate Prize in Criminology and the 2007 Nigel Walker Prize from the University of Cambridge, and the 2008 Distinguished New Scholar Award from the American Society of Criminology Division of Corrections and Sentencing.

Rex Newton has more than 30 years of experience working in the Oregon corrections system. He has served in various mental health positions, including prison psychologist, program director of the alcohol and drug residential treatment program Cornerstone, program director of the prison parenting program Parenting Inside Out, and mental health consultant. His clinical interests include early childhood intervention as a crime prevention strategy. He has facilitated many prison-based therapy groups with incarcerated men. A common focus in those groups has been on dealing with early childhood trauma stemming from emotional, physical, and sexual abuse, and subsequent problems with post-traumatic stress disorder, substance addictions, and ongoing involvement in the criminal justice system. Dr. Newton is currently developing an in-prison inmate mentoring program using older inmates to mentor younger prisoners to help prepare them for life back in the community.

Caitlin M. Novero is a doctoral student in the clinical and school psychology program at the Curry School of Education, University of Virginia. She has worked with forensic populations in prison rehabilitation programs in Boston, Massachusetts, and central Virginia.

Susan D. Phillips is an assistant professor in the Jane Addams College of Social Work at the University of Illinois at Chicago. She began her career as a social worker at Centers for Youth and Families in Little Rock, where she was responsible for developing and coordinating direct service programs for children of incarcerated parents. She cofounded one of several programs that was chosen to be a federal demonstration project several years ago and is a former state chairperson for the Mothers in Prison, Children in Crises Campaign. Her research includes seminal studies describing the experiences of children who are present when their parents are arrested, the needs of grandparents who are caring for children whose parents are in prison, and factors influencing recidivism among mothers. Dr. Phillips is known not only for her research on children of incarcerated parents, but also for her part in national projects to translate research into practice.

Eve E. Reider is health scientist administrator in the Prevention Research Branch in the Division of Epidemiology, Services, and Prevention Research at the National Institute on Drug Abuse. Dr. Reider's areas of focus include selected and indicated populations, HIV prevention in the context of drug abuse prevention, health services research, and gender issues in prevention research.

Jean Rhodes is a professor of psychology at the University of Massachusetts, Boston. She is currently principal investigator on grants from the National Science Foundation, the Picower Foundation, and the Edna McConnell Clark Foundation. Professor Rhodes is chair of the Research and Policy Council of the National Mentoring Partnership. Dr. Rhodes sits on the board of directors of the National Mentoring Partnership and on the advisory boards of many mentoring and policy organizations. She also serves on the editorial boards of several journals in community and adolescent psychology.

Elizabeth B. Robertson is the chief of the Prevention Research Branch at the National Institute on Drug Abuse. Since taking this position, Dr. Robertson has broadened the branch mission of preventing drug abuse and drug-related HIV infection to include a developmental focus from early childhood through adulthood in multiple contexts such as the family, community, social service and clinical settings, and the media.

Rebecca J. Shlafer is a postdoctoral fellow at the University of Minnesota. Her research interests include the study of child and adolescent outcomes in the context of early risk and adversity. She is particularly interested in parental incarceration and family criminality as contexts for children's development. Dr. Shlafer's current research emphasizes the importance of children's early relationships for their future development, considering the complex pathways of risk and resilience, as well as the role of intervention in modifying these pathways.

Christopher Wildeman is an assistant professor of sociology and faculty fellow of the Center for Research on Inequalities and the Life Course at

Yale University. Before joining the faculty at Yale, he was a Robert Wood Johnson Foundation Health & Society Scholar and postdoctoral affiliate in the Population Studies Center at the University of Michigan. His primary research interest is the consequences of mass imprisonment for American inequality. His dissertation research was published in *Demography* and won the Dorothy Thomas Award from the Population Association of America as well as graduate student paper awards from three American Sociological Association sections.

Liza Zwiebach is a doctoral candidate in clinical psychology at the University of Massachusetts, Boston. Ms. Zwiebach is currently involved in a wide range of research projects, from a study of psychopathology in survivors of Hurricane Katrina to the creation of a measure assessing developmental capabilities pertinent to emerging adulthood.

Index